The Mounties
As They Saw
Themselves

The Mounties As They Saw Themselves

William Kelly

The Golden Dog Press

Ottawa – Canada – 1996

Canadian Cataloguing in Publication Data

Kelly, William, 1911–
  The Mounties as they saw themselves

ISBN 0-919614-67-1

  1. Royal Canadian Mounted Police I. Title.

FC3216.2.M68 1996   363.2'0971   C96-900732-9

Cover design by The Gordon Creative Group of Ottawa.

Typesetting by Carleton Production Centre of Nepean.

Printed in Canada by AGMV "l'imprimeur" Inc., of Cap-Saint-Ignace, Québec.

Distributed by:

  Oxford University Press Canada,
  70 Wynford Drive, DON MILLS, Ont., Canada, M3C 1J9.
  Phone: 416-441-2941   *   Fax: 416-444-0427

The Golden Dog Press wishes to express its appreciation to the Canada Council and the Ontario Arts Council for current and past support of its publishing programme.

THIS BOOK IS OFFICIALLY LICENSED BY THE ROYAL CANADIAN MOUNTED POLICE. A PORTION OF THE PROCEEDS FROM ITS SALE WILL BE DONATED TO COMMUNITY POLICING PROJECTS ACROSS CANADA.

Table of Contents

The North

Humour

RCMP in Wartime

Horses

Policework

Maps

Foreword

The RCMP *Quarterly* has been an important means of communication for the Royal Canadian Mounted Police since its publication began in 1933. That year, Commissioner James H. MacBrien authorized the magazine in recognition of the Force's sixtieth anniversary hoping that it would be "of interest and possible assistance to the members of the Force in the performance of their duties and in the maintenance of our standard of 'Esprit de Corps'." The *Quarterly* was well received not only by members of the RCMP but by former members and the public as well. In commenting on the first issue, the *London Free Press* stated, "The *Quarterly* is full of interesting and enlightening articles, presented in a manner that makes them of national value." This standard and tradition has been continued since 1933, with the exception of two years during the Second World War when publication ceased as a wartime economy.

Another event occurred in 1933 which proved also to be of great benefit to the Royal Canadian Mounted Police — the engagement in the Force of a young recruit, Constable William H. Kelly. His early years were spent in the province of Saskatchewan where he learned police work in the traditional way, sometimes even patrolling on horseback to perform his duties. During this period he met and soon married Nora Hickson, an accomplished writer, who would be his lifelong companion. Kelly's abilities soon singled him out for advancement and promotions came quickly. In 1939, he was transferred to Ontario where he was employed in criminal investigations including wartime black marketing, winning promotion to Detective Corporal two years later. In 1946, he became a commissioned officer with personnel duties in eastern Canada.

In 1951, Inspector Kelly was transferred to England as a Liaison Officer to European police forces and intelligence organizations and the RCMP representative to Interpol. Three years later he returned to Ottawa and duties at the national Headquarters. In 1959, he won promotion to Superintendent with responsibilities for security and intelligence. By 1965, he was the Directory of Security and Intelligence with the rank of Assistant Commissioner. His final position in the RCMP was assumed in 1967, when he became Deputy Commissioner Criminal Operations. Deputy Commissioner Kelly retired in 1970. My first knowledge of him was in October 1970 when, as a commentator for the Canadian Broadcasting Corporation, he brought informed background and perspective to a confused and troubled nation in the throes of the FLQ crisis.

I later learned that in addition to his skill as communicator in the electronic media, Deputy Kelly has displayed considerable ability as a writer in the course of his RCMP service and thereafter. While conducting investigations into the wartime black market in 1941, Kelly produced his first article for the RCMP *Gazette*, warning other police forces about the deceptive operations he had discovered. In April 1946, Kelly wrote his first article for the *Quarterly*, a piece entitled "Agent Provocateur", exploring the undercover aspects of police practices. After that he became a prolific contributor to the *Quarterly*, with about a dozen articles in print so far. In addition, Deputy Kelly had co-authored two books with his wife, Nora: *Policing in Canada* (1976) and *The Horses of the Canadian Mounted Police: A Century of History* (1973).

The RCMP *Quarterly* encompasses a broad spectrum of material relating to the Force, everything from social notes to celebrated criminal cases. Deputy Kelly obviously was faced with a difficult task in selecting articles from 60 years of back issues. I do not know exactly what selection criteria he used but the result has been excellent. His articles cover the entire span of publication with samples from each of the last six decades. There is an emphasis on history here, with contributions by historians writing about the past and also with contemporary accounts by members of events which now form the RCMP's history. Articles about the Arctic, our prairie past, the wartime, horses and significant personalities fall within this category. But Deputy Kelly has a well practised sense of humour as well and several articles are chosen for their elucidation of the lighter side of life in Canada's national police force.

A few of us are fortunate enough to have complete collections of back issues of the RCMP *Quarterly* and thus access to an important source of information on the life of the Force. In the pages of the *Quarterly* we can find a record of many historical episodes and most significant public events which have involved the Royal Canadian Mounted Police over the last 60 years. For those who do not have this advantage, William H. Kelly's book will be a valuable addition to the home library and a very interesting read. It is also fitting that this book will appear as the Royal Canadian Mounted Police prepares to celebrate in 1998 the 125th anniversary of its formation. This book is a suitable historical literary companion to this event.

William Beahen
RCMP Force Historian

Introduction

The RCMP *Quarterly* has been published from July 1933, except for a period of about two years during World War II.

Most of the articles chosen reveal aspects of Canadian history, through the work of the RCMP, of which the general public is seldom aware. Many of the articles are personal accounts of the experiences described. Most of the others were written by persons employed by the Force, such as the various *Quarterly* editors, most of whom were civilian members, but their articles are based on official records.

Some expressions in certain early articles referring to aboriginal people are highly inappropriate today. The language is part of the historic context. Editorial consideration was given to changing such expressions to more appropriate ones, but the decision was made not to change the original writing. At the time the articles were written the terms were, unfortunately, generally accepted.

W.H. Kelly, Editor

Ottawa 1996

The Prairies

1

Massacre in the Hills

John Peter Turner, RCMP Historian

Countless deeds of perfidious robbery, of ruthless murder done by white savages out in these Western wilds never find the light of day ... My God, what a terrible tale could I not tell of these dark deeds done by the white savage against the far nobler red Man! Major W.F. Butler in *The Great Lone Land*

Food—Festivity—Firewater—Fighting!

Within the scope of these four words may be found the more noticeable indulgences of life along the Western frontier three-quarters of a century ago; indeed all four might avail to signify common usages, past and present, among practically every race of humankind. In varying degrees, man's tendencies are much the same the world over. Without bodily nourishment life ceases; without diversion, festive or otherwise, it dwindles; "firewater" by any other name has ever been a favourite medium of unpredictable possibilities; and the tendency to shed another's blood (witness the world today) has thus far proven to be quite impossible of eradication.

Of these pronounced indispensables, so inseparable from early western days, one—the imbibing of intoxicants—has been forbidden absolutely to the Indian; and save to uphold the honour of the nation, the fourth has long since been regarded as an offence at large. But, within the memory of a few still living, time was, in one portion of Canada at least, when these four "ways of the flesh", inflated as they often were to excesses, swayed, as nothing else could, the vagaries of human subsistence and endeavour.

In the early '70's, a barbaric battleground and buffalo pasture occupied the country now embraced by southern Alberta and Saskatchewan and the more northerly parts of Montana. This was the last major portion of the continent remaining to the Indian: a land in which the western intrusion had as yet made small impression, save to introduce, conjointly with the barest benefits, the undermining corrosions of civilization. For the most part a veritable ocean of perennial grass, veiled from the world by utter solitude, flanked by the Missouri watershed along the south, by the Saskatchewan on the north, by the slowly advancing settlements of Manitoba and Dakota to the east, and by the Rockies on the west, spread immeasurably to the horizons. Along the 49th parallel an international boundary, on the verge of being surveyed, divided the dual sovereignty of this distant land. Rivers, large and small, coursed through its breadth. At its very heart on the Canadian side of the line, the Cypress Hills, accessible by horseflesh from every compass point, rose in broken and irregular configurations above the plain: a weird arena of utter savagery, a neutral tract, tenanted by resident wild creatures — buffalo, elk, moose, deer, grizzly bears, antelope, and other game — and visited by transient Stone-age men — Blackfeet, Crees, Assiniboines, Saulteaux, and Sioux. Far aloof, at widely separated points, trading establishments flourished, drawing from the wild plains hunters an enormous yield in skins and fur.

Fort Benton at the head of navigation on the upper Missouri, reeking with tawdry saloons, bawdies, gambling hells and unkempt trading counters, commanded an activity that extended northward into Canada; Fort Edmonton on the North Saskatchewan, a staid, well-ordered, almost baronial emporium of the fur trade, stood behind stout palisades at a discretionary distance from the warlike Blackfeet Confederacy towards the south; and Fort Qu'Appelle, to the east, on the margin of the Great Plain, had had its inception as near the vast pastures as safety would permit. Upon these strategic forts encroaching civilization relied in order to tap the resources of the last great Indian wealth; and hither, as well as to a few subsidiary posts, both north and south, red-skinned riders had learned to come spasmodically to barter the products of the hunt and avail themselves of proffered benefits and evils.

At this period, the Montana frontier, the very opposite of the orderly Saskatchewan field of trade, blazed with illicit licence. South of the line, a flagrant disregard for civilized amenities was rampant. The law of the trigger prevailed. White men and red continually vied for mastery. Crime of every description waxed bold and dominant. To be expert on the draw was to boast an enviable superiority. Gold dust was useful, but horses were wealth, power, prestige, and the only quick transport on the plains; and horse-stealing — a deeply-rooted Indian virtue — probably the most unforgivable malfeasance of the West, had become by adoption a popular expedient among a host of hardened freebooters. In glaring contrast to the ethics followed by the Hudson's Bay Company in the North, trading methods in proximity to the Missouri consisted largely of ghastly inhumanities. For the most part, the decalogue was scoffed at. Calloused persecution of the tribes grew to be a custom — the only good aborigine a dead one.

Once stripped of his possessions, the Indian was vermin. Frontier heroes, exponents and expungers of the law, side-armed sheriffs, murderers and degenerates — all the good, bad and indifferent strata of civilized life — constituted a blunt and bloody spearhead that had sunk deeply into the vitals of the West. Benton had grown to be a rough-and-tumble slattern of a place — the congenial rendezvous of reckless adventurers from eastern and southern communities and the haven of gold-seeking backwashes from the western mountains.

Buffalo products furnished the all-important quest; but the big wolves that dogged the shaggy herds provided profitable pelts, as well as ready employment to hard-living profligates and men of shady record. Young squaws were not immune from current prices; the small, wiry horses of the Indian, procurable by fair means or foul, held variable values. Simple commodities were traded to the red men; but liquor held the stage. A tin cup of poisonous firewater would fetch a buffalo robe, sometimes a piebald pony, or a girl with raven braids.

Recognizing no international boundary, the more obdurate Benton traders had instituted a reign of murder and debauchery throughout the Canadian portion of the Blackfeet realm. The establishment, in 1868, of Fort Hamilton (later to bear the more appropriate appellation of Fort Whoop-Up) and the subsequent erection of smaller posts such as Stand-off, Kipp, Conrad, Slide-out and High River presaged a state of lawlessness that promised evil to the Canadian scene. By the autumn of 1872, the trade in firewater had spread towards the east with the building of several log trading huts on Battle Creek in the Cypress Hills, chief of which were those of two "squaw-men", Abel Farwell and Moses Solomon. In sheer defiance of the laws of Canada and the United States, brigandage now straddled and controlled the boundary line. Utter ruination of Canada's Indians of the plains was under way.

And so to our story, gleaned from participants, eye-witnesses and conflicting records.

The year of 1872 was drawing to its close. The leaves had fallen in the wooded bluffs along the prairie streams. With colder weather threatening, a band of hunting Assiniboines, under Chief Hunkajuka, or "Little Chief", pondered the selection of a winter camp-site. Far to the north, on the heels of the buffalo masses, the nomadic wayfarers had gathered a goodly supply of pemmican and dried meat. Men, women and children were happy; for in food, above all things, lay the magic gift of life. Not far removed, on the banks of the South Saskatchewan, a camp of Crees — friends and allies of the Assiniboines — were already settled, and thither Hunkajuka decided to repair. There would be festivity aplenty; inter-tribal gatherings of "friendlies" had ever been conducive to sociability. Besides the interests of both camps would be well served, and the long months of cold would pass amid many pleasantries.

During the early winter, there was little to be desired. The dusky tenants of the tapering lodges revelled in sheer contentment. Security and plenty prevailed; festivities, whether rituals or carnivals of food, so dear to pagan hearts, followed one upon another. An occasional buffalo hunt replenished the fresh meat supply and tended to conserve the fast-dwindling pemmican and "jerky". But soon the latter commodities were all but gone; inherent prodigality had joined with an all-too-free abandon. Worse still, for reasons unknown to the wisest soothsayers, the buffalo herds drew off to other parts. The nightmare of famine, of want beset by winter, loomed as an imminent danger. Desperation fell upon the camp, and quick decisions followed. Little Chief bethought him of the Cypress Hills, hundreds of miles southward, across the whitened plains. It were better to risk the rigours of such a journey than to stay and starve. So, with gloomy forebodings, the Assiniboines bade their compatriots farewell and turned to a bitter task.

Week followed week as the hunger-scourged travellers trudged on. One by one, the aged and decrepit dropped out to die. Ponies and dogs were eaten; and, as these dwindled, the tribulations of the squaws increased. Buffalo skins, par-flêche containers, leather — all articles that offered barest sustenance — were turned to account as food. Wherever old camp-sites were found, discarded bones were dug from the snow, to be crushed and boiled. Hunters ranged desperately to no avail; while, ever closer and closer, the grim spectre of famine trailed the struggling waifs. The cold bit to the marrow. A youthful couple, seeing their only child succumb, decided it was the end; but, so weakened was the crazed young warrior following a self-inflicted knifethrust in his vitals, he lacked the strength to complete the pact. So his helpmate survived.

The threat of death confronted all! But at last the Cypress Hills was reached; and, camping in a sheltered vale close to Farwell's post, the exhausted band, having lost some 30 lives, slowly recovered from its recent ordeal. Buffalo were numerous; smaller game abounded about the coulees and brush clad slopes. Though helpless to travel farther without more ponies, the Assiniboine remnant, released from its bondage of cold and hunger, resumed the normal activity of tribal life. Spring was at hand; buds were now swelling on the aspen trees.

Meanwhile, a related episode was being enacted far beyond the boundary.

South of Farwell's post, a matter of a hundred miles or more, in Montana, there lies another hilly outcropping — the Bear's Paw Mountains. Working out from here, a small gang of "wolfers" from Benton had spent the winter trapping and poisoning the thick-coated harpies of the buffalo herds, and doing some trading. April of the historic year of 1873 had come, and the members of the party—all seasoned and unscrupulous frontiersmen—had packed up and were on the move. Mostly, they were men who lived hard, shot hard, and, when opportunity offered, drank hard of "Montana Redeye" and "Tarantula Juice", the principal medium of border trade and barter.

With horses loaded, they struck for Benton to "cash in" and indulge in such attractions as they craved. At the Teton River, ten miles from their destination, a last camp was made, and here, while all slept, a band of Canadian Crees, accompanied by some Metis, ran off some 20 of their horses. Arrived at Benton, the maddened dupes, doubtlessly abetted by much liquor, planned a swift revenge. A punitive expedition of about a dozen desperadoes, including the wolfers, well mounted and under the leadership of an erstwhile Montana sheriff, Tom Hardwick, of unsavoury reputation, was forthwith pledged to the recovery or replacement of the stolen stock and to the fullest possible accounting in red-skin blood. At the Teton, the trail of the Cree raiders was picked up and followed, only to be lost some miles to the northward. Nevertheless, resolved to loose their venom upon Indian flesh, the potential murderers pushed on.

While Hardwick and his co-searchers were casting northward, all was not peaceful in and about the diminutive trading posts in the Cypress Hills; nor in the Indian camps nearby. From time immemorial the place had been a general battleground of warring tribes, and more recently the scene of bitter hatreds engendered by the whiskey trade. Horse-stealing and spontaneous killings were confined to neither side. Testimony criss-crosses and is entangled in every attempt to lift the veil from the utter depravity attendant upon the first trading incursions from Benton to this historic spot; records left by one side contradict the other; details are muddled in keeping with the drunken brawls and liquor-crazed homicides staged by whites and Indians. But from sworn statements of whites and the obviously faithful chronicles and memories of several Assiniboines involved—who still live—an account, to all intents and purposes varying slightly from the truth, emerges.

Besides Little Chief's followers who, devoid of food, had run the long gauntlet of the winter plains, several bands of the same tribe were en-camped in and about the hills—principally one under Chief Minashina-yen, who had wintered in one of the many sheltered coulees, and lost a number of ponies to enemy raiders. None of these Indians had been south of the boundary during the winter. With each and every camp the whiskey traders had been driving a brisk and unscrupulous trade for buffalo robes and furs; but, with the first days of spring, the camps began to move to

7

summer haunts. In addition, 13 lodges of Wood Mountain Assiniboines had drifted in from the east and joined Little Chief's camp on Battle Creek, doubtless attracted by the presence of the traders. And some 40 or 50 lodges stood clustered below the shelter of a steep cut-bank, on the east side of the creek, directly across from Farwell's post.

Ten days previous to the arrival of Little Chief's band from its painful trek, a story became current that three horses had been stolen from Farwell's by passing Assiniboines. Perhaps they had strayed, as the corral gate had been left open. In any case, whiskey was flowing freely, and George Hammond, the owner of two of the horses, seemingly an advance member of the Benton gang, had worked himself into a frenzy and sworn vengeance upon all Indians in the neighbourhood. But Little Chief's Indians, who had consumed or worn out all but five of their own mounts, had picked up one of Hammond's missing horses on the way in and returned it to its owner.

That same night, in the budding month of May, Tom Hardwick, with part of his gang, rode into Farwell's. Within the log trading post the lid was off!

Next morning, the rest of Hardwick's men arrived. Drinking grew boastful. Farwell kept his head, but Moses Solomon joined in the festivities. Meantime, two kegs of liquor found their way, gratuitously, to the Assiniboine camp. Someone at the post, in his cups, turned the horses out from the corral, and, soon afterwards, Hammond announced in whiskey-sodden expletives that his horse, returned to him only the day before, had again been stolen—by the very Assiniboine who had brought it in. Farwell argued otherwise, and offered to have two horses from the Indian camp delivered to the complaining Hammond backing his word by striking out, across the creek, for that purpose. Little Chief readily complied with the request, offering two horses as security. Meanwhile he sent out some young Indians to search for the missing animal, which was found quietly grazing on a nearby slope.

It was now past midday. While Farwell talked to the chief, several of the Benton gang called to the trader to get out of the way. Well fortified by liquor, they were obviously out to kill! Startled, Farwell shouted back that, if they fired, he would fight with the Indians. He urged the gun-men to hold off until he went to the post for his interpreter, Alexis Le Bombard, in order that both sides might talk the matter over. This was agreed to; but barely had he left when shots rang out.

What followed has been the subject of many versions. From intoxicated minds stories would naturally disagree; falsehoods would spring from the guilty; exaggerations from onlookers. The truth would have it that many of the Assiniboines were hopelessly drunk. Thanks to the liquor purposely bestowed upon them, few of the Indians could offer resistance. The chief of the Wood Mountain band, which had recently been added to the camp lay helpless. Little Chief was in his senses, and the few who were sober, notably the squaws having sensed imminent trouble, strove frantically to bring the helpless warriors to their wits. The first shots fired may have been from one or more of these — though it would seem that ammunition was woefully meagre in the camp. The 12 men under Hardwick were joined by others including Hammond, their apparent leader, as well as by Moses Solomon, the trader. Two had been left behind to guard the buildings.

No matter the nature of the preliminaries, bloodshed to a certainty was close at hand. Murder, cold-blooded, besotted, and, under the circumstances, particularly merciless and ghastly, was inescapable. Little Chief's people assuredly had had no part in the horse theft on the Teton. They had committed no greater evil than to drink the white man's poison. But, in the minds of the Benton gang, it was sufficient for the purpose that they were Indians.

That May-day afternoon was to witness stark tragedy on Battle Creek. Life in the Cypress Hills was functioning true to form; but utter savagery had of a sudden been confronted by a wave of civilization more savage still. Blood-lust, rendered wild-eyed and determined by copious drinking, must needs vent itself — and the Assiniboines had offered the coveted opportunity. On no account would Benton gossip have grounds for ridicule. The robbery on the Teton, even if amends in kind were not achieved, would be well and truly brought to frontier satisfaction by unerring triggers. Indians must pay. Murderous premeditation on the part of Hardwick and Hammond and their satellites has been proven. Had not the gangsters seized a position along a cut-bank commanding the Assiniboine lodges after first speculating upon the lay of the land, the affair that followed might be said to have occurred on the spur of the moment. A galling fire was poured upon men, women and children indiscriminately. Pandemonium reigned among the lodges. To the credit of Little Chief and the few men he could muster for defence, several futile attempts were made to dislodge the murderers by courageously charging the cut-bank. But each sortie was repulsed by the unerring storm of bullets hurled upon it.

Their position helpless, with dead and wounded piling up, the Assiniboines raced towards the Whitemud Coulee directly to the east and on the gangsters' left. Here they attempted to make a stand, but Tom Hardwick and one John Evans mounted their horses and outflanked them. They were submitted to deadly fire from the higher ground, and driven to the cover of the brush. Little Chief tried to outflank the flankers, but several men were sent round-about to Hardwick's support. One of these,

Ed Grace, attempted a short cut and was shot through the heart by an Indian, who bit the dust a moment later. And so the killing proceeded. Hardwick and his supporters drew in from their outpost, killing Indians by picked shots wherever they appeared. The Assiniboines were murdered, routed and scattered to the winds. As the sun sank, the camp was charged, but none save three wounded men, who were promptly dispatched, and several terror-stricken squaws, remained. According to the story handed down, the unfortunate women were taken to Farwell's and Solomon's posts, there to face a night of drunken bestiality and outrage.

Next morning, the Assiniboine lodges were rifled of such valuables as they contained, and were then piled with all the Indian equipment and set on fire. Two horses were found and probably claimed by Hammond. Dead bodies lay everywhere, but the number was never to be known. Many victims, grievously wounded, had been dragged away by the survivors. A ghastly reminder of the outrage was Little Chief's head on a lodge pole high above the smouldering camp. The one dead white, Ed Grace, was buried beneath the floor of Farwell's post, which was then burned down. With that, the Benton colony in the Cypress Hills loaded its wagons, vaulted to the saddle and hit the trail to Benton.

Food (or the lack of it), festivity, firewater and fighting had contributed to bring about a bloody climax which Canada could not and would not countenance.

Then the North West Mounted Police! The famous march across the plains; the erection of Forts Macleod and Calgary in the Blackfeet realm, and Fort Walsh on Battle Creek — the coming of law and order and square-dealing.

Editor's Note

The 1873 massacre was reported to Ottawa by Lieutenant Governor Morris. He wrongly informed the government that the gang responsible were Americans from Fort Whoop-Up, near present-day Lethbridge. Actually they came from Fort Benton, Montana, and included at least one Canadian. The government had already been informed of the massacre by the U.S. government. Sir John A. Macdonald had considered for some time a police force for the great western area known then as the North-West Territories. The Massacre prodded the government to take action. On September 25th that year an Order-in-Council announced the formation of a "Mounted Police force for the North-West Territories". Recruiting for the Force began soon after.

J.P. Turner was the Force's historian for many years. He authored two volumes of the definitive history of the North-West Mounted Police for the years 1873–1893, and was published by the King's Printer.

2

Maunsell's Story

ex-Sub/Const. E.H. Maunsell

The following story is an old timer's tale about whiskey trading, patent medicine, and carpenters' levels. We enjoyed reading it and think you will too. The author, ex-Sub. Cst. E.H. Maunsell, was one of the earliest members of the Force — Reg. No. 380. His entire life was as remarkable as the few brief years he describes here.

Born in Ireland on October 14, 1854, he joined the North West Mounted Police on June 11, 1874, and journeyed with the Force on the famous "march west". His brother, George W. Maunsell (old service number 386) joined the Force a year later at Dufferin on February 20th. Ned took his discharge on June 25, 1877 (time expired), to take up ranching just outside Fort Macleod, Alberta. George took his discharge on May 31, 1878, to join his brother in forming the well-known IV Ranch adjoining the Peigan Reservation. They were joined in 1881 by a third brother, Harry Frederick, who came out to Alberta from the old country by way of Fort Benton.

In his later years, prompted by the 50th anniversary of the Force, Ned Maunsell wrote this chronicle of his early life in the NWMP on the Canadian frontier. His story begins here. Ed.

Few people have seen our vast country change from a wilderness into what it is now. When I visit Calgary and stay at the Palliser Hotel I feel like a second Rip Van Winkle. To one who has not had my experience, it would require a vivid imagination to see Indian tepees on the ground now occupied by the hotel and envisage large herds of buffalo grazing on the town site of Calgary. This vast change could never have taken place if the Mounted Police, or some similar force, had not first established law and order.

In 1873, the North West Mounted Police was formed. It consisted of three troops, A, B and C, and comprised 150 men. This Force was dispatched over the Dawson route, the trail joining Port Arthur's Landing (now Thunder Bay, Ont.) to the Winnipeg area, and wintered at Stone

Fort, Manitoba (now Lower Fort Garry, some 20 miles north of Winnipeg). Later the Force was increased to three hundred and D, E and F troops travelled through the United States as far as Fargo, North Dakota, by train, having left Toronto in the eary summer of 1874.

I was among the latter group. At Fargo we got off the train and, after getting our wagons together, marched about 150 miles north to Dufferin, Manitoba, which was about a mile or two north of the international boundry line. There we were joined by the other three troops who had journeyed south from Stone Fort to meet us. We camped at Dufferin for a few weeks, getting our transportation into shape while awaiting the arrival of supplies which came down by boat on the Red River from Fargo. Each troop was provided with a number of the famous Red River carts, hauled by oxen and driven by half-breeds under the charge of a man whose name was, not surprisingly, Driver.

We all knew that we were being dispatched into the Northwest Territories for the purpose of suppressing the sale of whiskey to the Indians and that our objective was Fort Whoop-Up which was supposed to be strongly fortified and garrisoned by several "desperadoes". In order to demolish this Fort, we brought with us two nine pounders and two mortars.

We fretted much at being delayed at Dufferin as we were anxious to start our crusade. At Dufferin I had an opportunity to observe that not all my colleagues were "abstainers". Manitoba was not "dry" in those days; in fact it could be described as "extremely humid". No matter how small a settlement might be, a saloon appeared to be a necessary adjunct. There was not a settlement at that time around Dufferin, still it boasted two saloons. Their only justification for existing was that Royal Engineers wintered there. The Engineers were employed surveying the forty-ninth parallel. They had left by the time the police arrived and the saloons, not expecting us, had allowed their stocks to run low. Those Mounties who were not teetotalers dried up the place by the simple expedient of consuming all the contents.

On the first week of July, we started on what proved to be the longest cavalry march on record. Owing to the large number of wagons and Red River carts, we presented a most imposing appearance. We started out in great pomp; a large advance guard of mounted men in extended order and a large rear guard. At night, we were guarded by nine mounted sentries. However, our eastern horses, not being used to the prairie grasses, failed rapidly and we soon abandoned a good many of these frills. In fact, we did not go very far before we were converted from a mounted, to a dismounted force, and had to depend on shanks' mare. On arrival at Roche Percée, "A" Troop was detached from the main force and dispatched to Fort Edmonton. This troop was under command of Colonel Jarvis and had for sergeant-major the later General, Sir S. Steele.

At Old Wives Lake we encountered the first aborigines. To those of us who had formal, preconceived ideas from reading Fenimore Cooper and other authors, it proved a bitter disappointment. I was particularly angry with Longfellow, for, on carefully looking over the whole band, I did not see a single Hiawatha or Minehaha — even allowing for a poet's license.

The impoverished condition of this band of Indians led to much debate as to the existence of the whiskey traders. Some argued that if all the Indians were as poor as these, no whiskey trader could make a living out of dealing with them. Others advanced the idea that their poverty was caused by dealing with the whiskey traders. The only touch of romance that we observed was that all the bucks were armed with bows and arrows.

We obtained some mementoes from these Indians which we long treasured. Unfortunately, we pitched our tents in one of their abandoned camping grounds. The spot might have better been called a cleansing station because it was there that the Indians got rid of their parasites. The moment we set up camp those creatures became very much attached to us. The fresh pastures which we afforded them were evidently most suitable for they increased and multiplied at a malicious rate. This plague was aggravated by the fact that after leaving Old Wives Lake we travelled through a country where water was scarce and we had no opportunity of washing. To make matters more uncomfortable, we were also reduced to very small rations.

The gloomiest days ever experienced by the Mounted Police were, undoubtedly, the days of short rations. In the morning each man was issued a small lump of half-baked dough and a cubic inch of boiled bacon. These were promptly devoured in a few mouthfuls. We then had to fast till the following morning. All day we tramped over the endless prairie, suffering the pangs of hunger by day, devoured by parasites by night.

This was very different from what we had pictured ourselves doing when we joined the Force. We were all young men and inspired with a spirit of adventure. We had imagined ourselves mounted on spirited horses chasing desperadoes over the prairies. We had also thought that perhaps the Indians might not appreciate the motive of our coming and prove hostile. All of which would have been much more exciting than fighting hunger and cooties. The shortness of supplies was, however, somewhat alleviated when we got into buffalo country.

It was most providential that we met the buffalo when we did as we had completely run out of provisions. We were now put on a straight ration of buffalo meat and although the quantity was not limited, our appetite was not really appeased. The buffalo we first met were the old bulls, those which had been driven out of the herds. Their meat was very tough and the only way we could cook it was to boil it until it disintegrated into strings. In a few days, however, we got to where the buffalo were numerous and some discrimination could be used in selecting animals for slaughter.

The method adopted for cooking was primitive. Buffalo were killed every day, more or less according to chance. When we camped at night the cooks would chop their meat into large chunks and boil it. In the morning, each man was allowed to help himself to what he thought would suffice him for the day and it was marvelous what he could consume. We would fairly fill our haversack, and instead of having regular times for meals, it seemed as if we were eating all day long. In this way we easily consumed ten pounds per day. Even then we did not feel satisfied as our craving for vegetable food was intense.

I believe the aim of the Commissioner was to keep the line of march about a hundred miles north of the boundary and this distance was pretty well maintained. We skirted the Cypress Hills on the north and crossed several deep coulees containing many berry bushes laden with berries which we devoured ravenously regardless of whether they were ripe or not. The chokecherries were particularly welcome. We found they counteracted the laxative effect of consuming such a vast quantity of fresh meat.

For some time before we turned north the only water we had to drink was what we could find in half-dry alkali lakes. The land surrounding these lakes was just as bare as if a prairie fire had swept across it due to the vast herds of buffalo which fed there. The water in the lakes was also badly fouled by the buffalo.

When we turned north, we followed a long coulee which led us to a valley through which ran a magnificent river. This must have been either the Seven Persons coulee or else the coulee where Medicine Hat was later built. Here we remained for a few days and thoroughly enjoyed washing ourselves and drinking clear, cool water. Our poor horses seemed to equally enjoy the fresh water; they had been having a hard time both from shortage of water and grass.

While we were camped on this bottom, scouting parties were set out to see if they could find Fort Whoop-Up or any other human habitation. They returned without results and we started on the trek again. This time, we travelled almost due south. The reason for the change in the direction of our march led to the wildest speculation amongst the men. We came to the conclusion that the government must have been hoaxed and that such a place as Whoop-Up did not exist. Having carefully searched the country where it was supposed to be, we were sure it didn't exist.

The yarn about the whiskey traders, we decided, was pure myth. What would whiskey traders want in a country where there were no Indians? We had been travelling for over two months and had not met one Indian, except the band at old Wives Lake. We had become so skeptical that some even doubted the existence of the Rocky Mountains! They thought that after travelling for two months and a half due west from Manitoba we should have caught sight of them. The men by now were a very disgruntled and disgusted lot. We had been marching for a long time, half starved of food, forced to drink the most vile kind of water, and bothered by parasites. Now it seemed we had been dispatched on a fool's errand and would become the laughing stock of Canada.

After travelling a few days, the tops of three hills came into view. These hills proved to be the Sweet Grass Hills, although at the time, we did not know what they were called. It was a great relief to the eye to see hills after observing nothing but monotonous prairie for so long. We were astonished, though, at how long it took to get near one of those buttes. Distance is so deceptive.

About the twentieth of September, we experienced a severe snowstorm and this day's march put me in mind of a picture I once saw of the retreat of Napoleon's army from Moscow! I was driving a Red River cart following the trail that the lead wagon made in the snow. Now and then, I would pass a wagon, the team of which was too played out to continue and was, therefore, waiting for the rear guard to give it assistance. We also had a number of saddle horses which were so weak they could not be induced to travel without being led. We used to tie seven or eight of these together in a line and a man would lead each string. If one of these fell, sometimes the whole line would also tumble — like a lot of nine pins.

Because of the storm, the buffalo started moving south. The visibility, however, was extremely limited and, as a result, we were overrun quite frequently by bands of buffalo which did not seem to notice us in the thick snow.

That night, we camped on some high ground and it was sunrise the next day before the rear guard got in. During the night, the snow had ceased and when reveille sounded in the morning, at about 5 o'clock, there was not a cloud to be seen. Soon we saw what we took for a strange phenomenon. Bright, rosy-pink objects appeared in the west well above the horizon. It came to my mind that this must be the light referred to by poets as "the light that never was on sea or land". When the sun rose, the source of this mysterious light was revealed. To the west stood the Rocky Mountains clad in new snow. The sun, before it became visible to us in the east, had illuminated the higher peaks to our west. The whole scene was a marvelous panorama. Not only were the mountains visible in the west, but south of us rising out of the prairie stood the three buttes of the Sweet Grass Hills looking like gigantic sentinels guarding the unknown.

The east also presented a sight which no eye will ever witness again. As I stated, we were camped on high ground and as far as the eye could see were vast herds of buffalo moving slowly south, their black bodies a stark contrast against the snow-covered prairies. The storm evidently had moved the buffalo from the north and they were now returning to their winter ranges. It was impossible to calculate their vast numbers. Who would have predicted then that the buffalo would almost become extinct in a few years!

From this point, Colonel French and Colonel Macleod and some other officers went to Benton, Montana, to obtain supplies. After a day or two, the Force moved east to a lake which I believe is called Wild Horse Lake. Our half-breed guide who was an old buffalo hunter advised us against moving onto the flats while the buffalo were so thick. They would be sure to stampede and if we were in the way the result would surely be a disaster.

We remained at Wild Horse Lake until the Commissioner returned. He came into camp after midnight and we were much puzzled to know how he had found our location in the dark. The explanation came in the morning when we found he was accompanied by a guide, Jerry Potts. In later days, I made several trips with Jerry and I am convinced that he was possessed of some special sense which is given to few. No matter how dark the night, no matter how great the distance, Jerry could lead you to any point you wanted to go. He was more familiar with this vast country than any settler was with his quarter section.

I was on guard the night the Commissioner arrived. After things were quiet, the corporal of the guard investigated the wagons and found one contained some sacks of potatoes. He "appropriated" some for each one of the guards. As we had a large fire of buffalo chips going, we proceeded to roast our potatoes. However, impatient, I could not resist eating one of mine raw. I enjoyed it more than any fruit I had ever eaten.

Next day everything was abustle. It was decided to leave three troops, B, C and F, in the country under the command of Colonel Macleod, while D and E Troops went to the Swan River area, the point that had been chosen for our Headquarters. All the strongest horses were selected for the two troops that had to return. This trip was an enjoyable one. We were well supplied with provisions and we made good time. When we arrived at Swan River we found that the construction of the barracks was still in the hands of the Board of Works and was far from being completed. We also found that the quantity of hay that had been put up for the Winter use of our horses had been burnt in a prairie fire, so Colonel French decided to leave E Troop at Swan River, taking D with him to Fort Garry where he arrived early in November. By this time, we were indeed an unkempt and ragged lot. Colonel French had us all weighed and much to our surprise we had all gained weight, notwithstanding the hardships and hunger we had suffered. We then moved from Fort Garry to Dufferin, the point from which we started, having completed a march of over two thousand miles. Here we occupied the quarters recently vacated by the engineers who had completed the survey of the international boundry line to the Rocky Mountains.

In the early summer of 1875, we moved to Swan River and met E Troop who had wintered there. Swan River was a point which would delight the heart of a prohibitionist. There was no possible way of anyone running whiskey into that area without being instantly detected. We remained at Swan River camp for about a year and only on two occasions was liquor brought in.

The first "culprit" was no less a person than Major General Selby Smith. General Smith was at that time in command of the forces in Canada — an Imperial officer. The General, having inspected the garrison at Fort Garry, decided to visit British Columbia, travelling through the Northwest Territories with a police escort. He had been requested by the government to inspect and report on the police, and for this purpose he and his staff visited Swan River barracks early in July. He camped in front of the officers' quarters which were a long distance from the men's quarters.

That night I was on guard duty and at about two o'clock in the morning a sentry reported to Sgt. Tom Lake, who was in charge of the guard, that D Troop's barrack windows were lit up. Lake took me and another man with him to investigate the cause of this extraordinary occurrence. I might say that the men's quarters were one huge building occupied by D and E Troops. Before we reached the room we heard a great deal of laughing. When we arrived there we found all the lamps lit and the men of D and E Troops dressed just as if they had gotten out of bed, and all acting in a most peculiar manner. The only one decently dressed was a man called Jack Beaudoin. He was decidedly under the influence of liquor! He at once rushed up to Lake saying, "Sergeant Lake, you are the very man I want. I was just going to see you. I want you to arrest General Smith for bringing whiskey into the Northwest Territories." Lake appeased him by saying he would attend to the matter in the morning and that the General had no chance of escaping. He soon sent all the men back to their beds and turned the lights out.

The next day after coming off guard I got an explanation of what caused this excitement. Beaudoin, a man who had the instincts of a

Sherlock Holmes, reasoned that it was highly improbable that General Smith and his entourage were making this long and weary journey without being provided with some stimulants. To test his theory, sometime after midnight, he searched the General's wagons and was rewarded by finding a five-gallon jug containing some suspicious fluid. He took the jug to the barrack room and woke up two of his special chums. These three worthies made a most exhaustive test of the contents of the jug! After several libations they became convinced both from its taste and effect that it was indeed whiskey. They then woke up the rest of D Troop, and having also roused E Troop, invited them all to partake. We expected there would be a great investigation into this matter but we were mistaken.

The next attempt to get whiskey was made by a police officer. I was forced to perform an unpleasant duty this time. During Summer and Fall a light wagon was used for bringing in the mail, but in Winter it came by dog train. An order was issued that nothing but letters and papers would be brought and we were warned not to send for anything else. At this time I was a clerk in the orderly room and one of my duties was to accept the mail from the mail carrier and sort it. A few days before Christmas the mail arrived and I emptied the contents of the sacks on the floor. I noticed a parcel addressed to Sub-Inspector Dickens.

Just as I had the Colonel's mail sorted he arrived in the orderly room and I handed him his letters. The parcel at once caught his eagle eye. He asked me to whom it was addressed and I said Mr. Dickens. I was then told to tell Mr. Dickens that the Colonel wanted to see him in the orderly room. When Dickens appeared the Colonel asked him if he had not heard the order about not getting parcels by mail. Dickens said he had but that he had sent for the parcel before the order came out. The Colonel appeared to accept this explanation and turned to go into his office when Dickens made a fatal mistake. He stooped and picked up his parcel and started to leave the orderly room. It seemed strange to me that he was in such a hurry to secure this parcel when he knew I would be delivering the rest of his mail in a very short time. It must have also seemed peculiar to the Colonel, for just as Dickens was going out the door he asked, "What is in that parcel, Dickens?" Dickens stammered. His stammering became worse with his increasing nervousness. After much stuttering he managed to say, "b-b-b-brandy, Sir." The Colonel then told him to hand the parcel to me and directed me to open it. I produced from it an imperial quart of Hudson's Bay brandy. I was then ordered to take the bottle outside and smash it. This was a most unpleasant duty.

Fortunately, at Swan River there were no substitutes for liquor such as the patent medicines, prevalent in those times. The only instance we had of the terrible effects of excessive drinking of patent medicines happened to a corporal named McCrom. He was sent on detachment to Fort Carlton, a Hudson's Bay post. After being there some months he was reported dead. Another man was sent to take his place and instructed to inquire into the cause of McCrom's death. In due time the man reported that he thought McCrom had died from excessive drinking of Perry Davis painkiller as he had found over eight broken bottles in McCrom's room.

The only person at Swan River who drank fairly constantly was a strange character named John Wymersburch, who hailed from Luxembourg. John had a job attending sick horses. Whatever these horses suffered from, many required a dose of sweet spirits of nitre. When John administered this he always took horn for horn with his patient. It did not seem to do him any harm.

Had I taken my discharge from the police at Swan River and left the Northwest Territories, I think I should have remained a lifelong convert to prohibition. I could see nothing in the enforced temperance that we were subject to, but what was beneficial.

In 1876 the Custer massacre occurred and the United States troops pursued the Sioux northward. Fearing the Sioux would be forced into Canada, D Troop was sent to Fort Macleod to reinforce C. On arriving at Fort Macleod as a member of D Troop, I expected conditions would be similar to what they were at Swan River. Indeed, nothing could have been more dissimilar — as far as drinking was concerned. At Macleod men were quartered in smaller rooms, nine men to a room. The room I was assigned contained men with whom I was quartered at Dufferin and whose habits regarding drinking I knew. Now, had we returned to Dufferin where there were two saloons, I feel sure that at least two of these men, besides myself, would have had no thought of visiting these institutions. However, after supper on the day of our arrival we were visited by a C Troop man who produced a bottle containing sufficient whiskey to give us all a drink. After our experience at Swan River we were much restrained. But one thing led to another and soon we asked the C Troop man if he could obtain any more. All subscribed sufficient funds to purchase two more bottles and for the first time in my life, I knew what it was to be intoxicated.

Now, I must recount the doings, as related to me by a C Troop man, of that part of the Force that left us in the Sweet Grass Hills in the Fall of 1874. He said that as soon as we separated at Wild Horse Lake they marched to Fort Whoop-Up under the guidance of Jerry Potts and had no difficulty in finding it. It was built where the St. Mary and Belly Rivers join. Bearing in mind reports that the fort was garrisoned and prepared to fight, Colonel Macleod approached it cautiously. The nine pounders and mortars were placed so as to command the fort. C Troop was the artillery troop. In the morning, long before sunrise, the other two troops were given extra ammunition and told to advance on the fort in extended order, being cautioned that if fired on to at once take cover and wait for the guns to do their work. As the men advanced and the sun rose, no sign of life appeared around the fort. When they had approached within two hundred yards they saw an Indian run from an outhouse into the fort. They expected the alarm would be given and they would be fired on at any moment, but nothing happened and they advanced right up to the fort. Colonel Macleod hammered on the gates with the butt of his revolver. It was opened by a man with a wooden leg who said, "Walk right in Colonel, you are perfectly safe." It appeared that he and his squaw comprised the entire garrison. The police carefully searched the fort but found neither liquor nor defenders, so the garrison was left in peace.

Jerry Potts then led the police to Fort Kipp, named after a half-breed, Joe Kipp. This fort was close to the junction of the old Man's and Belly Rivers. Here also they drew a blank. The next point of attack was Fort Weatherwax which was built on a gravel bar of the old Man's River about four miles east of the present town of Macleod. Here the police met great success. The fort contained a large quantity of merchandise such as the Indians traded for and a large quantity of whiskey. Beside these, there were a great number of buffalo robes. Everything was confiscated and a heavy fine was inflicted on Mr. Weatherwax. He was an American and had an implicit belief in the all powerfulness of his country. He told Colonel Macleod that as soon as he could get into communication with Washington, the Colonel and every Mounted Policeman would wish they had never been born.

From Fort Weatherwax the police moved up the river a few miles to an island where they built Fort Macleod under great difficulties, the Winter having set in. While some engaged in building, others were sent out under the guidance of Jerry Potts to capture every whiskey trader in the country. Chasing whiskey traders was most congenial work for us. As we viewed the matter, those who were engaged in the business must be unscrupulous; not only were they selling their poisonous whiskey to the Indians but they took advantage of the Indians' subsequent intoxication to obtain their buffalo robes for practically nothing. The Indians became very friendly towards the police, largely owing to the diplomacy of Colonel Macleod. He explained to them the object of the police coming and also the laws they were expected to obey. These he administered with justice and firmness and thereby gained the confidence of all.

In 1875, the I.G. Baker Company and the I.C. Powers Company, large firms from Benton, Montana, established stores close to Fort Macleod expecting that when the whiskey traders had been banished they would acquire the large Indian trade. They also catered to the Police. I do not remember which of these stores brought in substitutes for whiskey. The first of those substitutes was very near the real thing. It was put up in fruit cans and labelled, "Brandy Peaches". On opening one of these cans it was found to contain a few peaches immersed in a fluid that was highly exhilarating. "The authorities", however, saw through the thin disguise and placed an embargo on brandy peaches. Unfortunately, there was no restriction on patent medicine and those that contained alcohol found ready sale. This encouraged some enterprising person to smuggle in whiskey from Montana which was just as poisonous as the patent medicines. There was no doubt the rotten stuff was intended for trading with the Indians.

When I arrived in Macleod in '76, I found an extraordinary state of affairs which is difficult to relate. I will first deal with patent medicines. I found many of the men consumed them in large quantities. I forget the names of the most popular brands but everything that contained alcohol was eagerly bought. I never used them. If I had, I would not be writing these reminiscences today. Of course, these drugs were not always in stock in the stores; everything in those days was brought by bull train from Benton, Montana, and there would be long intervals between shipments. Occasionally, however, at the urgent request of some of the men, the stores would obtain a case or two through mail carriers.

All this reminds me of a man whom we called Doc. He told me some of his life. He was intended for the medical profession, but having become a victim to the drinking habit, his fond but deluded parents thought their son might become weaned from his vice if they got him into the Mounted Police and thereby sent to a bone-dry country. Doc, however, found no difficulty in adapting himself to the "wine" of the country shortly after he arrived in Macleod. He became a regular patent medicine fiend. He was on guard once when a case was brought in by the mail carrier. When the guard was relieved at five in the afternoon, Doc hurried down to the I.G. Baker store and asked John Smith if there was any of the medicine left. John replied that it was all sold, long ago. On the counter, close to where Doc was standing, lay a carpenter's level which Doc picked up. He asked Smith if he had any more and was told there were two more, which he at once bought. He took these to his barrack room, procured a screwdriver and removed the glass tubes which contained some kind of alcohol. These tubes he emptied into a cup and drank. Fortunately, he got very ill. No doubt that prevented carpenter' levels from becoming a popular beverage.

I believe that all those who drank patent medicines to excess had their lives shortened but I only remember one case where the effect was sudden. This happened in either '78 or '79 when I had started ranching. I came to

21

Macleod to see a man named Toni la Chapelle. I found him in a room at Taylor's Restaurant, together with all the elite of Macleod. The gathering was presided over by Captain Winder who was then in command of the Macleod post. They were evidently celebrating something. Amongst those present was Jerry Potts and another half-breed named Roche La Rue who was always called "Rock". On entering the room Captain Winder presented me with a bottle which was labelled "No. 6". I glanced at the label's directions and I think a teaspoonful was a dose for whatever ailed you. I followed the directions and it was not unpleasant to taste. While I was discussing my business with Tony someone suggested another round of drinks of which all partook, with the exception of Rock who was sitting on a chair apparently asleep. Captain Winder told Jerry Potts to wake him up. After giving him several shakes, Jerry turned and said he was dead. It appeared Rock had been the first to sample No. 6. It was a new brand and he had consumed a whole bottle before the celebration had commenced.

Eventually, the selling of whiskey to the Indians completely ceased. The Indians gave no trouble as there were still sufficient buffalo to supply them with all they wanted. So the only duty which the police had to perform was the one of trying to capture whiskey smugglers who were endeavouring to run in whiskey to sell to the police themselves. There was a sort of tacit understanding between the smugglers and the police. Every policeman was keen to capture the smugglers on their way in. If this happened, the smugglers' horses, wagons, and all wagon contents would be confiscated. If a smuggler was successful in running the blockade, he, to some extent, found sanctuary. He invariably cached his whiskey and brought it in to town in small quantities, disposing of it as opportunity occurred. The police greatly enjoyed the challenge of trying to capture the smuggler; it was certainly much more preferable than the monotony of barrack life. The police were handicapped, however, as there was no telling where or when the smugglers would cross the boundry line, and they always travelled by night. Eventually, they would be apprehended though — with the exception of one man, named Lawrence.

So successful was Lawrence in eluding us that we would have preferred capturing him to winning the V.C. He lived in a house in Macleod and made no bones about his livelihood. The police and he were the best of friends and would frequently join one another. Lawrence was kept under observation and if he was reported absent we knew he had gone to Montana for whiskey. After a few days, patrols would be sent out to try and intercept him, but as always happened, Lawrence turned up in Macleod smiling, followed in a few days by the disgusted patrols. Finding it impossible to capture Lawrence coming in with his cargo, it was decided

22

to worry him by fining him for having whiskey in his possession. Watch was kept on him at night with the hope that he would be seen leaving town to visit his cache; the intention being to catch him returning with booze.

One night the scout reported that he thought Lawrence had whiskey in his cabin as he had noticed several men entering and leaving during the evening. Sgt. John Birk and two men were sent to search. It being June, the sun was just rising when they entered Lawrence's cabin. They found two other men there, asleep on chairs. Lawrence was in bed and apparently asleep. Birk announced, "Lawrence, I have come to search your cabin." Now Lawrence was very alert. He said, "Alright, Sergeant, I will be with you in a minute", or something like that, which led the police to think that he realized he was caught and was prepared to go to barracks with them. He got out of bed, put on his trousers and boots, went to a washstand where there was a basin and jug, emptied the contents of the jug in the basin, and washed himself. He then combed and brushed his hair, and, having performed his ablutions, he did what was usual: took the basin and threw its contents out the door. When this was done, he turned to Birk and said, "Now go ahead with your search." The cabin was small, and after looking in every possible place the police could find nothing incriminating. What puzzled them most was that while Lawrence was perfectly sober he smelt like a distillery and so did his house. They had to return to barracks and report that they had not found anything. Some days later, Lawrence revealed the mystery; when the police had entered his cabin there was about a quart of whiskey in the jug which he emptied into the basin, washed himself with, then threw out.

When ranching started, the duties of the police were greatly increased. We were living close to Montana which then contained many lawless men. Horses were frequently stolen and driven across the border. This alone kept the police busy. Then when the buffalo entirely disappeared, as they did around 1879, the Indians at once took to killing cattle. Even after the Indians had been placed on reserves and were being fed by the government this offence did not cease. It took some time for the Indians to become accustomed to reservation life and cease their nomadic life. They were used to consuming vast quantities of meat. The rations of meat they were given on the reservations, although sufficient for a white man, were entirely inadequate for an Indian.

The police got every assistance from the ranchers in suppressing cattle rustling; but in another way, the influx of the ranchers added to their difficulties in controlling the liquor problem. It is safe to say that amongst these early ranchers not one prohibitionist could be found, nor could a single person be found who would not avail himself of illicit spirits if the opportunity presented itself. As a consequence, whiskey smuggling increased to such an extent that the entire police force, even if they had no other duties to perform, could not control it. It had a demoralizing effect on our men. They were trying to enforce a law, prohibition, which was disapproved of by all the settlers and for that matter, the police themselves. It must be confessed that if the reputation of the Force had to rest on their enforcement of prohibition, it would not have attained the high level it has. It can easily be understood that when the government at last recognized the impossibility of enforcing an unpopular law, the Force heaved a great sigh of relief. They were now able to bend all their energies towards suppressing other crimes.

In closing, I would like to make a brief summary of what the pioneer police undertook and accomplished. In 1874, three hundred green men, some very young without any experience of prairie life and few with the experience of discipline, were launched into this unknown country, told to put an end to the sale of whiskey to the Indians and to instill in the latter, some of the most savage tribes in North America, respect for law and order. This they accomplished well. They could not have done so if they had been men of an inferior class. When the Sioux under the leadership of Sitting Bull crossed the line in 1877 and 1878, after having defeated and annihilated the flower of the American Cavalry, they were handled by a few Mounted Policemen at Cypress Hills. They became as obedient to law as if the police were ten thousand strong. To appreciate what the police accomplished, in those early days, one has only to look at conditions as they existed in Montana: shootings were of daily occurrence and lynch law the only law in force.

Have I not reason to be justly proud of the boast that I belonged to that body of men who laid the foundations on which those who followed built such splendid traditions?

Editor's Note

It is rare to find a first-hand account of the final days of the March West. Maunsell took his discharge after his first term of service and became a rancher and a highly respected citizen in what is now southern Alberta. This article, written some years before it was published in the RCMP *Quarterly*, touches on a number of incidents, which have been the basis of other historical writings.

3

A Police Patrol
Skirmishes with Indians

Ex-Const. E.F. Racey

Following the engagement at Cut Knife Hill some 30 miles from Battleford on May 2, 1885, between Lt. Col. W.D. Otter's column and the Crees under Poundmaker, the victorious red men became wanderers in the Eagle Hills and Battle river country.

Food was scarce. The supplies looted from the Indian agency stores and settlers' homes had been consumed and Nature's larder was emptying fast. Gone were the days when the plains and forests abounded with game, when luscious trout and bass swarmed aplenty in the woodland streams and lakes. Rabbit meat had now become the main dish of the nomads who, to conserve their ammunition for future clashes with the white man, resorted to the primitive bow and arrow and the snare while hunting.

Yet hunger and want failed to dampen the aboriginal ardour for nightly wardances executed to the sombre throb of tom-toms and the weird shrieks of untamed spirits. Cavorting wildly in breechclout, moccasins, war paint and feathers, their shadows in the light of the camp fire flitting from tree to tree, the dancers produced a spectacle of demoniacal passion. Advancing with shoulders well back, they started with a sort of exaggerated goose step and as the tempo mounted so did their frenzy.

Some older bucks harked back to the days when they fought the Blackfoot and the Bloods, when scalps were plentiful and buffalo roamed the plains. Those good times, they prophesied, were destined to return after the white foe was exterminated and the prairies, as Riel had promised them, once again belonged to Indian and half-breed. The younger braves were imbued by a desire to emulate the deeds of their elders.

Such orgies kept the war flame glowing, the warriors' vehemence at fever pitch and helped to ease the pangs of hunger.

Meanwhile, the men in Colonel Otter's column, which had retired from the perilous position at Cut Knife Hill and camped just outside the stockade at Fort Battleford, spent most of their time training and sharing nightly outlying picket duty. The Mounted Police attached to the brigade patrolled the country daily in all directions. At an early hour each morning a patrol, consisting usually of an NCO in charge and four constables, started out; each day miles of almost impassable ground were traversed, and seldom would the weary patrol return before sundown. It was dangerous work in that savage-infested area, for the patrol might at any time meet up unexpectedly with a band of wandering Indians and either have to fight it out or, if too greatly outnumbered, work out their salvation in other ways.

I remember one such encounter which took place on May 14, 1885.

In the morning of that day we were instructed to ride a little further than usual in the area south of the Battle river, if possible to a certain settler's cabin. The settler had been forced to flee, but before doing so had buried two guns in his back yard. our task was to unearth the guns and bring them to camp. Our search was to be in a section unfamiliar to us of the Eagle Hills which was a favourite stamping ground of wandering enemy bands, and to find the small cabin was going to be difficult — that much we knew.

We left camp at 7 o'clock with Reg. No. 670, Sgt. J.C. Gordon in charge of our party which comprised besides myself four other constables and a halfbreed guide. After a few miles the trail was little more than an indistinct thread. It wound tortuously through rough hilly country well wooded with poplar bluffs that made ideal cover for anyone bent on ambush. For several miles we followed our usual routine of examining the ground a mile or so in from the trail on both sides.

At noon we stopped beside a small stream for a lunch of hard tack and spring water. A short rest, then we decided to push straight on for the settler's cabin. The trail got worse as we went along, but that was nothing to what awaited us at the top of one hill we ascended. We rode into a large band of Indians travelling in the opposite direction.

For a moment they were as startled as we. A glance satisfied us that we were hopelessly outnumbered, about 20 to one, and that our only hope was to make a running fight of it.

Rifles barked — theirs and ours — and the Indians made a concerted rush forward, yelling like fiends. We emptied a few of their saddles, then turned and rode for cover. To our dismay we saw a large party of Indians bearing down on us from the crest of a hill on our right. To think of stopping and making a stand was out of the question, so we rode like mad. One of our men, Reg. No. 983, Cst. W.I. Spencer, kept on going. As he dug both spurs into his horse, we cursed him heartily, checked the Indian advance and retreated further.

Another of our party, Reg. No. 973, Cst. F.O. Elliot, was shot from his horse, but we were being pressed too hard to stop and see whether he was dead or not. Common sense dictated the only sensible course open to us. Elliot's horse had bolted, and to stop and try to help our unfortunate comrade, or to investigate, would have been sheer suicide.

All we could do was retreat a few yards at a time, seek cover, fire one or two rounds, then retreat again. We kept doing this until in about an hour and a half the Indians forsook the chase, fortunately before we suffered more casualties.

Back at Battleford we learned that Spencer was under the care of Dr. Strange of C Company, Royal School of Infantry, one of the militia surgeons. Then only did we understand why he had fled, leaving us behind. During the first exchange of shots he had been wounded in the back. The bullet had been deflected by a cartridge in his belt, entered his body to the right of his spine, made a sort of half circle and emerged through the front of his belt, taking some of his revolver ammunition. He had ridden to within a short distance of the Battle river when he was taken from his horse and conveyed in the ambulance to the field hospital. Deciding that a man who, with a bullet hole in his innards, had ridden seven miles or more over a rugged, ill-defined trail through bush country had grit to spare, we forgot our grudge against him.

A large rescue party and a wagon drawn by four of our fastest horses were immediately made ready to go for poor Elliot. We of the scouting party just had time to replenish our cartridge belts, saddle fresh horses and grab a mouthful of food. Two trails led up into the Eagle Hills. One, known at that time as "the new trail", was in general use; it curved along the top of a ridge flanked on both sides bv heavily-wooded ravines. But it was not as steep or dangerous as the other which forked off to the east about a quarter of a mile; the latter, called "the old trail", had a surface of very heavy gravel, mostly round filed stones that made poor footing for horses. From these hills it was about four miles to our objective.

At the scene of our skirmish we had little difficulty in locating the spot where Elliot had fallen. On foot we followed the Indians' tracks through bush and over hills until we reached a part of the Battleford-Swift Current trail that circled a dune. Here we saw a gruesome thing. Elliot's dead body had been buried in sand taken from a badger mound nearby, but his head was uncovered — left to the mercy of any wild beasts that chanced by.

In silent rage we gazed at our departed comrade, realizing that in the fast-approaching darkness it would be impossible to convey his remains to the wagon over the rough ground we had travelled; to attempt it would be foolhardy. Nor was there any way of moving the wagon to the other more passable trail without returning to Battleford. While we pondered this problem, another point came up for consideration. The Indians, confident that we would come back for the body, had made sure it would be easy to find. But their strategy was obvious to all of us; the spot they had chosen for burial was ideal for an ambush. Well aware of their intention and preferring to run the risk in daylight, we returned to Battleford to wait for dawn.

Next morning at 4.30, a squad of 20 men together with a light wagon and a four-horse team, set out along the Swift Current trail. We rode south from Battleford, crossed the Battle River about half a mile from camp, then proceeded through hilly country lush with poplar bluffs.

At the junction of the two trails, just before they entered the Eagle Hills, was a high bald-faced elevation, from the top of which a person with binoculars or remarkably good eyesight could spy on the activities in the camp at Battleford. Here, one of our men who had recently patrolled that locality drew attention to a clump of young poplars.

"Those trees grew up mighty fast," he announced.

Upon investigating we found that the trees had no roots. They had been merely stuck in the ground, making a U-shaped screen behind which were signs that someone had recently lain hidden there.

We resumed our march, rode up the new trail and through the wooded hills until we came to the dune. Our comrade's body had not been disturbed. Cautiously we circled the clearing, our senses alert to detect any movement in the surrounding bush. The wagon was wheeled round and the body dug up and placed in it.

And at that moment the Indians broke cover and were upon us. They swarmed from all directions. The corpse was hurriedly roped down and, as the signal to return to camp was given, rifle fire poured in on us. But marvellous to relate, not one of our party was hit.

We were soon in full retreat, returning the Indians' fire as we urged our horses to utmost speed. I happened to be one of the advance guard and some instinct caused me to swerve to the old trail, despite the shouts of Reg. No. 594, Sgt. Major T. Wattam who was riding with the support. My two companions stayed with me, and fortunately the whole troop with the wagon followed us.

It was a wild ride that got wilder as we plunged down the steep hill. A group of Indians in ambush on the new trail awakened to the fact that we had changed our route and rushed toward us, shooting as they came. We of the advance guard wheeled at the bottom of the hill and emptied our guns with good results. Soon the support was aiding us, covering the wagon's descent.

The wagon rolled down at terrific speed, bouncing and jolting along with an incessant clatter as it passed over the many rocks. The lower part of the dashboard was knocked out and the corpse, shaken loose from its hastily-knotted bindings, slid forward along the wagon pole. The off man threw himself into the wagon box and gripping Elliot's hand held him steady. At the foot of the hill, the old four-wheeler trundled past us and scudded under cover for repairs.

We also took cover and engaged the attention of our enemies who seemed to be closing in on a wide front. The weird beat of tom-toms sounded from the top of the hill; war-whoops and yells resounded on all sides, and rifles barked harshly. We went about the business methodically and kept up a steady fire. Finally the Indians retreated; our resistance was evidently stiffer than they had expected. They made one or two attempts to draw us into the open, but, failing in this, withdrew.

Meanwhile the wagon had been repaired and the corpse fastened down firmly. Battleford was reached without further incident, and Elliot's remains were buried in the Mounted Police cemetery there.

Subsequently, following their surrender and the end of the rebellion, we learned from the Indians that Fate had favoured us. The Indian scout stationed on that hill behind the poplar screen, not expecting us so early in the morning, had fallen asleep. Barely getting clear himself, he had scurried from his hiding-place a few minutes before we arrived. Belatedly he carried news of our activities to his brother savages with the result that they had not sufficient time to perfect their plans for the ambush they had in mind.

Editor's Note

Ex-Constable Elliot's Rebellion 1885 medal is held at RCMP Headquarters, Ottawa. Information from any of our readers regarding his next of kin would be appreciated. Address: The Commissioner, RCMP, Ottawa, Ont.

4

When Sitting Bull Came to Canada

George Shepherd

When the Sioux nation began its migration to Canada in 1876 bloodshed seemed inevitable. Sitting Bull was a power not to be ignored. Yet a few North West Mounted Policemen marched into his camp, and before he realized it, his power was gone — supplanted by British law.

Sitting Bull, the Sioux, Cypress Hills, Wood Mountain, Fort Walsh — what a wealth of memory these names stir in the historian's breast! How vividly they recall that never in the history of the Mounted Police was there a more gruelling task than that of policing the Cypress Hills-Wood Mountain region when the Sioux sojourned there from 1876 to 1881.

The onerous duty of maintaining surveillance over approximately four thousand warlike Sioux, more than seven hundred of whom were warriors, was undertaken and accomplished by a mere handful of Mounted Police. That not a single life was lost on either side ranks this as one of the outstanding achievements in Canadian history. Perhaps the secret of success was in the manner Inspr. James Morrow Walsh and his men won the Indians' respect and esteem. Their story is full of interest.

Late in May 1876, Asst. Commr. Acheson Gosford Irvine of the North West Mounted Police, who was then stationed at Fort Macleod, received word from the Department of Justice, Ottawa, that owing to United States operations against hostile Indians of Dakota and Montana near the Canadian boundary there was a strong possibility the Indians would seek refuge in Canada. The Wood Mountain area was mentioned as the likely point of entry, and instructions were given to keep a sharp look-out for indications of such an undesirable influx.

In June, Inspector Walsh, the officer commanding the Cypress Hills district, was at Hot Springs, Arkansas, taking health treatments. From Ottawa he received a telegram advising him of the Custer massacre on the Little Big Horn River in the United States, and requesting that he return to his post. He left immediately for Ottawa where he conferred with departmental officials, then proceeded by way of Chicago and the Missouri River to Fort Walsh, arriving early in August. His first act was to order two scouts (one was the well-known and trustworthy Louis Léveillé) to watch the boundary country to the south-east. He also instructed them to shadow the movements of the Sioux, and to learn if possible their intentions and approximate strength.

The information in Léveillé's report enabled Walsh to warn trading posts and Indian agencies south of the international line along the Missouri and Milk Rivers of impending assault. As a result these traders and agents forestalled the Indians and saved themselves from attack.

Meanwhile a large band of Sioux had assembled on Rock Creek, ninety miles east of Fort Walsh and several miles south of the United States boundary. In October Inspector Walsh proceeded with a Mounted Police patrol to the Wood Mountain country, and from a point where Rock Creek crossed the boundary, kept about one thousand Sioux under close observation. The band was still south of the line, and in due course the inspector was convinced that the expected raids on the Milk River and Missouri posts would not materialize, for the time being at least. He accordingly retired to Fort Walsh, leaving scouts to keep an eye on the Indians.

The Sioux occupied their time hunting the buffalo between the boundary and the Missouri River, and it was not until November that their advance line entered Canada. Sub-Inspr. Edmund Frechette with a small party of police and scouts immediately set out to visit the camp which consisted of fifty-seven lodges. During the trip the patrol suffered frequent delays and great hardship from storms and cold.

Inspector Walsh became uneasy at Frechette's continued absence and, taking along twelve policemen and three scouts, set forth to investigate. On the way to Legare's trading post at Wood Mountain, which he reached on December 21, he met Frechette and his party, weary from exposure and hours in the saddle. At Wood Mountain he learned that Black Moon of the Uncapapa Sioux, who was Sitting Bull's uncle and the hereditary high chief of the Sioux Nation, had arrived there two days previously with fifty-two lodges, increasing to 109 the lodges that had crossed the boundary. The Indians of these lodges with their 3500 horses and thirty U.S. army mules, represented various divisions of the Sioux, numbering about five hundred people. This number was eventually to increase to between four and five thousand by additions from the south.

About four miles east of the old Wood Mountain boundary commission buildings was a small settlement of half-breeds that had been established some years earlier. There also was the camp of White Eagle of the Santee band who, with some 150 lodges composed of refugees from the Minnesota

Massacre of 1862 had occupied that neighbourhood for years. The new arrivals from the United States had joined White Eagle who since crossing the border had been peaceful and law-abiding and resented the intrusion of other Indians even though they were of his own nation, unless they were prepared to abide by the orders of the Mounted Police.

Among the newcomers, most of whom had participated in the annihilation of Custer and his command six months previously, the most important were Black Moon, Little Knife, Low Dog and the Man Who Crawls — all Uncapapas — a formidable array of savage war-lords compared to the single police officer and handful of men who had come to face them. A council was held during which Walsh laid down hard and fast rules that were to govern the Indians' conduct while they remained in Canada; he then inquired regarding their intentions. They answered that they had been driven from their own country and were seeking peace. They begged for pity from the White Mother. They were starving and, other than lassoes, spears and arrows, had no means with which to hunt the buffalo. Like the Indians who had preceded them they pleaded for ammunition, and Walsh authorized Legare to give them limited supplies. Thenceforth the Sioux were kept under constant observation by the red-coated representatives of law and order.

Early in March, 1877, the inspector again set out, this time to visit a camp of newly arrived Sioux on the White Mud Creek near the boundary. Hastening to meet them, he travelled with three half-breed scouts in advance of his party. As he pressed onward he sent Scouts Léveillé and Daniels in one direction, choosing another for himself and Joe Morin, the third scout. Soon he came upon a fresh Indian trail. After some reconnoitring he followed it, speedily out-distancing Morin. Presently he saw an Indian on a hill-top; a few minutes later as he raced on he saw another, then another and within a matter of minutes he was in the midst of a camp in the course of erection by the main body of the Sioux.

The sudden appearance of Walsh caused a wild commotion. Because the policeman had ridden in from the south they at once supposed him to be the advance guard of attacking Americans. Women and children became panic stricken; screaming and yelling, they started to pull down the partly-erected lodges. Horses stampeded, and a wild rush of fear-crazed Indians ensued. Medicine Bear of the Yankton band and Four Horns of the Tetons were the chiefs in charge. With their warriors they assembled on the opposite side of the White Mud Creek. Meanwhile Walsh was trying to explain the situation to them; but at the wrong moment Léveillé and Daniels, who were searching for Walsh, dashed out at break-neck speed from behind a hill. The shocked and bewildered Sioux trained their guns on the inspector and warned him not to advance across the creek. Léveillé thereupon grew angry and drew his gun to protect his superior officer.

The situation grew tense. Inspector Walsh realized he was in a precarious position. Calmly however he instructed Léveillé to put up his gun; firmly and patiently he stood his ground. After a lengthy discussion he and his scouts were permitted to cross the creek; the Indians were reassured, and began again to erect their lodges. Walsh learned that this particular band had suffered so much from treachery and raids on their camps, that the women and children had been denied even the merest semblance of comfortable sleep for a year. Eventually he was conducted to Four Horns, the leader, who said, "We are Tetons and followers of my adopted son, Sitting Bull, who is yet south but looking this way."

A council was then held in the usual manner, and the chief made pleas similar to those made by his brethren who had preceded him — pleas that were granted as the others had been.

In Mid-May Sitting Bull, the renowned commander-in-chief of all the Sioux crossed the boundary with 135 lodges and moved northward up the White Mud. Inspector Walsh immediately departed from Fort Walsh with four constables and two scouts, picked up the trail south of Pinto Horse Butte about fifteen miles east of the White Mud and soon came upon the main camp. There were then in Canada about eight hundred lodges of American Sioux, representing some 4000 Indians.

The police were given a hearty welcome and requested by Spotted Eagle, the war chief, to come among them. Such was the climax of months of faithful watching and scouting. At last the Mounted Police were in the camp of the redoubtable Sitting Bull. A dramatic moment of Western history had arrived. It was said to be the first time in Sitting Bull's career that white men, soldiers or socounts, had marched into his camp and pitch their tents beside his own. Afterwards Sltting Bull said in effect, "This is the most wonderful day in my life. Yesterday I was fleeing from white men, cursing and reviling them. Today they enter my camp and pitch their lodges beside mine. Boldly and fearlessly they enter my camp. Their White Forehead Chief (Walsh) walks to my lodge alone and unarmed. Alone and apart from his soldiers he quietly sits himself down cross-legged beside my lodge, giving me presents of tobacco and the hand of peace. It is a different world. What has happened? Is my reign at an end?"

These thoughts obviously confused Sitting Bull, and, though he knew it not, he had surrendered his power for ever.

Upon being invited to speak to the camp, Walsh told the Indians about the laws of the Great White Mother and warned them there was to be no bloodshed, no fighting. Canada was not to be used as a base from which to carry war across the boundary.

Spotted Eagle, chief of one of the many bands—the Sans Arcs or No Bows—, replied first. He voiced his people's grievances: they had been driven this way and that by American troops, and in order to save their women and children had been forced to cross the boundary.

Inspector Walsh was struck by the fine physique and bearing of Spotted Eagle. Immaculate in dress, handsome of face, his voice deep and resonant, this war chief was one of the most impressive savages on the plains. He carried a frightful weapon—three blades of steel in a long shaft—which Walsh eventually obtained. Before guns had been procurable, the Sans Arcs had used lances to hunt and fight with instead of bows and arrows—hence their name. Later, Spotted Eagle together with Stone Dog and Broad Tail by their influence helped Walsh defeat in council Sitting Bull who wished to go south of the boundary line and attack General Nelson A. Miles of the United States Army.

After Spotted Eagle had spoken other chiefs told of tribulations suffered by their bands.

That night Walsh and his escort slept in the Indian camp. The next morning Sitting Bull and his followers were given an opportunity to witness how the law they had just promised to respect was enforced.

Three Indians leading five horses had just ridden into camp. Solomon, one of the half-breed police scouts, recognized the new-comers as aliens belonging to the Assiniboine branch of the Sioux. One, named White Dog, a notorious character on the plains, was considered a great warrior. The previous year Sitting Bull had tried to bribe him with three hundred horses into joining the camp for the summer.

Upon looking over the horses White Dog and his companions had brought in, Solomon discovered that three of them belonged to Father DeCorby, a Roman Catholic priest of the Cypress Hills. The scout passed the information on to Walsh, stating that Léveillé agreed with him that the horses had been stolen. Inspector Walsh made sure of his ground before proceeding. He sent Solomon and Léveillé to examine the horses again. When they returned and assured him that they had not been mistaken—that the animals truly belonged to the priest—the inspector decided to make an example of the three horse thieves. He accordingly instructed Sgt. "Bob" McCutcheon to make the arrest.

White Dog was standing with his companions among a group of fifty or sixty warriors, telling them of his trip across the plains. Sergeant McCutcheon took two or three men and arrested the Indian trio. White Dog hotly demanded the reason; when the sergeant told him, the indignant warrior retorted that the horses were his and that he would neither give them up nor submit to arrest.

The inspector, realizing that if McCutcheon gave ground or retired for further orders police authority would be jeopardized, joined the group.

By this time the whole Sioux camp was in an uproar; hundreds of excited savages pressed around in an attempt to witness the outcome, and White Dog, apparently under the impression that the entire camp would stand by him, was more than arrogant.

Walsh stood before him and queried curtly, "You say you will neither be arrested nor surrender these horses?"—the scouts had caught the animals and brought them close. Putting his hand on the Indian's shoulder the inspector said, 'I arrest you for theft." He then ordered McCutcheon to seize White Dog's weapons, and before the Indian or his friends had time to resist he was disarmed.

The camp grew silent and tense. Walsh called for leg irons to be brought, then standing in front of White Dog, he held them up and said, "White Dog, tell me where you got those horses, how you got them and what you intend to do with them, or I shall put these irons on you and take you to Fort Walsh for trial."

For a moment no-one spoke; the camp was still as a grave.

White Dog's confidence suddenly deserted him. With evident reluctance he made a statement to the effect that he had been crossing the plains east of the Cypress Mountains when he found the horses wandering unattended over the prairie. He claimed he did not know it was a criminal act to take them, as it was the custom on Milk River below the boundary to assume ownership of stray animals until claimed by the owner. Walsh, although he knew the Indian was lying, accepted the statement, and warned him never again to molest other people's property in Canada.

White Dog realized only too well that he had been disgraced before the entire Sioux nation. It was a bitter pill to swallow. As he was about to turn away he sneered at Walsh and muttered threateningly in his own language, "I shall meet you again."

The inspector immediately halted him and called an interpreter, then ordered White Dog to repeat his words. The Indian stood silent and sullen, refusing to speak, and when Walsh put into words his own interpretation of what had been said White Dog remained stubbornly silent. Walsh again lifted the leg irons. "White Dog," he said, "withdraw those words, or I shall put you in irons and take you to Fort Walsh for threatening a police officer."

The Indian was completely subdued, and said he had not meant the words as a threat. Walsh knew that this statement also was a lie, but, having won his point, accepted it as true. He had humiliated White Dog in the presence of the whole Sioux camp, had made him show fear of the law.

The lesson was long remembered by Sitting Bull. Within twenty-four hours of their arrival in Canada the Indians had witnessed British law in operation. Nine or ten men in a hostile camp of six or seven hundred warriors had brought to submission one of the most feared and desperate chiefs of the plains.

Upon his return to Fort Walsh the inspector made a full report to Assist. Commr. Irvine, who had arrived from Fort Macleod, and it was decided to strengthen the detachment at Wood Mountain. Preparations were made for this undertaking, but before the expedition got under way six fine-looking warriors arrived with word that three Americans had been detained in the Sioux camp. Sitting Bull, realizing that the prisoners' lives would be in grave danger should any of his young braves decide to take vengeance, had sent the warriors to the police for instructions. He did not know the white man's procedure regarding prisoners.

The envoys carried American cavalry carbines and belts full of ammunition, which they had taken from Custer's men during the battle of the Little Big Horn. They also carried coup sticks — strong, slender shafts of wood with round stones attached to the striking ends; Sitting Bull's nephew, who was in the party, had dispatched twenty three of the enemy with his coup stick and proved it by the notches in its handle.

The next morning at six o'clock Assistant Commissioner Irvine started out for Sitting Bull's camp at Pinto Horse Butte. With him were Inspector Walsh, Inspr. Edmund Dalrymple Clark, Sub-Inspr. Edwin Allen, a few constables and scouts and the six Sioux warriors. The journey was accomplished in two days of hard riding. The police were greeted by a long line of savages, each of whom insisted upon shaking hands with the white visitors. Walsh had succeeded beyond all expectations in gaining the respect of these 'tigers of the plains'.

Afterwards the police discussed the three American prisoners with Sitting Bull. One, the Reverend Martin Marty, a Roman Catholic priest, was apostolic missionary of Dakota territory, another, John Howard, was General Miles' chief scout and the third was an interpreter.

They had been sent by General Miles to ask the Sioux to return to the States — an ironical request, as Miles had been pursuing and fighting these Indians for years. The priest said he had been a prisoner for eight days. All three were immediately given their release.

Later the assistant commissioner and his men noticed some American horses among the Indian ponies.

Late that night Sitting Bull went into the lodge especially set aside for the assistant commissioner and told Irvine how Custer and his command had ridden blindly into the Indians; how the soldiers and Indians had fought in utmost confusion, with Custer's men using the butts of their rifles.

"The soldiers could not load their carbines," Sitting Bull said, "and the Indians' pulled them off their horses killing them with knives and coup sticks. The horsemen were not even armed with swords."

Before the police patrol's return to Fort Walsh, the wily old chief expressed his pleasure at being in Canada and told of his intention to obey the laws of the Great White Mother.

In spite of his peaceful intentions, however, Sitting Bull found it hard to relinquish the power that once was his, and when a number of Nez Perces who were pursued by U.S. troopers to the border joined the refugee Sioux with tales of woe, it was the Mounted Police who prevented another blood purge of American soldiers south of the line.

With the swift destruction of the last buffalo herds and the consequent poverty of the Sioux refugees, many dejected bands reluctantly turned southward to accept rations from the U.S. authorities. Those who clung to Sitting Bull remained in Canada until July, 1881. The period of their stay was fraught with peril and hazard, like a keg of gunpowder ready at any moment to burst into unpredictable destruction. But the Mounted Police sat tightly on the lid.

5

The First Vice-Regal Tour of Western Canada

John Peter Turner

Canadians have indeed been honoured by the appointment of Field Marshal Viscount Harold Rupert Leofric George Alexander, G.C.B., C.S.I., D.S.O., M.C., as their new Governor General. During the invasion of Sicily and Italy he had the 1st and 5th Canadian Infantry Divisions and Armoured Brigade under his general command, and throughout World War II won the esteem of all Canadians. One of Britain's most brilliant military strategists, a man of prowess and diplomacy, he has come to our Dominion preceded by his fame.

His coming makes it appropriate at this time to recall details of the first vice-regal tour through the Canadian Northwest. The year was 1881, and thus far the closest any Governor General had come to setting foot in this region occurred four years previously when the Earl and Countess of Dufferin visited Manitoba.

Sixty-five years ago a great transition was taking place in Western Canadian territory which but recently had resounded to the war-cry of savages and the tread of countless buffalo. The Indian was receding, albeit reluctantly, from his primordial way of life and settlers were deploying over the plains with gathering momentum. Explorer, corporate trader and finally the tireless rider in scarlet tunic had paved the way. All these things presaged a new and greater West and more and more the people were relying for guidance and protection upon the ubiquitous virile North West Mounted Police then in the ninth year of its existence.

There remained but one step to be taken — transportation. The Government of Canada, with an eye toward influencing the Crown colony of British Columbia to enter Confederation, had promised that a transcontinental railway would be built; in fact work on it had already begun.

Early in the year it was decided that His Excellency the Right Hon. Sir John Douglas Sutherland Campbell, Marquis of Lorne, K.T., G.C.M.G., P.C., Governor General of Canada, should visit Western Canada. Her Royal Highness the Princess Louise, daughter of Her Majesty Queen Victoria and charming chatelaine of Government House at Ottawa, was not included in the plan; it was deemed inadvisable for her to incur the discomforts and rigours of such a journey.

Late in the spring Commr. A.G. Irvine of the NWMP received instructions to arrange for an escort to accompany His Excellency on the tour, and preparations were started at once. Provisions were cached at suitable points, equipment and stores gathered, officers and men specially chosen, the best horses and vehicles selected.

Inspr. P.R. Neale went to Winnipeg in June to purchase horses, wagons and buck-boards which, with three army ambulances bought in St. Paul, Minn., and hired drivers, were shipped the 60 miles to Portage la Prairie the farthest point west on the new uncompleted Canadian Pacific Railway.

Meantime, while the nucleus of a selected escort, consisting of seven NCOs, 16 constables, 31 horses and three wagons with Reg. No. 13, Sgt. Major Thomas Lake in charge, left NWMP headquarters at Fort Walsh for Fort Qu'Appelle, a Hudson's Bay Company post 315 miles north-eastward, Supt. W.M. Herchmer with seven men and 14 horses set out from Battleford by main cart trail bound for the same destination, a distance of 280 miles.

Unforeseen difficulties arose and trouble beset seemingly everyone concerned in the preparations. At Portage la Prairie Inspector Neale had barely set up camp when a violent thunder-storm scattered tents, wagon-covers, bedding and other equipment; on the trail to Fort Qu'Appelle 100 miles from Fort Walsh the horses of Lake's party stampeded and 15 of them were lost, and to the north some oats which Superintendent Herchmer had intended to pick up at Fort Carlton, H.B.C. post midway between Battleford and Qu'Appelle, had been sent to Battleford. As a climax to this series of set-backs, three constables carrying Indian annuity money arrived at Carlton from Qu'Appelle on horses so jaded that Herchmer had to replace them with four of those he had selected for the tour.

Oats were an essential travelling commodity in those days and of course it was imperative for the success of the tour that they be made available in quantity at strategic points. Herchmer instructed that two tons of the oats at Battleford be returned to Fort Carlton and from there he took them to Qu'Appelle, arriving on July 21. While his men were laying in a cache in the Touchwood Hills and another at Humboldt, he learned that Lake's party, its rations almost exhausted, was slowly approaching from the south and immediately sent out supplies and assistance. On the 26th the travel-weary detachment arrived — its only reverse the lost horses and these were replaced by hired ones.

On July 31, his mission at Qu'Appelle finished, Herchmer with eight NCOs, 32 constables and 50 horses, one light and five heavy wagons set out for Fort Ellice, principal H.B.C. post on the upper Assiniboine — his object being to store oats at suitable points along the trail. Next day a messenger overtook the party, with instructions from Ottawa for Herchmer to go to Portage la Prairie and there take over the transport from Inspector Neale.

Herchmer pushed on to Fort Ellice where he hastily completed his arrangements, then, leaving Lake in charge of the main escort party encamped in good pasture-land a few miles from the settlement, moved on to Portage la Prairie.

Inspector Neale had in his care nine hired men, two police recruits doing teamster work, 39 horses, two of them incapacitated, and 12 wagons. Herchmer relieved him of his command, and on August 8 took charge of more transport and stores that had been shipped to the end of the newly-laid steel of the C.P.R., several miles west of Portage la Prairie. Five miles further west he made camp.

All now was in readiness — a spick-and-span get-up awaited His Excellency's arrival.

The wait wasn't long. As a brilliant afternoon was waning, smoke was seen in the east and the vice-regal train rolled slowly on unballasted rails to the end of the line. Accompanying the vice-regal party was Asst. Indian Commr. Elliott Galt who had brought along two wagons loaded with presents for the Indians. Herchmer consulted with the Governor General's military secretary and it was decided that His Excellency should take a steamer up the Assiniboine to Fort Ellice where he would be met by the Mounted Police escort.

Following upon these arrangements Herchmer retraced his steps to Fort Ellice and on August 12 camped near where Sergeant Lake and the main escort were staying. The escort presented a fine appearance — the men in white helmets and new tunics, the horses groomed to a glossy sheen, the transport teams choicely matched.

Next morning shortly before the steamer bearing His Excellency was due Herchmer and 20 men on horseback trotted down the winding road from the high plateau on which Fort Ellice was perched and were lined up at the landing place as the boat steamed to shore.

The distinguished visitor disembarked and acknowledged the "Royal Salute", sounded by the trumpeter, after which he remarked favourably on the pleasant spectacle before him and followed by his aides inspected the escort.

While the baggage was being unloaded, a four-horse team got out of hand and bolted. Before the high-spirited animals could be brought under control the wagon had upset throwing the teamster to the ground and breaking his collar bone; the injured man was sent to Winnipeg on the returning steamer for medical attention.

The Governor General's party consisted of a chaplain, the Rev. Dr. Mc-Gregor of Edinburgh; a surgeon, Dr. Sewell; a military secretary, Lt. Col. F. De Winton; aides-de-camp, Major Chater, Captain Bagot of the Royal Artillery and Captain Percival of the 2nd Life Guards; an artist, Sidney P. Hall of the *London Graphic*; correspondents of the *Toronto Globe* and the *London Times*, and a French chef and six servants.

In the lavish entertainment that followed, Chief Factor Archibald Mc-Donald of the H.B.C. and his wife were hosts. A keg of Demerara rum was broached and to round out an occasion that was replete with Western hospitality a sumptuous repast was served. His Excellency attended an Indian council that afternoon and was guest of the McDonalds for the night.

Next afternoon the party left by trail for Fort Qu'Appelle, His Excellency riding in one of the army ambulances.

Countless details devolved upon the Mounted Police throughout the tour. Apart from serving as escort, they performed such duties as unpacking and repacking the baggage and equipment, pitching and taking down the tents, fitting and repairing the saddlery and other harness. The regular nightly routine provided for two reliefs — one from 10 p.m. to 2 a.m., the other from 2 to 6 a.m. In the daily routine, reveille usually was at 3 a.m., with the cavalcade on the trail by 6, a stop being made at 10 for breakfast and another at 3 p.m. for dinner — then a further advance was made to suitable camping grounds for the night. This schedule was altered at Mounted Police and H.B.C. posts.

At the mission of Lebret Father J. Hugonard and his assistants had erected an arch of green boughs under which the visitors passed to be met by a large gathering of half-breeds and Indians who presented an address and in turn were addressed by His Excellency.

A few miles further on was Qu'Appelle. The travellers arrived there in the evening of August 17 and were met by an escort led by Inspr. S.B. Steele. Here the civilians who had been hired at Portage la Prairie were paid off, and the Force henceforth assumed all transportation duties.

Half-breeds and Indians gathered to stare at the son-in-law of the Great White Mother, and the setting sun shone on a colourful picture. Lodges of the red men dotted the river bottom, lithe young warriors in gaudy costumes astride their ponies galloped back and forth on the plains, and the flashing scarlet of the Mounted Police lent a special touch of brightness to this thoroughly Western scene.

During his brief stay at Qu'Appelle the Governor General was made comfortable in the H.B.C. post by Chief Trader W.J. McLean and his wife, the former having met His Excellency at Lebret.

On the 18th, with Inspector Steele in charge of the guard, His Excellency attended a council of the Indians who afterwards held a big war-dance in his honour. On the morrow the cavalcade wended its way out of the valley and after six days of easy travelling through the Touchwood Hills and across the Salt Plains came to Gabriel's Crossing on the South Saskatchewan where the well-known Metis plainsman, Gabriel Dumont, operated a scow-ferry.

Crossing the river was arduous work. Some of the escort swam the 80 horses over and others made numerous trips transporting the baggage and wagons. Each time, the loaded ferry drifted downstream a mile or so before reaching the opposite bank and had to be hauled up to the landing-place with ropes for the next passage. "The men," said Superintendent Herchmer afterwards, "worked admirably — their handiness and cheerfulness under most trying circumstances were most favourably commented upon."

At Duck Lake Chief Beardy, decked out in his most brilliant raiment, embraced the Marquis warmly and in Cree and broken English showered him with encomiums. The Cree chief had always been a trouble-maker, but judging from his present conduct a new-comer would have thought him one of the most fervent and law-abiding of the Queen's subjects. He capped this highly-effusive reception by holding the vice-regal hand tightly and solemnly declaring that they were blood relatives — his father was reputed to be a white trader called Sutherland, a name connected with His Excellency's forebears.

Though amusing the situation was startling and His Excellency, laughing aside the intimate pretension, presented a souvenir token of his visit and lost no time in resuming the journey. That evening he arrived at Fort Carlton where he and his party found quarters for the night awaiting them in the H.B.C. post.

In the morning, after attending an Indian powwow, the visitors sailed down the North Saskatchewan on the company's steamer *Northcote* and at Prince Albert changed over to the steamer *Lily* which took them to Battleford, capital of the Northwest Territories. Shortly after the vice-regal departure from Carlton, Herchmer with the escort and transport took the overland trail westward and in the morning of the 29th arrived at Battleford. In the preliminary preparations for the tour, a relay of horses had been sent to this point from Fort Walsh by Commissioner Irvine who had correctly calculated that the animals purchased in Winnipeg would bring the Governor General's party this far.

His Excellency reached Battleford the day after Herchmer did and was escorted immediately to Government House, residence of the Hon. David Laird, lieutenant-governor of the Territories.

That afternoon hundreds of Indians and whites took part in a grand powwow with Lord Lorne, at which Inspr. W.D. Antrobus was in charge of the guard of honour, and the following day His Excellency inspected the NWMP barracks.

Calgary, the next important stop in the itinerary, lay 300 miles to the south-west.

Indian Commr. Edgar Dewdney, who later succeeded Laird as lieutenant-governor, joined the party at Battleford, and on September 1 they set out with an escort of 45 men and 80 horses. John Longmore, commonly known as Johnny Saskatchewan, acted as chief guide and assisting him were Poundmaker, one of the foremost Saskatchewan Crees, and Louis Laronde, guide and interpreter of D Division, NWMP.

Through virgin country, in which water and wildfowl were ample but wood was scarce except around Sounding Lake, the cavalcade blazed its own trail, and in many places was forced by obstacles of Nature's own designing to pursue a roundabout course.

A week after leaving Battleford the travellers sighted a small herd of buffalo near the Red Deer river. Three of the animals were bagged and Poundmaker caused consternation among some of the Easterners when he sat on one of the carcasses, tore out the quivering liver and calmly ate it raw.

Near Sounding Lake the party overtook a supply train that Herchmer had sent ahead from Battleford on August 24. The train, carrying fodder which would be needed before Calgary was reached, had made very poor time and Herchmer was reluctantly forced to transfer some of the oats to his own already overloaded transport.

The nights grew colder, bringing discomfort to members of the escort who were travelling light with little warm clothing or bedding, and in the mornings the tents were covered with hoar-frost.

Longmore had planned to cross the Red Deer at a point south of Hand Hills, but the river banks were so steep that no crossing could be made there and the travellers had to go considerably out of their way before a suitable place was found. Longmore said that he knew nothing whatever of the country on the other side of the river so he was sent back to Battleford and Poundmaker replaced him as chief guide.

Herchmer aware that the party was behind schedule was concerned. Their indirect course had taken more time than had been anticipated and there was danger of the provisions running out. To go directly to Calgary would in the circumstances be imprudent, Herchmer thought, so they struck out for Blackfoot Crossing where supplies were obtainable. A cold drizzle that lasted 12 hours set in shortly after the Red Deer was left behind, but when the weather cleared good time was made and on September 9 the vice-regal party reached the famous crossing.

To the south-east from Fort Walsh Commissioner Irvine and his adjutant Supt. John Cotton, with some NCOs, men and horses had gone to Fort Macleod from where the Commissioner sent oats and a relay of horses to Calgary. The Commissioner and his adjutant arrived in Calgary on August 24 and settled down to await the vice-regal party. Unaware that His Excellency's itinerary had been changed he dispatched several carts of oats to the Red Deer, but later, upon receiving a letter from Herchmer advising him of the altered plans, he set out for Blackfoot Crossing with more oats and some spare horses.

At the crossing on September 10 the day after the vice-regal party arrived there, a large number of Indians including Crowfoot chief of the Blackfoot, and many other dignitaries congregated and took part in a grand powwow. His Excellency and staff in full-dress uniform mounted a platform of a sort erected for the purpose, while the guard of honour under Herchmer drew up on both sides of them and Indian Commissioner Dewdney and Chief Crowfoot walked to their appointed places. Though the guard had been assembled at a moment's notice and preparations had necessarily been hurried, efficiency was the key-note; in his report Superintendent Herchmer said:

> The men turned out in a manner that would have done credit to any troops stationed in permanent stations. His Excellency and party were loud in their expressions of admiration at the men's appearance. ... Notwithstanding the fact that they had travelled over 850 miles of prairie, they were thus enabled to supply a guard of honour at a few minutes' notice fit to appear on a general inspection.

No sooner had the Governor General sat down than over 200 mounted Indians galloped up and in their wake flowed a horde of men, women and children on foot. Rifles cracked and bullets whistled overhead ominously close, and De Winton, entirely unaccustomed to displays of Indian exuberance, sidled up to Herchmer and inquired in a low voice, "Are your men loaded?"

As the ceremony got under way the copper-skinned hosts in war bonnets and robes of state ranged themselves in a long semicircle, some of them squatting on the ground, others remaining on their ponies—a striking picture of frontier might and grandeur which Hall subsequently painted and titled "The Last Great Council of the West".

Crowfoot then addressed His Excellency. He dwelt on the failure of the Government to provide the Indians with sufficient food and supplies, but voiced appreciation of the fair treatment accorded his people by the Mounted Police. An hour or more passed with speaker following speaker in much the same strain. The interpreter was Jean L'Heureux an old country Frenchman who some years before had cast his lot with Crowfoot and even shared the chief's lodge.

In the afternoon the march to Calgary was resumed but prior to the vice-regal departure Blackfoot Crossing felt the fury of a sudden and violent hail-storm that forced everyone to run for cover. Toward the end of the next day Commissioner Irvine and Superintendent Cotton met and joined the cavalcade which was in need of the extra horses and oats they brought.

On the 12th, under the direction of Cotton, the party crossed the Bow River, entered Calgary and occupied the camp previously set up by the Commissioner.

Westward the glimmering peaks of the Rockies drew the attention of the Marquis who gazed spellbound at the beautiful scene before him. In high spirits he visited the H.B.C. and I.G. Baker stores, the Mounted Police barracks and many of the settlement's humble dwellings.

Among the latter was that of an Irishman named Sam Livingstone who in 1849 left his homeland for the California gold-fields. He became an expert Indian fighter, buffalo hunter and trapper and was associated with Kit Carson. Crossing the Rocky Mountains to the Bow River country in 1870 he had wandered here and there along the North Saskatchewan until eventually he settled down on the north bank of the Elbow River. His Excellency was so interested in this well-known pioneer that he stayed and took pot luck at the old man's table.

While the cavalcade rested at Calgary, His Excellency beguiled the time fishing and hunting and exploring the district.

On the 15th His Excellency and staff escorted by Herchmer started from Calgary for Fort Macleod. Commissioner Irvine and Superintendent Cotton had preceded them by a day. At a leisurely pace the cavalcade proceeded, visiting the Indian Department farm at Fish Creek and at lunch time stopping at the ranch of "Honest" John Glenn who apologized profusely for being obliged to ask his distinguished guest to eat meat and pudding from the same plate.

Further on, when about half way between Calgary and Fort Macleod, the column came to a wayside eating place — the little log shanty of Joe Trollinger and his bride Lucy, a Blood squaw. His Excellency paused there long enough to eat and rest, and added his name to the unrecorded list of famous personages who at one time or another had partaken of Lucy's cooking which was acclaimed far and near for its matchless delectability.

Near High River a stop was made at the Emerson and French ranch, and "The Leavings" on Willow Creek, 25 miles north of Fort Macleod, was selected as a camp site for a night; at the latter point the column received fresh horses and a load of oats which the Commissioner had forwarded from Macleod.

On the 17th, in the morning, the vice-regal party met Irvine and Cotton about eight miles from Macleod; the two officers had ridden out to welcome it to the father of all police posts in the far West.

At the head of the escort that followed the Commissioner and Cotton was Supt. L.N.F. Crozier, officer commanding C Division at Fort Walsh who had arrived at Macleod with a large number of his men several days previously. Behind this escort was a crowd of Indians, whites, and half-breeds, some on horseback, some on foot. A salute was fired from two 9-pounder field-guns that had been moved from the fort to a high ridge overlooking Willow Creek, and Mounted Policemen lined the trail at intervals as the distinguished visitors crossed the Old Man's River; at the main gate of the fort a guard of honour under Inspr. F.J. Dickens awaited them.

Seldom if ever had the old fort witnessed such pageantry. Indians by the hundreds, Blackfoot, Bloods and Peigans, resplendent in paint and gay attire, mingled with lean and stalwart cattlemen, freighters, store-keepers and half-breeds. The Mounted Police were everywhere, and gracing the entire assemblage was a sprinkling of white women dressed in the best finery of their limited wardrobes.

Lt. Col. J.F. Macleod, C.M.G. (ex-Commissioner, NWMP), and his wife were greeted heartily by His Excellency and commended for the conspicuous part they had played in building the West.

While preparing for the reception, Mrs. Macleod discovered that her only garment befitting the occasion, a black plush coat trimmed with silver fox, was gone at the elbows (fine clothes rarely came to Fort Macleod), but with true Western resourcefulness the good lady had blackened her elbows.

Macleod himself had also been faced with a problem — he had a black frock coat but no silk hat, and the black, broad-brimmed felt he substituted was incongruous. Never was any man more ill at ease than he as alternately he smiled toward His Excellency and frowned in irritation at the offending head-gear; he seemed barely able to repress a desire to tear it from his head and tramp on it.

The occasion was of course sufficient reason for a long powwow among the Indians, intermittent speeches, horse racing, dancing and singsongs.

In the background during these activities was the ceaseless beat of raw-hide drums. Traders at improvised booths benefited from the easy-flowing money and Canadian one-dollar bills which had but recently appeared were displayed as novelties.

Next day Commissioner Irvine received the following letter:

> Fort Macleod, 18th September, 1881.
>
> Sir, I am commanded by His Excellency the Governor General to desire you to express to Superintendent Herchmer his entire satisfaction with the admirable manner that officer has performed his duty while in command of the force of Mounted Police which has escorted His Excellency from Winnipeg to Fort Macleod. I am further to request you to convey to the non-commissioned officers and men who formed the escort His Excellency's thanks for the services rendered by them while on the march, and the pleasure it has afforded him to witness the discipline and efficiency of the corps.
>
> I have the honour to be, Sir, Your obedient servant,
>
> F. De Winton, Lt. Col., Mil'y Sec'r.

Unmistakable signs of winter were in the air, and it was decided that the D Division part of the escort should return immediately to its headquarters at Battleford. Accordingly in the morning of the 19th, Herchmer turned over command of the escort to Superintendent Crozier.

In the afternoon the Marquis held a council with the Bloods and Peigans, and Herchmer, who had not yet departed, commanded the guard of honour. Years later, "Norrie" Macleod, Colonel Macleod's nephew, in referring to the doings of that afternoon said it was the "best turn-out of Indians" he had ever seen, "so many genuine costumes, bows and arrows, not to mention the old brass, bell-mouthed blunderbuss carried by Button Chief".

Commenting on the tour, Herchmer later reported that the "percentage of loss in horses had been small, taking into consideration the length of the trip, the loads carried and the pace of travel, and bearing in mind also that the majority of the horses employed were remounts" and that "the old police horses had in nearly every case been working hard up to the last moment".

Regarding the men in the escort, he stated:

> I cannot close this report without drawing your attention to the great assistance rendered me by ... Sergeant Major Lake. Of this non-commissioned officer's conduct I cannot speak in too high terms, nor can I overrate the cheerful manner in which the whole escort, non-commissioned officers and men, performed their several duties, some of which were particularly arduous ones ... duties, it must be remembered, that did not cease when camp was pitched each evening.

Day and night, the horses received the greatest care.... I believe it to be unprecedented that not a horse was incapacitated from work by sore back or shoulders. I attribute this entirely to the great care and attention exercised by Staff Sergeant Horner. From His Excellency, his staff and the gentlemen accompanying him I and my command received the greatest kindness, consideration and assistance.

Next day, September 20, following a consultation with Colonel De Winton, Commissioner Irvine and a small party rode southward with news of His Excellency's intention to visit Fort Shaw in Montana, U.S.A. By steady riding he and his men travelled the 200 miles to Fort Shaw in record time, arriving on the 22nd, and were heartily greeted by Col. Jacob Fort Kent, the officer commanding.

Pleased at the prospect of a visit from the Governor General of Canada, the genial commandant, after sending an escort under Lieutenant Todd to meet the vice-regal column, set about with his officers and men making arrangements for the forthcoming reception. Next morning, assured that all would be in readiness, he with the Commissioner rode out to welcome His Excellency. Meanwhile, escorted by Superintendent Crozier and the men of C Division, His Excellency and entourage had left Macleod on the 20th and gone to Pincher Creek where quarters for the Marquis were provided in the home of Colonel and Mrs. Macleod while a camp for the other visitors was established nearby. Next day His Excellency visited the farm of the police, also that of the Indian Department.

Bad weather prevented a detour that had been contemplated to Kootenay Lake, and on the 22nd the journey to the United States was resumed. The travellers passed across an open plain, leaving in their wake a well-defined path known afterwards as the "Governor General's Trail", crossed the Kootenay, Belly and St. Mary's Rivers and turned due south on the Sun river trail to American territory.

The weather changed, and a bright sun in a cloudless sky revealed in great detail the vast sweep of plains and the bold outlines of the Rockies which here near the international boundary culminate in the huge obelisk of Chief Mountain. Deeply impressed His Excellency penned these fitting lines to the towering massif:

Among white peaks a rock, hewn altarwise,
Marks the long frontier of our lonely lands.
Apart its dark tremendous sculpture stands,
Too steep for snow, and square against the skies.
In other shape its buttressed masses rise
When seen from north or south; but eastward set,
God carved it where two sovereignties are met.
An altar to His peace, before men's eyes.

48

Camp that night was on United States soil a short distance beyond the Milk River, and after dark while out gathering fuel with some companions one man made a gruesome discovery. He came upon a dried-up Indian corpse sewn inside an old buffalo hide and thinking it was wood took it along. For days after he was the butt of much good-natured banter.

Next night camp was pitched on the South Blackfoot Reserve near Hamilton and Hazlett's trading store which dispensed a variety of comestibles and liquid refreshments. Jerry Potts, famous guide and interpreter of the Force who had conducted the party from Fort Macleod, imbibed freely of the latter, worked himself into a bellicose frame of mind, and recalling a difference he had had with a local Indian decided to settle it in true Western fashion. Fortunately the police picquet took a hand in the matter and despite Jerry's protests bound him, put him in a wagon and left him there to cool off for the night.

The following day, September 24, the troops under Lieutenant Todd arrived and the entire train moved southward to Birch Creek where camp was made. During the night the American horses stampeded and in the morning could not be found. An extensive search would have entailed too much delay and the party moved on without the animals, though the men stopped long enough to brush up and burnish their accoutrements. Colonel Kent reached the Blackfoot Agency with the Commissioner and afterwards, meeting up with the party, took practical charge of arrangements for the remainder of the trip.

Late in the afternoon of the 28th they arrived at Fort Shaw. Seventeen guns boomed a salute to His Excellency; the entire garrison paraded and presented arms; a guard of honour was furnished, and the regimental band played "Hail to the Chief", then broke into "God Save the Queen" as the vice-regal conveyance swept past curious spectators and drove under an arch which had been specially constructed over the main gate for the occasion.

Unaccustomed to such fanfares several of the police horses, disturbed by the music, reared and plunged threateningly, but steady hands quietened them.

Then a near-calamity occurred — the Governor General's team bolted. With experienced hand the police teamster gave the frightened animals their heads. Skilfully he manoeuvered them into a running circle until they eventually drew up in front of the commanding officer's quarters where the Marquis alighted unhurt and entered the building, which had been kindly placed at his disposal.

That evening with Colonel Kent as his guest, His Excellency dined with several members of his staff. A splendid reception was given to the others of the party; Commissioner Irvine and Superintendent Crozier were guests of the American officers, and after taking full charge of the horses, the American soldiers threw their mess room wide open. Cigars, beer and sandwiches were supplied and everything possible was done for the comfort and entertainment of the red-coated Canadian police.

The barracks at this military post were more elaborate than those of the Mounted Police. The adobe buildings had wide verandas, shade trees lined the four sides of the square, and throughout there was a spacious comfort not associated with the small log buildings typical of the initial outposts of the NWMP.

In the morning, arrangements were made for His Excellency's departure. The military band marched and played reveille to the tune of "The Regular Army", while Crozier and his men paraded for the last time in their capacity of escort to the Marquis of Lorne.

In bidding them farewell His Excellency said:

> Officers, non-commissioned officers and men — our long march is over, and truly sorry we feel that it is so. I am glad that its last scene is to take place in this American fort where we have been so courteously and hospitably received. That good fellowship which exists between soldiers is always to the fullest extent shown between you and our kind friends. This perfect understanding is to be expected, for both our Empires, unlike some others, send out to their distant frontier posts not their worst, but some of their very best men. I have asked for this parade this morning to take leave of you, and to express my entire satisfaction at the manner in which your duties have been performed. You have been subject to some searching criticism, for on my staff are officers who have served in the cavalry artillery, and infantry. Their unanimous verdict is to the effect that they have never seen work better, more willingly, or more smartly done while under circumstances of some difficulty caused by bad weather or otherwise. Your appearance on parade was always as clean and bright and soldier-like as possible. Your force is often spoken of in Canada as one of which Canada is justly proud. It is well that this pride is so fully justified, for your duties are most important and varied. You must always act as guardians of the peace. There may be occasions also in which you may have to act as soldiers, and sometimes in dealing with our Indian fellow-subjects you may have to show the mingled prudence, kindness, and firmness which constitute a diplomat. You have, with a force at present only 250 strong, to keep order in a country whose fertile, wheat-growing area is reckoned about 250 millions of acres. The perfect confidence in the maintenance of the authority of the law prevailing over these vast territories, a confidence most necessary with the settlement now proceeding shows how thoroughly you have done your work. It will be with the greatest pleasure that I shall convey to the Prime Minister my appreciation of your services, and the satisfaction we have all had in having you with us as our escort and companions throughout the journey.

By 9 o'clock His Excellency was again on the road, accompanied by the Mounted Police and a detachment of American troops. At the parting of the ways a few miles out a halt was made and each man in the police escort was presented to the Governor General who had expressed a wish for an informal good-bye. He shook hands with all and smiled adieu.

Finally amid cheers the vice-regal party, with the American infantry now in charge of the escort, moved off in the three army ambulances bound for the terminus of the Utah Northern Railway at Dillon in south-eastern Montana.

At Helena a public reception was declined as the United States was in mourning for President Garfield who had died on September 19, a victim of an assassin's bullet.

Immediately after the Governor General's parting with the Mounted Police, Commissioner Irvine struck out on his return to Fort Macleod; next morning, that of the 30th, Crozier and the escort started after him. Near the South Blackfoot Agency cold weather and snow-storms were encountered and Crozier had to leave several horses with ranchers along the way. He and the escort crossed the Milk River during a blinding blizzard but they reached Fort Macleod without mishap on October 7.

Some of the escort who were members of B Division, Qu'Appelle, stayed at Fort Macleod for the winter rather than attempt the hazardous journey across the plains, and those from Fort Walsh remained for a short time because Star Child, a Blood Indian accused of murdering Reg. No. 335, Cst. M. Graburn in the Cypress Hills two years earlier, was about to be tried; there were disturbing rumours afloat and it was deemed advisable to have as strong a force on hand as possible.

The NWMP escort travelled many miles during the vice-regal tour — from Fort Walsh to Fort Ellice, 443 miles; from the end of the C.P.R. tracks to Fort Shaw, 1,229 miles, and finally the mileage involved when the men returned to their respective posts.

Lord Lorne's tour did much to cement that feeling of kinship which today prevails throughout the British Commonwealth. In reporting the tour, Commissioner Irvine drew attention to the great benefits accruing from it to the country:

> The interest shown by His Excellency in everything concerning the prosperity and welfare of the settlers has left a lasting impression on them. He at all times took every opportunity of visiting their homes and conversing with them on their personal welfare and their plans for the future. He gleaned from all the information that could be obtained in reference to their opinions as to the prospects and natural resources of the country. The personal interest shown by His Excellency in the settlers will, I am aware, ever be remembered with feelings of loyalty and pride.

Among the Indians, too, His Excellency's visit has been productive of much good. As the direct representative of Her Majesty the Queen, His Excellency's presence in their midst, and the trouble and care taken to enquire into their wants, has had the effect of strongly impressing the Indians with the kindly devotion of the Great Mother towards her red subjects. . . .

The numerous and exceptionally great kindnesses extended by His Excellency to the Police Force shall ever be proudly fostered by the corps. No words of mine can adequately express the earnest and heartfelt appreciation that prevails throughout all ranks.

In due course the Governor General returned by rail to Winnipeg where during an address to a large audience he paid this tribute to the Force:

Canada has been fortunate in organizing the Mounted Police Force, a corps of whose services it would be impossible to speak too highly. A mere handful in that vast wilderness, they have at all times shown themselves ready to go anywhere and do anything. They have often had to act on occasions demanding the combined individual pluck and prudence rarely to be found amongst any soldiery, and there has not been a single occasion on which any member of the force has lost his temper under trying circumstances, or has not fulfilled his mission as a guardian of the peace. Severe journeys in winter and difficult arrests have had to be effected in the centre of savage tribes, and not once has the moral prestige, which was in reality their only weapon, been found insufficient to cope with difficulties which, in America, have often baffled the efforts of whole columns of armed men. I am glad of this opportunity to name these men as well worthy of Canada's regard — as sons who have well maintained her name and fame.

6

Letters from the North-West

Const. A.R. Dyre

This instalment, which concludes the Dyre letters, tells something of the happenings during the North-West Rebellion.

Fort Calgary, Apr. 7, 1884.

Dear Trevuss:

Two years ago today I joined the Mounted Police and in that time have saved only $100 which you refuse to accept — all right, " 'nuff sed". If you were to live in a police fort for a month you would wonder how I had been enabled to save even that small amount, but then two years ago money was flowing like water up in this country, for everything was so dear a feller had to live on Government rations and could therefore save his pay. Now our mess, washing, tobacco, a dance now and then and other things too numerous to mention, take up all our pay and unless we nab a whisky dealer or some cuss setting the prairie afire or gambling, we never get much ahead. But what's the odds as long as you are happy?

If you come up here in August or any other time I can get you a pass to show you around, for as long as I like, that is if I am not out on detachment, but we are so peculiarly situated here that we don't know what minute we will be "fired" perhaps 100 miles away. The Negro was strung up here on the 29th of last month and died game.

I heard from home last mail, they are all well except Mother who is rather poorly. I heard lately that Ella Lees at Macleod was going to be married, but could not find out who to. Remember me to my cousins and write soon to

Yours as ever, A.R. Dyre.

Columbia Crossing, Sept. 22, 1884.

Dear Trevuss:

I received a very short letter from you about a month ago. Since then I have been removed up here to the crossing of the Columbia and a wild place it is, but I think there is more chance of being keeled over by mountain fever than by a tough pistol. However, as cold weather is coming I expect to escape both. I have just returned from a trip into the Selkirks after a horse thief. Sergeant Ward and I followed him nearly to the summit of the Selkirks, but as he had 24 hours' start of us and intended to go right through to the Coast we were obliged to turn back. As it was we ran out of grub and were a day without any. Our horses were as bad off as ourselves as we could not get any feed for them, so after a 50-mile ride on played-out horses we arrived at our camp weak with hunger and fatigue, and worse than all, no prisoner with us. I heard lately that two toughs whom I used to know in Calgary had been lynched by cowboys in Montana, for horse stealing, and my most earnest prayer is that the same fate may overtake the coyote who led us such an unsuccessful dance into that most magnificent but dreary region, the Selkirk Mountains.

I am very glad to hear of Mother's recovery from her sickness. I am very much obliged to Mr. Dickinson for his kindness, but notwithstanding the strenuous efforts made by the two little sheets printed there, Calgary is not growing a little bit, and lots there are at a discount, or soon will be. But I must close now so hoping to hear from you soon, I remain,

Yours as ever, A.R. Dyre.

Address — Columbia River, B.C.

Columbia Crossing, Nov. 13, 1884.

Dear Trevuss:

Yours of October 10 received and while you Eastern people are having your financial troubles, and Livy and her gallant knight of the axe are trying to stave off the old man "with a bang and a clang and ring-ding-ding the world goes merrily on" as the song says, with me, and I live well and make plenty of pocket money capturing the festive whisky trader and the maudlin drunk, and I spend it too as it is impossible to save money in the country even if I were so inclined, which I am not.

The CPR are building barracks here for us which will be finished in about two weeks, and you bet I'll be glad to get into them as I have had about enough camping for one summer. Although the weather is splendid for this time of year still it is no joke hustling into one's clothes before the fire is lit in the morning. There will be eight or ten of us here this winter and a couple of us are going down to the mouth of the Beaver, but as they are building quarters for us there I don't care whether I am sent or not.

I hope Livy's affianced will be more faithful to her than mine has been, that is if she cares for him as I did the "false" faithless creature that enslaved my boyish fancy. Ah Jesus that is a wound from which I am only now recovering and like an old maid I console my seared and bleeding heart by lavishing my affection on pets — a dog and a bear cub a fellow gave me are the recipients of my surplus love and kicks.

It was when I was over in the Rockies last winter that I received the last letter from my charmer and after writing to her till now, I have come to the conclusion that she wants no more truck with me and I have decided to save my ink and postage stamps. In regard to Kate marrying the bushwacker I don't see why she shouldn't if she wants to and it is pretty evident she does want to. The end of track will be here in about ten days. You had better address your letters to me in care of C.P. Mail Coy. as the last one had been to Victoria before I got it. Remember me to my aunts etc., and believe me,

Yours as ever, A.R. Dyre.

Beaver Creek, Feb. 24, 1885.

Dear Livy:

Yours of the 10th was only 11 days coming here. Talking about snow-shoes and squaws, I must tell you I never saw a squaw with them on. There are no Indians up here except an occasional hunting party of Shushwups or Kootenays. We are too far west for the Stonies or "John McDougall's Indians" as I call them, who are the most westerly tribe in the N.W., too far north for the Kootenays and too far east for the Shushwups, who are spread from Shushwup Lake to the Coast. Our snow-shoes are about four feet long and about 18 inches wide. What cock and bull story is that you told me about Dr. Jesse Hurlburt and the $125,000,000?

March 2. While writing the above Sergeant Fury came in and told me I would have to start for the Summit immediately with a dispatch for the detachment stationed there. It was then 4 o'clock in the evening and snowing hard and with a curse not loud but deep at such beastly weather, I saddled up and started, reaching the Summit at half-past eight. The distance is 25 miles. The snow is eight feet on the level up there while here it is a little over three. The Coy's store at the Summit is completely covered by a snow slide and the snow has drifted around all the other shacks so that all you can see is a little smoke coming out of a snow bank where the stove-pipe sticks through the roof. To get inside you go down about a dozen steps cut in the snow, at the bottom of which is the door.

They have to shovel the snow away from the doors and windows every day as it snows there nearly all the time.

Six teamsters have been blotted out up there by snow slides and two or three more who are missing are supposed to be under a slide. The weather is getting mild now and slides come thundering down every day and it is as much as a man's life is worth to travel at all. I have seen a few slides and a more awful sight cannot be imagined. Thousands of tons of snow and ice come thundering down the mountain side carrying rocks and trees and everything else that is in the way and the noise is deafening. It is all chance work when travelling. If you happen to be in front or have not come to it you can enjoy a magnificent sight, but if you are going along that part of the road where that particular slide is going to sweep over, you can imagine the result. I only stayed one night at the Summit. On my way home I met Mr. Hogg, the chief of the old T & O Survey. He is one of the chief engineers on this road and is stationed over near the Second Crossing of the Columbia.

I received the cuffs and identification badge all right for which many thanks. I think you might venture to send the slippers now. They may come all right. I can get them soled here. Write soon and let me know how the invalids are getting along.

Love to all,

Yours as ever, A.R. Dyre.

Beaver Creek, B.C., Mar. 30, 1885.

Dear Livy:

I received your letters and the slippers all right, many thanks.

Riel and his red devils are raising the very devil in the North-West. Ten of our fellows were killed the other day in an engagement and a lot more wounded, Fort Carlton burned and Major Crozier forced to retreat. About a thousand troops are coming up from the East to help quell the devils, and there are 25 of us in the mountains who will probably be kept here while the other boys are winning fame, or at least dying bravely. I tell you it is rough and we mean to ask to go and contribute our mite. Calgary is in danger from the Indians around there, and there will be a bloody war in the whole North-West before the rebels are crushed, which will put that beautiful country back a good many years as settlers will not come where they are likely to lose their hair. You will follow proceedings by reading the Herald and whenever I can write I will if I am not bowled out. We receive telegrams every day and I will not close this letter till mail day, so that I can let you know the latest.

I always was unlucky and it's just my luck to be cooped up in these damned mountains, which I have begun to hate, since they keep me from joining the brave fellows who are trying to overcome that scheming, copper-colored devil Riel. Our hopes were raised today by a telegram from the Mayor of Calgary, asking us to go down as the Blackfoot were rising, but a damper was put on our spirits by a later telegram from Inspector Dowling saying there was no immediate danger, and it looked as if we were to stay here like "Patience on a tombstone", till all the fighting was over or until this cursed CPR was finished.

March 31. I am on guard today and among other prisoners we have a madman who is to be sent to Winnipeg next train. We have to keep him shackled and tied down in his cell, and he yells, curses and groans nearly all the time. He broke loose about an hour ago and started to batter his head against the wall. I have often heard of the strength of crazy people but never saw anything like this before. He grasped me as we were tying him down and every muscle in him appeared to be as strong as steel. As I write he is lying down growling like a dog and I don't care for any more crazy people. Another telegram came today from Calgary, saying it was all quiet there.

April 1. We have heard nothing more about the war, think the wire must be cut. I am to escort the east-going mail as far as Laggan tomorrow on the train. Love to all.

Send this to Trevuss. A.R. Dyre.

Edmonton, May 2, 1885.

Dear Mother:

I left Beaver Creek on the 16th of last month. They have special police in the mountains now as we were wanted here in the North-West. We only stayed two days in Calgary and have been till yesterday coming here. We had to travel slow as we had four companies of militia with us, about 150 teams for transportation, so our horses are fresh even if they have come 250 miles from Calgary. We have another 200 mile trip to Fort Pitt east of here. The Crees under Big Bear have captured Pitt from the Police and we are going to take it back or lose our hair. There were only about 25 in the fort when it was besieged by Big Bear. Our fellows made a tunnel from the fort to the river and escaped in the night. Big Bear has two white women and a policeman prisoners, and report says the poor women, whose husbands were killed, are nearly dead. Those of us who were in the mountains are used as scouts and advanced guard, along with the civilian scouts and we have our old commander over us, Mr. Steele, and if any man can lead us to victory he can. General Strange is head of the expedition but Steele runs the whole thing. General Middleton had a battle with Riel and his breeds and came out about even I think, but you have heard more about it by this time than we have as we have been on the prairie so long. Coming from Calgary one morning shortly after striking camp we saw a mirage. The Red Deer River, 50 miles away, was laid out before us, the trees and a solitary horseman appearing right before us.

Edmonton is the best town I have seen in the North-West, and Fort Edmonton an H.B. post, is well built and protected. Fort Saskatchewan, where a detachment of our fellows are, is 20 miles down the river. I saw Mr. Jacques at Calgary and he said he was going to write to Pa. I shall write from Pitt and let you know how we get along. When you write address to Regina in care of Major Steele, and it will be forwarded to wherever I am. Love to all

Yours affectionately, A.R. Dyre.

Battleford, Sept. 3, 1885.

Dear Trevuss:

I received yours of August 9, last mail. I suppose you have heard from them at home an outline of my adventures during the rebellion. I did not draw the long bow in the least, indeed I did not tell them half the danger I was in at times as I only knew it would upset Mother and as I am a miserable writer I can only hope to give you a verbal report of the thing sometime if I am not knocked out before I see you. At the first engagement I was in, a bullet grazed so close to the hand I was holding my rifle with as almost to burn it, while others struck the ground between my long legs and whistled round my head like devils let loose. McRae was shot in the leg not two feet from me. Again at Loon Lake I had a similar experience but there we carried the day and killed 16 red devils outright and wounded a great many more, as the Globe of July 3 containing the only true and authentic account by Major Steele, will tell you. "C" School and "A" Battery are camped here yet. It is amusing to see how the volunteers were received on their return East. ... Tell Milton, if he will be a soldier to first acquire a military education and join some corps as an officer, but if I ever hear of him becoming a private soldier he will get a combing from me when I see him.

I don't know whether we are to be stationed here permanently or not. We are only attached to this troop at present, but I think when Steele gets command of a troop he will send for us, as he swears by the men who kept the Rocky Mountain toughs in order and fought for his honor at Loon Lake.

I think Livy did right in firing her knight of the axe. It seems strange to hear of Eva having lovers. She must be quite a grown-up young lady. Give my love to all the family and write soon to, Yours as ever,

A.R. Dyre

P.S. Address Battleford,

A.R.D.

(The following letter is from the Adjutant, Inspector Allan, to T.H. Dyre, brother of the late ex-Constable Dyre.)

Battleford Barracks, Nov. 23, 1885.

T.H. Dyre, Esq., Barristers Thornbury.

Dear Sir:

I am just in receipt of yours of 5th instant, inquiring about your late brother's death. In reply I beg to inform you that he died in hospital here on the 31st day of October last of typhoid fever and was buried on the morning of the 2nd instant with military honors in the burying ground close by the Fort here, and side by side with those of his comrades who fell at the Battle of Cut Knife Hill and Frenchman's Butte. The service was read by the Rev. Mr. Pritchard and all that then remained of the poor fellow was followed to his last resting place by his comrades and troop officers. He was quite conscious up to the time of his death and seemed quite resigned to meet the worst. He was not a man of very robust constitution, still he had done a lot of hard service during the Rebellion under Superintendent Steele, between Edmonton and Fort Pitt, a service which entailed long and hard riding by day and night, constant exposure to all weathers and hardships, such in fact is the service required to be performed by the Police. He is reported to have been an excellent soldier, always ready to perform any duty assigned to him by day or night and without a murmur. He was much thought of by his comrades in the northern district where he had served principally. His accounts have been gone into in the regular manner as prescribed by the Queen's regulations by a Board of officers, and the whole proceedings together with the proceeds of the sale of kit and the balance of pay due him, etc., amounting to $169, together with a package of letters and photographs, a silver watch and an Indian relic, all of which have been forwarded to Regina, the Headquarters of the North-West Mounted Police, where by writing to the Commissioner, Lieutenant-Colonel Irvine, establishing your identity or that of his father as the nearest of kin, the whole will be forwarded to you if it has not already been done.

I remain, dear sir,

Yours truly,
John Allan
Inspr. and Acting Adjutant

Editor's Note

When the writer mentions receiving money for arrests, he refers to part of the costs assessed by the magistrate. In the early days members were able to keep the money. Later the policy was changed and the money was put into a fund to be shared by all members of the Force. This procedure was discontinued many years ago.

7

The Chinook

Inspector A.F.C. Watts

The wind-filled West seemed terror-filled — and I? — I fear it's bringing, Next moment, 'neath that very self-same sky, A lark came —
singing!   — Egbert Sandford

The cold snap had held the country in its grip for nearly three weeks.
Day after day the sun had shone with a cold glare, dulled by the frost
particles that drifted through the still air like sparkling coruscations of
glass; at night the Aurora Borealis marshalled its myriad flickering lights
along the northern sky, advancing and retreating, now blazing, then dying,
till the sky lightened for the dawn.

The thermometer that hung outside the door of the ranch-house had
registered ten, twenty and thirty below zero, and was still dropping, the
mercury threatening to retreat into the bulb altogether. At night, after
with numbed hands, we had scattered hay to the lowing cattle round the
corrals and fed and blanketed our stabled horses, we would heap high the
woodbox behind the big heater in the living-room, load it to the lid with
dry poplar, open the dampers, and sit down before the blaze to take off
our steaming mocassins, thanking our lucky stars that there was plenty
of wood anyway, and a quarter of beef hanging in the meat house.

The frost was thick on the window-panes and lined the wall just inside
the door where the cold air had penetrated. The cattle in the yards, their
coats white with frost, would bed down close together under the sheds at
night, while those out among the hills, that had been left out on the range
for the winter to "rustle" their own sustenance, sought the pine bluffs
on the slopes, — not the valleys, for there the frost strikes the hardest.
Even those hardy little vagabonds of the hills, the coyotes, kept to their
dens at night, and their weird outbursts of nocturnal serenading were
seldom heard.

Then one day the change came; when the day dawned, the tense cold
was still apparent, but the sky was a shade more blue, and the frost
particles were no longer falling. We had a busy half hour on the creek ice

cutting a slope down to the water-hole for the cattle, for the water had sunk over a foot and they could not drink without kneeling.

The yearling colts in the feed-lot were playfully biting and kicking at each other as they lined up at the freshly filled hayrack. And even the more tactiturn cows, after raising their noses and scenting the air, wended their way along the trail to the pasture, their first move from the vicinity of the corrals for weeks.

We were riding that afternoon on the slope of a long range of hills to the west, looking up the cattle that were failing in flesh owing to the protracted cold, and that would have to be taken in to feed. We pulled up our horses in an open space in the poplars, where we could view the masses of white hills rolling up to the base of the frowning mountain range in the background. And then we heard it—just a faint far-off murmur at first, like the distant sighing of the sea. Over the mountains to the south-west some white fleecy clouds were rising, and masses of them completely hid the higher peaks and tumbled down their slopes towards the lesser hills.

We rode on, and the sound that was before distant and vague, grew clearer. It was a wind that was coming over the ranges and down the valleys from the south-west. Across on the next hill it reached a bluff of snow-laden pines, and scattered the snow from their branches in a white haze. A puff of wind fanned my cheek; it was not the stinging frost-laden breath of the Arctic, but a deliciously warm breeze that had its origin in the far Pacific ocean itself, had swept clear through the grim fastnesses of the Rockies, and, gathering strength and swiftness as it came, would not expend itself until the welcome warmth had been felt for two hundred miles out on the Alberta plains.

This was the "Chinook", that comes unheralded across the mountains, often in the depths of winter, and usually after the longest cold snap of the season. Many theories have been advanced as to its origin and power, some of them sensible and some fantastic; but that afternoon scientific theories did not trouble us. We turned our horses' heads towards the homeward trail, knowing that now our range cattle would continue to "find their meat in due season" in perfect safety.

Next morning the transformation was complete. Our thermometer had amply justified its existence and had risen nobly to the occasion — over the freezing mark. The mountain ranges stood out clear against the sky, but above them was a sweeping crescent of white cloud, its edges dropping to the tips of the hills to the north and south. It appeared as if a vast curtain was being slowly raised by the hand of the Creator, to disclose one of the sublimest spectacles of Nature—a mountain range, snow-clad, shining in the sun. This was the wonderful "Chinook Arch", which, although not of the variegated colour of its twin brother, the Rainbow, is a more substantial and potent symbol of the "Hope that springs eternal".

On the open slopes of the foothills the snow had almost gone, and the cattle wandered there and fed in content, their backs to the wind. Nearby, the snow, instead of rustling underfoot like powdered sugar, was soft and slushy, and little pools of water appeared in the yards and on the three foot thick ice of the creek. That afternoon we discarded our mitts, fur caps and mackinaw coats, and worked in our shirtsleeves, while ever the snow faded like magic from the hills, and the eternal harmony of the wind sighing in the trees filled our hearts with gladness.

Usually in a few days, the Chinook will blow itself out, or be beaten back by a stronger snow-laden wind from the north. It cannot be Spring that has come, two months before its time. But we have no cares for the future; we drink our fill of the balmy air, with gay abandon get our boots wet through in the slushy pools, and sing as we go bareheaded about our work.

Then, if for a space, the silence of winter again enwraps the white hills; if once again the cattle seek shelter from the cold, while the Aurora Borealis stabs the northern sky, we will still go forth to our labour with a song. For have we not seen the little hills clap their hands and sing and the mountains bow themselves before one of God's sublimest gifts, the Chinook Wind!

Personalities

8

Jerry Potts

John Peter Turner

A brief picture of one who was full of wisdom in all that pertained to tracking and trailing — a firm friend, a rough though affectionate and respected man, an honest and faithful servant.

Autumn winds swirled around old Fort Benton which for years had been the American Fur Company's principal post on the Upper Missouri River in Montana. Inside the building a sixteen-year-old lad loitered near the trading counter, staring moodily at nothing. His was a problem, and a heavy one. His father, John Potts, trader and factor, was planning to return to Scotland. The boy didn't want to go; he didn't want to attend school in Edinburgh. He liked frontier life; he wanted to stay where he was. On the other hand, his father had spent many years of tireless industry in the New World, and deserved a rest in his ancestral home.

Jerry Potts shifted his position at the trading counter and became more disgruntled than ever as he weighed his prospects. The factor had gone upstairs to close the shutters against the oncoming evening, a job usually attended to by a post employee. The latter had just had a bitter altercation with a vagrant Blackfeet who had sought to obtain some goods on credit. To terminate the argument, the factor had sent his helper on an errand, and so the routine had been changed.

Suddenly the lad stiffened as the sharp bark of a rifle sounded. His breath caught as he saw his father's body tumble from an upper window. Out in the dusk, an Indian — the same Blackfeet who had argued with the servant — sprang from near-by cover and vaulted to his pony's back.

Young Jerry stood frozen to the floor. Then suddenly the primal instinct of the wild — his mother's Piegan blood — laid hold upon him. His eyes flared; his lips set grimly. As he saddled his favourite pony he realized what had happened. The disgruntled Indian, in seeking to square matters with the post employee, had shot down the factor by mistake.

The young frontiersman made deliberate preparations, took one last look at the old fort and rode away in pursuit. Mile after mile across the plains, day after day, through long and lonely nights, the teen-age avenger

67

followed stubbornly, persistently. Finally, within the Blackfeet realm far to the north in British territory, he overtook his victim and pierced him to the heart.

Factor John Potts had been known far and wide for his ever-ready counsel and square dealing; his name was honoured and respected. And his son, by his boldness, added stark courage to the name. Bravery was the highest ranking virtue in the Blackfeet code. The boy had executed a daring retribution, had earned a pass to death; but, amid plaudits from a thousand throats, he turned unharmed to the vagaries of frontier occupation.

From that day on the adventurous youth enjoyed the freedom of the Blackfeet camps as had no other man of white extraction, pure or mixed. Among other recognitions, he received a crowning initiation to the inner councils of the proud Confederacy — Blackfeet, Piegans, Bloods and Sarcees.

Buffalo were unusually plentiful on the Belly plains that autumn and young Potts threw in with a large hunting camp of Bloods and Piegans.

But from the east, a war party of Crees under Chief Piapot, augmented by Assiniboines and Saulteaux, ventured to penetrate the forbidden Blackfeet territory. While spying on their hereditary enemies the invaders came upon a group of Piegan women and children gathering wood along the Belly River. The little group was wiped out — all but one small boy who escaped to give the alarm.

The fight that followed was bitter and prolonged. Under the exhortation and leadership of Potts, the Bloods and Piegans drove their foe beyond the river. Outwitted and demoralized, the Crees fled in disorder; many were killed as they floundered helplessly in the water; others were pursued far out upon the plain. Again and again they attempted to make a stand, but scores were cut down and slaughtered. Several hundred of Piapot's following forfeited their lives.

Jerry returned from the bloody encounter with a gaping wound, an arrow in his body, and nineteen grisly scalps. His fame grew and became imperishable. Four years earlier the Qu'Appelle Crees, on the South Saskatchewan, had repulsed the Blackfeet; and now, in this fight of 1870 the defeat had been avenged. Moreover, the strategy and leadership of Potts had held the Blood and Piegan losses to a minimum. This sanguinary clash — the last tribal battle of the northern prairies — took place on the site of the present City of Lethbridge, the forces of Piapot being driven across the river where the General Hospital now stands.

In the summer of 1874 the newly formed North West Mounted Police made their famous 800-mile march across the prairies. While visiting Fort Benton to secure supplies and communicate with the government at

Ottawa, Asst. Commr. James F. Macleod engaged young Potts as guide and interpreter for the Force. Fort Macleod — the little outpost that was to be erected on the Old Man River in the heart of the Blackfeet country — would be called upon to exert a salutary influence in taming the populace in the last arena of savagery in Canada. It was therefore important that a competent man be selected to assist in establishing law and order — one who knew the wiles of the Indians and spoke their language.

The adventurous plainsman became one of the first essentials in the ticklish task confronting Assistant Commissioner Macleod and his troopers. As a trailer and scout he was to prove himself a marvel, even among the most experienced Indians. His ability to travel through blinding storm or blackest night was uncanny. Across wide stretches of open country he charted his course and invariably arrived safely at his destination. In daylight he, doubtless, after the custom of the Indian, followed a sequence of landmarks. But even when visibility was reduced to naught, he was seldom known to hesitate. Intuitively he knew which way to go, what direction to take. The late Sir Samuel B. Steele, for long a conspicuous member of the Mounted Police, once said of him:

> He possessed an uncanny sense of locality and direction. Others could guide travellers through country they had visited before, but this man, who was made war chief of his mother's nation, could take a party from place to place by the quickest route, through country altogether unknown to him, without compass and without sight of the stars. Unlike other guides, he never talked with others when he was at work. He would ride on ahead by himself, keeping his mind fixed on the mysterious business of finding the way. He was never able to give any clear explanation of his method. No doubt his gift was largely the result of heredity. He had travelled in his youth for long distances from points in Western Canada to points in the Western States before there were any railways, and his early experience certainly counted for much. Though he had not before journeyed through many parts of the country, his Indian ancestors had, and that is probably the true explanation of his weird ability.

But Potts, precise as he was in his duties as super-plainsman, had that composite nature of dependability and abandonment so common to the frontier West. He worked hard, and he played hard. He was the superlative as a servant of the Mounted Police; he was the superlative in seeking diversions that satiated his native unrestraint and freedom. He was no prairie innocent; no frequenter of pink teas, and, like most outstanding men, he mixed his failings with his virtues.

Among other frailties, he possessed an unquenchable thirst — and boasted of it. Often he would say he had something a camel might have envied, and as his position with the Force was unofficial, he never in off hours grew intimate with prohibition. When not on duty he indulged freely if the spirit moved him. Jamaica ginger, essence of lemon, Perry Davis' Pain-Killer — all were tolerable substitutes; and with such in his system, his interpretations of the English and Blackfeet languages might have seemed a trifle weird, perhaps too choicely punctuated, but always understandable.

In appearance he was, at first sight, more or less unprepossessing; but, though short and slope-shouldered, he was tough as nails, and his nether limbs were admirably moulded to fit the saddle. His eyes were keen and piercing. He was in his own way picturesque and fascinating, a man of mingled emotions, one who harboured a strange complex of the white man's understanding and the Indian's elemental instinct. Always his integrity and loyalty were above reproach.

On July 14, 1896, Jerry Potts died from a lung afffliction and was buried in the Police Plot near Fort Macleod. He had served twenty-two years with the Force. To those who knew him, he had been a pillar of dependability in hundreds of difficult situations, in danger and emergency. His influence among the Indians had often suppressed bickerings that might easily have lead to barbaric war and bloodshed. His faithful services to the scarlet troopers of the plains should never be forgotten.

9

A Mountie's Wife in the North

Martha Cameron

They say "The Mountie always gets his man!" Well, in my case, it was the other way 'round—I tried to get the Mountie and found it was no easy task.

This big chunk of RCMP, G.I. Cameron, came to Dawson City in 1925 when I was a young Yukon chick. After some careful angling, he took the bait, but I had a tough time actually landing him.

In those days, it was really hard to get permission to marry in the Force, and after three years of courting, the Officer in Charge finally said we would be able to get permission by the following June.

So, we went ahead with our wedding plans. But on New Year's Eve, at the annual ball, the Officer in Charge died of a heart attack, and his successor, when he finally arrived in the Yukon, laid down his own decree: No married constables in the Territory. And that was that.

Cam decided we had waited long enough, however, and on the morning of June 16, 1928, he "purchased" out of the Force. That evening we were married in St. Paul's Pro-Cathedral at Dawson City. So, I had won a Mountie, and he had won a bride, but we had no job.

Cam and I headed for Ottawa, his hometown, to start a new life, but things just never panned out during those depression years, no matter how hard we worked. By 1934 we had returned to Vancouver. There, some of his RCMP friends suggested he join up again as they were looking for good men. So Cam applied and was off to the Yukon on transfer in June, 1935.

We were given our first married post at Fort Selkirk, on the Yukon River, and there we spent 14 happy years before Cam went to pension in 1949. Since then he has been with the Yukon Territorial government in a number of capacities, and after his retirement from the Territorial Civil Service, he was named sergeant-at-arms for the Yukon Territorial Council.

Ours was certainly an interesting time at Selkirk, still in the age of the dog team, no roads, no planes. When Cam went on patrol, as he did

71

regularly, that was it — maybe three weeks later he would turn up. There was no way of communicating from the day he left home.

One night at Selkirk, as I was rocking our baby daughter Ione to sleep, she sat up and said, "Mommy, I wonder if the coyotes have eaten Daddy yet?" What a pleasant thought in our little cabin on the Yukon riverbank! It was never lonely, however, with about 10 other white folk in the village and Indian families at the far end of the settlement.

When the policeman was away, his wife was often called on to take his place . . . most unofficially, of course. One night I heard a rap on the detachment door; it was the missionary in charge and he said, "Martha, can you help me out? A couple of Indians are causing a fuss in the village and I cannot do a thing with one."

I took the leg irons and handcuffs. I had never seen Cam use them, but as he was many miles away, it seemed the logical way to keep our Indian brave quiet until he slept off the effects of the home brew. So away we went. In one of the cabins we found the chap very much under the influence of something or other. As the missionary held him, I clamped on the handcuffs, and for good measure, the leg irons.

When I got home, I realized there might be serious consequences for this — I'd done something I had no right to do and knew nothing at all about. The deed was done and I worried all night. In the morning, we went down and let him free . . . with me expecting him to get even with me! But no. Selkirk Indians after that said, "Policewoman worse than policeman." I really had overstepped my traces, though I don't know what anyone else would have done under the same conditions . . .

We were always busy in that small village. We had wood to cut, water to carry (or, when it worked, the pump to handle, always remembering to leave a bit to prime it). In winter we cut a hole in the ice or melted snow, which we did for washing in any case. It was a full-time job, along with cooking and cleaning, and we did a lot of knitting and crocheting as well.

Once I took a contract from the wood man to saw all the 4-foot logs we bought for the detachment into 16-inch lengths. We didn't need any keep-fit classes in those days!

As the years passed, we began to see aircraft in the North and finally got weekly plane service at Selkirk.

I took the contract to keep the landing field rolled. The company sent down a two-ton "cat" and roller which, I must say, was a pleasure to have. All the kiddies would ride as I went up and down the field! I was also agent for the airline, which meant handling all the mail and freight.

We had two stores, or trading posts, where we could get almost anything in the way of food, warm clothing and so forth. I handled the medicine and first aid chest for the Indian Department, and when anyone was ill, arranged to send them by plane to the hospital. But a lot of medical treatment was done right there, the Mountie pulling teeth when necessary, and doing the odd bit of stitching sometimes needed.

I well remember the first needle I gave—the doctor had shown me the procedure and I practiced on a lemon. So along came my first patient and I debated whether I should have someone there in case I couldn't go through with it. But I decided to do it alone and my Indian patient was an excellent model. He said, "That's the best needle I ever had," so it never bothered me after that.

It was really a pleasant life. Whenever folks came to Selkirk, the detachment was the place where they stopped to ask about things. We were a good group, never more at one time than 15 whites and a few Indians. Of course, at Christmas time, all that were able came in off their traplines for miles around and then it was a continual celebration, with dinners and parties and dances.

The Indian village had a huge log house where we all danced and made merry one night during the season. They were a good group of Indians, and to this day, 22 years after Cam retired, we still have many friends among the Selkirk people who are always glad to see us when we are down their way, or if we meet in town.

During the war years, our little group at Selkirk sent a huge bale of knitted goods to the Red Cross at Dawson regularly and our days were never long enough. In winter we skied or went snowshoeing or skating (after first clearing off the river ice). Everything was done the hard way but we made it into fun. I have seen the temperature go down to 86 below zero, but ours was not an official recording because we were not a "Met" station. On days like that we stayed home and just kept piling on the wood!

At Christmas we all got together in turns, so no one sat alone for dinner. I generally made boxes of home-baked goodies for the old bachelors. I remember one year, an old chap came back in tears and said no one had ever given him anything like that in his life, and told me how much he enjoyed every bit of it.

But at New Year's, at 80 below zero, his cabin burned. Cam was away on patrol so I went along to help with the fire pump on my back. It was so cold, the pump wouldn't work. All we could do was save what we could, then just watch the cabin burn. When the small porch dropped off, a carton slid to the snow ... and there was my fancy box of goodies, intact! "That old man!" I said to myself, and pitched it into the flames.

The next day, he came to the detachment after inspecting the ruins of his home, and said, "Do you know what? I think someone must have stolen my box of goodies. I had them up on the roof of the porch ... it was far too nice to eat. I just liked looking at them!" So I had to get busy and make him another box.

Being agent for the airline was another good way to make friends. When a plane was forced down for weather, we had the passengers stay with us for as long as a week. One planeload of 14 was billeted around the homes in the village. Everyone pitched in and it was more like a picnic than work. Every day they would take off with lunch packed and each night come back again, not able to get over the mountains between us and Alaska. This particular plane had come from Dallas and was on its way to Fairbanks. One of the Indians came to the house one night and "made medicine" for them, and they did get through the next day.

We had a two-way radio with regular scheds connecting trappers in the area. I would read the *Dawson News* over the air once a week. By spring I had built up quite an audience!

It was still the day of sternwheeler riverboats and they were an important part of our daily life in summer. In the autumn when it got dark, the boats would often tie up at Selkirk and the crews would all gather at our place for coffee and a visit.

The last boat was an annual highlight, as was freezeup, when we could walk across the ice to the farm eight miles away. In the spring at breakup we would walk to the top of Victoria Mountain to watch the ice move out, and there we would gather the first spring flowers. Then followed the first boat, trailed by the small boats of trappers, who landed to unload their furs at the trading post. That was usually early in May and on Mother's Day it was a treat to let Mom climb the mountain for a picnic; there was still enough snow in the draws to make a good pot of tea.

We put up river ice in the spring so we could make ice cream most of the summer, hauling the ice with our dog teams and storing it in an old cabin cellar full of sawdust. We had two huge freezers—the hand-cranking kind—and during the summer we had many good outdoor parties. When the trappers came in to get their outfits there would be a big ice cream feed ... lots of work but it was fun.

The dog teams needed a lot of care and exercise, summer and winter. Our daughter could play with any of them, in no danger. She grew up learning to handle a team and to handle a gun as well as the best of them; gun practice was frequent in the spring. Besides the dogs, Ione had her pet sheep, which lived with us all the years at Selkirk and had to be put to sleep before we left.

I tried to teach our daughter at home but she soon knew more than I did, so we sent her to boarding school on Vancouver Island. She always came home for the summer and tried a time or two to get to Selkirk for

Christmas but the weatherman didn't always cooperate! We didn't get annual holidays in those years.

The Selkirk detachment had no prisoner's cell, so prisoners were kept in our house and it meant 24-hour duty for us. If the prisoner was male, Cam attended him and could only snooze a bit during the day when I could carry on. If it were a woman, I was on 24-hour duty, with Cam keeping an eye from his office while I slept during the day. We had no indoor plumbing in our home, so we had to accompany the prisoner to the wee house in the backyard, as well.

Each spring on his patrols to isolated trappers, Cam found some dead and had to bury them; others who were ill, he cared for or brought in to the hospital. In a detachment of our kind, we were called on for everything, particularly when there was no one at the Mission. We never did perform weddings, though we were witnesses to many and prepared the food for the parties afterward, but now our daughter, Ione, is more than making up for that lack. After she grew up and married her geologist, Art Christensen, and had two boys of her own, she became a magistrate and juvenile court judge and is often called upon to officiate at civil marriages. We are glad they are in the Yukon with us, living right next door.

I could go on and on, but this is not supposed to be a book-length story. It was a wonderful time for us, those 14 years at Fort Selkirk, and we have no regrets. Staying in the North means we can keep in touch with our old friends, and with the new, younger members of the Force, which last year celebrated its 100th birthday. I am certainly glad I chanced to write some of its history.

Editor's Note

The wife of a member of the Force was expected to act as a "second man" when living on a single-man northern detachment, although this was never officially acknowledged. Mrs. Cameron's activities obviously went beyond the call of duty. Written in 1974, the article first appeared in the October 1974 issue of *Alaska, The Magazine of Life in the Past.*

10

The Pedley Story

RCMP *Quarterly* Staff

The man who made one of the most publicized and yet probably one of the most tragic patrols in the history of the Force 55 years ago this Winter has died. Reg. No. 3613 ex-Sgt. Albert Pedley passed away at Salisbury, England, June 3 at the age of 81.

Albert Pedley originally came to Canada at the close of the 19th century from Cambridge, and after farming for about a year in Manitoba enlisted in the North West Mounted Police at Regina on Apr. 18, 1900. He was then 22. Three months later he was sent to G Division headquarters, then at Fort Saskatchewan, NWT, about 20 miles north-east of Edmonton. His next posting was to Fort Chipewyan, NWT, and it was from this northerly settlement that he started out on his renowned patrol. (In 1905 Fort Chipewyan became part of the province of Alberta. It is at the northwestern end of Lake Athabasca and roughly 100 miles south of the Northwest Territories boundary.) Despite the fact that at the time the trip was widely publicized, and that Hollywood later even made a motion picture supposedly based on it, there is little in official records at Headquarters concerning the journey. In fact, the only account on file of the first part of the patrol is contained in Constable Pedley's meagre report to his Officer Commanding, Inspr. D.A.E. Strickland, dated Jan. 9, 1905.

On Dec. 17, 1904 — it was during this year that the prefix "Royal" was added to the name of the Force — Constable Pedley left Fort Chipewyan by dog team with an interpreter and a seriously ill mental patient, bound for Fort Saskatchewan, some 400 miles to the south. Excerpts of Constable Pedley's account of the trip follow:

> I left Fort Chipewyan on December 17 with the interpreter and two dog trains and the lunatic ... in my custody. After travelling for five days through slush and water up to my knees, I arrived at Fort McKay on December 22.

> Owing to the extreme cold of this morning the prisoner's feet were frost-bitten. I did all I could to relieve him and purchased some large moccasins to allow more wrapping for his feet.

I proceeded next morning and reached Fort McMurray. I purchased fish here for dog feed. On December 24 purchased more fish (and) travelled without accident till December 27, reaching Big Weechume Lake. Here I had to lay off a day to procure a guide as there was no trail. I had to buy moose meat for the dogs as there was no fish. Next day I reached Big Jackfish Lake and secured fish enough to take the dogs to Lac la Biche which is three days from here.

I arrived at Lac la Biche at 11.30 a.m. December 31 and secured a team to carry me to Fort Saskatchewan.

Special Constable Damies attended a dance here, and he came to me about 10 p.m. and reported that there was a fight on. I went over and arrested (a man) who was crazy drunk and making trouble. I searched the premises of (a second) and found some brandy and in another house I found a part bottle of whisky. I arrested them both, and on the morning of January 2, started for Fort Saskatchewan with the intention of having the prisoners tried by the nearest magistrate. I had to hire another team for these prisoners.

On January 4 arrived at Saddle Lake and laid Information against Lac la Biche prisoners before Mr. Carrol, J.P., and tried them next day and convicted all three.

On January 6 made Andrew at noon and I was delayed here on account of damage to one of the sleighs.

I reached the barracks (Fort Saskatchewan) on January 7 and reported.

During the earlier part of the trip the prisoner was very weak and refused to eat, but towards the latter part he developed a good appetite and got stronger. I made arrangements along the trail for fish and moose meat for the return trip.

The mental patient — believed to be either a priest or a missionary — was then transported to the RNWMP guardroom at Calgary for treatment by Assistant Surgeon Rouleau of the Force, and subsequently to a hospital.

"He was badly frozen about his feet, and the exposure to the cold had caused paralysis of the tongue for several days. Every care and attention was given him at the hospital, with the result that he was discharged on Feb. 23, 1905 with the loss of only the first joint of a big toe. His mind and speech were as good as ever. His life was saved," remarked the Surgeon.

Unfortunately, however, the story did not end there. Constable Pedley had some dental work to be attended to prior to journeying North again, and so commuted between Fort Saskatchewan and Edmonton for the next month. On Feb. 8, 1905, he left the Fort with Cst. George D. Ferris and Cecil E. Denny, who at the time was a special constable in the RNWMP.

Pedley appeared to be in good health when the party started out, but after three days on the trail again, other members of the party noticed that his health was deteriorating and by February 13, he had become violently ill. Denny reported later that Pedley had neither eaten nor slept for five days. It was at Lac la Biche that his health was in such a serious state that it was decided to return immediately to Fort Saskatchewan.

Later that month, Constable Pedley was transferred to a hospital at Brandon, Man., where he remained until Oct. 4, 1905. Following this, Commissioner Perry granted him three months' leave and early in 1906, Constable Pedley returned to active duty at "Depot" Division, Regina, where he continued to serve with the Force until retiring to pension on Apr. 17, 1924. He was promoted to the rank of corporal on Oct. 1, 1916, and to sergeant four years before he terminated his 24 years of service.

After taking his pension, ex-Sergeant Pedley remained in Regina for nearly ten years, after which he returned to England.

A son, George A. Pedley, also served in the Force, retiring to pension with the rank of corporal in 1955. He now resides in Webb, Sask.

In 1952, the Metro-Goldwyn-Mayer Studios in Hollywood released a motion picture entitled "The Wild North" which was billed as being based on Constable Pedley's patrol, but there were really no similarities in the two stories whatsoever.

11

The Man from Idaho

RCMP *Quarterly* Staff

As the year 1903 dawned a considerable influx of settlers came into the Northwest Territories from sections of the U.S.A., and while many were anxious to establish homesteads, inevitably a number of "drifters" came to look the country over and as was the custom, carried one or two guns on the hip. Members of the NWMP warned these immigrants that the practice of carrying revolvers was prohibited in Canada, and this generally had good effect but numerous arrests were made when men failed to comply with this law.

The quiet town of Weyburn was enjoying a bright summer day when the peace was much disturbed by an individual who liked to be known as "The Man from Idaho". He had travelled the west through the earlier years and arrived in Weyburn with two cohorts a few weeks earlier. These appeared to be his "cheering section", their chief job seeming that of advising the local citizens what a "bad hombre" they had in their midst in The Man from Idaho.

In the afternoon, receiving considerable encouragement from his cohorts, "The Man" walked the centre of the main street shooting holes through various buildings and threatening all and sundry. The first citizen who poked his head through a window to see what all the shooting was about promptly had his hat shot from his head and was told that if he left his head out he would acquire a couple of holes in it. He proceeded to mind his own business.

Becoming emboldened, the gunman encountered another citizen and making him hold his hat above his head he shot it full of holes. This man was made of sterner stuff and refused to be cowed telling the gunman he had better settle down or the Mounted Policeman would provide a cell for him. He was informed that no Canadian could arrest him and offered to bet $25 that the North West Mounted Police couldn't do the job.

The citizen promptly accepted the bet and telegraphed to Halbrite for Cst. Henry (Larry) Lett who rode into town later that night and began to look for the wild and woolly man from Idaho. He located him in the boarding house where he was busy relating tales of his past prowess to a somewhat skeptical audience. Constable Lett immediately grabbed the man when he made a move to reach for his gun, took it from him, then decorated the "Idaho Kid's" wrists with a pair of handcuffs.

Taking his prisoner with him he quickly located the two henchmen and completed the three arrests within 30 minutes of entering town. Of course, Constable Lett immediately acquired a true friend in the citizen who won the $25 and in addition, became the toast of the town. Shortly afterwards he was promoted to corporal for his work on this and other previous occasions. The *Moose Jaw Times* in reporting the incident stated "Constable Lett should receive at least several stripes for his cool courageous work."

The above incident occurred in the present town of Weyburn, Sask., on May 15, 1903. The man making the arrest was Reg. No. 3156 Cst. Henry (Larry) Lett, who engaged in the NWMP on Sept. 9, 1896 and was discharged to pension on Dec. 31, 1918 with the rank of sergeant major. He died at Regina, Sask., on Jan. 16, 1934.

12

Police Heroism Rewarded

RCMP *Quarterly* Staff

Once again the RCMP has been honoured by one of its members, Reg. No. 11973, Cpl. Hugh Cecil Russell, receiving the rarely-conferred King's Police and Fire Services Medal, the award being approved by His Majesty in November, 1947.

The facts surrounding Corporal Russell's heroic exploit briefly are these. On a farm two miles from the small town of Gunn, Alta., 40 miles north-west of Edmonton, two well diggers were busy at their trade just before noon of blustery Nov. 25, 1946, and had drilled down about 45 feet when one of them, Kenneth Walter Callioux, 21, rushed into the farm-house and shouted to the farmer that his companion, Edgar Belrose, 22, was at the bottom of the well hole overcome by gas fumes. The two men hurried back to the excavation where Callioux slid down the rope to rescue his co-worker. A minute or so later the farmer realized that something had gone amiss with him for the only response to his calls were groans and it soon was evident that the second workman also had collapsed.

Notified of the mishap, Corporal Russell and Reg. No. 13035, Cst. (now A/Cpl.) John Edward Mead of nearby Stony Plain Detachment procured two 60-foot lengths of rope and lost no time getting to the scene.

Steam issued into the cold air from the incomplete well which consisted of a circular hole 21 to 24 inches in diameter and 45 feet deep and over which was a boring apparatus comprised of a large wooden turn-table and an auger drill on a winch. The turn-table was connected to the winch by a lever-controlled gear, and it was clear that during the operation of this contraption constant vigilance would be essential lest signal and rescue ropes get fouled with the suspension cable. Beyond doubt the gas threat in the well was very dangerous, for pending the arrival of the police a lighted lantern had twice been lowered into the hole and both times had gone out less than a quarter of the way down.

Sizing up the situation at a glance, Corporal Russell instructed Constable Mead to supervise surface operations while he himself descended the well. Then with a water-soaked scarf over his mouth and nostrils he was secured to the cable and lowered by a hand crank. He had difficulty breathing in the confined space and in this first attempt succeeded only in partially looping the rescue rope about the uppermost accident victim before he signalled to be hauled up for air.

Second time down he took along a pair of ice tongs, intending to use them for lifting the body while he tied the rope into position, but they slipped and proved of no help. On this and all subsequent attempts a horse was used to wind the cable and ropes on the winch. Adding to the danger of a cave-in and the difficulty of keeping the ropes and cable from getting entangled with one another was the fact that the entire well-digging rig revolved over the well mouth. Besides the cable, which was used for lowering the rescuer, there were three ropes — one for signalling, one with a flashlight attached to it, and the other to raise the victim — and all had to be let down and wound up together. On his third descent the corporal was dropped too quickly and unseated from the steel hook which he straddled, and when hauled aloft following the unnerving experience was hanging precariously to the cable. In the rush there had been no time to pad the hook but though his spine was wrenched slightly in the fall fortunately he sustained no permanent injury. For the fourth time down he had a gas mask, brought to the farm by a neighbour, but it had to be discarded because the visor clouded up and obscured his vision. However on this try he managed to place the rope around the arm of Kenneth Callioux whose body soon afterwards was raised. Stimulants were given this victim and artificial respiration applied but it soon was apparent that life was extinct and he was pronounced dead.

Meanwhile the rescuers went about retrieving the other body. About this time the strain was beginning to show on the corporal, and on his fifth trip into the death shaft calamity almost struck. At the foot of the excavation he lost consciousness and was pulled to safety just in time. Revived, he was given hot coffee and took a short rest. Observing the corporal's physical and mental exhaustion, Constable Mead spoke up and said it was his turn to go down. But even as he did so he knew that his unusually large body — six feet 2 1/2 inches and weighing over 20 lbs. more than Russell — would prevent him from accomplishing anything worth-while jammed in a hole of such narrow dimensions. Corporal Russell, himself a six-footer but of sparer stature, wouldn't hear of it, and on his feet again, returned to the well and was lowered to the bottom. This time he got the rope in place, but it slipped off as the body weight shifted. Up to the top once more for a short breather and back to his task, finally the second dead body was lifted out, and the ordeal was over.

At the well opening Constable Mead had the situation in hand throughout the operations and his actions are deserving of high praise. In sub-zero temperature with a wind blowing and snow flurries, his was a difficult painful assignment in which he had to use his bare hands to keep the various lines from fouling. Though only recently transferred to the prairies and therefore quite unfamiliar with the operation of the crude antiquated machinery upon which they relied, he calmly and efficiently supervised and directed the work of the half-dozen men who made up the surface crew. While his participation was less spectacular than Russell's, and it is true that he did no more than his duty as a member of the Force, the proper handling of his end of the job was none the less essential to the successful outcome of the whole undertaking, and the fact that no further fatality or accident occurred has been attributed largely to his cool behaviour.

Corporal Russell, actuated solely by the possibility that there might still be a chance, if only a slim one, of saving the two men, and fully aware of the hazards involved accepted the initiative without the slightest hesitation or thought of himself. He properly refused Mead's offer to take over, for the constable's bulk would have denied him practically any freedom of movement in the cramped space while the effort might have added to the tragedy without in any way helping matters. In addition to asphyxiation, the corporal faced the risk of cave-in, while the outmoded equipment used in lowering and raising him could have contributed nothing to his peace of mind. All in all it is small wonder that he was practically exhausted by the time the bodies were extricated. "I must say", remarked one of the men present at the rescue operations and interviewed later, "that Corporal Russell displayed fortitude, his whole object being to get the boys out without any thought of his own safety beyond taking the necessary precautions, and save them if at all possible. He displayed courage and perseverance and I for one wouldn't have gone down that well for anything. He never hesitated or delayed until he had both bodies out. It must have been a great physical and mental strain, but he stayed with it."

Corporal Russell's actions are worthy of the highest traditions of the Force, and the *Quarterly* congratulates him on his courage, determination and initiative and the fact that he came through his exploit unscathed. Like all its predecessors, this latest award of the King's Police and Fire Services medal reflected honour not only on the recipient, but on the whole Force, and all ranks will be gratified that Corporal Russell's gallantry has thus been recognized.

13

The Northern Men

Ex-Sgt. Jack Fossum

During our recruit training period we were advised that we could volunteer for Northern service but that there was a waiting list. The application form listed certain qualifications required, including some skill as a carpenter. If accepted, the applicant was required to make his will prior to his departure for the North. Northern service included service in the Yukon and the Northwest Territories. Men who were accepted were required to remain in the North for a minimum period of two years, after which they could re-engage or return to the "outside".

Those were the days before the advent of aircraft, snowmobiles and two-way radio communication in the North. Living conditions were primitive and isolation complete except for the visit of the Arctic supply ship once a year. The silence and loneliness was compounded by darkness in the long winter months. Travel was by dog team only and the Husky shared the hardships of the trail with his master. This sort of life called for a man in good physical condition, of an even temperament, who was capable of coping with cabin fever as well as rugged travel. Such a man was known in the Force as a Northern Man. His role as policeman in the North was similar to that of his colleague "outside" but with one important difference: he was entirely on his own in whatever situation he might have to face.

Such a man was Henry Stallworthy. He was a typical Northern Man and yet he was more than that. His career during thirty years of service, twenty of them in the Yukon and the High Arctic, is regarded as outstanding. Today, when Canada is struggling to assert and maintain sovereignty over its vast Arctic region, Stallworthy's accomplishments are of particular significance, for they contributed towards establishing that sovereignty. He was an explorer as well as a policeman. The northern tip of Axel Heiberg Island bears his name: Cape Stallworthy.

Stallworthy joined the Force in 1914 at the age of eighteen and served for a while in the Yukon before joining the RCMP contingent and being sent to France during the World War. At the end of the war he returned to the Yukon. Like so many others, he had come under "the spell of the North".

In 1923 he joined Corporal Petty and Constable Robinson at the detachment at Chesterfield Inlet. In 1924, Staff Sergeant Clay and his young wife Maggie arrived on transfer from the Mackenzie River area. One of the few white women in the Arctic at the time, she enjoyed Northern life and looked forward to the new and different living conditions in this tiny, isolated community. The four men at the Hudson's Bay Company trading post and the two priests at the Catholic mission were the only other white people in the area. However, the Eskimos employed by the RCMP on a permanent basis, a floating population of hunters who came and left with the seasons, their wives and children and their many dogs made for a lively community.

That year the Hudson's Bay Company traders made a fall patrol in their large motor schooner up the Back River to Baker Lake. Clay joined them to acquaint himself with his new territory and to meet the native people in the interior. He would be gone for an indefinite time during which he would have no communication with Chesterfield. In his absence, Maggie contented herself in her new surroundings, always cheerful and active. She walked a lot on the beach where there were often children, and many dogs which were allowed to run loose in the settlement during the summer.

One afternoon, Stallworthy became aware of a dog fight on the beach. When he heard Maggie scream he ran and was horrified to see her on the ground surrounded by the snarling dogs. They were tearing at her leg and had stripped the flesh from knee to ankle, leaving the bare bone exposed. He beat off the dogs, picked her up and carried her up the slope to her home. The leg was badly damaged, with blood spurting from torn arteries. There was chloroform in the medical supplies — but very little. The men worked quickly to stop further loss of blood. They made Maggie as comfortable as possible, then turned their attention to the larger problem.

They knew, and Maggie knew, that the leg would have to be amputated. In fact, she pleaded with them to do it as quickly as possible. There were no antibiotics in those days and infection was a constant threat. The settlement had a basic supply of surgical tools, medical supplies and the pitifully small amount of chloroform. There was also a comprehensive medical text, *Pye's Surgery*. They spent the night studying the book and consulting with each other. None had any previous experience in dealing with an emergency of this magnitude.

Towards morning they had reached an agreement, assigning each other to the necessary tasks. Father Duplesne was to perform the surgery, assisted by Norman Snow, the trading post manager. Stallworthy would take charge of the instruments and administer the anesthetic. Before starting the operation they wrote out the following statement, which they all, including Maggie, signed: "We believe that the amputation of Mrs. Clay's leg is necessary. We have every reason to believe that we can succeed. We believe that this will save her life."

Stallworthy lifted the girl onto the dining room table. He sterilized the instruments and took charge of the chloroform. On a signal from him Duplesne began the cutting, but when he came to sawing the bone he faltered. Stallworthy hastily handed the chloroform to Maria, the post's Eskimo interpreter and a competent woman, and went to the priest's assistance. He finished removing the leg just as the chloroform gave out.

Maggie awoke almost immediately and when Stallworthy carried her to her bed she asked, "Is my leg off? I feel so much better." And later, a poignant remark, "I won't be able to dance again, will I?"

At first it was thought she might recover but because of lack of recovery facilities and antibiotics, shock and loss of blood, she failed rapidly. The two priests tried to talk to her about converting to their faith so they could administer the last sacrament. This upset her and she asked Stallworthy to stay at her side so that she would not give way in her weakness. This he did and made notes of her thoughts and messages to her husband, whom she knew she would never see again. He gave her sips of tea and comforted her as best he could, remaining at her side constantly. At about midnight of the third day she died.

A rough coffin was made. Maria lined it with duffel and fine white cloth. Stallworthy and the other men led the little procession up the barren hill behind the detachment. He read the Anglican burial service from a prayer book. They built a rock cairn to cover the coffin. Then, completely exhausted from lack of sleep and overwhelming emotion, he fell into a long sleep.

In the weeks that followed he watched for and dreaded the return of the schooner. The others had delegated him to meet the ship and break the news to Clay. The day finally arrived. When the schooner anchored, Clay shouted, "Where is Maggie?" He immediately sensed something was wrong. When told, he went to pieces and had to be given close companionship by the others during the months that followed.

In the spring Stallworthy and Clay left the Inlet and journeyed south to Fort Churchill, thence overland to Winnipeg and down the Niagara Peninsula to Maggie's family. Again Stallworthy told his story, this time to the grieving parents who had, of course, been unaware of their daughter's fate. Shortly afterward, Clay took his discharge from the Force.

After a quick visit to his home in England, Stallworthy again turned his thoughts to Northern service and waited for another posting. In the meantime he was stationed at Jasper, Alberta Detachment and there he met Hilda Austin, a school teacher, who was later to become his wife. Finally he got his wish and was transferred to Bache Peninsula on Ellesmere Island. This was the detachment he had been hoping to get all along, a spot near the top of the world in the land of the Arctic explorers — Greeley, Amundsen, Nansen, Cook and Peary. He would employ Eskimos who had travelled with these men. He was filled with enthusiasm.

When he reached Ottawa he was told that the German expedition of Dr. E.K. Krueger, who had been given a permit to travel across Ellesmere Island to Axel Heiberg Island, had failed to return and it was feared it might have been lost. It was a small party consisting of three men: Dr. Krueger, a distinguished scientist, his companion, Bjar, a Dane, and one Eskimo. They had one sled and a poor dog team, with very inadequate equipment. They had definite plans to travel as far west as Meighen Island, depending on game conditions in the area.

The expedition had been at Bache the previous year and had not been heard of since. Stallworthy was told to be on the lookout for them and to consider they might have come out by another, more northerly route. Their chances for survival were considered poor.

Arriving at Bache in the summer of 1930 on the S.S. *Beothic*, Stallworthy was now far beyond any human habitation. The Canadian government employed Greenlanders from Etah to work and travel with the RCMP members at Bache. They would cross Smith Sound on the ice in winter, bringing their strong dog teams, their travelling gear, and their wives who made the bearskin pants, sealskin boots and other equipment for the RCMP members. Some of these men had travelled with polar explorers since the days of Peary. In fact, one of them proudly claimed to be a son of Peary.

The RCMP maintained a detachment in this remote and uninhabited place primarily to maintain sovereignty. Denmark was casting covetous, expansionist eyes across Smith Sound to the land mass of Ellesmereland [as Ellesmere Island was called by the Danes], although on the map the Canadian archipelago borders were defined by east and west longitudes to the North Pole. But Greenlanders had travelled and hunted across Smith Sound from time immemorial, oblivious to the white man's boundaries.

After leaving the usual cargo of supplies, reading material and other amenities for the detachment members, the *Beothic* headed back south, not to return for another year. It was now known that nothing had been seen or heard of the missing Krueger expedition.

Stallworthy now had a new and vast domain to patrol. He had experienced Eskimo travelling companions and would share the solitude with a junior constable for the next year. They turned their attention to the immediate task of transporting the mountain of supplies to the detachment some distance away, settling in to the detachment quarters, and securing dog food—walrus, seal and narwhal—for the coming winter. It was all hard work but a most necessary part of the routine life in the far North. Unlike life in the "outside", there were no deadlines to meet, no telephone to answer and no time clock to punch. When hunting was good or when they were on long patrols they often worked around the clock. Time meant nothing. Getting essential projects done in the rapidly diminishing daylight hours was a driving necessity. It was no life for a lazy man.

Stallworthy's first winter at Bache passed quickly. With Constable Foster (in his second year at the detachment) and two capable Eskimos, Inuituk and Noocapinguaq, as travelling companions he made winter patrols whenever weather and moonlight made it possible. In the spring the serious business of looking for Krueger began. As soon as the sun reappeared he set out with the two Eskimos and travelled south along the coast of Ellesmere Island.

It was a gruelling journey on the rough sea ice in blizzards and low temperatures. They reached the abandoned RCMP post at Craig Harbour in six days, only to find that Krueger had not gone that way. This narrowed the field of future search, but they had to make haste to get back to Bache while it was still possible to travel on the sea ice.

On the way home they were fortunate to sight two polar bears. They shot one and took it down to sea level for badly needed dog food. Stallworthy followed the other up the glacier. Always aware of danger at this time of the year when a thick layer of snow still covered and concealed the crevasses, he tested each step ahead with the long metal rod they carried for this purpose. A rising welt in the flat surface indicated an updraft from below. Suddenly the snow in front of him fell away with a sickening rush, revealing sheer walls of ice. He scuffed a runway behind himself and made a running leap across the gaping chasm, took two careful steps ahead, then dropped like a stone down a lateral crack leading to the crevasse. As he fell he let out a shout. He jolted to a stop, wedged between the ice walls about twenty feet down, and his parka, which he had been carrying on his arm, slithered away into the depths. Then he blacked out. He was aroused by the Eskimos shouting at him from above. They had heard his shout. The crack in the ice, acting like a conduit, had carried his voice down to sea level. They let down a harpoon line but he was afraid to move for fear of losing his fragile hold. Inch by inch he managed to get the noose under one armpit and with the free hand grasp the line above his head. As his companions pulled him, cut and bruised, to safety, they wept like children. The bond of friendship which had developed between them was to endure and strengthen as they shared dangers and hardships in the year ahead.

After his return to the outside two years later, Stallworthy was amused to read an article in the *Toronto Star* relating the incident. A full-page color illustration showed him in full dress uniform — scarlet serge, breeches, boots, spurs and all — upside down in the crevasse, Stetson hat firmly in place.

They reached Bache with a good load of meat and polar bear skins for pants, which would be made by the Eskimo women. The rest of the season passed without event and early August brought the *Beothic* with the annual supplies for the isolated post. The RCMP had planned to close Bache and station the detachment at Craig Harbour, below the narrow passage of Smith Sound where the floating icepack had proven over the years to be an impassable barrier. However, when Stallworthy boarded the *Beothic* and reported to Inspector Joy the result of their spring patrol in search of Krueger, this changed all the plans. Joy told them the German government was pressuring Canada to continue the search for the Krueger expedition. He instructed Stallworthy to leave the supplies at Bache and to carry out an intensive search the following spring with the help of more Eskimos and dogs who would come over from the Robertson Bay settlement on the Greenland coast.

After unloading mail and supplies the *Beothic* began her return journey. Two new men, Constables R.W. Hamilton and Art Munro, had arrived with the ship on transfer to Bache and Constable Foster was returning south. Hamilton, an experienced Northern Man, would take part in the spring search for Krueger.

During the months that followed, caches of food for dogs and men, coal oil, ammunition and other supplies were laid along the routes the searchers would follow in the spring. In March, three experienced Eskimo travellers, their wives, seven children and eighty-six dogs came across from Etah, Greenland. The women and children would be guests of the RCMP during the upcoming search. The women worked continuously making bearskin pants, sealskin Kooleetahs and footwear up to the last minute.

Three parties would take part in the search. Hamilton with two Eskimos, three sledges and forty-seven dogs would travel south on Eureka Sound and search the islands off the southern tip of Axel Heiberg. He would rendezvous with Stallworthy at Cape Southwest a month later. After leaving a cache of supplies at Cape Southwest, a supply party of two Eskimos and fort-yseven dogs would return to Bache. Stallworthy, with three Eskimos, three sledges and fifty-four dogs would completely circle Axel Heiberg Island.

On March 20 they were on their way. At first they had to traverse some very rough terrain. For forty-eight hours it was a case of packing and relaying, climbing up over rocky hills for about four miles, then descending to the river ice leading to Bay Fiord for about a mile down a dangerous incline. This took twelve hours. They would join harpoons together and let each sledge down singly with one man to guide it while the rest of the men dug in their heels and paid out line. At a point about 200 yards down the hill the sledges were blocked and the process repeated until all sledges were at the bottom. They worked continuously for two days.

They now had excellent sleighing downgrade on the river ice to Bay Fiord where they arrived three days later. Here they had to unload the sledges and file and polish the steel runners with emery paper after the passage over rocky terrain.

On March 25 the patrols parted. Hamilton turned south and Stallworthy north on Eureka Sound with his three Eskimo companions, Eetookasuaq, Quaviarsuaq and Kahdi. They followed the line of caches and at first were in no danger of running out of supplies. On any lengthy patrol men and dogs must count on living off the land. Game must be found along the way to feed the dogs. Without their dogs, the men would be without transportation and without transportation for their supplies they would perish. This, Stallworthy was convinced, was what had happened to the Krueger expedition. He had no expectation of finding the men alive but hoped to find some evidence of where they had been and where they had perished.

They had fair going on Eureka Sound and made steady progress to May Point, arriving there on March 28. It was known that Krueger had reached that far in April 1929. The following day they travelled west to the mouth of Mokka Fiord, but found no signs that the Krueger expedition had visited there.

They had expected to find bear on Eureka Sound but were out of luck. The prolonged diet of canned meat was not sustaining the dogs very well in the cold weather and a heavy feed of bear meat would have restored their strength. The patrol was now nearing an area where bears are seldom seen because there is no food for them, so much against his will, Stallworthy was forced to kill some musk oxen for dog food. These animals were a protected species and, of course, as a policeman charged with enforcing the regulations he was doubly reluctant to contravene them himself. But he had no choice; the dogs had to be fed.

On April 5 they left Skraeling Point and followed the coast for about five miles but found no sign of Krueger's passing, and no indication that he had visited any of the points in the area. They passed what was shown on the map as Schei Island, and found it to be a peninsula joined to Axel Heiberg Island by an isthmus about two miles wide.

On April 9 they reached a point opposite Cape Norman Hubbard (later renamed Cape Stallworthy) at the northern tip of Axel Heiberg Island. There they located a cairn on one of the capes. One of the Eskimos knew of a cairn in that area built by Peary. Stallworthy left the others a short distance from the cape and, taking a snow knife with which to hack his way up to the top, went to examine the cairn.

Here he found his first trace of the missing expedition, a note dated April 24, 1930, left by Krueger. As it was written in German he did not fully understand it, but it was evident that the party had been at Lands Lokk and at this cape. The note was signed by Krueger, Bjar and the Eskimo Akaio. Stallworthy concluded that at this point they were in good condition since from what he could glean from the note they intended going to Meighen Island across the frozen strait. Krueger had apparently changed his plan to go north from here, presumably intending instead to look for new land to claim for the fatherland.

The cairn had been built by Peary in 1906 in his trip from the north coast of Ellesmere Island and visited in 1914 by MacMillan. Records in the cairn showed that Peary's original papers were lifted by the explorer MacMillan and that MacMillan's in turn were taken by Krueger. Stallworthy made copies of all the records and placed them in a cylinder in the cairn, giving the date, April 10, 1932, his own name and those of his travelling companions and the purpose of the patrol.

The German expedition had reached the cairn in thirty-seven days and, considering that they had visited Lands Lokk and walked the distance from Bache Peninsula, Stallworthy felt they had made very good progress. Stallworthy now had good reason for believing that Krueger had visited Meighen Island and he decided to cross Sverdrup Channel and continue his search there. They left the Cape and travelled south along the west coast of Axel Heiberg, covering ninety miles in two days. On the second day they encountered pressure ice and tough going. There was not much to choose between following the shore ice over the rocks or the rough sea ice but they decided to travel on land in the hope of finding traces of the expedition. On April 16 they reached Cape Levvel opposite Meighen Island. Climbing to high ground, Stallworthy could see the island through his binoculars some seventy miles away. The rough sea ice extended as far out over the channel as he could see.

However, during their journey down the coast they had seen only one lone caribou which they had shot and fed to the dogs. They were now running out of dog food and the dogs were put on short rations. In their weakened condition it would not be possible to attempt crossing the channel. Not only would the search now have to be abandoned but with the total absence of game of any kind the men were in danger of meeting the same fate as those for whom they were searching. They had no choice but to press on toward Cape Southwest where they knew a food cache would be waiting for them.

But Cape Southwest was still a long distance away. The dogs were so weak that some of them had to be lifted to their feet to get going after the more and more frequent rests. Stallworthy was also getting concerned about his companions. Going for days without rest and with little food they had become so gaunt that their eyes were sunken back into the sockets. He had no way of knowing that he looked the same.

On April 20, after forty-eight hours of almost continuous travel they found themselves only about fifteen miles from Cape Southwest. During this time they had fed the dogs their spare seal skins, their mittens and extra footwear. They had also given them what was left of their bacon and pemmican. They were now completely out of food themselves.

The cape where the food was cached was in plain view but the dogs did not have the strength to continue. They built an igloo and killed six dogs to feed the rest. But there was little meat on their bones.

The next day they decided to lighten their loads by leaving behind their heaviest equipment, but though the going was much improved they could only move at a crawl. It took them sixteen hours to cover the last few miles to the cache. They remained there for two days, feeding the dogs often and lightly on the canned meat and pemmican that had been stored there, and searching the area for game, but without success.

On April 25 they took the rest of the supplies and left to hunt for game. But the dogs soon lost their early stamina. After travelling some ten miles, Khadi, the crackshot of the group, found and shot seven caribou, and they fed all the meat to the dogs.

Three days later they set off through the deep snow to Hyperite Point, but the dogs could not exceed a walking pace and were soon staggering again. When a blizzard blew up they stopped, built an igloo and camped for the night. The following morning they had to sacrifice another five dogs to save the others. Two of the men went with Stallworthy to look for anything alive. One of the men was left behind with the dogs to keep them from eating their harness. But they returned empty-handed. That night they slept in the open as the snow was too soft to hold up for blocks.

On May 4, Stallworthy, looking through his binoculars, spotted a seal on the ice about a mile away. The others watched anxiously as Khadi crawled forward to get within shooting distance. The shot broke the seal's neck. The next day they got another, quite large seal. This was obviously a land of feast or famine. The blubber of the seals was about three inches thick, and offered more nourishment than half a dozen caribou. A turning point in their fortunes had been reached at last. The next day a large bear was spotted near their camp. Two experienced bear dogs held it at bay until it was shot.

They now had plenty of meat. Men and animals were recovering from starvation, happy to know that they would have no difficulty getting back to Bache. Stallworthy sent two teams back to Cape Southwest for the tent and supplies left behind, a distance of about ninety miles. They were away for nine days.

On May 18 they left Ulvingen Island on the home stretch. There was plenty of game in the area of travel, and on May 22 they reached the detachment.

The patrol had taken sixty days. Counting side-trips in search of the missing expedition and in search of game, Stallworthy estimated the distance covered at not less than 1400 miles. Hamilton had returned from the south on May 7. He had found no evidence to indicate that Krueger had returned by a southerly route.

"*Nascopie* fails to reach Bache Peninsula — Three Mounted Policemen marooned." This headline appeared in Canadian newspapers in October 1932. There had always been the danger that the annual supply ship might some year not be able to reach Bache due to ice conditions.

Now it had happened, right on the heels of Stallworthy's return from the hazardous Axel Heiberg Island patrol. Stallworthy, Hamilton and Munro were stranded for a year without supplies.

The three men had no way of communicating with the outside but Ottawa RCMP headquarters, greatly concerned, sent messages over public radio stations in Canada and the U.S.A. ordering transfer of the detachment to Craig Harbour. However, the transfer could not be undertaken until the following spring when the 200-mile journey to the southern tip of Ellesmere Island would be made by dog teams. The men had prepared the building for permanent closure in 1932. They would now have to get themselves up again, hunt walrus, seal and narwhal to feed their dogs during winter patrols and for the sledge journey to Craig Harbour in the spring. With no fresh supplies arriving, they would have to ration themselves in order to eke out what they had to carry them through the fall and winter.

They were lucky enough to get seven walrus although it was late in the season. The larger livers were sliced, frozen and rationed to one meal a week for each man. This was their insurance against scurvy, the dreaded illness of northern explorers. Their supplies of all food had been badly depleted, owing to the presence of extra Eskimos for the Krueger search.

When the sun returned in the spring they made their journey south to Craig Harbour without incident. There they found an abundant supply of food left by the *Nascopie* the year before and for a while there was great feasting. In August the supply ship appeared over the horizon with men to relieve them. At last Stallworthy and his companions could head back to civilization.

In Ottawa, Stallworthy was interviewed by the Commissioner, Sir James MacBrien, who was most anxious to hear about all that had happened during the past two years. But he also had disturbing news. He wanted Stallworthy to go back to Bache Peninsula in the summer of 1934 to guide a scientific expedition from Oxford University, headed by Edward Shackleton, son of the Antarctic explorer, Sir Ernest Shackleton. The group had plans to travel and explore the large northern territory of Ellesmere Island and use Bache as their headquarters. They wanted an experienced Northern Man to guide them. The Commissioner had the right man, or so he thought.

But Stallworthy had other plans. He had decided he was through with the North. He wanted to get married. He wanted a long holiday in England with his family. He would need time to consider the Commissioner's proposal. It was not an order. Like all Northern postings, it was on a voluntary basis. In any event, next summer seemed a long way off and he would have time to do many of the things he had planned.

During the years since he had left Jasper his relationship with Hilda had flowered in spite of the long periods of separation. They had been together during his brief spell out of the North. The annual visits of the supply ship had brought reams of letters from one to the other. They had both known that for them there could be no-one else.

She now came to see him in Ottawa. He met her at the Union Station early one November morning and at noon they were married, with three of his best friends as witnesses. For their honeymoon they sailed to England where his mother and members of his large family welcomed him and his Canadian bride.

The Commissioner had asked him to meet and confer with the young men who formed the nucleus of the proposed expedition. They met at Oxford and spent days poring over maps and making plans. They had hundreds of questions for the man who had the answers. He suited them. They wanted him and no-one else. Inevitably, Stallworthy agreed to go. Hilda had known he would — all his paths had led in the same direction, northward. Her sustaining hope was that this would be his last sojourn in the land of ice and snow.

The expedition left London's St. Catherine dock on July 17. On board the Norwegian sealing vessel *Signalhorn* with Stallworthy and

Shackleton were three young Oxford graduates, Ev Moore, Robert Bentham and Haig-Thomas. The oldest member of the party was Dr. Noel Humphreys, a medical doctor who had taken part in other scientific expeditions but never travelled in the Arctic regions.

The aim of the expedition was to penetrate the northern interior of Ellesmere Island farther than Peary who had navigated the northern coastline westward to Axel Heiberg Island earlier in the century. The group was interested in the flora and fauna, ornithology, geology and in the surveying and mapping of the region. But the major interest was the adventure of travel and exploration. Stallworthy's interests matched those of his charges. The journey would take him farther north than any member of the Force had ever been. Ellesmere Island, some 80,000 square miles in area, only slightly smaller than England and Scotland together, is Canada's northern-most land mass. His presence in its largely unexplored northern region would also serve to strengthen Canada's sovereignty on her polar frontier.

The group agreed to split up into three parties. Stallworthy would travel with Ev Moore and two Eskimos, Inuituk and his old friend Noocapinguaq, to Grantland. Humphreys and Haig-Thomas would attempt a crossing of Grinnell Land. Shackleton and Bentham would cross Smith Sound on the ice to Bache which they would use as a base to carry out exploration and geological studies.

After spending the winter in Greenland, the three parties set out on April 4 on their separate journeys. Moore proved to be a tough and hardy Arctic traveller, always fired with enthusiasm to reach their goal. However, because of the poor game conditions they had to abandon their plan to reach Grantland and settle for a crossing of the United States Range to plant the British flag between there and the coast. Only one of the two white men could go; the other would have to remain at their camp on Lake Hazen and try to catch fish to feed the dogs. Stallworthy insisted that Moore go on with Noocap, and when they returned four days later they brought news that they had reached latitude 82.25, longitude 71.45. Then they had turned south, leaving the Union Jack fluttering in the breeze.

In his book, *Arctic Journeys*, Shackleton tells the story of the 15-month journey into the Canadian Arctic, and the adventures of the other two patrols. The journey back to England on the *Dannebrog*, a small Danish schooner, proved to be an added adventure. In one of the worst storms of the year the vessel lost a blade from its propeller and had to finish the voyage under sail.

Stallworthy spent the rest of his days in the Force on the "outside". He retired to pension in 1945 at the age of fifty with the rank of sergeant major.

In the summer of 1956 Stallworthy returned to the North, this time as security chief on the DEW Line, a string of radar stations being strung across the Arctic. He was also there on behalf of the Canadian government to look after the welfare of the Eskimo people during the construction phase. After an absence of over twenty years he found a strange and new Arctic. Instead of shouts of mush! mush! the Arctic stillness was broken by the roar of machinery. Instead of the dog teams there were motorized caravans with heated accommodations. Instead of pemmican there were beefsteaks, fresh fruit and vegetables.

The only dogs he saw around Frobisher Bay were gorged on the meat and other refuse thrown from overfilled mess hall plates. While previously he had communicated with the Eskimos in their own language, he now found that those employed on construction spoke some English. They had leaped almost instantly from the Stone Age into the modern world with ease and dignity. Stallworthy could not help but wonder what the future might hold for these people that he had come to love and respect.

This account of detachment life in the Arctic and the life of one whom Edward, now Lord Shackleton, has called one of Canada's greatest Arctic travellers would not be complete without a little postscript. In 1973, Stallworthy was again called to Ottawa. At the age of 78 he was invested with the Order of Canada by none other than the Queen herself. Hilda was at his side during this crowning event of his adventurous life. In a brief conversation the Queen turned to Hilda and asked, "And what were you doing while your husband was away from you so far and for so long?" Hilda replied, "I counted the months, the weeks and the days waiting for his return." Stallworthy died on Christmas Day, 1976, in Comox, B.C., where he and his wife had made their home since his retirement. His name — like that of another Northern Man, Henry Larsen — has a place in the history of the Force.

Editor's Note

Many members of the Force became expert northern travellers in the course of their service, but Henry Webb Stallworthy takes pride of place. As a result of his leadership in the Oxford-Cambridge Arctic Expedition he was made a Fellow of the Royal Geographical Society. Later because of his accomplishments in the North, he became an Officer of the Order of Canada.

This article is an excerpt from the book, *Cop in the Closet*, by ex-Sergeant Jack Fossum. It was published by Hancock House Publishers Ltd., Vancouver, B.C. The book was serialized in the RCMP *Quarterly*.

The North

14

The Missing Krueger Party

Vernon Lachance

Gleaming glaciers, ice-locked hills, wind-swept rocks, precipitous snowdrifts, and a sparcity of vegetation: the Arctic Islands of Canada present a picture of infinite desolation to the newcomer.

And of all the Arctic Islands that known as Ellesmere is one of the most bleak. The winter climate is intensely cold, cold far beyond the recorded temperatures, when the howling winds sweep down with icy breath from the glaciers dominating the island.

The Royal Canadian Mounted Police detachment at Bache Peninsula on Ellesmere Island was established in the summer of 1926. It is situated at a point only eleven degrees from the North Pole: the most northerly police post in the world.

It was the sudden uproar of the Eskimo dogs, one day in March, 1930, that warned Constable McLean of the approach of someone. The sky was overcast, but there was no wind, and the Constable could soon hear sounds of approaching sleighs.

A few minutes later his eyes widened in surprise. Visitors were rare at Bache Peninsula, but here were five bulkily clad figures approaching with three dog-drawn komitiks. The sleighs were heavily loaded. Two of the men were white; the other three were natives, obviously Greenland Eskimos.

Within the detachment's shelter, McLean was soon receiving explanations. The leader of the party was Dr. H.K.E. Krueger of Darmstadt, Germany, a scientist and explorer who wished to add to the world's knowledge of the geology and geography of the Canadian Arctic. The other white man was his assistant, Mr. Aare Rose Bjare, a native of Denmark. The three Eskimos had accompanied the white men from Greenland where Dr. Krueger had passed the winter; two of them were to remain with the others only part of the way on their intended journey, and then return to Greenland.

Dr. Krueger was ill, suffering from severe cramps. He explained that he and his assistant had suffered unusual hardships while conducting explorations in Greenland a few months earlier. This had happened when, at a point just south of the Humboldt Glacier, they had been overtaken by darkness and caught by a storm. With practically no food they had been compelled to hibernate for several days, during which time they had been reduced to eating, raw, their dogs which had frozen to death. The experience had not yet shed its effects. Bjare was still suffering from a frozen foot as a result of the adventure.

But Dr. Krueger was determined, he said, to carry out the explorations and scientific work which he had planned for the Arctic Islands.

Because of the white men's condition and in order to give their dogs a rest, Constable McLean urged the German scientist to stay at the detachment for a few days, an invitation which the party was not slow to accept.

They stayed for a week. Dr. Krueger outlined the route he intended to follow in his work. He would first make for Axel Heiberg Island to the west, he said, by way of Flagler Fiord and Eureka Sound; then, in due course, work north, around the head of Axel Heiberg Island, and continue down the west coast and back through Baumann and Makinson Inlets to Bache Peninsula, or swing south to Craig Harbour. This would permit him to arrive in time to intercept the Canadian Government ship *Beothic*, on its trip to the outside world in the late summer.

McLean was not impressed with the scientist's plan to send two of his three natives back when he had reached Axel Heiberg Island. This would leave him with only one komitik and fifteen dogs to haul a tremendous load. And the condition of the dogs was not too good.

But the German doctor, with no slightest sign of egotism, impressed the Constable with his ability to look after himself. He had done considerable exploration work in Africa, McLean learned, and had a few summers' work in Greenland to his credit, in addition to his recent arduous experience in the same country. With a sufficiency of supplies, McLean reasoned, and following the route outlined, the party should reach the southern part of Axel Heiberg Island, where game was usually abundant, before encountering serious difficulties.

On March 19th, armed with much of the knowledge and experience gained by the Mounted Police in the Arctic Islands since 1922, the Krueger party left Bache Peninsula on the first stage of its trip.

It was April 11th before the two Greenland Eskimos arrived back at Bache Peninsula. They were Ilkoo and Kahlgnah. Akkea had stayed with the two white explorers.

They had left Dr. Krueger at Depot Point on Axel Heiberg Island, the two natives reported. The progress of the party had been very slow. All the food, clothes, ammunition, camp equipment, heavy scientific instruments and a pneumatic boat had been loaded on the one komitik. A heavy deep-sea sounding wire made up the load.

It had required the combined strength of the dogs and all the men to move the heavily loaded sleigh, when Ilkoo and Kahlgnah started back. Dr. Krueger was leading, breaking trail ahead of the team; Bjare pushed behind with Akkea pushing at the side of the sleigh and whipping up the dogs.

Ilkoo and Kahlgnah brought with them some geological specimens already collected by Dr. Krueger; also several letters for delivery when the *Beothic* arrived in August. One of the letters was for the captain of the ship; others bore German addresses. Leaving the specimens at the detachment, the Greenland Eskimos, after a day's rest, pushed on for their own country.

McLean was relieved by the report. The worst of the planned route had been overcome and the party should be able to reach Bache Peninsula or Craig Harbour, comfortably, before the ship arrived.

But August and the *Beothic* came, and still no word from the party. The letter from Dr. Krueger to the ship's captain explained the delay. It mentioned that if the party had not returned by August it would mean that they were spending the winter on the west coast of Ellesmere Island and would only return in the spring, in order to travel with the spring mail from Thule to Godhavn, Greenland.

With the *Beothic* was Inspector A.H. Joy, of the Royal Canadian Mounted Police, pre-eminent among Canadian Arctic travellers. Joy had met Dr. Krueger on the inward voyage of the ship in 1929. Like Constable McLean, he had been favourably impressed with the quiet confidence and undoubted capabilities of the German scientist. To Joy, Dr. Krueger's letter dissipated all doubt. Evidently his party had encountered interesting geological or other specimens and had decided to wait over for the full, but all too short, summer season's work. It would then be too late to reach Bache Peninsula or Craig Harbour in time for the ship, but communication and travel via Greenland, would be available in the spring. The late fall or early spring should see the party safely returned.

It was only back in Ottawa, in the late spring of 1931, that affairs assumed a less favourable aspect. When the Greenland mail brought no word from Dr. Krueger, his friends in Germany communicated with the Canadian Government and revealed hitherto undisclosed ambitions of their countryman. Apparently in some of his letters to Germany, Dr. Krueger had remarked that when he reached the north end of Axel Heiberg Island, instead of turning south on the west coast as announced to Constable McLean, he planned to continue out on the Arctic Ocean for about 200 miles, to a point approximately 82′ 22″ north latitude and 105°

west longitude. He would then turn south to the head of Isachsen Island and continue along the north side of the Ringnes Islands down the east side of Amund Ringnes to Cape Southwest, and from there follow on to Hyperit Point and then to Bache Peninsula, or turn south through Baumann Fiord across the Island to Makinson Inlet, where he could choose Craig Harbour to the south or Bache Peninsula to the north, to meet the *Beothic*.

This startling information had its confirmation in the deep-sea sounding wire carried with the party's equipment. It removed the expedition from the apparently safe trip explained to Constable McLean, to one of extreme hazard. If the latest information were correct, Inspector Joy knew that Dr. Krueger had chosen the worst section of all the Arctic Islands for a party not too well planned or equipped.

It was a region almost destitute of game. Donald McMillan, the United States explorer, had attempted the trip northwestward on the Arctic Ocean from Axel Heiberg Island in 1916, but, after only a few days on the polar ice, with a considerable quantity of provisions and all the necessary equipment, he had encountered insurmountable difficulties through the ice continually breaking. It was only with the greatest difficulty that he finally managed to return to land.

To Joy, the Krueger party's gravest danger would lie in the possibility of the loss of their one komitik containing all their food and equipment.

When the *Beothic* reached Bache Peninsula in the late summer of 1931, Inspector Joy learned that the police there were still without further word from the party. A special searching patrol to Craig Harbour had seen no sign of the missing men; nor had there been more cheering news at Cape Sparbo or Dundas Harbour. Several routine patrols by the police and natives had no news to report, while still another special searching patrol to the west coast of Ellesmere Island had fallen short of its objective, due to lack of snow on the only practicable route.

During the ship's brief stop at Bache Peninsula Inspector Joy made arrangements for further special patrols to take up the search during the winter of 1931–32. His instructions were sweeping and thorough. To Corporal Stallworthy, a seasoned veteran in Arctic work, now in charge of the Bache Peninsula detachment, he outlined the routes to be followed.

Two police patrols, Joy instructed, were to proceed to the west coast of Ellesmere Island and then make a search of Eureka Sound and the shores of Axel Heiberg Island, Meighen Island and Isachsen Island.

It was a stupendous program. The season of travel in the Arctic depends on the reappearance of the sun around February 1st. For about two months after that date travel is fairly safe: — unless the ice breaks up sooner than expected; unless the fiords and rocky expanses are found to be bare of snow and the runners of the komitiks will not slide; unless the dogs' feet are cut to pieces on the mounds, turrets and pinnacles of rough ice thrown up along the shoreline, for stretches extending miles out to sea; unless any one of the other thousand and one obstacles met with in the Arctic Islands, proves unexpectedly serious.

Joy's instructions were detailed. The searching party would include two members of the Force and six Eskimos, with sufficient dog teams. On their arrival at the mouth of Bay Fiord, they were to divide and take different directions: two Eskimos and one Mounted Policeman, with two or three komitiks, were to go north on Eureka Sound around the head of Axel Heiberg Island, and southward along the west coast to Cape Southwest, touching if possible, the southern tip of Meighen Island. A similar second party was to proceed southward on Eureka Sound, then continue along the south coast of Axel Heiberg Island, across to Amund Ringnes Island, and follow the south coast on to Ellef Ringnes Island. If food supplies permitted, the search was to be continued along the west coast of Ellef Ringnes Island north to Isachsen Island, and then, again if possible, along the north side of these islands to the east side of Amund Ringnes Island, returning to Cape Southwest to meet the northern searching party.

To carry out these elaborate searches, Joy added, it would be necessary to have a supporting party of two Eskimos with dog teams loaded with fuel and provisions. This third party would accompany the southern searching party part of the way, build a substantial cache and deposit their loads at Cape Southwest in readiness for the northern searching party. If the supporting party found indications of game along the south coast of Axel Heiberg Island, they were to remain there for a few days to hunt and thereby augment the cache's supplies.

The sweeping instructions went even further. Should the two searching parties arrive at the arranged meeting place without having discovered any trace of the Krueger party, they were to cover the only remaining territory likely to reveal a trace of the missing men. The combined party were to continue along the south coast of Axel Heiberg Island and across to the head of Bjorne Peninsula; then they would again divide, one party following the east side of Bjorne Peninsula, the other the west side. The western party, on reaching Great Bear Cape, would travel overland and meet the eastern searchers at the foot of Baumann Fiord or at Hoved Island. The last stretch would take the combined force overland to Makinson Inlet and up the east coast of Ellesmere Island to Bache Peninsula.

Thoroughness could go no further. With clear, deliberate appreciation of the enormous size of the undertaking, the decision had been reached to search every inch of the coast line of the huge district likely to have been visited by Dr. Krueger's party. Joy knew, perhaps better than any other living man, the extent of the task he had imposed on Stallworthy. For he himself had covered most of the territory to be scoured, a large part of it in two patrols which will always live in the annals of Arctic travel. But Joy's patrols had been in the nature of exploration and not search; Stallworthy's greatest difficulty would be the race against time, the necessity for examining every inch of coastline during the short winter season of travel; the ever present possibility that they would run short of food for themselves and the dogs; that the dogs would play out and die; that there would be insufficient snow for the komitiks to slide along; that an early thaw, or a delayed return, would present the insurmountable barrier of open water between the islands; that there might be accidents, even fatalities.

When the *Beothic* steamed out of Bache Peninsula on the way back to civilization, Inspector Joy knew that everything humanly possible would be done to locate and bring back to safety, if they were still alive, the three members of the Krueger party.

The ambitious search was well under way in the winter of 1931–32, although full details of the patrols could not be known until the ship again reached Ellesmere Island, for communication with Canada's Arctic Islands is infrequent and uncertain. The Government ship is still the most reliable means of contact with the police detachments; and even this method, at best, occurs only once each year.

To reach Bache Peninsula each summer, the ship has to race against time and changing ice conditions, but since the establishment of Bache Peninsula detachment the Government ship had managed to reach it, or at least to approach close enough to ensure that supplies were available, each year. 1932 saw the first failure. The ship could not, except at grave risk of being caught in the ice, attain its objective. The annual menace, at last realized, determined the authorities to abandon Bache Peninsula in favour of Craig Harbour; the first detachment opened on Ellesmere Island in 1922. But the anxiety concerning the Krueger party, and the failure of the ship to penetrate the ice, postponed the change for another year.

The reports received by the ship from the police detachments to the south of Ellesmere Island failed to alleviate the anxiety of the authorities concerning the fate of Dr. Krueger's party. For nothing had been seen or heard of the missing men, despite much hard work in surmounting bad ice and other conditions.

So the period between the summer of 1931 and the winter of 1932–33 did nothing to pierce the wall of silence surrounding the fate of the missing men, but added a new anxiety concerning the police searching for them. The imaginations of those familiar with Arctic conditions quickened into anxiety. So many things might have happened! . . .

But out of that same Arctic silence, in May, 1933, came a message bringing a mixture of relief and dwindling hope. It was a radio message sent via Godhavn, Greenland. Perhaps one of the Greenland Eskimos who had been engaged for the search, had carried the message from Bache Peninsula to his own country. It was from Corporal Stallworthy and gave the result of the ambitious undertaking laid down by Inspector Joy for the winter of 1931–32.

Laconically, the message read that, altogether, 3,000 miles had been covered by the searching patrols. At the northwest corner of Axel Heiberg Island the northern patrol had discovered, in Peary's Cairn, a record left by the Krueger party. The record, dated April 24, 1930, bore the signatures of Dr. Krueger, Bjare and Akkea. The Krueger party, the message continued, had visited Lands Lokk, north of Axel Heiberg, and intended proceeding to Meighen Island, apparently having decided against continuing north out on the polar ice.

But because of bad ice, scarcity of game, and the loss of too many dogs, Stallworthy's message explained, the police patrols had not been able to reach Isachsen and Meighen Islands. And no trace of the missing men had been discovered elsewhere. When the two police patrols finally reached the west coast of Ellesmere Island on the return journey, 29 dogs had perished.

A terse message, but it suggests more than enough to the initiated. Bad travelling conditions, no game, the loss of almost half the dogs ... If that had happened to the police parties, well-equipped, experienced, familiar with the country, what could be the fate of the missing men without most of the advantages of the searchers? And with only one komitik and 15 dogs in poor condition to tempt disaster?

When the Government ship brings out Corporal Stallworthy and his reports this fall, more will be known of the details of the patrols, the hardships met and overcome, but the fate of Dr. Krueger's party, missing since 1930, is still a mystery locked in the ice-bound spaces of the grim islands of the Arctic.

Editor's Note

Further information on Stallworthy's efforts to locate the Krueger Party can be found in the article, "The Northern Men", elsewhere in this collection.

15

The Bathhurst Inlet Patrol

Const. C.I. Adam

It was in 1911 that two white men, H.V. Radford and T.G. Street, undertook a journey to the far North. The former an American explorer-biologist, and his companion a Canadian and native of Ottawa, intended to study the flora and fauna of the northern territories, and collect specimens of musk ox and wood bison for museums. Radford had been engaged in similar endeavours before, and on the last occasion — in 1909 — had spent some time in the Fort Smith District. On December 1 of that year, fortified by the protection of a permit to secure specimens of game for scientific collections, he had shot a giant Wood Bison, of which he said: "My big Wood Bison is of course the largest wild animal — of which record exists — ever killed on the American continent — North or South America." He went on to say that his specimen was even larger than Hornaday's Plains Bison.

After nearly two years of preparation for his latest expedition, Radford and his partner passed the winter of 1911–12 near Schultz Lake and reached Bathurst Inlet early in 1912. Their destination was Fort McPherson, westward along the Arctic coast. At Bathurst Inlet they came across an encampment of Eskimos who had had few dealings — if any — with white men. The Eskimos who had brought them so far turned back and the travellers arranged to obtain assistance from those among whom they now found themselves.

The following spring reports reached civilization to the effect that Radford and Street had been murdered by Eskimos in June 1912. In spite of the years which have mellowed the memories of those who are intimately acquainted with the case, records show that Harry Radford was a man ill-equipped to venture into the northern wilderness. Impulsive and impatient, he was to quote the words of a northern resident, "utterly helpless and can do nothing for himself — a trip of this arduous nature is simply madness for him to tackle". Recently a letter to Headquarters from a man who knew both adventurers confirmed these opinions; corroborated too the statements of others that George Street "was a good lad" whose misguided sense of loyalty to his contract with Radford resulted in an untimely death.

On May 31, 1913, Sgt. W.G. Edgenton in charge of the RCMP Fullerton Post Detachment, reported the occurrence. A few days later one of the Eskimos who had travelled with the ill-fated men from Schultz Lake, came to Chesterfield Inlet and told the story to H.H. Hall, manager of the Hudson's Bay Company trading post there, who relayed it to his immediate superior in the following letter:

June 11, 1913

Dear Sir:

The Eskimo Akulack who took the Radford party from Schultz Lake to Bathurst Inlet, arrived today and reported that both Mr. Radford and Mr. Street were murdered by Bathurst Inlet Eskimos. . . .

Akulack left Mr. Radford about the 5th of June. . . .

When Akulack parted from Mr. Radford, it appears that everything was in good order, he had his men engaged, and all preparations were completed for his departure.

Mr. Radford was about to make a start, in fact, the man supposed to go ahead had started when the other backed out and would not go, and Mr. Radford to enforce obedience struck him with a handle of a whip; a fight ensued and Mr. Radford was speared in the back by another native. Mr. Street made a run for the sleigh, but was murdered before he had time to put up any kind of a fight.

According to the story told Akulack by one of the natives who was supposed to have witnessed the fight, Mr. Radford put up quite a fight before he gave in, and had to be speared several times before he fell, and as life still lingered as he lay on the ground, he got the finishing touch by getting his throat cut. Akulack, on being asked why the Eskimo refused to accompany Mr. Radford, said that the man's wife was suddenly taken ill, and Mr. Radford, not understanding the Eskimo language, must have taken the wrong meaning and tried to enforce obedience. Akulack named the principal murderers as 'Hull-la-lark' (Hala-lark) and 'Am-me-ker-nic'.

This report, like all others from the Indians, might be false, but . . . Akulack is considered a first class and reliable Eskimo. . . .

While I was inland, I had an Eskimo trading with the same band named 'Ka-kami' and from what I learned from him, the majority are still in their primitive state and are still using bow and arrow and that all quarrels and disputes are generally settled by death of one of the combatants.

Mr. Radford wrote to Mr. Fred Ford from Bathurst Inlet, dated 3rd June and everything seemed to be Ok then, and he also expressed his thanks for the assistance given him. Conditions must have changed very quickly, for five days later, after Akulack's departure, they were murdered.

107

For some time uncertainty prevailed as to the truth of this account, and one or two false reports concerning the men's reappearance at remote places had to be investigated. The region where the tragedy occurred is almost inaccessible; an investigation would be extremely difficult and tedious.

In September 1913, Superintendent Starnes estimated that the capture of those responsible for the killings would take approximately two years. He recommended that the police party be made up of one officer, an NCO experienced with Eskimos, winter travelling and boating, two or three constables and a good interpreter.

Superintendent Starnes also suggested that a small schooner be sent to Churchill, load up with supplies for two years for the party, its prisoners and witnesses, then proceed as far as possible up Chesterfield Inlet to establish a base for supplies. From that point the party could work by boat or canoe to the end of the open water, and there establish a second base from which the overland journey with sleds and dogs could start.

Later, Superintendent Demers, Officer Commanding "A" Division suggested that the expedition should be equipped for three years. A number of untoward circumstances including the wreck of the Hudson's Bay Company's schooner in the autumn, prevented further investigation in 1913.

Early the following year the Government sanctioned the sending of an expedition as recommended by Superintendent Starnes and approved by Commissioner Perry.

Inspr. W.J. Beyts was appointed to lead the party which included one NCO and two constables. In the schooner *Village Belle*, which had been purchased for the expedition, the police sailed from Halifax on July 31, 1914. Owing to unusually bad weather the Hudson Bay coast was not reached until too late in the season to carry out the plan of establishing a post at Baker Lake.

In 1915 Inspector Beyts organized the advanced post at Baker Lake, and this proved unexpectedly tedious, owing to rough weather on the lake and the difficulties of transportation.

Inspector Beyts made two attempts to journey from Baker Lake to Bathurst Inlet in the winter of 1915–16. Both of these were frustrated, principally by the scarcity of deer on which the party had to rely for dog feed. The absence of fuel also aggravated the difficulties so far encountered.

In the summer of 1916 Inspector Beyts was relieved by Inspr. F.H. French, and the autumn and winter of that year were spent in making more preparations.

During this period, additional information about the murders was obtained from time to time. Inspr. C.D. LaNauze in his patrol to arrest the murderers of Fathers Rouvière and LeRoux, heard an account of the tragedy which coincided with the story of 1913 and the subsequent conclusions reached bv Inspector French himself.

The Commissioner's instructions to Inspector French were as follows:

> It will be your duty to get in touch at the earliest possible moment with the tribes said to be responsible for the deaths. You will make inquiries and take such statutory declarations as may seem necessary in order to obtain a full and accurate account of the occurrence. From information received, it is assumed that there was provocation. If this is found to be the case, it is not the intention of the Government to proceed with prosecution. If, however, there is found to be no provocation, the Government will consider what further action is to be taken.

The Patrol

Inspr. F.H. French accompanied by Sgt. Major T.B. Caulkin and four natives left Baker Lake Detachment at 9 a.m. on Mar. 21, 1917. They had with them three teams of dogs — 25 in all — sleds and two canoes.

The small party struck out to the west across Baker Lake, taking rations and supplies for one month from the first cache along the route. This was all they could carry on a journey which was to last ten months. Afterwards they were to subsist as best as they could on game and from the hand of Providence. Not only did they have themselves to think of, but also the dogs, who virtually speaking, would be their only lifeline with civilization. It was an inspiring undertaking, made even more so by the vast expanse of the unknown, and only partly mapped territory which they had to traverse.

For five days the weather held clear and cold and the party arrived at Schultz Lake on March 26. Then a storm commenced and lasted until April 2, when the travellers broke camp and proceeded towards Aberdeen Lake. The lull did not last long; for four days until this lake was reached, the little party struggled through a howling gale, half frozen and blinded by swirling snow.

On April 5, at the east end of Aberdeen Lake they came across an encampment of Shan-ing-i-ok-muits and one Pad-i-muit family in whose camp they built an igloo. It was here that the services of a native were procured, to carry a reserve of venison as a precaution against a shortage of dog feed. So far the game had been just sufficient to meet requirements. Proceeding overland in a north-westerly direction, the party followed a twisting course along numerous ravines, as there was no snow on the ridges. The weather stayed fine and clear but the quantity of snow was diminishing. Deer appeared to be getting more plentiful and prospects seemed generally good.

But nature evidently took a delight in turning the tables. The weather changed abruptly on April 10, becoming so foggy and stormy, that a halt had to be called. The native guide decided to return to his own camp and they were left alone in a strange country with which none of the police natives was acquainted. Compasses were little more than rough guides because of the great magnetic variations in that area.

The blizzard continued until April 15, foiling several attempts at a start. When eventually they were able to break camp, it was only to be confronted by a long stretch of absolutely barren, rocky country which was found to be impassable. This forced the party to make a long detour to the north-east until Lake Garry came in sight; or what was taken to be Lake Garry, since it did not conform in any way to the map.

At this time the object of the patrol was to locate the Shan-ing-i-ok-muit encampment but due to a sudden fog which descended, the effort proved fruitless. The expedition then headed west towards Lake Pelly but as the fog continued it was impossible to locate the outlet from this lake into Backs River. The weather remained unchanged for several days, until on April 24 a break was made through to the river and down it as far as the first Eskimo encampment.

Of this Inspector French writes:

> At this time I had made up my mind to follow Backs River up to Lake Beechey and strike north from there, as it appeared to me that we were losing considerable time, what with fog and storms and having no knowledge of the country ahead. . . .
>
> However, on meeting the natives at this point, I was told that to proceed upon such a course was impossible, for between Lake Beechey and Bathurst Inlet there was a large stretch of country consisting of high, barren, rocky hills on which there was usually very little snow and considered by the natives as practically impassable for sleds, so that they consequently never used this route.
>
> One of them informed me that the route travelled over by the Eskimos coming south from the Arctic coast followed a river which extended inland, east of Bathurst Inlet. He also stated that he himself knew this river and had been along the route as far as the Arctic coast.
>
> I endeavored to obtain this man's services as a guide across country to this river. At first he demurred, saying that it was a country of starvation and hardship, but I offered him a rifle and ammunition to accompany us. However, it was not before a good deal more conversation that he consented to do so.

On April 26 the patrol broke camp and proceeded north. But again a howling blizzard which continued on and off all the way up to the Arctic coast, made their weary journey practically intolerable. The coast line came in sight on the night of May 7, approximately 15 miles west of the mouth of the Ellice River upon which—unknown to them until much later—they had been travelling. It was known to the natives as 'Coog-nay-ok' (Ku-nai-uk).

They continued north-west up the coast of Queen Maude's Sea, following recently-made native sled tracks and managed to kill some much needed deer, on Melbourne Island. The tracks wound through Blue Inlet into Melville Sound, but once again severe blizzards forced them to halt. On the morning of May 13 which broke fine and clear, the party started for the north-west. It was the first warm day since the men had left their home base, and as they proceeded to the west-end of the Kent Peninsula they made a detour of several small islands, hoping to find some signs of a native camp. Next day sled tracks were sighted running in a south-westerly direction towards Bathurst Inlet. These were followed until a large Eskimo camp on an island in the mouth of Bathurst Inlet came into view. This was at noon on May 14, 1917. The camp contained about 36 natives, but evidently the men were away seal hunting for the day. When the women sighted the patrol, they ran into their tents and igloos, but reappeared when members of the party raised their hands in a friendly gesture.

Shortly afterwards the men returned and seeing strangers in the camp, advanced at the double in extended order, each carrying a spear or snow knife at the trail. However, on seeing that everything was in order they entered into conversation with the guides and became amicable.

This procedure had to be repeated at nearly all the native settlements visited en route.

These Eskimos supplied seal oil for lamps, helped build igloos and furnished information. Their assistance was invaluable.

Inspector French's report states:

> From May 14, 1917 until our arrival at Bernard Harbour on June 13 we were constantly meeting fresh bands of natives and carrying out our investigation of the murder of Messrs. Radford and Street. We took many statements from natives some of whom were present when the white men were killed. Practically all the natives had heard of the affair. . . .
>
> The most important were those who were present in the camp and eyewitnesses of the affair when the unfortunate Messrs. Radford and Street met their fate. I have incorporated in this report, the statements made by these individuals.
>
> In the first encampment I took statements from three men and one woman who were present, the first being a native named "An-ing-nerk", who was a headman, and had under his control a band of 35

people at the time of our meeting. His statement, which is herewith attached was interpreted by Police Native Joe.

Police Native Joe is not what I would call a first-class interpreter, but taking him all around, he did very well.

Oo-Shing-Mu-Ya Camp May 14, 1917

Statement of An-ing-nerk — Bathurst Inlet Native:

"About five winters ago, two white men came from the south and they had their huskies with them, and they came to an island on the salt called Kwog-Juk. One was named Ish-Yu-Mat-Ok and the other Ki-Uk. The one white man called Ish-Yu-Mat-Ok was bad, but the other white man named Ki-Uk was good. The three huskies who came with the white men went away again to the south and the white men could not speak to us and we did not understand them but they made us understand a little by making signs.

"They wanted two men to go away with them to the west, two men, Har-La and Kan-E-Ak, were going with them but Kan-E-Ak's wife was sick, she had fallen on the ice and was hurt, and Kan-E-Ak did not want to leave her there. The white man called Ish-Yu-Mat-Ok got very mad and ran at Kan-E-Ak and hit him with a whip, the other man (Ki-Uk) tried to stop him. The white man was shouting all the time. He dragged Kan-E-Ak to the water edge, the other white man went with him, they were going to throw Kan-E-Ak in the water. Everybody was frightened the two white men were going to kill Kan-E-Ak. Two men, Ok-It-Ok and Hal-A-Lark (Hull-la-lark), ran out and stabbed Ish-Yu-Mat-Ok, he fell on the ice, the other white man ran off shouting towards the sleigh and Ok-It-Ok ran after him and caught him and Am-E-Geal-Nik stabbed him with a snow knife. He was running towards the sleigh; he tried to get a rifle. The two white men were covered over and left on the ice. I do not know what became of their property. . . .

"I do not think that this would have happened if the white man had not beat Kan-E-Ak with the dog whip, or if we had understood the white man. . . .

"We do not want trouble with the white men, we want them to come here and trade with us. I cannot remember all as it is a long time ago now, there were only a few men in the camp, the others were away hunting when the fight started. We went and told the huskies who came from the south with the white men, what had happened to the white men."

Witness: F.H. French, Inspector
(signed) his X mark
An-ing-nerk

"I certify that the above is a true interpretation of what I have heard and interpreted to you from the above-named witness."

(signed)
Police Native Joe,
Interpreter.

112

Similar statements were taken from other natives, and in each case Radford appeared to be regarded by them as a bad man, while they spoke of Street as a good man. No doubt these reputations were carried along the trail and spread from one tribe to another.

Inspector French quotes similar experiences of natives refusing to accompany his party at the last moment. However, with a certain amount of discretion, the difficulty could either be overcome, or a new guide procured. In his opinion the Kill-in-e-muits — members of which tribe were responsible for the murders — were the best class of Eskimo he met.

It should be said here that as a result of a very thorough investigation into the murders of Messrs. Radford and Street, no attempt was made to prosecute those responsible for the deaths. It was a case of self-defence through fear, by those who knew no better than the primitive laws of nature. Both victims lived with this tribe of natives for over a month before the incident, at the time of which there were few natives in camp, undoubtedly therefore premeditation was absent.

When we digressed from the narrative of the journey itself, it may be recalled that the party encountered the Kill-in-e-muits at the mouth of Bathurst Inlet. At this time it was their intention to proceed south down the Inlet, past the scene of the crime, all the while continuing their investigation. After experiencing great difficulty in traversing the ice, now covered with some 15 inches of water, the expedition reached the foot of the Inlet on May 24. It was impossible to proceed farther. Ammunition and supplies were entirely finished, and the men's diet consisted of half-rotten deer meat. In fact the case looked hopeless until the party met a band of Eskimos who had followed their trail. These natives had come from the west and from them it was learned that there were three ships along the Arctic coast — about nine days' travel.

Inspector French decided to go west to these ships, try to obtain supplies and ammunition to last through the summer, then return again to the foot of Bathurst Inlet and wait till the freeze-up before proceeding overland to Baker Lake.

A native was hired to travel with the party. Wending their way north, up the west side of Bathurst Inlet towards Coronation Gulf, the travellers crossed the mouth of the Arctic Sound, rounded the inlet on to the Arctic coast, and continued west.

The dogs now began to show signs of lameness, cutting their pads on the pointed ice which was fast breaking up. The weather was getting steadily warmer with continued rain and sleet; the sea ice was rotten in places and much difficulty was experienced getting both dogs and sleighs over. Sometimes it was necessary to detour for several miles.

On June 2 a snowfall made it impossible to discern the ice-cracks, and Sergeant Major Caulkin and two natives fell through the ice while guiding the dogs. Two days later the party reached the mouth of the Tree River where they met a small band of Killi-shuk-to-muits on an island. The Eskimos said a white man was living nearby; a Swedish trapper named Albin Kihlman. He, too, told the police that there was a trading vessel three days west from the camp.

And here the last of the venison was used up. Grizzly bear meat became the principal food and though palatable it made everyone sick — adding to the many discomforts already being endured.

After four days of intolerable hardship battling their way through sleet, rain and snow, the sick and hungry patrol finally located the schooner on June 8. The boat, the United States gasoline schooner, *Teddy Bear*, with Capt. J. Bernard in command, was frozen in near an island at the mouth of the Coppermine River.

From Captain Bernard the police party obtained some provisions but the kindhearted skipper could spare no ammunition. At any rate these stores were not sufficient to permit the party to carry out the original intention of wintering at the foot of Bathurst Inlet, therefore Inspector French decided to proceed farther to the north-west in an endeavour to locate a Hudson's Bay Post which the *Teddy Bear*'s skipper said was located at Bernard Harbour. Two days later the journey was resumed towards Cape Krusenstern, and on June 13 Mr. Phillips, post manager of the Hudson's Bay Co., met the patrol.

Here Inspector French voices his thoughts:

> Mr. Phillips informed me that it would be impossible to proceed farther west by sled, as the break-up was liable to occur any time now, and that if I attempted it I would get stranded somewhere along the coast. He further informed me that the Hudson's Bay Company's boat would arrive as soon as the ice cleared ... so we pitched camp near the post.

> ... I must say that it has been the hardest trip I have ever made, and we suffered much from cold and exposure.

> These we felt all the more when our supplies ran out, and when towards the end of our journey our deerskin clothing got the worse for wear and the hair started falling out and the winds pierced through the seams and holes.

> Most of us were continually frozen about the face and hands and ... we were suffering from snow-blindness more or less during the whole journey, the natives particularly showing a weakness in this direction ... I must say this was due to the inferior quality of the glasses, but these were the best I could procure before we started.

> Both myself and Sergeant Major Caulkin were in very poor shape as regards to health — undoubtedly due to the straight meat diet which

we had been on for the past six weeks ... and even this eaten mostly half raw ever since the time of our being out of coal oil for our lamps. Mileage travelled

to date:	
Distance travelled over routes	1,835
Distance travelled deer hunting	284
Distance travelled seal hunting	114
Distance travelled looking for native camps	250
Total	2,483 miles

After staying about two months at Bernard Harbour, Inspector French decided to move camp to the Coppermine River and there await the freeze-up which would permit a return to Baker Lake. This decision was reached owing to the increasing scarcity of game in the vicinity and the diminishing supplies of the Hudson's Bay Post; barely enough for the next winter after two months' supply had been purchased by the patrol.

A further small quantity of food was obtained from the cache left by the Canadian Arctic Expedition. Ammunition proved to be the greatest worry since there was none of .303 calibre to be had. In the end, two 30–30 rifles were bought from Mr. Phillips along with a small number of cartridges.

On Sept. 1, 1917 the patrol left Bernard Harbour in two whale boats. Three natives travelled across country to the Coppermine with the dogs. Albin Kihlman, the Swedish trapper, had joined the party. Evidently a former member of the *Teddy Bear*'s crew, the man did not possess sufficient supplies to see him through the coming winter. In all probability, if left on the coast, he would have become destitute.

While French's party was at Coppermine a band of Indians arrived overland from Fort Rae and Great Bear Lake districts on a trading visit to Charles Klinkenberg, a Danish settler who trapped at the mouth of the river. Before the Indians left for home Inspector French gave one of them a letter in the hope that it would reach civilization and furnish a clue to the expedition's fate and whereabouts.

On Oct. 16, 1917, the party made a start by sled from the Coppermine River. Travelling proved difficult; progress dropped to a mile-an-hour average as the rivers and lakes had hardly frozen enough to bear the weight of sleds. Returning to the Arctic coast the patrol proceeded towards the mouth of Bathurst Inlet. The intention was to reach the head of the inlet by the time the gulf became frozen over, for it was then the deer would begin to cross from Victoria Land and Collaston Islands.

The journey along the coast became increasingly hazardous. A man had to walk ahead of the teams to test the ice and many times it was touch and go whether the sleds would break through. Although temperatures

115

remained high for this time of year — at a point so far north of the Arctic circle — storms and wet snow continued to soak them all to the skin, adding to the many other discomforts.

Bathurst Inlet was reached again on November 12. By this time the dogs were suffering from undernourishment and overexertion after the hard haul along the coast. Fortunately five deer were sighted in the inlet and subsequently shot.

The soft deep snow in Bathurst Inlet retarded progress and by November 18 food supplies were getting dangerously low. One third of the journey had not yet been completed and it was necessary to discard various non-essential items to tighten the loads. Luckily on this same date the party reached an Eskimo encampment where they were able to trade for a small quantity of dried deer meat. In this settlement were several relatives of the native woman "Solomon" who had accompanied the patrol. Because she had been suffering from an abscess of the ear all summer and fall, it was decided to leave her with her uncle, notwithstanding her usefulness in repairing clothes.

It had been Inspector French's intention to proceed to the foot of the inlet, then south. But the natives said there was a river in Gordon Bay which started somewhere near the Ellice River. By following this route the party would reach land and consequently deer, in a shorter space of time. On November 21 the expedition changed direction, travelled south-east over Gordon Bay and next day came to the mouth of this river. Here they found a large quantity of deer carcasses strewn along the banks under the snow. Evidently these had been speared from kayaks by the natives before freeze-up, and only the skins taken. Arrival of the patrol dispersed large numbers of wolves, wolverines and ravens who had been feasting on the carcasses. They were quickly replaced by the hungry dogs.

Throughout the month of December, prospects of the patrol ever reaching civilization looked extremely dim. Although the weather remained calm but cold, the barren country was almost devoid of snow, precluding the possibility of approaching deer, on which the men were now entirely dependent. Clothing and footgear constituted another problem and badly needed repair. The party had been continually wet during the fall travelling and were now constantly frozen by the cold spells.

After crossing the Ellice River on December 4, the patrol reached Backs River on the 12th, and then camped near the Jervois River. Inspector French decided to turn south from here in an attempt to locate Inspector Beyts' cache made at the timber in November 1916. For the next two days the dogs were not fed. One sled and tarp were abandoned and the dogs split up among the other teams.

"On December 17," said Inspector French, "we had no luck again and got no deer. We had to resort to a method of feeding the dogs which struck deep into all of us, for we shot five of the weakest dogs and skinned them for the night's dogfeed."

Next day the remaining dogs ate a bag of deerskin clothing.

By December 22 several dogs were exhausted and fell from time to time. Five more of them had to be shot for food. Here the first stunted spruce trees were sighted. Fresh musk ox tracks crossing the Thelon River were followed by two of the natives with the patrol. They returned to say that they had shot ten of the animals.

So it was that on Christmas night the weary patrol enjoyed a big feed.

A week later Sergeant Major Caulkin and Native Joe went south to look for the Beyts' cache. This they discovered about 16 miles from camp. But the cache had been broken into — probably by wolves — flour was scattered, lard pails bitten through, even the molasses keg had been shattered and the tops bitten off tins containing salt, pepper and baking powder. All that could be salvaged was some flour, oxo, candles and tobacco. The latter was greatly appreciated since the men had been smoking dried tea leaves for some time.

On January 3 the journey was resumed. After another two weeks of struggling through heavy blizzards it became necessary to shoot more dogs. And one night in particular starvation was averted when one of the bitches produced a litter of seven pups. Somewhere south of Schultz Lake, another sled was burned and discarded.

All members of the patrol were now subsisting on a thin soup. Too weak to talk and care very much about anything, their clothing nearly in rags, the men stumbled along the trail urged on by the necessity to keep going. The cold was almost unbearable. It became a case of touch-and-go whether the natives would quit. But good fortune came their way on January 2 when 15 deer were sighted and ten shot. Had it not been for this stroke of luck it is doubtful whether Baker Lake would have been reached.

It is fitting here that Inspector French should take up the tale and in his own words conclude the story of one of the greatest feats of endurance ever undergone by man.

> The ten deer cheered us up, the dogs were well fed and we had a big banquet of back steak and blood soup. January 23 we travelled north-east. On the 24th we remained in our igloo as it was very cold and stormy. Native Bye-and-Bye went ten miles north-east and found a river running north with several sled tracks on it. On January 25 we proceeded along this river to the north. Its banks are very low and in some places it is so wide that it resembled a lake. On January 26 we continued along it and at 9.30 a.m. came to the mouth and found

ourselves at the south-west end of Baker Lake. The day was fine and clear; we could see the island where the Hudson's Bay Company's post was and we were greatly overjoyed to see some land we knew, after an absence of over ten months.

We made the Hudson's Bay Post in the afternoon and were kindly greeted by Mr. Ford, the post manager and given the best food.

We stayed there until the 27th and thawed out a little. Next day we made a long point to the south shore. On the 29th we arrived at the detachment, all well and glad to get home.

Inspector French ends his report thus:

> I again respectfully wish to bring to your notice Reg. No. 4557 Sgt. Major T.B. Caulkin. This NCO has been of the greatest assistance to me and I have always found him absolutely trustworthy and reliable and he has at all times proved himself to be a man.

> I also wish to bring to your attention Police Natives Joe and Bye-and-Bye. These natives put their hearts entirely in the trip and under most trying circumstances always stood by me, and I consider that they should receive some suitable reward, over and above their wages, as a recognition of their services.

Inspector French reports January a "terribly cold month", average temperature being 60° below zero. On January 24 the thermometer registered 72° below zero.

The Commissioner's report of the RNWMP 1918 says this patrol was a remarkable achievement in the way of travel; Inspector French computes the distance travelled, on the outward and return journeys to Bernard Harbour as follows:

Outward Journey

Mileage establishing caches along the route	150
Mileage securing natives to accompany patrol on journey	200
Mileage from Baker Lake to Bernard Harbour (approx.)	1,835
Mileage deer hunting en route (approx.)	284
Mileage seal hunting en route (approx.)	114
Mileage hunting for Eskimo Camps (approx.)	250

Return Patrol

Mileage from Bernard Harbour to Coppermine River (whale boat)	175
Mileage from Coppermine River to Baker Lake (approx.)	1,720
Miscellaneous Mileage, deer and musk ox hunting and native camps (approx.)	425
Approx. Grand Total	5,153 miles

Author's Note

This is Inspector French's story — perhaps it should have been written by him. The events which occurred as they did during World War I, have never appeared to receive sufficient acclaim, although Inspector French was awarded the Imperial Service order. Only recently the Province of Saskatchewan honoured this ex-officer by naming a lake after him.

For his share in this heroic endeavour, Sergeant Major Caulkin — who retired as assistant commissioner — was awarded the King's Police and Fire Services Medal.

Most of the quotations used in this article are from patrol and crime reports as set forth in Commr. A. Bowen Perry's annual report for the RNWMP on Sept. 30, 1918. Other extracts, and photographs have been drawn from the case files. This does not alter the fact that the writer, or better still rewriter, has experienced a sense of inadequacy in perforce trespassing on the property of another. C.I.A. . . .

Editor's Note

This was probably one of the most arduous northern patrols ever made by members of the Force, not only because of difficult conditions but also because the patrol covered 5,000 miles in ten months.

16

Kingualik and the Coronation Medal

Supt. C.J. Dent

After arriving at isolated Baker Lake Detachment (G Division, N.W.T.) by boat in a typical September snowstorm during the fall of 1953, my first task was to unload one year's supply of food, fuel and maintenance materials. When this was properly stored, the second responsibility was to familiarize myself with what was required of an operational and administrative nature at the detachment. Uncovered in the detachment safe was a sealed, registered, official, OHMS envelope.

Inside was a Coronation Medal and scroll which identified the recipient as E2-109, Ooyoumut, an Eskimo believed living somewhere in the Back River area. The Force had been asked by the Director of Indian and Northern Affairs to make an official presentation in ceremonial dress to Ooyoumut, take photographs, and send the photos to Ottawa. Ooyoumut was described on the accompanying parchment as being:

"An outstanding hunter and provider amongst the native people".

Not knowing who this soon-to-be-honoured Eskimo might be, I asked E24, S/Cst. Ooyoumut, if he knew who he was. "That's a relative of mine," but he went on to say, "He's been dead for a long, long time." Checking the death certificates which were maintained by the Force as Registrars of Vital Statistics in the Northwest Territories, I learned E2-109, Ooyoumut, had indeed died ten years earlier. E2-110, Kingualik, his wife, was still alive, however, and believed living somewhere along the Back River. She was not known to have ever visited the settlement of Baker Lake, and it was highly unlikely she ever would.

I communicated this revelation to the commanding officer of G Division at Ottawa, who after conferring with the Indian and Northern Affairs Dept., agreed with my suggestion to award the medal posthumously to E2-110, Kingualik. Correspondence in reply reiterated the initial dictate to perform the ceremony in red serge, forwarding the photographs to Ottawa.

I wasn't quite sure how to go about undertaking the arduous two hundred mile trip to the Back River area by dog team in the dead of winter, and comply with instruction to the letter. My dilemma was resolved the following spring when an RCAF single engined Otter aircraft dropped into the settlement on a training flight. The pilot asked if I wanted to visit any of the more distant, remote camps to check on native conditions. It took about thirty seconds to remember the ceremonial presentation to Kingualik. The RCAF crew agreed to try and find the Back River camp, affording an opportunity to visit other isolated camps as well, and check on native conditions in general.

Enquiries conducted at a camp near Pelly Lake led us northeast along the Back River towards Chantry Inlet, where we finally located Kingualik's camp.

For anyone unfamiliar with the primitive nomadic life experienced by these inland caribou Eskimo, survival, almost void of worldly possessions, depended primarily on individual resourcefulness. Although they may have lacked material wealth, they possessed an abundance of sociality, greeting us in a very friendly fashion.

It was still quite cold, and you may be able to appreciate the astounded expression on faces of young and old when I took off a long outer caribou parka, revealing the red RCMP serge tunic, boots and breeches. As I put on my Stetson, I told S/Cst. Ooyoumut that what I wanted to do was stand with Kingualik long enough to take a photograph, then, hopefully, we could join them in their igloo for a cup of tea during which I would explain what the occasion was all about.

The Eskimo started laughing. The RCAF crew were doubled over with laughter to such a degree tears were actually flowing. The more they laughed, the more Kingualik laughed and it indeed became difficult to gain control of the situation long enough to capture the significance of the occasion on film. That finally being accomplished, everyone—ten Eskimos, S/Cst. Ooyoumut, four RCAF air crew and myself—crammed into the igloo and assumed as comfortable a position as possible while tea was brewed.

With S/Cst. Ooyoumut interpreting, I tried to explain to Kingualik what this once in a lifetime occasion was all about. I related to her that she could indeed be proud of her departed husband who had been selected amongst all Canada's Eskimo to receive the Coronation Medal commemorating the crowning of Princess Elizabeth as Queen of England. Her husband had been recognized as an outstanding hunter and provider amongst his people.

At this precise moment, and without any hesitation, Kingualik raised her hand denoting silence and boldly stated, "Wait a moment! That's not true! Many winters I was hungry." After recovering from her candid expression I then tried to impress upon her that she should treasure this medal, that with the passing of time, handing it on from grandparent to grandchild, it would increase significantly in personal family value.

Departing from Kingualik's camp some two hours later after shaking hands once again from adults to and including all children, I felt richly rewarded to have shared the emotion, compassion, and joy of meeting these friendly, proud people. I thought, too, that this would probably be my one and only encounter with Kingualik. Such proved not to be the case!

The Hudson's Bay Affair

One year later, the following spring, Sandy Lunan, a thirty-five-year northern veteran and Hudson's Bay manager, cranked up our detachment land-line phone and demanded, "Dent, what the hell did you tell Kingualik up on the Back River?" Lo-and-behold, Kingualik had made the trek into the settlement from the Back River with her son and was at that precise moment in the Bay store to trade.

She had entered the Bay warehouse and, acting like an experienced customer, had commenced telling Mr. Lunan what she wanted. First on her list was a 22-foot Peterborough freighter canoe and outboard motor. She also wanted a .250/3000 rifle and a case of ammunition. That was followed by a request for a case of tea and then tobacco.

Realizing the sizeable sale, Mr. Lunan enquired as to where her fox pelts were, and how many did she have. Much to his astonishment, Kingualik pulled her "Coronation Medal" out of a small duffle bag and, as she pushed it across the counter towards him, said, "The policeman told me the medal was very, very valuable." She explained to Lunan that she hated to part with it, but the supplies were needed more than the medal.

The intrinsic value of the medal was soon explained to Kingualik. Fortunately, her son did have some foxes and caribou skins to trade, which coupled with Family Allowances, enabled them to purchase most of the items required. Kingualik returned to the Back River after I had the opportunity to reinforce the proper significance of the medal through the able interpreting abilities of both Mr. Lunan and Canon W.J.R. James, the Anglican Missionary.

Caribou did not migrate through the Back River area during the fall of 1956 or the spring of 1957, resulting in severe hardship for all and death by starvation for fifteen of the Eskimo scattered throughout this area.

THE CORONATION MEDAL

When I returned to Baker Lake again in 1958 after a two-year absence, Kingualik and a grandson, 14-year-old Ooyoumut, were living at the post. A school had been constructed during my absence and Ooyoumut, for the first time in his life, had the opportunity of attending school.

Very much a proud hunter following in his grandfather's footsteps, he rushed excitedly home from school one day in mid-October, telling Kingualik that he had heard there were caribou about four miles northwest of the settlement. Although unfamiliar with that terrain he was confident of his hunting abilities and desperately wanted to kill a caribou for his grandmother. She told him to let the teacher know and, if given approval, it would be all right to go hunting.

He returned home that night elated with his hunting success, telling Kingualik and the teacher that he had shot a caribou and would return to it the following day with his dog to back pack the meat home.

Three days later he had not returned, three days during which the winter's first serious snowstorm diminished visibility to zero. Kingualik went to S/Cst. Sceteenak's home and told him that her grandson had failed to return home with the caribou he had shot three days before. Up until this moment, we did not know Ooyoumut was missing.

The task ahead was next to hopeless considering weather conditions and Ooyoumut's unfamiliarity with the countryside around Baker Lake. Commandeering every available experienced adult Eskimo living on the post we organized a fan out search of the area north of Baker Lake. Temperatures had been well below zero, and, with the wind chill factor, survival was doubtful.

When we failed to locate Ooyoumut on that first day's search, the result was inevitable. At search headquarters we had reconstructed what probably happened. When Ooyoumut went back to recover the caribou kill, a southwest wind began blowing. Snow, coupled with wind, dimmed visibility to inches. Ooyoumut would have thought, "If I keep the wind on my left shoulder as I walk I will reach the north shore of Baker Lake within a few hours." Once he encountered the shoreline it would be a simple matter to continue west until he came across canoes, wintered along the shore; oil barrels, buildings and home. Good logic.

What he didn't realize was that the wind shifted very gradually from the southeast to southwest. This would then caused him to walk in a semicircle and pass north of the settlement. Exhausted and freezing, death would have been inevitable. In all probability his body would be found northwest of the post.

During the evening, as exhausted searchers returned and were accounted for, the wind and snow subsided. Clear skies set in and the temperature plummeted.

At noon the next day one of the searchers scanning hillsides about four miles northwest of the settlement spotted slight movement. Zeroing in with his telescope he identified Ooyoumut's dog sitting up. When he reached the site, he found Ooyoumut's body partially covered with snow, lying on his back, hands crossed over his chest, frozen like granite.

Rather than relate his find first to the police he went to Kingualik and told her that he had found Ooyoumut, dead. He then came to tell us. By the time I got to where Kingualik had been living, she had gone. Her friends told me she was in a state of emotional shock and had wandered off over the hill by the cemetery.

I immediately sent one of our special constables to find her and bring her back. The other special and a local Eskimo were dispatched to bring in Ooyoumut.

Lashed to the Komatik

S/Cst. Seeteenak brought Kingualik back towards the settlement by dog team. Rather than permit the sleigh to bump across a steep hill I picked her up and, carrying her, walked to the Anglican Mission. I almost made it. I slipped and, rather than let Kingualik strike the frozen ground, I tried to cushion her fall by clutching her in my arms at the last moment. My back cracked. I was left motionless and could not move or straighten up. Kingualik walked to the Mission, and I was taken home lashed to the komatik, carried into the house and put in bed.

The special constables attended to funeral arrangements, making a coffin, taking the body to the church for service then to the cemetery overlooking Baker Lake for burial.

Kingualik came to the detachment office some two weeks later with one of the special constables to act as interpreter. With tears flowing freely she produced the "Coronation Medal" and, pushing it across the desk towards me, said, "I cannot keep the medal any longer. Were my husband alive, Ooyoumut would not have perished. I do not deserve to have it".

Considerable time was spent convincing her she must keep the medal. No one could have prevented what happened. "Ajurnarmat", I said to her, an Eskimo word that covers a multitude of misfortunes regardless of circumstances, "It cannot be helped". This fatalistic perspective she accepted.

However, Kingualik once again surprised me. From her duffle purse-like bag, she produced a small ball of something green, similar to a small marble. She painstakingly took it apart, eventually unfolding and flattening out a one dollar bill. Where on earth she came into possession of currency, I do not know, as it was only shortly after this incident that the Hudson's Bay Company converted from tokens to money. Currency had not been used. Probably some white person had paid her for sewing, or domestic chores with this legal tender. Whatever its origin, as an alternative to my accepting the Coronation Medal she felt obliged to pay the police for the services of searching for and locating the body of Ooyoumut, and for assisting so much with the funeral.

Emotion and pride were so evident it was indeed difficult not to join in openly shedding tears with Kingualik. The matter of payment for services rendered was resolved when Kingualik agreed to write a letter to one of the Baker Lake Eskimo confined in the Clearwater, Manitoba, Sanatorium, putting the letter and money in an envelope, and mailing it.

Today the Inuit

Today these Northerners are called Inuits. To me, with all the warmth, compassion, and recollection it is possible to muster they are still Eskimo. My life, and that of my wife, have been significantly enriched through our exposure to, and dealings with, these Eskimo of by-gone decades. After my retirement in the not too distant future, there is little doubt our fondest recollections will generate from our postings north of 60 — particularly those years spent living with the Eskimo.

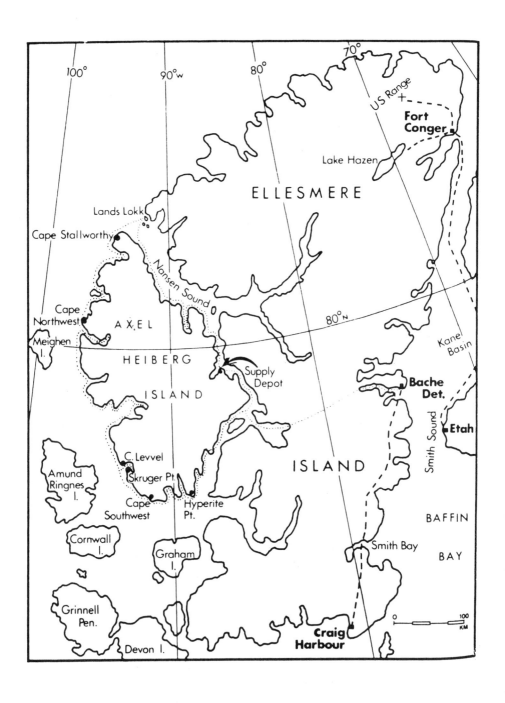

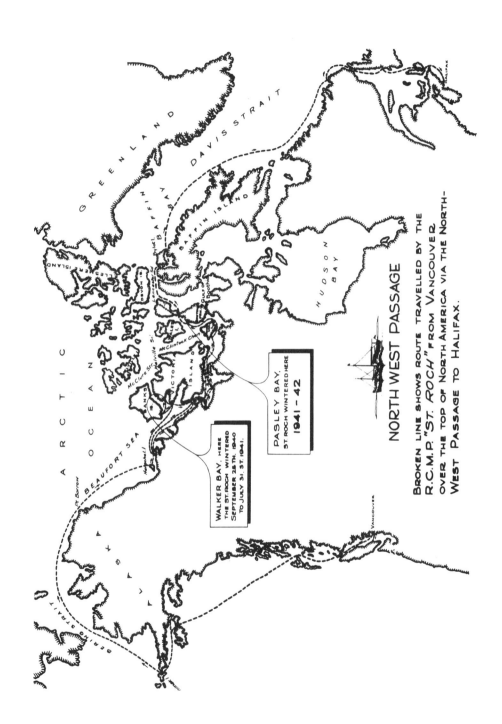

NORTH WEST PASSAGE

BROKEN LINE SHOWS ROUTE TRAVELLED BY THE
R.C.M.P. "ST. ROCH" FROM VANCOUVER
OVER THE TOP OF NORTH AMERICA VIA THE NORTH-
WEST PASSAGE TO HALIFAX.

PASLEY BAY,
ST ROCH WINTERED HERE
1941 ~ 42

WALKER BAY, HERE
THE ST. ROCH WINTERED
SEPTEMBER 26TH 1940
TO JULY 31 ST 1941.

GREENLAND

DAVIS STRAIT

BAFFIN BAY

BAFFIN ISLAND

HUDSON
BAY

ARCTIC

OCEAN

BEAUFORT SEA

BERING STRAIT

ALASKA

VANCOUVER

17

An Arctic Expedition

A/Sgt. H. Stallworthy

The Voyage North

On the evening of July 17th, 1934, a Norwegian sealing schooner left St. Catherine's Dock, just below London Bridge, and headed down the River Thames towards the open sea and the far North, amid the cheers of a host of friends and well-wishers. On board were five members of the Oxford University Exploration Club, eight hardy Norwegian seamen, and myself, representing the Canadian Government, and acting in the capacity of technical advisor to these ambitious Explorers who were embarking on a strenuous expedition, which would take them to the extreme limits of the Canadian Arctic Archipelago. Great interest centred around the departure of this Expedition due to the fact that one of its members was Edward Shackleton, son of a famous father, whose last voyage to the Antarctic started from this same dock. Although the *Signalhorn* was a very small boat for such an undertaking, our Captain, who was the only English speaking member of the crew, had no fears for her safety, either in the gales of the North Atlantic or in the heavy ice of the Arctic, which we were bound to encounter before the termination of our outward voyage.

The Universities of Oxford, Cambridge and Nottingham were represented on this Arctic Expedition. Dr. Humphreys, the Leader, is a Surveyor, Botanist and Medical Doctor. One of his most notable achievements was his recent successful ascent of Mount Ruwenzori, the highest snow-capped peak in the mountain range of Central Africa, for which he was awarded the Murchison Grant by the Royal Geographical Society. On this expedition he was particularly interested in the opportunity to make a complete Botanical survey of Ellesmere Island. Edward Shackleton, organizer, had previously been on an expedition to British North Borneo, where he climbed Mount Mulu, the highest peak in Sarawak. A.W. Moore,

Biologist and Photographer, had also been a member of the Borneo Expedition. To Robert Bentham, Geologist, and youngest member of the party, Ellesmere Island presented a rich field for investigation. David Haig-Thomas, Ornithologist, had recently returned from hunting big game in Abyssinia, and was looking forward to hunting the big sea mammals to be found in Arctic waters. His scientific interest in the Expedition was the study of bird life. But apart from all these individual scientific interests, they were all looking forward to the main objective of the Expedition, namely, the crossing, mapping, and geological survey of Grant Land (Northern Ellesmere Island), the interior of which had not, at that time, been explored.

The Expedition had received the full support and some financial assistance from the Royal Geographical Society, the Oxford University and the Canadian Government. Other financial assistance came from many Educational organizations and private individuals interested in exploration and its scientific results. Many prominent British manufacturing firms presented equipment, provisions and fuel. Although most of the members had travelled in various parts of the world, none of them had previously ventured into the Arctic or Antarctic regions, and were most anxious to gain some experience in the frigid zone.

Few people realize the geographical position or the extent of Ellesmere Island. It is Canada's farthest north island and is some five hundred miles in length, with an approximate area of nearly eighty thousand square miles, or only slightly smaller than England and Scotland together. Cape Columbia, on the north coast, lies within four hundred and eighty miles of the North Pole. It was from this point that Peary, in 1909, made his final and successful dash to the Pole.

The *Signalhorn*, after passing through Pentland Firth off the North coast of Scotland, battled her way across the North Atlantic to Cape Farewell, South Greenland. During the whole crossing we had experienced a succession of storms with furious opposing winds. Many times during the twelve days which it took to make the crossing to Cape Farewell, we were at a standstill, barely holding our own against the mountainous seas. The ship was loaded to her utmost capacity before we started, with coal, provisions, clothing, equipment and oil, sufficient for a two years' sojourn in the Arctic. With heavy seas breaking over her, we were constantly in danger of losing our deck cargo. On one occasion, when some lash ropes were broken, a number of cases of pemmican and oil went overboard, but according to the Captain, they came aboard again on the next breaker. Some of the members not used to such rough travelling conditions, were quite ill on this part of the voyage, but off the West coast of Greenland we had calm seas and fine weather, and enjoyed the run of about fifteen hundred miles to the north end of Greenland.

The scenery along the west coast of Greenland is very impressive and the glaciers, gleaming in the sun, resemble gigantic immobile waterfalls, pouring down thousands of feet into the sea from the inland ice-capped mountains. The reflections in the water from these glaciers, and the immense icebergs which break from the active ones, floating in the calm sea, is a sight one does not easily forget.

Several calls were made at some of the Eskimo settlements along the coast to pick up dogs, Eskimo equipment, clothing, and dried fish for dog feed. We also took on board a quantity of lumber and other materials to build our winter quarters, which had been sent out from Copenhagen earlier in the season on a Danish supply ship. At Godhavn, on Disco Island, we met Dr. Rosendahl, the Colonial Governor, who entertained us at his home and showed us round this interesting settlement. Here we saw their Eskimo Parliament building, their well-equipped hospital and their school, where the native children are taught to read and write both the Eskimo and Danish language. Here, too, we met Dr. Porsild, father of the Porsild brothers, whose names are well known in Northern Canada in connection with their work in establishing reindeer reserves in the Western Arctic. Governor Rosendahl was our guest as far as Jacobs-havn, where we found the Danish North Greenland supply ship had just anchored. We were entertained on board their ship, the *Dannebrog*, by the Administrator of North Greenland, and other officials, with whom we discussed Expedition plans. All the Danish authorities with whom we came in contact on this and subsequent occasions, were extremely courteous and most helpful to the Expedition.

At these settlements seventy dogs were purchased to take north for our future sledging journeys. The Eskimos had plenty of dogs for sale, and I was able to select some very good ones. Collectively, they would compare very favourably with the best sledge dogs in our own Arctic areas of the Dominion and were all what are termed "Husky" dogs and had been raised by the local natives.

On continuing our voyage, the deck cargo had been increased so much with lumber, equipment, dogs, and about five tons of dried fish for dog feed, that there was no room to walk. We were lucky to meet with very satisfactory conditions crossing Melville Bay, where we saw only a few scattered ice floes. The "Melville Pack", so well and unfavourably known to Arctic navigators, has often beset ships for weeks at a time, and not a few exploration and whaling ships have been crushed and lost trying to force their way through the immense ice-pack, which usually moves to and fro with the tides during the summer months.

We were still favoured with splendid weather when we arrived at North Star Bay, and dropped anchor at Thule Settlement, which is the headquarters of the Cape York District. Here we were met by the missionary and Mr. Hans Neilsen, the local Governor, who invited us to tea. There were many natives at the settlement awaiting the arrival of the Danish supply ship, which was now a few days behind us. The Eskimos of the farthest North districts of Greenland only see a ship from the "outside" once a year, when they come to the settlement, consequently they have had very little association with white men. Their lives are dependent entirely on their skill as hunters. Their clothes, made from Polar bear, seal, Arctic blue and white fox, and Arctic hare skins, are very picturesque, and at the same time are the most practicable form of clothing for these happy people who reside farthest North on the globe.

Destitution is practically unknown amongst these Eskimos, although North Greenland certainly could not be termed a paradise for game. Apart from migratory birds, in the short summer, their food consists almost entirely of seal, walrus and narwhal, which accounts for all the men being such experts with kyacks and harpoons. The North Greenland Eskimo, unlike his brothers in Canada and further south in Greenland, cannot go inland to hunt caribou, or live at inland lakes where fish are obtainable. The whole of the country, excepting a few narrow fringes along the coast, is covered with inland ice or "ice-cap" as it is more popularly termed. To travel inland always means a hard climb to ascend the glaciers and generally necessitates the crossing of dangerous crevasses to an altitude of two to six thousand feet, before one can reach the interior, which is the home of the blizzards and, of course, is absolutely devoid of game. It is surprising indeed that even with all these disadvantages and the dark period of the mid-winter in this latitude, these natives are the most cheerful and carefree people one could wish to meet.

I was glad to see some of my old friends among the Eskimos, who had been my travelling partners when they were attached to the Police Detachments on Ellesmere Island. After trading for more native equipment, and arranging for some Eskimos to join us at Robertson Bay, over one hundred miles farther north, we left Thule with the good wishes of Mr. Neilsen and the Eskimos, some of whom would have liked to accompany us.

The sun was a blaze of colour at midnight on August 12th as we steamed out into Smith Sound. Thus far, we had encountered very little ice, which could not be taken as a good indication of what might be in store for us. Robertson Bay, which is the most northerly Eskimo settlement in the world, was reached the next day. The arrival of an Expedition ship from "white man's land" is a great event in the lives of these people, some of whom had been with Peary, MacMillan and Rasmussen.

Owing to the extremely short season of navigation in ice-infested Smith Sound and Kennedy Channel, we made only a short stay. Two Eskimos, Noocapinguaq and Inuatuk, and their wives, joined the Expedition. They were soon on board with their kyacks, kometiks (sledges), twenty-five dogs, and their household effects (which included a sewing machine and a portable gramophone), happy to be chosen to accompany us and to have the opportunity of seeing new land to the North.

A course was set for Bache Peninsula, where we had hoped to establish our winter quarters, but we were soon surrounded by heavy ice floes and, to our great disappointment, the next day the whole of the Sound between Greenland and Ellesmere Island was blocked with heavy ice. Advancing towards Ellesmere Island, we found ourselves confronted by a great barrier of pack-ice through which it was impossible to force a passage. We cruised along the edge of the pack, crossing and re-crossing the Sound, hoping to find a lead in the ice running towards the North. Kane Basin was packed tight and there was no water in sight as far as could be seen from the "Crow's Nest" with a powerful telescope. It was decided to drop back to Etah Fiord to a safe anchorage and to await more favourable conditions. On making further attempts for two days, we found the ice conditions unchanged and with no indication of any leads opening up, although these attempts were made during the period of "Spring tides". Very reluctantly we returned to Etah, where we were forced to establish our base, which is in Danish territory and was some four hundred miles south of our objective in Northern Ellesmere Island. We were at least within striking distance for sledging parties and in a comparatively good location to procure walrus, which we needed for dog feed in addition to the dried fish and pemmican that had been brought for this purpose on the vessel.

While cruising among the ice-floes in Smith Sound we had obtained eight walrus, which made a welcome addition of about five tons of meat and blubber. The walrus is very fond of sleeping on floating ice-pans during the warm days. They are easily killed by rifle fire. If they are killed instantaneously by an accurate shot through the neck they remain on the ice. Indiscriminate shooting of walrus on ice-pans or in the water results in the loss of many of these large mammals, unless a harpoon and line is used to prevent them from sinking. Walrus, seal and narwhal meat is by far the best food for sledge dogs in these latitudes, as land game and fish never have the percentage of fat which is so essential to dogs in the winter.

The unloading of our supplies had been rather slow with the ship's lifeboat, assisted by our motor boat and a small dory. This work was completed on August 22nd. The seventy dogs, apparently none the worse for their voyage, were temporarily placed on an island in the Fiord about a mile from the camp.

Since the ship's charter had now expired, and as further delay would entail the risk of her crew having to winter in the Arctic without adequate supplies and clothing, the Captain made preparations for their homeward journey. This was our last opportunity to send messages to those at home waiting anxiously for our letters. After a farewell party on the deck, at which one of the crew played an accordian, to the great delight of our Eskimos, the *Signalhorn* steamed slowly out of the Fiord and headed toward the South and civilization, sending a message of farewell in Morse Code on the ship's hooter. We watched her out of sight, then turned to the many tasks which had to be completed in the short time at our disposal before the coming of the long Arctic Night.

The Base and Preparations for Winter

The Expedition's work had now started in earnest and we began to look like explorers. Beards were very much in evidence, as our toilet requisites had not been in demand since leaving London. The most urgent work was the establishment of pemmican and other supply depots as far north on the Greenland coast as possible, and the construction of the Expedition house. I took charge of the building, assisted by Bentham, who was chief engineer for the motor boat as well as assistant carpenter. The others carried the heavy supplies, coal and lumber up the steep bank to the building site. Six tents of various types were pitched for the stores and temporary sleeping quarters and a mess tent was organized. Dr. Humphreys took first turn at culinary duties.

At the end of August, Bentham, Haig-Thomas and I, accompanied by Noocapinguaq, left for the North with two boats loaded with pemmican and other supplies to establish caches as far North as possible, but on reaching Cairn Point, a distance of about twenty-five miles, we found further progress impossible. The ice conditions in Kane Basin were still unchanged. The ice was pressed tightly against the cliffs and no water could be seen to the north. We cached the supplies well above high tide mark and returned to Etah with a view to taking more pemmican to Cairn Point at a later date and possibly proceed farther North if an opportunity presented itself. The establishment of depots well to the north would have meant so much to the future sledging parties. Six other attempts were made with the boat before the freeze-up in early October, but with such bad ice conditions, unfortunately only a minimum of success rewarded our efforts.

On one occasion Shackleton and Moore had remained at Cairn Point to relay supplies farther North with a dory and outboard motor. They had a somewhat exciting experience when they were returning from a short distance North, following an open lead some distance off shore as a result of a temporary calm and the presence of so much heavy ice, some new ice quickly formed which prevented them from getting ashore. However, they were able to haul the boat on to a small ice-pan and drifted South for a considerable distance, passing the point where they had left their heavy sleeping robes and food. Fortunately an on-shore wind sprang up the next day and broke up the new ice which enabled them to run their not too reliable outboard motor and reach the shore near Littleton Island. During these boat trips they were usually accompanied by one of the Eskimos. From a cache-laying point of view these trips were not very successful, but a number of walrus were killed and stored for future use on these trips.

The house was a two storey frame structure 24 by 14 feet including a porch. The construction had been a very slow process owing to the fact that it had been assembled in Copenhagen and each timber and board had been carefully marked and taken down again, but as the instructions for reassembling it were written partly in Danish it proved to be quite a jig-saw puzzle. I would have much preferred bulk lumber to work with. However, it proved to be a well-planned and solid house, and was quite comfortable and warm, but rather cramped for six men. We later built a lean-to on the windward side which provided accommodation for some of the stores as well as a place to recharge radio batteries during the winter.

The dogs were then brought from the Island and divided into six teams, each dog being fitted with a harness and a sealskin trace approximately fourteen feet in length; winter quarters were also arranged for the teams.

We realized as a result of some bones being found on the Island that four of the dogs had been killed and eaten by the others, but there were now seventeen missing, some of which might have left the Island and become stranded on ice-floes. It is very difficult to make a fair division of food when feeding so many loose dogs. Unfortunately we lost a number of animals later in the year through feeding them shark meat, which acted as a poison. This meat evidently had not been properly dried by the Eskimos farther south from whom it was purchased.

Etah proved to be a most undesirable location to spend the winter. The days were now getting extremely short and with the dark period rapidly advancing, the winds blowing down the Fiord, so well known to the Eskimos and previous Explorers, seemed to increase. Our local sledging trips were curtailed as the prevailing Easterly winds, blowing with great force from the mountains of Greenland, continually carried out the ice along the coast both north and south of the Fiord, and left only the length of the Fiord on which to exercise the dogs. Regular trips were made to Brother John Glacier at the head of the Fiord, a distance of about four miles, to bring fresh water ice, this being our only water supply. Other short trips were made to walrus and seal caches near at hand to haul in feed for the dogs.

On the 23rd of October the sun did not show itself above the horizon at noon, and we settled down for the winter. Cooking proved to be one of the chief occupations, and an entirely new departure for most of the members of the expedition, especially the making of bread. However, they soon mastered the art and we were never without good bread at the Base Camp. On November 1st an attempt was made to reach Robertson Bay and Thule, with a view to getting more Eskimos to help us on the first stage of our journeys North after the dark period. But this had to be postponed until the end of January owing to the darkness, the continual blizzards on the ice-cap route, and the open water along the coast. Our chief pastime in the winter was reading and preparing for the spring journeys; the care of dogs; and making sledges, clothing, and a thousand and one minor preparations occupied a good deal of our time. The radio kept us in touch with world events. There was always a good supply of music available, in fact, between the radio and a portable gramophone, we generally had a continuous programme. Through the courtesy of The Canadian Radio Commission and Westinghouse Station KDKA at Pittsburg, we were able to receive news from our relatives and friends on Saturday nights. On December 23rd, we clearly heard some musical numbers especially directed to us by a dance orchestra at the Mayfair Hotel, London. We spent a most enjoyable Christmas, our Eskimos being the guests of honour. Through the kindness of Lady Shackleton, we enjoyed a splendid Christmas dinner which had been especially packed in England five months previously.

Dr. Humphreys and Haig-Thomas left at the end of January with Noocapinguaq and Inuatuk and two teams of dogs following the ice-cap route to Robertson Bay. They returned in the middle of March accompanied by a number of Eskimos. They had visited Robertson Bay and also Thule where they had communicated by wireless with England. A few days later some more Eskimos arrived with their dog teams to work for us. There was now a total of over 170 dogs in the camp, which presented quite a problem as our dog food supply was running very low. Many of the Eskimo dogs were very thin, and some of the Expedition dogs were only in fair condition for the long trek North.

Owing to the fact that we had to winter so far from Grant Land and to the fact that many of the dogs were not fully equal to such a hard trip, it was decided to change our plans and split into three parties. It was arranged that Moore, who was very keen on travelling, should accompany me to Grant Land, where, if possible, we were to explore the interior and cross to the North Coast. Shackleton and Bentham were to visit Bache Peninsula and carry out a survey as far North as possible on the East coast of Ellesmere Island, while the Doctor and Haig-Thomas would attempt a crossing of Grinnel Land where they expected to do some plane-table mapping. The six dog teams were then made up into three teams. Bentham was very considerate in giving his best dogs to Moore and myself; he was to have been my partner in a previous arrangement, and our dogs had worked well together, but owing to the change of plans it was considered that more time for geological work would be available if Bentham did not go on the longest journey. At the request of the Doctor, I made the distribution of the Eskimos and dogs for the three parties. There were now twelve Eskimos available with dog teams, which gave each party two Eskimos for the duration of their journeys and two Eskimos with support teams, making five sledges to each party. For the next few days each party was very busy working individually and getting their dog feed and rations advanced along the trail. By April 3rd we had all started on our long journeys and were glad to be on the trail after a somewhat monotonous and inactive winter.

Sledge Journey of Grant Land Party

As I am not thoroughly conversant with details of the other sledge journeys made during the course of the Expedition, and as space will not, in any case, permit me to do them full justice, in the following account I must necessarily confine myself solely to the experiences of the party which travelled to Grant Land and of which I was a member. This party consisted of Moore and myself, assisted by Noocapinguaq and Inatuak, who went all the way with us, and Eko and Rasmise who acted as our support party.

On April 3rd, in the early morning, we finished carrying the last of our outfit up the hill and then took up three empty sledges with the fifty-nine dogs. There was a very cold wind and drift as we loaded the five sledges and set out over the rough going across country to Cape Hatherton.

We had some trouble in lifting our loads over boulders before we descended to the shore ice a short distance north of Littleton Island, where we picked up some pemmican from one of the depots. On nearing Cape Hatherton, where the ice foot (shore ice) was hanging precariously to the cliffs, we decided to wait until high tide to travel along this narrow shelf, which stood about twelve feet above the open sea at low tide. Inuatuk shot a seal here in the open water, which drifted towards the shore. By utilizing an ice pan for a raft, we got it ashore and had a good meal of boiled meat, which was very acceptable, as the weather was cold and we had plenty of time to spare. The Grinnel Land Party had built an igloo here and had stayed for the night.

The going on the shore ice proved to be quite good, although in some places it was only just wide enough to edge the sledges around the cliffs. At the point of Cape Hatherton the ice was piled up about 25 feet high against the cliffs, and skirted on the outside by open water. The Grinnel party had done a lot of work here in chopping their way over the high ridges, a distance of about one hundred yards. Four of us took the sledges over, one at a time, without accident. It would have been a very easy matter to drop a heavily loaded sledge into the sea when passing over some of the ridges. The Eskimos show remarkable skill and patience at this work. A little further north we picked up ten more cases of pemmican, and reached the main depot at Cache Point in the early hours of the morning. The Doctor's party was encamped on the shore ice with two tents and we pitched our tent as well, there being no suitable snow to build an igloo, which we would have preferred with the temperature at 32 degrees below zero and a fresh wind blowing from the open Sound.

At noon the Doctor's party left to cross Smith Sound. Their head native told me that some of their dogs were very hungry and needed seal meat as the pemmican was "not alright". After seeing them off, we brought more dog-pemmican, coal oil, and sugar from the cache to our camp, and loaded up the sledges. The total weight of our outfit was not far short of 3,000 pounds, the heaviest item being, of course, the dog-pemmican of which we had 1,500 pounds. Rations 480 pounds, coal oil 240 pounds, robes, skins, spare clothing, etc., arms, ammunition and hunting gear amounted to approximately 750 pounds. When distributed, the dead weight on four sledges was about 650 pounds each and the fifth sledge, driven by Rasmise with a small team, had a load of 400 pounds. We left a note for Shackleton's party, which we expected would arrive at this point later in the day. We then left to follow the Greenland coast north.

We were now embarked on a long journey, full of determination to travel into unknown Grant Land as far as possible. With Noocapinguaq in the lead we made short work of crossing Force Bay on the hard packed snow. Before reaching Rensselaer Bay, where the snow was loose and deep, we climbed on to the shore ice between the tidal hummocks and the gigantic cliffs. Here we found a good right of way, covered by a recent snow fall where we maintained a steady trot. As we advanced along the shore into Kane Basin we saw that there was crusted snow and irregular patches of rough ice.

We were indeed fortunate to have level going for our heavy loads along the shore ice, although we had to follow every indentation of the coast line to Cape Russell, which we reached after three days of steady travel. At this point we met two Eskimos who had been north on a bear hunt, with two dog teams. They were not a very prosperous looking pair and had certainly had a lean time. Having seen no bear and having only obtained one seal in two weeks, their dogs were in very bad condition. They had been obliged to kill five and had just killed two others when we arrived at their camp. One man had only four dogs left and the other seven. To add to their troubles one man was a cripple and the other had frozen his face badly. We gave them a good supper and a feed of pemmican for their remaining dogs. These two Eskimos were returning south after visiting Cape Calhound where they had expected to obtain seal in the open water at the Cape but unfortunately, contrary to their expectations, had found the ice pack solid.

It was useful information for us to know that there was deep snow on Peabody Bay, where we planned to cross. We left the next morning, keeping well out into Kane Basin, and found the going slow, but not nearly so bad as it would have been had we travelled further in on the Bay along the foot of the huge Humbolt Glacier, which is not less than fifty miles across the foot.

Shortly after setting out on the 70 mile trek across to Cape Calhound, we came across a tidal crack in the ice, where the dogs soon scented seal. This seemed to be Noocapinguaq's lucky day, for he got three without any delay when they came up to breathe at their holes in the crack, which was frozen over with new ice; and while we were pitching the tent to camp for the night Inuatuk secured another. After leaving the shore ice, the going had been very hard in the deep, loose snow, and with the low temperature the dogs had to be driven hard to maintain a slow walking pace. The fresh seal meat was, therefore, a most welcome change for them, as they were not getting proper satisfaction from the pemmican ration. Although we had not been on the trail long they were becoming very thin and tired.

Opposite Scoresby Bay we found the fresh track of a polar bear near a large iceberg. It was just about time to end our march for the day, so Moore, Rasmise and I established camp, while Inuatuk, Noocapinguaq and Eko left at once following the bear tracks with empty sledges and taking only their rifles, knives and a primus lamp. About 12 hours later they returned with their bear. It was an animal of average size and made a fair feed for the 99 dogs, considering that they had recently been given a good feed of seal meat, and what was perhaps more important from an Eskimo point of view, they had also obtained a fine skin for making two pairs of trousers.

We stayed at this camp long enough to rest the dogs. Most of the day was spent drying our sealskin footwear and mitts over the primus lamps in the tent and eating the heart and other delicacies of bear meat. The bear skin was cached by suspending it on a sealskin line about 30 feet above the ice on the perpendicular wall of a large iceberg.

The dogs were feeling better after a good feed and rest and the forty miles or so to Cape Calhound were covered at a good trot. After climbing onto the shore ice again we made lunch. Here we found a good many fossils embedded in limestone. We collected a number of these, which we thought were interesting corals; they were left to be picked up on our return.

A large bearded seal was lying on the ice about a mile from the cape, but unfortunately it slid into its hole when Noocapinguaq was approaching for a shot. We continued along the shore ice on excellent going for about eight miles, and camped where we encountered some more high pressure ice at the northern point of Morris Bay. The weather thus far had been quite good. The mean temperature, since leaving the open water further south, had averaged from 33 to 39 degrees below zero.

On the following morning, April 14th, we made a cache of dog feed and provisions for our return, and re-arranged our sledge loads. Since we had expended some of the supplies and had laid two caches, we decided that this would be the best time to send our support teams back, rather than risk their accompanying us farther north, where there was expected to be a shortage of seal at this season. They were issued with enough supplies to take them back to the Base. We then continued north with our three large sledges, carrying loads of about 900 pounds each. Our stock of dog feed was now 1,048 pounds of pemmican and a small quantity of seal blubber.

We found travelling on the shore ice much better than on the ice of Kennedy Channel, although getting around some of the high capes necessitated a great deal of work chopping our way through, or over the huge piles of ice pressed up against the cliffs. The shore from Cape Calhound to Cape Bryan is by no means as straight as the present maps would lead one to believe. From Cape Constitution, for a considerable distance north, there was a complete absence of snow on the ice, which was all of new rubble variety and blue in colour. The rough nature of the ice showed that the Channel must have been very choppy when it was freezing up in the fall. At Cape Constitution we saw the large seam of coal which was investigated by Dr. Lauge Koch, Danish Geologist, in 1921, and I was fortunate enough to obtain a photograph of the Cape which shows the seam running parallel with the coast, a short distance above the high tide mark.

We had quite a lot of trouble in rounding some of the cliffs before we finally got to Cape Bryan. At some points the pressure ice was piled 30 to 50 feet above the sea level, against the cliffs, giving every evidence that the currents in Kennedy Channel are very strong. After staying over for two days during a terrific wind, where we sheltered behind a pressure ice ridge, on April 19th we started across the rough ice to cross the Channel to Ellesmere Island.

Our camp had been anything but comfortable on the windswept shore, where there was no snow with which to build an igloo. The wind died down during the first part of the march, but the ice was rough and the going consequently slow with the heavy loads. The weather suddenly became calm and a thick fog descended and at times we could not see the other teams. The ice conditions improved and we were able to break into a slow trot, with Noocapinguaq appearing at times in the fog ahead of us. We were glad to see, when the fog cleared, that we had almost reached Ellesmere Island. Inuatuk had lost sight of us, but he soon caught up when we got clear of the rough ice. Owing to the good judgment of Noocapinguaq, we had travelled more or less in a straight line from Cape Bryan. After lunch we made fair progress on the level ice, and pitched the tent a short distance from Cape Baird.

A strong breeze arose, with the result that this also proved to be a very uncomfortable camp. One of my dogs was badly lamed as a result of a general fight at feeding time. Owing to the cold winds and the fact that there had been no snow to lie on and also to the fact that the dogs had necessarily been tethered on the glare ice for several consecutive nights, they were becoming very thin and weary. One female in my team was quite played out and had to be destroyed.

We were now a comparatively short distance from Fort Conger, and we expected that it would be an easy march to cross Lady Franklin Bay, but it proved to be the most strenuous day of the whole journey. The Bay was filled with an old polar ice pack covered with snow, waist deep in some places. To avoid as much of this as possible, we kept outside the pack on Robeson Channel, but we had to cross approximately fifteen miles of it to get into Discovery Harbour. The snow between what appeared to be rolling hills of old ice, was very deep and crusted, and although the crust was about six inches thick, the loaded sledges continually broke through and had to be dug out.

This march of about twenty miles had taken us as many hours before we reached Discovery Harbour, the winter quarters of the British Arctic Expedition of 1875 and 1876 under Captain Nares. The large house built by the Greely Expedition, and named Fort Conger, had later been taken down and built into three small huts by Peary. Moore and I occupied the one known to the Eskimos as "Peary's house". There was a stove and some coal from the local deposit. This proved to be very useful to dry out our clothing and sleeping bags which had become "iced up". We were also able to make bannocks and so conserve our supply of coal oil. The two Eskimos slept in one of the other small huts. The third hut is in a very poor state of repair. We were unable to find the tablets erected to the memory of C.W. Paul and J.J. Hand of H.M.S. *Discovery*, British Arctic Expedition. They were, no doubt, under the deep snow drifts.

The last visitor to Fort Conger was Dr. Lauge Koch, in 1921, on his Journey around the north coast of Greenland. The year previous to Dr. Koch's arrival, Captain Godfred Hansen had established a cache of provisions for Roald Amundsen in connection with his plans to fly over the North Pole. About 60 pounds of pemmican were found to be in good condition, considering that it had been there for fifteen years, but other supplies consisting of canned meats, chocolate, sugar, tobacco and clothing had been spoiled by the dampness.

During our stay Moore took a number of photographs, a subject in which he is very interested. He also climbed to a cairn on the top of a hill, a short distance inland, and deposited a record of our visit. We had expected to obtain plenty of Arctic hare in this district, but after a walk inland I could not see a single track. Noocapinguaq had expected to see muskoxen on the hills, but the absence of land game here was undoubtedly due to the heavy snow.

On April 23rd, in the early hours of the morning, we left for Lake Hazen, travelling through Black Rock Vale in preference to the longer route via the Ruggles River. The going was very slow until we reached the height of land, where there was less snow. In Lady Franklin Bay we travelled along the shore of Mount Belloc Island and the north shore of Sun Peninsula, amongst the ice hummocks, rather than on the Bay, where the snow was about a foot deep.

On the south side of the Peninsula we saw the first muskoxen, with the aid of binoculars. I could see four cows and three young calves. It seemed to me that this was rather early to see calves at foot (April 23rd). We made camp between two small lakes in Black Rock Vale, and found it extremely cold, although the thermometer registered only 30 below zero at midnight, when the sun was just above the horizon. We had travelled a long day but had not gained much distance.

The dogs had been given a straight ration of one and one-half pounds of pemmican per day and were getting into very poor condition. We were now very anxious to get to Lake Hazen, with a view to obtaining plenty of fish for them. At this camp, when shovelling snow from a gravel bar, we found small pieces of coal, and a kind of resin, which burnt readily when a match was applied.

The next day proved to be a very hard one for the dogs, over bare rocky patches and loose snow, and we had to camp when the dogs played out only a few miles from the lake. During the day we saw a herd of 16 grown muskoxen and also a number of small calves. When we approached they went over a hill on the south side of the valley.

We found a depth of fourteen inches of snow on Lake Hazen, which we reached about noon the next day. The exhausted dogs, whose feet were sore and bleeding owing to the rock surface and crusted snow over which we had just travelled, were just able to pull the sledges across a bay in the lake to a point where we decided to camp and fish. We had seen no signs of caribou or Arctic hare, and our only chance of getting enough feed to condition our dogs for the strenuous trip into Grant Land would depend on the success of our fishing. We were naturally excited and somewhat impatient to start fishing. While we were chiselling the first holes through the ice, Moore and I had visions of pulling out large salmon trout (char) and feeding the dogs all the thawed fish they could eat.

Water was struck at four feet seven inches. We had expected the ice to be much thicker. The heavy snowfall on the ice, which had apparently been early in the fall, had prevented the ice from becoming very thick. Ice to the depth of ten feet or more has been known to the Eskimos at Lake Hazen in the past. I have personally seen seven feet of ice on Baker Lake, which is over 1,200 miles south of this point.

To our great disappointment, only a few small fish were hooked at these holes. We made another hole over deeper water and cleared a large patch of snow around the hole to let more light into the lake, but the fishing did not prove to be any more successful. We cut new holes and fished for about six hours, and then pitched the tent on the ice and tethered the dogs. After a meal we continued to fish for about 24 hours with the same disappointing results, although we hooked two fish about two feet six inches long. All the fish we caught were very thin. Collectively, we had not caught enough to give the ravenous dogs a pound each, and we had to feed pemmican as well. The fishing method employed was known as "jigging", with baited spoon hooks. The top of the fishing holes had to be stirred often to prevent the water from freezing over. We "jigged" almost continuously for three days, and our average catch did not exceed 36 pounds per day, which amounted to rather less than a pound per dog.

We could see that the first part of the journey into Grant Land would be a hard climb through the Garfield Range, which skirts the north side of the lake, and the prospects of obtaining game would be very small. For four days we had seen two muskoxen grazing on some foothills on the north side of the lake, but owing to the Game Laws, a part of which is framed for the express purpose of preservation of this extremely rare and almost extinct species of animal, it was decided that they should not be molested notwithstanding the very meagre rations of the party.

We had left a small cache of pemmican at Fort Conger, and the next cache on our homeward journey was across Lake Franklin Bay on the Greenland coast, just to the south of Cape Bryan. On our return journey we could not rely on getting seal until nearing the south end of Kennedy Channel, a distance of not less than 100 miles. We therefore found ourselves in a difficult if not a dangerous position, as regards making any further progress. I am sure that, at this stage, if our dogs had been subjected to absolute starvation, we should have found ourselves without any means of transportation. It was quite evident, then, that the whole party could not venture into Grant Land for any length of time without starving a number of dogs (unless we resorted to killing muskoxen), which would have made it very difficult, perhaps impossible, to get out of the country. It was therefore decided that Moore and Noocapinguaq, with the pick of the dogs and one sledge, should travel as far as possible into the unknown country, while I stayed at the lake with Inuatuk to fish at various places, with a view to getting sufficient fish ahead for their return, and if possible, to get the thinnest dogs into condition for the return journey.

I volunteered to remain at the Lake in order that Moore (who had not previously been in the Arctic), should have the opportunity of travelling as far North as possible, knowing that he would probably obtain some good panoramic photographs of the unknown country. He also had more practice than I in taking Aneroid readings. It was naturally a disappointment to me not to travel north from Lake Hazen, after our strenuous work in getting this far. I had every confidence in Noocapinguaq's judgment and ability to take Moore as far as possible, consistent with safety under these adverse conditions; while I felt keenly my responsibility in the safe return of the party. I may say that Moore, although very ambitious to go on himself, very sportingly offered to cast lots as to which of us should proceed, but on taking everything into consideration, I felt that it was better for me to remain at the Lake and act as a support party in case of emergency.

Having decided that these plans best suited the exigencies of the situation, Moore and Noocapinguaq left in the afternoon to climb the Gillman Glacier, which appeared to be the only Pass through the Garfield Range to the interior. They had 17 of the best dogs, 136 pounds of dog-pemmican, and a small quantity of fish. The weight of their equipment and rations, including one and one-half gallons of coal oil, had been reduced to a minimum.

The weather, during our stay at the Lake, was very good, but decidedly cold about midnight when the sun was shining in the North. It may be interesting here to note the variation in temperatures, which ranged from minus 28 to plus 30, between midnight and midday. During the following four days Inuatuk and I continued to fish. We moved camp three times, hoping for better luck in different places, finally locating at the northeast end of the Lake. We fed the dogs about 1 pound each per day, and were only able to put aside about 60 pounds of fish, which together with 96 pounds of pemmican (that had been retained at the Lake) would at least get the whole party as far as Fort Conger on our return journey. We had cut 23 fishing holes in the ice since we arrived on April 25th, and the fishing had been going on almost continuously, but we were never able to give the dogs a full feed. However, the amount we did procure enabled us to make a short stay in the country. I had retained less than two pints of coal oil at the Lake, in order that Moore and Noocapinguaq should have enough to carry them over their difficult journey for at least six days. After a few meals of raw, frozen fish, we found that even the best of them were very unpalatable, being practically tasteless; but we could not afford to use our scanty supply of coal oil more than once a day to make cocoa, which we found very beneficial before turning in to our sleeping bags after the long cold days spent lying on the ice "jigging" at the fishing poles.

At midnight on May 5th we saw the explorers returning. They were travelling slowly along the Lake towards our camp. Inuatuk had just returned from a short excursion on the north side of the lake, and had bagged two Arctic hare. I immediately began preparations for a hot dinner (using the last of our coal oil), thinking that the travellers would be cold and hungry. But before they reached us, Noocapinguaq called out in his own language, "We have caribou meat". When they arrived in camp they were full of news concerning the new country they had seen, and of the new range of mountains, which, it is believed, had never been seen before. They had found a good pass via the Gillman Glacier, and had to bear a little to the west before turning north. They had found the United States Range to be entirely out of place as shown on the maps. The party's furthest north position was approximately Latitude 82.25, and Longitude 71.45, where they climbed a mountain, and could see through to the mouth of Markham Inlet, and to the ice hummocks in the Arctic ocean. Many peaks of the Challenger Range were also seen, as well as many important peaks showing through the ice-cap of central and north-western Grant Land.

Noocapinguaq stated that the whole area is very rough and mountainous, and very difficult for sledge travel. It is quite apparent that a ground survey could not be carried out successfully by sledge parties without a Base and adequate supplies, either at Lake Hazen or on the north coast.

Moore took a number of photographs on this journey and is also writing a detailed account which, it is understood, will be available later. He reports having seen one very aged muskox; evidently an old bull which had become separated from a herd. Noocapinguaq had obtained three caribou (of the small Arctic species), the meat of which proved a welcome addition to their rations, and to their meagre supply of dog feed. This game was obtained on their return journey, and they brought some meat back to the camp, which was appreciated very much.

After fishing most of the following day (May 7th) without much success, we left our camp, following a small river bed southwards from the east end of the Lake. We soon reached our old trail and found the going up grade very slow. The dogs started well from the camp, but in a few hours, they were pretty well exhausted, and the next day, in travelling to Fort Conger, they could not exceed a walking pace even when they were going down hill on good snow. Four of the dogs in my team, which had been resting at the Lake, were so exhausted that they were staggering with weakness before reaching Conger. Inuatak killed two of his dogs before we reached Fort Conger and Noocapinguaq was also forced to kill two of his. In passing through Black Rock Vale we saw three muskoxen, and later the track of a lone wolf, which had followed our trail and had paid a visit to Fort Conger. My four exhausted dogs, which on the outward journey had been the best in the team, were now too far gone to work; but we decided not to destroy them, because within a few days it might be possible to get seal.

In order not to lose more time than absolutely necessary in getting south to the location where seal could be found sleeping on the ice, we arranged the dogs into two teams and discarded one sledge and some of the equipment. Our team was divided between the two Eskimos, making 16 dogs in each team. During our short stay at Fort Conger, I obtained some samples of the coal from the large deposit, which has been well described by the British Arctic Expedition and also by the Greely Expedition. I have retained a small sample of this coal to bring to Ottawa, which might be of some interest.

As the weather was becoming warmer during the day, we decided to travel at night for the benefit of the dogs and to make longer marches. Before leaving, we fed them a small quantity of the canned meat from Amundsen's cache, together with sealskin footwear and dog harness cut into small pieces. Moore left an Expedition record in the form of a brief report, giving some useful information in regard to the route we had taken and the fishing possibilities at Lake Hazen. Since this was the farthest North patrol by a member of the Force, I wrote a short official record of our visit, with a request that the finder forward it to Headquarters at Ottawa.

We camped about seven miles from Conger in order that the dogs should not be exhausted in crossing the crusted snow on the old Polar ice in one march. Our progress the next day was slow, with Moore and I walking ahead of the Eskimos who drove the teams. At Cape Leiber, to the south of Cape Baird, we collected a few specimens of rock. Before reaching Cape Bryan we were reduced almost to a crawling pace, although we had good sledging across the North end of Kennedy Channel, excepting a few patches of rough ice. We found the case of pemmican intact at our old camp site, as well as a small quantity of sugar and some tobacco. It was after two long days of slow travel, with Moore and me walking ahead, that we reached Cape Constitution, where we got our first small seal; but this was only an appetizer for the thirty-two hungry dogs. The first two attempts at hunting seal were unsuccessful; one failure being the result of bad marksmanship, which often proves to be the case when there is a scarcity of food and one is in dire need.

Our next camp was south of the Franklin Islands, where we had parted from our supporting party. We were glad now that we had left two cases of dog-pemmican here. We also found the small cache of rations and spare clothing in good condition. Leaving here the next morning, we were pleased to find a large patch of open water at the point of Cape Calhound. Our Eskimos obtained a very small seal after we made our camp on the shore ice. In the morning Inuatuk shot a bearded seal (Ukjuk) in the water, quite close to the tent. There was a frantic scramble to save it from sinking. As it floated towards the ice in the strong current, we pulled it up on a floating ice-pan, cut it up, and quickly hoisted it with ropes to the shore ice about ten feet above the water level, only just before the pan was turned up on its edge by the current, and disappeared under the main pack.

Our concern over dog feed, which had been a serious problem on this journey, was now at an end. The meat and blubber weighed about hundred pounds. The dogs fed to their entire satisfaction, in fact, this was the first time I had seen our dogs with more than they could eat since they had joined the Expedition. A portion of the seal blubber was kept for cooking as we were out of coal oil. It was now May 17th and the days were warm and pleasant. Inuatuk walked a considerable distance back on our trail for one of his dogs, which was in too starved a condition to keep up with the remainder and should have followed after a rest; but unfortunately he could not find him.

We made a more thorough search for fossils along the cliffs to the north of Cape Calhound and found that corals were very numerous. I photographed some of the largest ones which we could not have transported, also some other good specimens embedded in the rock. Some of the broken rock at the foot of the Cape seemed to be a conglomeration of nothing but fossils. We gathered what seemed to be the best specimens, which I later handed over to Bentham, at the Base, with a few other geological specimens.

After a good rest, we left to cross Peabody Bay, again finding it expedient to keep a considerable distance from the Humbolt Glacier to avoid the deep snow. The going was very heavy before reaching Cape Kent, but seal were plentiful and the dogs well fed. One could hardly believe that these dogs, which were on the verge of staggering with weakness a week ago, were the same animals that now strained on their traces with their bushy tails curled over their backs, apparently enjoying their work, while we rode on the sledges.

At Rensselaer Bay I visited a small island with Noocapinguaq, where we saw an arrow engraved in the rock which apparently indicated the position of the ship of the American Expedition, led by Dr. Kane in 1853, when their vessel was frozen in.

We found the going excellent on the broad shore ice. Our sledges were now light and, with fine weather, we found a sixty to sixty-five mile march quite enjoyable. While crossing Force Bay we obtained another good sized seal. This, with one of the two killed the day before, would be ample to last for the remainder of the journey. At the site of the main pemmican cache we saw the tracks of the other two sledge parties, which had returned from Ellesmere Island. After a careful study of the various tracks, our Eskimos concluded that they had all returned safely and that their dogs were not hungry.

On May 25th, we made our last camp at Cape Hatherton cache, where we found a note written by Shackleton. The weather was stormy and the sky over-cast when we left the next day for Etah, after picking up two boxes of geological specimens, and a field radio set. On leaving Hatherton Bay and climbing the hills on the land crossing to the Base, we had to travel into a very strong blizzard, and we were soon covered with the wet driving snow. It was a relief to get down into Etah Fiord, where there was not so much force to the wind.

We narrowly escaped a serious accident here, when descending the very steep incline. I was helping Noocapinguaq in letting our sledge down, when a large boulder became dislodged and started to roll down, following an impression directly towards Moore and Inuatak, who were several hundred feet further down. We ran forward to shout to them, when I noticed our sledge coming down backwards over loose rock, dragging the dogs behind. They heard our warning, however, just before the boulder bounced past them, missing them by a short distance.

We arrived at the Base in the afternoon, May 26th, and were welcomed by the Doctor, Shackleton and Bentham. Thomas had left with the Eskimos for Robertson Bay to do ornithological work, during the early summer. We had been on the trail for fifty-five days, during which time we had travelled nine hundred miles. This mileage was compiled by Moore and myself as accurately as possible, by comparing diaries and making calculation with the aid of an Admiralty Chart, making allowances for the extra distance travelled in following the winding shore line on the Greenland coast and detours necessary when hunting or avoiding difficult sledging. The two Eskimos, both of whom I had travelled with on long journeys before, are good hunters and dog drivers, particularly Noocapinguaq, who has had vast experience and knew most of the country over which we travelled. With these two natives and average luck as regards game on the trail, and better dog pemmican, I am sure we could have crossed Grant Land to Cape Columbia and return without any serious difficulties.

The Short Summer at Etah

After giving their dogs a day's rest, Noocapinguaq and Inuatuk left to join their wives at Robertson Bay, and we were without Eskimos until Noocapinguaq returned with some of his relatives at the end of June. For the next few days we had much to tell each other about our journeys. Both of the other parties had visited Fram Havn and the Police detachment house at Bache Peninsula. Shackleton and Bentham had made a good collection of geological specimens in the Bache Peninsula district. They had also travelled as far north as Scoresby Bay, where they made the first rough survey of the Bay which has so far been accomplished. They were fortunate in obtaining seal in the open water near Bache Peninsula. Their dogs were kept in good condition and were able to haul the heavy rock specimens back to Etah.

The Doctor's party had not been able to reach the interior of Grinnel Land, owing to the very heavy snow they encountered on the ice-cap after climbing the glacier from Princess Marie Bay. They then returned to Bache Peninsula and made a journey through to the West coast of Ellesmere Island. This party saw a number of muskoxen and caribou on Bay Fiord, and killed a Polar bear during the course of their expedition.

One of the most interesting Eskimos I met was Ootah, who is proud of the fact that he stood at the North Pole with Peary in April, 1909. He still supports a good team of twelve dogs, and although advanced in years, he is quite able to wrestle with a heavily loaded kometik in rough ice or to climb a steep hill with a hundred pounds of pemmican on his back. He informed us that he and Matt Hansen (Peary's negro assistant) are the only two survivors of the party who attained the North Pole.

As the Expedition did not now require a large number of dogs, most of them were given to the Eskimos. Only one team of ten was kept at Etah for hunting seal and local trips.

In the latter part of May and the whole month of June, we enjoyed the "Eskimo Summer". The weather was very warm with the sun shining overhead day and night. Due no doubt to the strong reflection from the ice, the sun seems to have more effect in these latitudes, or perhaps it is because we appreciate its health-giving rays after the long months of dark and cold during the winter. We became quite tanned at this season and the Eskimo complexions became very dark, even the colours in the dogs' coats were faded by the fierce light of the sun. Seal and walrus lay on the ice to bask in the sun and thousands of little Auk swarmed along the fiords where they nest in the rocks. Arctic flora is also very much in evidence. All of this, for the time, seems to make life in the Arctic well worth while.

During this season biological specimens were collected from the sea by means of dredging, and Doctor Humphreys was absorbed with his large botanical collection. During the first two weeks of June, Moore, Bentham and myself, after being assisted by the Doctor and Shackleton to get the boat out to an island with a dog team, left for Littleton Island on an egg collecting trip, which we had been looking forward to for some time. We had a flat calm sea, and with the outboard motor recently overhauled by Bentham working satisfactorily, we soon reached a small island near Littleton Island. It was not long before we had gathered two thousand fresh eggs, and had eighteen in the cooking pot over the primus lamp. The three of us made short work of them, an excellent meal after a prolonged diet of canned foods and occasional seal meat. We now had an ample supply of fresh eggs, sufficient to last until the arrival of our relief ship which we expected towards the end of August.

Thousands of Northern and King Eider ducks nest in this vicinity. Their eggs are pale green and somewhat larger than domestic duck eggs. The ducks themselves are protected from the time they arrive until September 15th, and as far as North Greenland is concerned, the open season automatically closes itself when they migrate South in October. Insofar as the eggs are concerned it is contrary to existing regulations to take these eggs after June 17th, as the ducks would continue to lay as long as their nests were being robbed, with the result that the young ones would be hatched so late in the season that they would not be able to fly South before the sea freezes over. Arctic foxes could then reach the islands and the young ducks would become easy prey for them. During an unusually early freeze-up, thousands of young ducks have been known to be frozen into the ice.

Early in August, the Doctor, Shackleton and Bentham left with one Eskimo in the motorboat to visit Robertson Bay and locate Haig-Thomas. Moore and I remained at the Base and engaged ourselves making preparations to leave. We dismantled the storehouse and made boxes for packing the expedition's specimens and equipment which were to be taken to England.

It was August 22nd when the Danish Motor Schooner *Dannebrog* arrived at Etah. They had located Haig-Thomas at Robertson Bay where they had all joined the ship. Captain Petersen, the veteran ice pilot, was master of the ship, and Mr. Hans Neilsen, a good friend of the expedition, was on board. The Missionary had also arrived, and some Eskimos who had brought their kyacks to hunt walrus in Smith Sound while the ship was in the vicinity of Etah. The next day they secured ten large walrus which made their excursion quite a profitable one. The walrus were hoisted on board to be taken back to Thule where there was a shortage of dog food. The expedition's surplus stores were taken on board to be stored at Thule station in case they should be required by future expeditions.

The Homeward Voyage

On leaving Etah on August 25th, there remained only Noocapinguaq and his family, who, I believe, are the most northerly residents of the world. Noocapinguaq now owned the Expedition's motor boat and was left with sufficient supplies to last for several months. Farewell shots were heard from rifles on shore, to which the Captain responded with the ship's hooter. We were on the first stage of our long voyage from the Arctic back to civilization "and all that it means". Turning south from the fiord we had the last glimpse of the house. We reached Robertson Bay the next day and said goodbye to Inuatuk, who had been very popular with the expedition members. A very strong wind was blowing from the shore when we left the Bay and the next day we were hove to in a heavy gale, having drifted a considerable distance away from Thule settlement. After a change in the wind we reached Thule on August 27th and stayed for a few days. Here we visited the school and hospital, and were entertained by Mr. Neilsen and Dr. Holm. We also attended a farewell dance at the invitation of the Eskimos.

Ice conditions were good when crossing Melville Bay, but we were prevented from calling at Upernavik on account of the heavy fog along the coast which denoted ice near the shore. We next visited Jacobshavn and Godhavn, where we renewed our acquaintance with the Danish oficials, while the crew, assisted by some Eskimo women, loaded about forty tons of rock on the ship for ballast. The last call was made in South Greenland at Ivitut. We were rather surprised to see an up-to-date mining settlement and a ship being loaded with electric hoists at a concrete dock. We were given a friendly reception by the mine officials, who invited us to make use of their baths and a very well appointed club house. We were shown around the mine and the electric plant by the Manager, and found much to interest us. We were then entertained at lunch and dinner by the staff. I was informed that the Ivitut Mine is the larger of the only two Cryolite producing mines in the world, and is operated by the Danish Government. We were given samples of Cryolite, some of which is pure. This is an important mineral used in the making of Aluminum.

During a north easterly gale on September 20th, we rounded Cape Farewell and said goodbye to Greenland. A course was set for the North of Scotland. We expected a fair wind to that point which we should have reached in twelve days' time, and hoped to arrive in Aberdeen in another two days, where the expedition would disembark before the ship proceeded to Denmark. The gale increased, with very heavy seas. We appeared to be proceeding slowly stern foremost towards Newfoundland instead of making any headway, and after two days of this weather also found that we had travelled a considerable distance south of our course. The wind then changed to the north and we made good progress for several days until we encountered another north easterly gale, which blew with such force that the Diesel engine had to be run full speed ahead into the wind to hold our own. After two days of this the propellor was broken, due probably to coming in contact with an ice floe, and one blade dropped off. It was then found that the vibration from the propellor shaft had caused a leak in the stern, which prevented any further use of the engine. We finished the crossing under sail.

We were now about seven hundred miles from Scotland and for another two days we were hove to before the storm subsided. A welcome change in the wind took place at this juncture and with all sails set our progress was good until we sighted the small island of St. Kilda, where the wind died down, leaving a heavy swell to remind us of the storm we had experienced. For the past ten days, conditions had been rather bad on board, and as the date of our landing was so indefinite, the captain had found it necessary to ration the fresh water. Our food consisted mostly of salt pork, salt beef and salt fish, which was most unpalatable without sufficient water to prepare it properly. After seventeen days of bad seas and worse food, we were thankful to know that we were almost within sight of Scotland.

As a result of being blown to the south and the ship being partly disabled, our course was changed from Pentland Firth to Stornaway, and the next day with a fresh wind from the northwest, it was decided to put in to Barra Island, where it was hoped that repairs to the vessel could be effected. On the succeeding morning we ran before the wind towards Barra Island, which is the most southerly of the outer Hebrides, and put in to Castle Bay. While entering the harbour at a fast clip, we narrowly avoided being wrecked on a hidden reef.

After anchoring at Castle Bay, we were glad to get ashore where we quickly found our way to the hotel in the fishing village. We first sent messages to our anxious relatives, who had no idea of our whereabouts, as the *Dannebrog* carried no wireless and we were now long overdue. We then made a raid on the hotel dining room where we enjoyed great quantities of the wholesome Scottish fare. In the next few days, several attempts were made to beach the *Dannebrog* to make repairs and fit a new propellor. Two fishing boats were used in this work, as well as a life boat which was loaned by the British Admiralty, but owing to stormy weather and insufficient variation in tides, all attempts were unsuccessful. It was therefore decided to send to the mainland for a tug to tow the ship to a dry dock at Oban.

During our enforced stay at Castle Bay, we were entertained at a dance by the hospitable inhabitants, who were greatly interested and amused at the unexpected arrival of a somewhat rough looking party of Arctic explorers in their quiet fishing village. It was almost like being in a foreign country, as all the Islanders spoke Gaelic in preference to English, but we greatly enjoyed trying to dance in the eightsome reels and other Highland dances to the tune of the bagpipes.

When it was found, on October 11th, that the *Dannebrog* would be delayed much longer than we had first thought, it was decided that we would cross to Oban by mail steamer, where connections could be made with London trains. Bentham volunteered to stay with the ship until she crossed to Oban, to attend to the forwarding of the expedition specimens and stores. We were sorry to leave Captain Petersen and his Danish crew at Castle Bay. They all spoke English and we had become very friendly on the long, trying voyage.

Arrival in London meant the end of my long and very enjoyable association with the members of the expedition, who now had to their credit an excellent knowledge of Arctic conditions and valuable experience gained in the technique of Arctic travel. Unless I am very much mistaken, a further five individuals may now be added to the list of those who know and understand the "call of the North". Exploring for new lands, to a major degree, in the Arctic, is more or less complete, but there still remain many thousands of square miles in these regions to be covered by exploration parties, particularly in the fields of Geological and Geographical survey, besides many other branches of scientific investigation. Some of the explorers of our party will undoubtedly, it is felt, at some future date, respond to the desire to return to the Arctic to carry on this work. I appreciate the opportunity afforded me by the Force, which enabled me to accompany this expedition and to associate with its members who, after the rigours experienced in the Arctic, have been successful in bringing back to civilization a wealth of extremely valuable information.

Editor's Note

This article published just over 60 years ago is a stirring tale of exploration in Canada's far northern regions; a tale of Arctic travel which would be hard to duplicate. Only a man with Stallworthy's experience as a "northern man" could write about it and highlight the difficulties, dangers and pleasures so clearly.

From my conversation with him many years ago it was clear that he admired the ability of the Eskimo to live under the most difficult conditions. He valued very highly the contribution they made to the white man's travels in the Arctic.

Other information about Stallworthy and his work in the North can be found in the article, "The Northern Men", elsewhere in this collection.

In Tribute

From: Lord Shackleton, KG, PC, OBE.

As from: 6 St. James' Square, London, S.W. 1.

Commissioner M.J. Nadon, Royal Canadian Mounted Police, 1200 Alta Vista Drive, Ottawa, Ontario

Dear Commissioner:

17th January, 1977

I was very sorry to learn of the death of Sergeant Harry Stallworthy, formerly of the Royal Canadian Mounted Police, and would like to pay a tribute to him.

As the organiser, and now sole survivor of the Oxford University Ellesmere Land Expedition of 1934–35, I would like to say how much we all owed to Harry Stallworthy. This Expedition, which has now been pretty fully described in the past, owed a very great deal to the help of the Royal Canadian Mounted Police, and in particular to their attachment to us of Harry Stallworthy.

Harry Stallworthy — like Inspector Joyce — was one of the greatest of Arctic travellers. His journey searching for the lost German explorer, Dr. Krueger, north-west of Axel Heiberg, provided one of the epic sledge journeys. I refer to this in the introduction to my book, *Arctic Journeys*.

> As explained above it was our intention to winter in the North, but as none of us had Polar experience, it was of vital importance that we should find someone else for the Expedition who had not only travelled and lived in the Arctic, but also had a good deal of knowledge of the methods of travel that were necessary in the country which we were aiming to visit. When therefore I was in Canada in the summer of 1933, and had the opportunity of discussing the plans of the Expedition with the Canadian authorities, Major-General Sir James MacBrien, of the Royal Canadian Mounted Police, very generously offered a great deal of valuable support to the Expedition, including the loan of a really experienced "Mountie" would knew the Arctic regions. This was undoubtedly the greatest help we could have received, and we were very fortunate that the man who should have been chosen to go with us was Sergeant Stallworthy. Not only had he spent nearly thirteen years in the Arctic regions of Canada, but the three years previous to the time we met him he had been in charge of the Bache Peninsula Police Station. In the course of these three years he had carried out a remarkable journey round Axel Heiberg Land, searching for the lost German explorer, Dr. Krueger. Although he failed to find Krueger he had found traces of him in the form of a note placed in a cairn, which gave an indication of Dr. Krueger's proposed route, and his probable fate from starvation in the neighbourhood of Meighen

Island. Stallworthy himself had an extremely difficult journey and very nearly starved out. Twenty-nine of the dogs of his party had to be killed, and, as he would be the first to admit, if it had not been for the skill of the Eskimos, he might never have returned. His chief hunter, it is interesting to note, was Etookashoo, and he, in the course of this journey with Stallworthy, actually pointed out the spot where, he said, Dr. Cook took photographs which the latter claimed afterwards to have been taken at the North Pole. This was approximately at latitude 82° North, within sight of land. For the rest of Stallworthy's career, his home town was Cirencester in the county of Gloucestershire, but he had emigrated while in his teens to Canada, and he there spent twenty years of his life in the Royal Canadian Mounted Police. During this time he saw service overseas, and his last appointment before the expedition had been that of NCO to the Bache Peninsula Detachment.

Harry Stallworthy carried through a similar remarkable journey with A.W. Moore, as a result of which they penetrated into Grant Land across Lake Hazen, and, more subsequently climbed up the Gilman Glacier through the United States Range to Mt. Oxford — a number of new features are on the map as a result of this journey.

Harry Stallworthy, though by far the more experienced traveller, generously allowed his younger companion to make the journey into Grant Land while he stayed at Lake Hazen fishing for dog feed.

I could tell many anecdotes of Harry Stallworthy and of his contribution to the Expedition. The fact that we achieved anything at all and indeed survived, owed so much to this remarkable Polar man. He taught us Eskimo; he taught us to drive dogs, he taught us everything about Arctic living, including how to make sour dough hot cakes — and I remember him with affection and admiration.

Editor's Note

Lord Shackleton is the son of the late Sir Ernest Shackleton, famous Antarctic explorer. On behalf of Oxford University Lord Shackleton took part in two expeditions of exploration, the latest as organizer and surveyor for an expedition to Ellesmere Land in the Canadian Arctic, in 1934–35. After serving his country with distinction in World War II, he became a well-known political figure in Britain. He has served as Minister of Defence for the Royal Air Force, 1964–67; Leader of the House of Lords, 1969–70; Opposition Leader of the House of Lords, 1970–74; President of the Royal Geographical Society, 1971–74. In 1975 he was appointed Chairman of a Government Economic and Fiscal Survey of the Falkland Islands and their Dependencies.

18

Man Hunt in the Arctic

Const. T.E.G. Shaw

Twenty-eight years ago a routine police investigation developed into a hunt for a desperate killer in Canada's frost-bound northland. The tense drama involving the "Mad Trapper of Rat River" has been the theme of countless stories, but here are the facts of the case from RCMP files.

On the "mystery roll" of the man-hunt scroll is written the trapper's name,
But no-one knows just who he was, from whence or why he came.

—J. Robert Barrett

A stranger arrived at Ross River Post, Yukon Territory, Aug. 21, 1927 and after a cursory look around, made his way to Taylor and Drury's trading store. Although not too much information was volunteered, trader Roy Buttle learned that the newcomer's name was Arthur Nelson, that he was a trapper, and that he intended to stay just long enough to build a boat.

The store-keeper said he would lend a hand and Nelson, although not too enthusiastic at first, finally accepted the offer. Roy Buttle sized the newcomer up fairly well and in view of the fact he did not outwardly show too much curiosity or ask too many questions, the reticent Nelson did confide a few things to Buttle over the nine days it took them to put the boat together.

Roy Buttle found Nelson intelligent and highly rational in all conversations, but there was something in the man's make-up that made him seem odd. For one thing, Buttle was the only person around the Post the trapper would have anything to do with it. He camped about half a mile from the settlement and openly showed that he welcomed no guests. Also, the Indians living around the Post were visibly afraid of the stranger and would have absolutely nothing to do with him.

This was not because Arthur Nelson was a towering giant of a man either. Of average height, his well-proportioned frame packed about 170 pounds. His speech carried the trace of a Scandinavian accent and he seemed to walk with an habitual stoop as if he had been used to carrying an extremely heavy shoulder pack.

Nelson told Buttle he was an American and had been raised on a small farm in North Dakota. He appeared to be in his early 30s. He said he had reached Ross River via the headwaters of the Big and Little Salmon Rivers, having come from Teslin Lake. The previous Winter he had been trapping in northern British Columbia in the area between Teslin and Dease Lakes. Buttle learned that Nelson had come to the Dease Lake area by way of the Stikine River and prior to that had worked at the quartz mines at Anyox, B.C.

When the boat was finished, Nelson left the Post August 30, travelling up river. The Mounted Policeman at Ross River, Cpl. Claude Tidd, himself a newcomer to the district the Summer of 1927, was on patrol up the Pelly River at the time of Nelson's arrival. Although he returned a day or two before Nelson sailed up river, he did not meet the trapper, but did hear about him from Roy Buttle.

Arthur Nelson returned to Ross River Post June 16, 1928 and stayed around for a month until the trading store's annual supply boat arrived. He told Roy Buttle he had been trapping at Ross Lakes during the Winter. After the supplies came in, Nelson purchased a few provisions, a Savage .30–30 carbine and some .22 shells. He left suddenly in mid-July.

About a month later, three trappers, Oley Johnson, Norman Niddery and Oscar Erickson, were travelling up the south fork of the Stewart River. One morning as they were eating breakfast at Twin Falls, they noticed a stranger walking toward them. They invited him to join them, but he refused, saying he had camped overnight upstream a piece and had already eaten. He told them his name was Arthur Nelson and asked the way to Keno, Y.T.

Nelson said he had come from Ross River Post where he had built a boat and that he had hit the Stewart River above the Rogue River (a branch of the south fork of the Stewart). The three men did not see Nelson's boat as he was on foot when he approached their camp, and after learning the way to Keno, he hiked off in that direction.

Robert Levac who operated a trading store at Fraser Falls was the next man to come into contact with Nelson. The latter asked if he could stop over a day or two and Levac put him up in a spare cabin. Nelson wanted to get rid of some marten skins he had trapped, but Levac wouldn't buy them. He said he would bid on them, but suggested that Nelson take them to Mayo, Y.T., to sell.

Nelson kept pretty much to himself the two days he stayed at Fraser Falls, doing nothing but lie on his bunk. Occasionally he went into the store to buy something to eat, but he seemed moody and answered either a curt "yes" or "no" to any questions Levac asked. Before leaving, however, he did tell the trader that he had come from Ross River Post where he had built a boat the previous Summer, but that it had been wrecked up the Ross River. When Nelson departed, he did so without saying a word to Levac.

A few days later, Arthur Nelson appeared in Mayo. One of the first things he did was to peddle his marten skins at the Taylor and Drury store for $680. This transaction was completed between Nelson and Mr. W.H. Jeffrey of the firm on Aug. 30, 1928. Nelson received this amount in cash through an arrangement between Taylor and Drury and the Bank of Montreal in Mayo, as the store did not have that much cash on hand.

Before the Summer was out, Arthur Nelson joined trader James Mervyn who was ferrying his supplies up the Stewart River to his store at Lansing Creek. Mervyn put Nelson and his outfit off at the mouth of the south fork of the Stewart where the trapper spent the Winter of 1928–29, and when Mervyn was returning to Mayo on his boat the following Summer, he passed Nelson who was on a raft. The trader offered Nelson a ride, but the latter refused.

Prior to this (in March 1929) trapper Jack Alverson who first met Nelson in Mayo in 1928, stayed one night at Nelson's cabin at the mouth of the south fork of the Stewart, but once again Nelson was in one of his reticent moods and other than some talk about trapping, the only thing Alverson learned from Nelson was that he said he was Danish.

The next two Winters, Arthur Nelson spent trapping in the Macmillan River district between Ross River Post and Mayo. On two occasions he visited the trading store at Russell Creek run by Mr. Zimmerlee. Although Zimmerlee did not see Nelson carrying firearms at any time, the trapper asked for some shot-gun shells on one occasion when he purchased supplies at the store.

In the Spring of 1931, trapper P. Fredrickson of the Russell Post area sold a canoe to Arthur Nelson who paddled off up the Macmillan River and later some Indians in the district found the canoe abandoned on the upper waters of that river. Nelson returned to Mayo shortly after leaving the Macmillan River area, stopping off long enough to pick up a few provisions including an abundant quantity of kidney pills. Clerk Archie Currie of Binet's Store was rather startled when Nelson bought six boxes of pills, but Nelson was so uncommunicative that Currie thought twice about engaging the man in any conversation.

In May 1931, Arthur Nelson headed north to Keno. He stopped there briefly, making a small purchase in the store then managed by Joe Clifton and began walking north again. Frank Gillespie was having a cup of tea at the mouth of Crystal Creek one morning when Nelson happened upon his camp fire. Gillespie offered the traveller a cup, but Nelson refused, asking where the bridge on the McQuesten River was located as he said he was going to Haggart Creek. At the time, Nelson was laboring under the weight of a heavy shoulder pack.

"Snoose" Erickson and his partner, Sullivan, had a cabin on the Mc-Questen River in May 1931 when Nelson passed that way at noon one day carrying the heavy pack and a small rifle. Erickson asked the stranger to have lunch with them, but he curtly refused the offer and kept walking in the direction of eightmile cabin near the head of the Beaver River.

And from the head of the Beaver River, Yukon Territory, in May 1931, trapper Arthur Nelson seemingly vanished just as strangely as he had first suddenly appeared at Ross River Post nearly four years earlier.

On July 9, 1931, a stranger arrived at Fort McPherson, North-West Territories, under rather unusual circumstances. This man drifted down the Peel River from the direction of the Yukon Territory on a raft consisting of three large logs, to a spot about three miles above Fort McPherson. There he abandoned his crude "craft" and apparently with either little or no outfit, walked the remainder of the way into the Fort where he purchased supplies. He was said to be well stocked with cash.

This information was passed along to Inspr. Alexander Neville Eames who commanded the Western Arctic SubDistrict of the Royal Canadian Mounted Police (with headquarters at Aklavik, NWT) by Bishop Geddes. Cst. Edgar Millen, in charge of the Force's detachment at Arctic Red River, was sent instructions to interview the stranger.

Constable Millen located the newcomer in Fort McPherson July 21 where the latter was purchasing more supplies. He told the Policeman his name was Albert Johnson, that he had come into the country via the Mackenzie River and that he had spent the previous year on the prairies. Asked about his plans, he said he was undecided, but had considered going over the Rat (River) portage. He told Constable Millen he would not live in the settlement as he did not want to be bothered with anyone and wished to live entirely alone. The Policeman was aware that Johnson did not wish to divulge much in the way of information about himself.

Constable Millen later learned from Northern Traders Ltd. and the Hudson's Bay Company that Johnson was definitely getting an outfit together for a trip over the Rat portage. On the next patrol to Fort McPherson in August, Cst. Ronald Melville found that Albert Johnson left the settlement on July 28, paddling down river in a canoe he had purchased from an Indian. The policeman learned from Arthur N. Blake who lived at the mouth of the Husky River, that Johnson passed his place looking for the Rat River, but had apparently missed it, because a few days later he returned and stopped at Blake's home.

Johnson then paddled up a creek behind Blake's place which leads to the Rat River by a chain of lake portages, even though the settler told him he didn't think it was possible to reach the Rat that way with a large canoe. Johnson told Blake that he was going into the Yukon Territory and not returning and after leaving via the nearby creek, Blake did not see him again.

Johnson was not heard of again until December when some Indians trapping in the Rat River district reported to Constable Millen at Arctic Red River that a strange white man had been interfering with their trap lines. They said the man lived alone in a cabin about 15 miles up the Rat and believed his name was Albert Johnson.

At 7 a.m. Boxing Day, Cst. Alfred W. "Bunce" King and Spl. Cst. Joseph Bernard left Arctic Red River by dog team in bitterly cold weather to investigate the complaint and also to see if Johnson had a licence to trap. The previous Summer in Fort McPherson Constable Millen had told Johnson he would have to obtain a trapper's licence either at Arctic Red River or Aklavik if he intended working the area, but there was no record of his having done so.

Constables King and Bernard stopped overnight at Fort McPherson and by evening the next day, reached the mouth of the Rat River where they set up camp. They left early December 28 to cover the remaining 15 miles to Johnson's cabin.

"I spent nearly an hour at the cabin, knocking on the door and calling to Johnson and informed him who I was and that I wished to speak to him, but he refused to open the door or answer," Constable King noted in a subsequent report to his Officer Commanding. "I saw him peeping at me through a small window near the door, which he immediately covered when he saw me looking at him."

King decided to mush on to Aklavik in view of Johnson's attitude and obtain a search warrant. This was issued by Inspector Eames. And in view of Johnson's peculiar attitude the O.C. strengthened the patrol by adding Cst. Robert McDowell and Spl. Cst. Lazarus Sittichinlis. The four men left Aklavik at 7 a.m. December 30 and arrived at Johnson's cabin at 10.30 a.m. New Year's Eve.

The location of Johnson's cabin was only a few miles above the junction of the Rat River and Driftwood Creek — a place which a third of a century earlier had been dolefully tagged Destruction City. It was here in the bitter Winter of 1898 that four men died of scurvy while waiting for a break in the weather before continuing their trek to the Klondike in search of a fortune. The Rat River at this junction is marked by a series of rapids so severe that at Gold Rush time, the banks were lined with the wreckage of equipment — hence the name Destruction City.

"Bunce" King walked up to the door of Johnson's cabin, knocked, and asked, "Are you there, Mr. Johnson?" He had hardly uttered the words when a shot rang out and he slumped to the ground. Struggling to his feet he staggered toward some brush nearby, while Constable McDowell poured rifle shots through the wall of the cabin to try and draw the fire away from his wounded comrade. But the shooting continued from inside the shack and two bullets narrowly missed the other Policeman.

Seeing that King's condition was serious, Constable McDowell abandoned the idea of attacking Johnson's cabin and thought only of rushing the wounded man to where he could get medical aid. The two dog teams left Johnson's cabin about 11 a.m. and after travelling all night, covered the 80 miles to Aklavik in 20 hours. King was placed in the All Saints Mission under the care of Asst. Surgeon J.A. Urquhart.

In view of the seriousness of criminal charges now facing the man known as Albert Johnson, Inspector Eames decided to lead a larger party to the lonely cabin on the Rat River. Others making the trip were Constables McDowell, Millen, Specials Sittichiulis and Bernard, trappers Ernest Sutherland, Karl Gardlund and Knud Lang and 42 dogs. The Inspector also obtained 20 pounds of dynamite with caps and fuse, figuring he might have to blast away the walls of the cabin if Johnson still refused to answer the summons.

The party reached the mouth of the Rat Jan. 5, 1932 and replenished the stock of dog feed at Arthur Blake's store on the Husky River prior to leaving for Johnson's cabin. Indian guide Charlie Rat was asked to return from Fort McPherson where he had been spending New Year's to lead the party along an Indian trap-line trail south of the Rat as it was felt that travel along the river itself afforded Johnson too many opportunities for ambush.

The lower reaches of the Rat run through a large canyon over 1,000 yards wide in most places with the banks varying in height from 200 to 600 feet. The river itself is narrow and the valley is well timbered and covered with brush.

Due to the insistence of the guide, the party camped late that afternoon at a spot he said was only four miles from Johnson's cabin. Next day, however, it was found the Indian had made a mistake because when they reached the river, they found they were six miles above the shack, and so spent the remainder of the day — January 8 — returning to the camp of the previous night. Travel was slow and tortuous due to the fact that temperatures since New Year's Day had been hovering around 45 degrees below zero and the footing through loose snow and willows was extremely hazardous.

A check of the dog feed at the camp showed there was less than a two-night supply left and no chance of securing extra within 80 miles, so Inspector Eames decided to storm Johnson's cabin the following morning. They arrived half a mile from the shack at noon January 9—about an hour and a half after day-break at that time of year. Securing the dogs in the timber, they moved forward and partially surrounded the cabin. Approaching from the river bank, the party could hear Johnson moving about so the Inspector called to him to surrender but Johnson ignored the order.

The Officer decided they would attempt first to break the cabin door down by smashing it with rifle butts, and the three Policemen and three trappers started to rush the cabin. But the wily Johnson was a step ahead of the party and commenced firing as soon as they clambered over the top of the bank. It was then noticed that he had cleverly fashioned out loopholes above the bottom logs of the cabin in eight different locations.

Despite the hail of lead, two of the party were successful in bashing in the door as they raced around the cabin, but this only led to Johnson pouring out a steady fire through the opening. When the six returned to the cover of the river bank, Knud Lang told the Inspector he had seen Johnson crouching on the floor of the cabin—which incidentally appeared to be four or five feet below ground level—with two automatic pistols.

The party was compelled to build a fire in order to thaw out as the temperature was still 45 below. The siege kept up until after 3 the following morning—15 hours in all—as it seemed Johnson had an unending supply of ammunition. About 9 p.m. small charges of dynamite were thawed out and thrown at the walls of the shack in the hopes that some of the logs would become dislodged, but as far as could be seen, they had no effect and most did not even explode. One of the group succeeded in rushing through Johnson's fire to throw a larger charge on the roof, but all it did was to blow a small hole in the roof and not stun Johnson as had been hoped.

The last of the dynamite—four pounds—was lobbed against the front of the cabin at 3 a.m. January 10 where it exploded successfully. Karl Gardlund and Inspector Eames ran forward with a spotlight intending to blind Johnson, but the latter heard them coming and commenced firing. Gardlund switched on the lamp anyway, but Johnson's accurate fire blasted the light out of his hand within seconds. The Police party then retired to catch an hour's sleep before returning to Aklavik through necessity—feed for the dogs. They arrived January 12.

Two days later Constable Millen was sent back to Rat River with orders to camp two miles from Johnson's shack to see if the fugitive was still in the cabin. Millen took along Karl Gardlund. And on January 16, a party consisting of Inspector Eames, ex-Cst. John Parsons, QM Sgt. R.F. Riddell and S/Sgt. H.F. Hersey of the Royal Canadian Corps of Signals, Noel Verville, Ernest Sutherland, Frank Carmichael and Special Constable Sittichinlis left Aklavik in another attempt to apprehend Albert Johnson.

Upon reaching the mouth of the Rat, the officer was handed a note from an Indian sent by Constable Millen who reported that Johnson had taken his outfit and left the cabin. Inspector Eames recruited a party of 11 Louchoux Indians camped at the mouth of the Rat to join the posse. The party set up camp on the river nine miles above the cabin. A severe windstorm January 15, 16 and 17 had obliterated all tracks, so for the next four days, the party fanned out along the whole of the Rat River canyon to the Bear River, visiting old cabins and Johnson's trap-lines, but no evidence could be found of his having been there recently.

Inspector Eames now found that it was impossible to keep so large a party supplied with dog feed and provisions, so the Louchoux Indians were dismissed. The supplies on hand were enough to keep four men going for nine days, so Constable Millen, Army Sergeant Ridded, Noel Verville and Karl Gardlund were chosen to remain and travel as far as the Yukon Divide if necessary. Sergeant Riddell was equipped with a portable shortwave transmitter and receiver, from which he was able to receive messages from Aklavik and occasionally transmit back. The Inspector and the remainder of the party left for Aklavik once more, arriving January 23. He planned to keep hauling provisions to the mouth of the Rat and replace the four searchers after their nine-day stint.

Constable Millen's party scouted a portage from near Johnson's cabin to where the Bear River joins the Rat and from there, into the higher hills that had not previously been searched. On January 28, an Indian who had been with the large party the previous week, overtook the four men and told Constable Millen that two shots had been heard the previous day from the region around the mouth of the Bear. The party returned and was successful in picking up Johnson's track which led to a thick patch of timber five miles from the mouth of a creek which empties into the Rat a mile north of the Barrier River.

On January 30, the four-man party split up, Constable Millen and Verville electing to rush down the hill into a creek near where Johnson had holed up and Sergeant Riddell and Gardlund taking the opposite direction. They could hear Johnson coughing. Johnson apparently heard Millen and Verville coming down the incline and once when Millen went past an opening in the timber, the trapper snapped off a shot at him. All four men fired a volley blindly into the timber where they figured Johnson was hiding and when there was no return fire, they believed he had been hit.

Millen and Riddell entered the patch of timber and a shot rang out at extremely short range. Riddell scrambled back over the bank for cover, but Millen remained and fired two shots into the thicket. Three rang out in answer. When Sergeant Riddell scrambled over the bank farther away, he saw Constable Millen lying in the snow.

Riddell and Gardlund sought the cover of large spruce trees and began pouring fire into Johnson's thicket. Gardlund watched his chances and while Riddell kept firing, he crawled forward and reached the feet of the inert Millen. He undid the Policeman's boot laces and tied them together to form a handle and pulled the body over the bank. An examination showed that Edgar Millen was beyond help. Johnson's bullet had been deadly.

Two days before this, Army Staff Sergeant Hersey and Special Constable Sittichiulis left Aklavik to bolster Constable Millen's party, but en route met Sergeant Riddell who was returning to report the Policeman's death. Sittichiulis returned with Riddell, and Hersey continued on to assist Gardlund and Verville who were keeping watch on Johnson's activities. Riddell brought the sad news to Aklavik Sunday afternoon January 31.

Shortly after this, Special Constable Hatting, Rev. Thomas Murray and Ernest Sutherland left Aklavik to relieve Gardlund and Verville and two days later, in response to an appeal by Inspector Eames over the local amateur broadcasting station, he left for the site with Sergeant Riddell, Special Constable Sittichiulis, ex-Cst. Constant Ethier, Peter Strandberg and E. Maring. En route they were further bolstered by Knud Lang, Frank Carmichael and later at Rat River by ex-Cst. Arthur N. Blake, August Tardiff and John Greenland.

Near the Rat they were overtaken by a messenger with news that an airplane was leaving Edmonton, Alta., to lend assistance. The large group reached the spot where Constable Millen had been shot February 5 and discovered that Johnson had taken to the high ground. They spent the day searching the nine-mile ravine. They were now in the larger foothills which contained numerous creeks, deep ravines and canyons running from the watershed. Between these creeks was frozen tundra covered with hardpacked snow from the ceaseless strong winds.

Fresh tracks made by Johnson were located February 6, 7 and 8 in three different creeks four to six miles apart showing that he had been crossing the tundra from creek to creek and circling eight to ten miles back over his own tracks.

The well-known bush pilot, Capt. W.R. "Wop" May flew over the area February 7 and seeing the scouting party on the Barrier River, landed two miles away from them on the tundra. Cst. William S. Carter from

Edmonton bolstered the searchers and Captain May returned to Aklavik to start ferrying in provisions and dog feed. Prior to landing, he scouted the area ahead of the party and saw where tracks — undoubtedly Johnson's — ended at the Barrier River, apparently a camping spot.

Another patrol joined the party February 8 headed by Cst. Sidney W. May from Old Crow Detachment in the Yukon, Spl. Cst. John Moses, two trappers and two Indians. They came via La Pierre House, Bell River, Loon Lake and the Rat. Next day a patrol led by Constable May went as far as the last timber on the Barrier River and found a recent track made by Johnson heading for the Yukon Divide. Earlier, Indians in the party had told Inspector Eames that it was not possible for anyone to cross the divide alone, so it appeared that Johnson was becoming desperate.

With the exception of Constable May, Special Constable Moses and Frank Jackson, the posse returned to the Rat River where it was decided supplies could be landed easier. These three stayed at the Barrier River camp and on February 12, Constable May and Indian Peter Alexis rode into the camp on the Rat with a note from a trapper at La Pierre House, Harry Anthony, stating that a band of Indians had spotted a strange snow-shoe track near La Pierre House. The description of the track was that of Albert Johnson's.

In view of this, a change of plans was necessitated, and the following men formed a party headed for La Pierre House: Constable May, Specials Moses and Sittichiulis, Staff Sergeant Hersey, Joseph Verville, Constant Ethier, Frank Jackson and Peter Alexis.

Inspector Eames, Sergeant Riddell and Karl Gardlund flew with Wop May back to Aklavik to obtain larger snow-shoes for the party and on February 13, they crossed the divide to La Pierre House, landing on the Bell River in deep soft snow. A sudden storm prevented further flying that day, but on St. Valentine's Day, Captain May scouted the Bell River for 25 miles and found Johnson's track which he followed as far as the mouth of the Eagle River in the Yukon where it was lost in a maze of caribou tracks.

Searchers scoured the Bell and Eagle Rivers February 16, finally camping about 15 miles from the mouth of the latter where they were able to follow Johnson's trail quite easily as the snow was softer and there was little wind. He had, however, managed to take advantage of the caribou tracks and had hiked without snow-shoes in these for about ten miles.

As the searchers believed they were narrowing the gap on the fugitive now, they broke camp early February 17. Also, another danger threatened. Johnson was headed toward the cabin of a trapper named Barnstrum and although no one in the party seemed to know the exact whereabouts of the cabin, it was felt the man should be warned of Johnson's treachery. To further complicate things, it had been planned to have Wop May search for the cabin from the air the previous day, but dense fog prevented him from taking off from La Pierre House.

Before noon, the patrol which consisted of eight men with dog teams and three on foot, was approaching a sharp bend in the river when Staff Sergeant Hersey, driving the lead team at the time, spotted Johnson coming down river only 250 yards away. Johnson saw the posse at the same instant and quickly laced on his snow-shoes. Then he made a dash for the river bank, rifle in hand.

Hersey and Joseph Verville — driving the next team — drew their rifles and started firing at Johnson from the centre of the river. They were quickly joined by Karl Gardlund and Frank Jackson, and in a short time, the whole party began moving up-stream, some on the river and others on either bank. All this time, Johnson was firing rapidly at the pursuers, but suddenly his fire ceased and he started to run back up river. Before he stopped shooting, however, his deadly rifle had taken a further toll — Staff Sergeant Hersey had fallen in the snow, shot through the lungs.

Johnson was running back in his own tracks, stopping occasionally to turn and fire, and was actually drawing away from the party. He was making for the opposite river bank which was not so steep. Called upon once again to surrender, Johnson ignored the command and kept running for the bank, whereupon the posse threw a concentrated volley at him. Reaching the bank, Johnson threw himself in the deep, soft snow and began to dig in, using his heavy pack as a cover. He then resumed firing.

But this time, the effect of numbers began to tell, and with men completely surrounding Johnson and a few on higher ground firing down on him, he was no longer shooting back.

"At 12.10 p.m., (February 17) it was found that Johnson was dead, having desperately resisted to the last," Inspector Eames noted later in his report. And so the 48-day "Arctic Circle war", which started out as nothing more than a routine investigation and ended in the deaths of two men and the serious wounding of two others, ended.

All of Albert Johnson's effects were gathered up and checked. A total of $2,410 in cash was found on his corpse in denominations of $20, $50 and $100 as well as two United States' $5 bills and one $10. There were also two small glass jars one containing five pearls (later evaluated at $15) and five pieces of gold dental work four dwt. ($3.20), the other, 13 dwt. alluvial gold ($9.36).

Firearms found in his possession included a model 99 Savage .30–30 rifle, an Ivor Johnson sawed-off 16-gauge shotgun and a .22 Winchester rifle, model 58 with cut-down stock. His supply of ammunition included 39 .30–30 shells, 84 .22 shells and four 16-gauge shot-gun shells. There were other miscellaneous items including packages containing a total of 32 pills.

Significantly enough, there was no trace of any written matter found either on Johnson's body, at his cabin or at any of the caches and camps he had made in the area of the Rat River. The two automatic pistols seen in Johnson's hand January 9 by Knud Lang were not located. An old canoe was at the cabin, and about 300 yards away, a carefully concealed stage cache containing a quantity of provisions.

Johnson's cabin was constructed of logs about a foot in diameter. The inside dimensions were roughly eight by 12 feet. The door stood four feet high, of which three feet were above ground level and the roof was made of heavy poles covered with frozen sod two feet thick. The walls were reinforced with extra logs and frozen sod 20 inches above ground level. The floor of the cabin was not as far below ground level as it first appeared, perhaps because of the depth of the hard snow outside. It was 38 inches below ground level, providing Johnson with plenty of protection when the seige was taking place.

A physical description of Johnson — after death — supplied by Assistant Surgeon Urquhart listed his height as five foot nine, estimated weight 145 to 150 pounds. He had light brown hair which was receding, pale blue eyes, snubbed upturned nose, moderately prominent cheek bones, lobed ears, low set and close to the head. The only mark on the body was a small wart or mole, two inches to the left of the spine in the mid-lumbar region. The Surgeon set his age between 35 and 40 years, the size of his feet as 9 1/4 inches and said his teeth had been well cared for but contained numerous fillings.

The task of identifying the man known as Albert Johnson was one that has never been successfully concluded. All but one of the few existing photos of Albert Johnson was of little use in helping establish the man's identity. All the Force had to go on was that he had told the late Constable Millen in Fort McPherson that his name was Albert Johnson; the Indians complaining about trapline interference said they too believed this was his name.

Fingerprints taken from his corpse were sent to both Ottawa and Washington, D.C., but they were not linked to anyone with a criminal record in either country.

First reports of the other stranger in the lower Yukon who called himself Arthur Nelson came to the RCMP in August 1933. From the physical descriptions and "lone wolf" attitudes of the two men, it seemed likely that they were one and the same, but this has never been proved conclusively.

There are, however, some facts that make it seem likely Nelson and Johnson were identical. Sgt. James R. Purdie of the Dawson C.I.B. made inquiries at the banks there to see if he could trace any of the currency found on Johnson's body. The Bank of Montreal traced two bills. One $50 bill was received at the bank as one of a shipment of 100 such bills on Sept. 7, 1926 and the other — also a $50 bill — was one of 100 bills sent to the branch at Mayo Mar. 22, 1928.

There is no actual record of either Johnson or Nelson having been in Dawson although Cpl. Arthur Thornthwaite of Old Crow Detachment in a report dated the same day Johnson was shot said that a local Indian gave a description of a man he worked with on the 12-mile dredge out of Dawson in 1930 and except for this man having brown hair (Johnson's was light brown) they seemed identical. The Indian said the man called himself Al Johnson and left the district in the fall of 1930 after telling the Indian he was going to the Peel River district to trap alone.

It is reasonable to assume that Nelson received the second $50 bill from Mayo, as on Aug. 30, 1928 — less than six months after the bill was sent to Mayo — Nelson received $680 in cash from the Bank of Montreal there from selling marten skins to the firm of Taylor and Drury.

The firearms found in Johnson's possession were not successfully traced due to company records having been destroyed, but it is significant to note that Arthur Nelson purchased a .30–30 Savage rifle at the Ross River Post, along with some .22 shells and two of Johnson's guns were a .30–30 Savage rifle and a Winchester .22. Mr. W.W. Douglas who worked for Northern Traders Limited in Fort McPherson recalled selling Johnson a 16-gauge single barrel shot-gun and a box of 25 shells on July 12, 1931, three days after he arrived at that post.

All the persons who had seen or talked to Arthur Nelson between Ross River Post where he was first seen and McQuesten River where he was last seen were eventually shown facial photos taken of Albert Johnson after death, and most thought it could be the same man, although none could be sure. Johnson was in such an emaciated condition at the time of his death (145 to 150 pounds) that it is explainable that his gaunt features would look somewhat different from the sturdy Nelson (170 pounds).

There was one other question that arose when attempts were made to link Johnson and Nelson and that was whether or not a man could travel from McQuesten River near Keno — Nelson was last seen there in May 1931 — to Fort McPherson, a distance of some 250 miles, in just over two months on foot — Johnson first appeared there July 9, 1931. To do so, he would have to cross over the Ogilvie Range. This was answered by Supt. Thomas B. Caulkin who commanded the RCMP at Dawson. He said he knew a man who left Mayo on June 28, 1934, went to Fort McPherson and returned to Mayo in the latter part of August 1934, thus doing double the trip in a two-month period.

Over the years since this bizarre affair, the Force has answered numerous inquiries from persons all over the world claiming to be relatives of "The Mad Trapper From Rat River" as he has been described in numerous articles, but in each case the RCMP has patiently checked photos and descriptions, and in all, has has had to write back, "we find that . . . is not identical with the man known as Albert Johnson".

19

The Darling Patrol
May–October 1910

D/Commr. W.H. Kelly (Rtd.)

D/Commr. W.H. Kelly's account of the Darling Peace-Yukon Patrol
gives a vivid picture of the hardships faced by the early members of the
Force. In 1910 Sgt. John (Jock) Darling, then 34 years old, Constables
Robert Cranford Bowen, 27, and Armand St. Laurent, 21, travelled 1,700
miles from Athabasca Landing in Alberta to Whitehorse in the Yukon. The
purpose of their trip was to follow and clear a trail built five years earlier
by Supt. Charles Constantine from Fort St. John, British Columbia, to
the government telegraph line north of Hazelton, British Columbia, and
then via Telegraph Creek and Atlin to Whitehorse in the Yukon.

Building the wagon trail through the Rockies was one of the most
unusual assignments ever to come the way of the Force. In the first year,
Constantine, along with two other officers and thirty men, built a total
of 94 miles northwest towards Fort Grahame. The following year 208
miles were completed, and by 1907 the road extended 104 miles north of
Hazelton where it was decided to use an existing trail for the remainder
of the route north to Whitehorse.

This was a period of great optimism and grand plans for the opening
of the Northwest Territories. The policy of the federal government was
to make Edmonton the gateway to the North and the wagon trail from
St. John to Whitehorse was intended to give the city access to the rich
natural resources to the north.

Constantine's work, however, was all to little or no purpose. When
Darling and his men travelled the route in 1910, three years after its
completion, they experienced much difficulty from fallen timber and encountered hardly a soul. Their story follows.   Ed.

For every major northern patrol made by members of the NWMP and RNWMP and recorded fully in written history, hundreds of lesser ones have received little attention. While doing research for a recent book on RCMP horses, I came across one such patrol: The Darling Peace-Yukon Patrol of 1910. Only a brief mention is made of the patrol in two RNWMP annual reports. Fortunately one of its members, a Constable Bowen, kept a diary and I was able to get a copy of it from the RCMP Museum in Regina.

Darling and his two constables, Bowen and St. Laurent, must have been filled with apprehension as they planned the patrol. They were undoubtedly familiar with the earlier hardships of the Moodie and Constantine parties. They would have known that Insp. Moodie who was sent out to explore the trail in 1897 lost 24 pack horses and six saddle horses either to the hardships of the trail or as feed for his dogs, and that Constantine, who had built the trail, had had an equally difficult time.

Nevertheless some members envied them their trip. Bowen's diary entry on May 3 describes how he spent the evening before the patrol: "Denny La Nauze and I lay on top of a haystack with a bottle of Irish — one long Irish lament because he was not going." Incidentally, La Nauze got his chance later. He became a northern traveller of outstanding ability and later an assistant commissioner.

On May 4, Darling, Bowen and St. Laurent left Athabasca Landing with saddle horses, a team and wagon, and eleven pack horses. Accompanying the patrol for the first twenty days was Frank Anderson. For his efforts he was paid $1 a day.

From the start the men found travel difficult. The first day they crossed through burnt timberland and then a stretch of heavy green timber. On the second day the wagon turned over twice and had to be reloaded. Not long after that delay the patrol was forced to stop and cut trees to hold back a bush fire. Later on the same day a pack horse fell on its back while crossing a creek.

The horses created special problems. Early on in the expedition it became apparent that the team and wagon could not keep up with the pack horses and always arrived in camp an hour or so after them. Another problem arose from the ease with which the horses were able to wander away at night, in spite of being tethered and hobbled. Much time was wasted searching for them in the mornings. More serious, the routine hobbling of the horses gave rise to stiffening of the fetlocks. This, combined with travelling through muskeg for long periods of time, created difficulties with their feet. Other problems were caused by the lack of good pasture on some parts of the trail. Describing his horse problems on one of the easier days, Bowen noted that "the team got bogged down" and that there was trouble "with a little sorrel, 'Teddy,' — easy, but had a bad habit of trying to chase his tail."

From time to time the patrol came across signs of human habitation — the occasional trapper's cabin and even a store. At one point on the trip they passed old flat sleighs left behind by the Moodie patrol of 1897. Occasionally they came across a police cabin built by Constantine.

By the time the patrol arrived at the RNWMP post at Lesser Slave Lake the horses were tired and it was necessary to spend a couple of days resting them.

The men, too, enjoyed the rest and the comfortable and pleasant quarters. They used the time to repair equipment and acquire supplies for the more arduous days ahead.

On May 16 they set out again leaving two pack horses behind. The first of frequent references in the diary to mosquitoes "being bad" starts here. Soon after setting out much of their time was spent chopping deadfalls out of their path. This entailed regularly sharpening axes as well as frequently shoeing horses.

May 18 was a steady day of rain. There was a Halley's comet that year and Bowen commented in his diary, somewhat dryly: "Halley's comet got its tail wet."

By May 24 the patrol had reached the Peace River, somewhere southwest of the present town of Peace River. The men now began to supplement their food supplies by shooting game birds. From Bowen's description of their early efforts it was a good thing they had supplies in the wagon.

Next, rain and snow made the going hazardous. One day the wagon got stuck in a muskeg and the men had to unload it, and pull it out with the aid of a block and tackle attached to the wagon pole. Within fifty yards of reloading the wagon it bogged down again breaking both whippletrees. During the delay required to repair the whippletrees a thunderstorm came up and when the patrol reached the Montaignais River the men had to build a bridge across its swollen waters. Even after such a disappointing day there was no complaint in Bowen's diary.

By May 29 the patrol had been on the trail 25 days and still had 139 to go. Bowen's entry in his diary for that day recorded more horse trouble:

> Packed ponies; sorrel frisky. Gladys kicked her pack under her belly and hit out. The rest followed, the black got hung up on a poplar and the whole outfit stampeded. All the packs except three strewn over four miles of trail, saddle and lots of straps broken. Camped at 1.30 p.m. having travelled five miles. Collected debris and had dinner. . . . Fixing shoes on horses, mending saddles and harness etc. until 10 p.m. Showery all day.

The next day Bowen made his first reference to making bannock. This activity became a regular item in his diary along with the shoeing of horses.

By now it was early June. Morning frosts were still common, but the cold mornings did nothing to curb the hordes of mosquitoes and black flies that appeared when the days warmed up.

Just before the patrol arrived at Fort St. John Constable Bowen recorded what he called a "desperate" situation. The men were fixing part of the trail when a landslide occurred creating more work before the trail could be cleared again. Soon after this mishap Bowen discovered that he had lost his one and only pipe while crossing a river. He hastened back across the river and after a lengthy and frantic search found his beloved pipe. This incident he included in his diary, but the last words for that day were: "Saint [St. Laurent] got a duck."

The patrol arrived at Lake St. John in British Columbia on June 5 and remained there until the 8th. Here they met Frank Anderson who had left the patrol on May 24 at the Peace River and was now working for the British Columbia government. He and some other friends royally entertained the group.

The next 600 miles were to be the most difficult of the whole patrol. This part of the trip took them through deep valleys heavily drifted with snow, over high mountains where deep snow covered what little trail existed, above the tree line, and over the Continental Divide.

Just west of Lake St. John, they found the first mile posts that had been erected by Constantine when he had built the road some three or four years earlier. They also found the bridges he had built — now rotten beyond repair due to his use of unpeeled poplar trees. Even when a bridge looked passable it could not be trusted and horses often put their legs through the floor poles. One horse put all four legs through and had to be physically rolled off the bridge.

In addition to the now more frequent deadfalls, rotten bridges and bad trail, the patrol began to encounter frequent bush fires. This required many hours of backbreaking work, often until late at night. There was never any complaint however, in Bowen's diary. The most he would say was that they were tired.

Entering good fishing country helped to improve their spirits, and Bowen's diary entries are not without their light-hearted anecdotes. He reports catching eight Arctic trout in Beaver Tail Creek and also a char which was found to have a beaver tail in its stomach! One wonders if the creek had its name before Bowen caught the char, or afterwards. The fishing at this point was so good that they remained to catch fish and smoke them so that they could be carried with them for some time without rotting.

The occasional bear created difficulties. On June 14 the patrol met a bear on the trail and the horses stampeded. The trail at this point was all but obliterated and the lead horse did not notice a rotten bridge until he was alongside it. Then he tried to get onto the bridge from the side and fell back into a muddy creek. The saddle was broken, and it was some time before it could be repaired and the patrol proceed. And of course, more time was lost in retrieving the horses that had run away.

The hard travel demanded that the men take a day or two off occasionally to rest. At mile 103 they took a typical rest day. They washed saddle blankets, repaired equipment, shod horses and did some fishing. When they started up again they found it hard going as a result of recent heavy rains. The team found the going particularly difficult and, as usual, lagged behind the pack horses.

In the distance now they could see the Rocky Mountains, beautiful and majestic, but a source of great hardship. The continuous rains and the melting of mountain snows affected the trails and the rising water in the creeks and rivers made them more difficult for the patrol to cross. On June 22 Bowen wrote that the patrol passed over "Devil's Canon [sic] Summit," probably near present day Mont Kenny. This was still a great distance from the much higher Continental Divide which they would have to cross in due course.

About this time Bowen recorded that one horse had taken a "header" into a creek and almost in the same breath that "forget-me-nots, greater and lesser celandine and wood anemone" had been noticed along the trail.

Bowen made his first complaint of the trip at mile 172 on June 23, when the patrol camped at the Ospika River. St. Laurent had cut his thumb with a knife thus making Bowen the permanent dishwasher, much to his annoyance!

To cross the Ospika the patrol had to cut green logs to make a raft. "This," wrote Bowen, "was the hardest day yet." First the horses had to be swum across the river. St. Laurent rode one of them and carried the hobbles to make sure the horses would not wander away while the men were rafting the wagon across. At 5.00 a.m. the men started to build a raft large enough to take the wagon and supplies across the river. Unfortunately the raft had to be rebuilt because it contained too much heavy, green, timber. The lighter raft, however, could only carry lighter loads and eight trips were required to complete the crossing. The river swells swept six inches over the raft. To make matters worse swift water carried the raft down river beyond the proposed landing point. As a result, a tracking trail had to be cut along the river from where the raft landed to the chosen landing place upriver so that the raft could be pulled back there and unloaded. It also rained all morning and most of the afternoon.

On June 28 the patrol reached Fort Grahame on Lake Williston, a very important supply point for Constantine's supply system in the spring of 1907. Darling expected supplies to have been delivered for him at this point, but finding none he pushed on, travelling now in high mountain country over the Omineca Mountains.

Horse problems continued. One horse got its foot caught between two rocks and cut off its hind hock as it released itself, "but not too badly," commented Bowen. Then St. Laurent's horse fell off the trail into a muskeg, requiring the help of all three before it was extricated.

By July 1 the patrol had been on the trail nearly two months and was making its way through high mountain passes. They could see snow falling on the mountain tops and according to Bowen the scenery was "alpine". By July 8 the patrol was at mile 308 and although the trail was somewhat better, the mosquitoes were still bad and the mornings brisk. Each morning found a quarter of an inch of ice on the water buckets. The patrol was nearing Bear Lake and running short of food. Instead of camping when they should have, however, they continued on another sixteen miles to Bear Lake. It was during this sixteen mile stretch that they crossed the Continental Divide, an especially arduous time because a trail through the heavy snowdrifts had to be broken for the horses. In this same part of the trail the patrol crossed two creeks. No doubt in reference to the crossing of the Continental Divide, Bowen noted: ". . . and a 10,000 foot summit with snowdrifts six to ten feet deep."

After this description one is surprised by the next item in Bowen's diary. It reads somewhat poetically: "passed a lake full of yellow water lillies . . . and crossed some beautiful little prairies full of ripe strawberries, the scent from which, crushed by the ponies' feet, filled the air."

When the patrol arrived at Bear Lake, almost the end of the trail built by Constantine in 1905–07, Indians met them with good news: from Bear Lake to Telegraph Creek (a distance of about 200 miles), the Indians said, the trail was reasonably good. When the men continued, however, they found instead "a regular goat track". Although there was no deadfall to cut through there were innumerable creeks and rivers each requiring a great deal of work cutting a track to pull the rafts back upriver from where they had been carried by the swiftly moving water during the crossing.

On July 18 the patrol came to within two miles of the Ashcroft-Yukon telegraph line. A camp was set up. Once again the horses wandered away and Bowen notes facetiously: ". . . they hit off for southern Alberta." By 11.00 a.m. the next morning, eight of the horses had been rounded up but it took most of the afternoon to find the others. The same day they met a telegraph lineman who informed them that King Edward VII had died.

Darling had been promised that supplies would be delivered for him at this point but like the earlier incident no supplies had arrived. Being near the telegraph line he was able to wire the commissioner at RNWMP headquarters in Regina who instructed Darling to patrol to Hazelton, about 100 miles to the south, to get supplies, and not wait for the pack train to deliver them.

By August 12 the patrol, freshly equipped with new supplies, set off from Hazelton on the return trip back to Telegraph Creek about 250 trail miles to the northwest. Crossing innumerable rivers including the larger ones such as the Klappan, the Skeena and the Stikine, they passed through territory that was probably the most picturesque and the most arduous of the whole patrol. They were often above the tree line and the mountain trails were tortuous. They had to travel many miles to advance only a few toward their goal.

It took them a month to get to Telegraph Creek. Upon his arrival Darling again wired the commissioner to inform him of his whereabouts. He was instructed to continue on as originally planned. After resting and enjoying the hospitality of the local citizens at Telegraph Creek for five days, they set off on September 19, for Atlin on Atlin Lake, about 200 miles north-north-west. They were about four and a half months out of Athabasca Landing.

It was on this section that the only horse to die on the patrol met its fate. It was Teddy, the sorrel who liked to bite his tail. Bowen describes the incident: "Teddy was found drowned in four inches of water in morning — hung up by hobbles on a stump and fell with head in a small creek."

The patrol arrived at Atlin on October 5 but it still had to go on to Whitehorse in the Yukon about 125 miles to the north. The commissioner had ordered Darling to proceed from Atlin to Whitehorse by land trail, but Atlin Lake ran north into the Yukon and Darling decided to take the steamboat, the S.S. *Atlin*, instead. Bowen's last notation in his diary reads:

> After this patrol, despite the orders of the Commissioner to proceed by trail, crossed over the portage [between Atlin Lake and Tagish Lake] on a wet rainy night in which the small steam engine stampeded the ponies into a particularly wet bush. Took the boat on Tagish Lake and arrived at Whitehorse on October 15th. Shipped outfit [presumably the team, wagon and supplies] from Carcross to Whitehorse by train and took ponies over the trail. A few miles out of Whitehorse met McLaughlin, who took Jock Darling away with him to hunt for a chap who had swiped some gold bricks. The patrol practically ended at Atlin.

Attached is an envelope containing forget-me-nots and other flowers picked on the Laurier [sic] Pass, Continental Divide etc. and maple leaves from the Skeena Valley.

No doubt Sergeant Darling submitted his own lengthy official report, but in the annual reports of 1910 and 1911, his commanding officer disposed of the patrol in a few brief words. In the 1910 report he mentioned that the patrol was underway, and in 1911 he said:

Sergeant Darling cleared the trail as much as possible and gathered some useful information regarding different routes in the northern part of British Columbia. The distance covered would be upwards of 1700 miles, over rugged and mountainous country.

There were no medals, no commendations, just a simple notation of a job completed.

20

Writing Home From Pangnirtung

Const. T. Bolstad

Mrs. Frances Fisher, Lumby, British Columbia, forwarded the following letter, excerpts of which describe life at Pangnirtung on Cumberland Peninsula, Baffin Island, Northwest Territories. The author, ex-S/Sgt. T.A. Bolstad, who was just a young constable at the time, served with the Force until his retirement on May 3, 1950, and became a member of the Okanagan Division of the Veterans' Association. Bolstad died April 29, 1990, at Oliver, British Columbia. Ed.

September 1, 1931

Dear Mother, Dad and Gene,

The old wisecrack about the ship coming in has finally come true for our small crowd at Pang [sic]. The least welcome thing was not my mail, so I might as well start off by thanking you all for your letters and the parcel; Gene's letter and the drawings were among the best.

As you all seem very interested in this new life of mine, I will endeavour to give you a few highlights of the past year. To begin with, I must say that all the talk of hardships and suffering in the North is rubbish. Of all the parts of Canada that I have been in, this country takes first place for climate and things of interest. Every new day holds a chance for some novel experience or event, and there is therefore a spice about the country that is not found outside. Only now and again does a person feel a few moments of lonesomeness, wishing to leave for a few days, but the country and most of the people in it do not allow this state to last. Time passes with a speed seldom never encountered anywhere else.

These following facts about the weather will undoubtedly startle you. When you probably experienced several occasions of −50°F weather and below, the lowest we registered on (only) one occasion was −44°F, and seldom did the mercury drop lower than −32°F. On January 2, 1931,

176

the temperature was 48°F, and on several occasions during midwinter, the readings were between 15 and 20°F. On the other hand, when you people swelter in the heat, which sends your old thermometer up around 100°F, we sit around quite comfortable in about 55°F; our highest this year being 63°F. From this you will readily see where we have a decided advantage over all the rich people who go South in the winter and North in the summer, for we can sit in one place and enjoy a good moderate temperature all year round without going to the bother of moving.

Another item which will probably surprise you is the comfort with which winter trips are made. All winter clothing for such trips is made of deerskins and is extremely comfortable. A complete issue of clothing consists of an outside "kooletak" with the hair turned out, an inside kooletak with the hair turned in, one pair of outside pants with the hair out, one pair of inside pants with the hair turned in, two or three pairs of (deerskin) socks, one pair of (deerskin) boots, and one or two pair of sealskin boots. About three pairs of mitts (one pair deerskin and two of sealskin) are of course necessary. The complete outfit requires nothing beneath it, but as a general rule it proves to be much too warm; so the inside kooletak and pants are supplanted by underwear, a sweater and a pair of ordinary pants. The entire outfit is very light and much less cumbersome than its appearance would make one think. When on the trail, it is necessary to keep this outfit dry. When entering the snow house at night, all snow must be promptly shaken from the clothing, mitts and socks, which are usually wet with sweat, and hung over the fire to dry.

Trips are usually made by one or two white men and one Native, generally with two teams of dogs. The average dog team consists of about 8 to 10 dogs, but for long trips the number is usually increased to about 15. The sleighs, better known as "komatik", are usually about 15 feet long, and there are anywhere between one-and-a-half to two-and-a-half feet between the runners. A good team will handle a load of well over a thousand pounds.

Another thing I have found quite erroneous is the bad reputation given to sleigh dogs by outsiders. I was inclined to be a bit leery of them when I first came, but I find now that they only want to be friendly with everyone. Unless badly frightened, they would not bite. Farther south and in the Mackenzie River district, it is necessary to keep dogs tied up for convenience. This naturally upsets their temper, so that in these places there are no doubt a good number of savage dogs, for they have reason to be. I am quite certain that no young pup ever cherishes the hope of some day growing up to be a famous mankiller. They are not very particular about the food they eat. In the winter when food is scarce, they chew anything that they can — all harness and whips must be piled on the top of the snow house, out of their reach, or in a snow cache. When the dogs get real hungry, young pups constitute a rare delicacy. No one, however, can blame the dogs for wanting to eat when they can, nor help but admire their splendid spirit, when one sees the way they carry on with a heavy load through cold and wet, often without food for days.

As there is no timber in this country, the cooking must be done on primus stoves which burn either gasoline or kerosene. Working on the same principle as a blowtorch or gas lamp, they put up very good heat, and besides being much quicker for cooking than a wood fire, they have the remaining virtue of being smokeless. The only drawback is that the fuel constitutes considerable weight on a long trip. The "grub" usually consists of hard biscuits, beans, bacon, oatmeal, tea and coffee and whatever game you run across in the course of the journey.

It doesn't sound very appetizing, but when a person has been travelling all day in the cold, anything that is eatable is good. A good illustration of the fact was given when Cpl. Margetts and Cst. Fisher were away camping for a month last fall. They were attempting to reach Pang by an overland route, but failed because strong winds prevented ice from forming in a fiord that they had to cross. They got lost getting back to their camp and were delayed for a day during which time Margetts froze his feet quite badly. When they finally got back, they had nothing to eat but frozen fish and biscuits. The fish had not been cleaned and it would take some time to do it as they were frozen solid. Refusing to wait, they dumped the fish as is, into a pot, boiled them up, and ate them.

My biggest worry when I first realized that I was coming into this country, was how people kept warm when sleeping outside in the dead of winter. I was certainly surprised at the absolute comfort of a snooze in a snow house. I had always wondered whenever I saw a picture of a snow house, how the Eskimo managed to keep the blocks in place. When I saw the simplicity of the scheme, I was ashamed that I had not figured it out for myself long ago. The key to the whole business is that a snow house is a spiral of snow blocks growing ever narrower until it reaches a peak at the top. Instead of having to stay in midair with no means of support, each new block is placed on top of the bottom row and jammed against the preceding block.

As the snow has a tendency to stick and freeze as soon as it melts, the blocks rest quite contentedly with only one corner unsupported. If properly set in, a block may be placed horizontally in this manner and a man can climb over the top of a finished snow house with no fear of its falling. When finished, all cracks are chinked with snow, a hole is cut in the top for ventilation, another for a door in the side; in you crawl, block up the door once again and there you are.

The bed consists of a large tarpaulin spread over the floor of the "igloo" to keep the remainder of the bedding dry (since heat from a sleeping body melts the snow beneath), one deerskin as mattress, and the marvel known as the eiderdown sleeping robe. This robe, when spread out, measures 90 inches by 90 inches, and folds over once, the bottom and side edges being closed with snaps. Once inside the bag, the icy chill soon leaves and though things get pretty frosty inside the igloo, once the primus stoves are put out, the occupant of the bag snores peacefully on, as though the cold never existed.

I made two long winter patrols and another by boat, last fall, besides going on the HBC's whale drive and numerous hunting trips. All three trips covered a distance of over 350 miles each and were overflowing with things of interest and wonderful scenery. The two overland trips to Davis Straits especially took us through some splendid country of mountains and glaciers that would gladden the heart of any tourist. Unfortunately, the poor light in winter makes it impossible to secure any good photographs.

There is nothing unpleasant about summer trips as they merely constitute a pleasant cruise in a motorboat, though a strong wind can suddenly make things very unpleasant. Fisher and Dr. Stuart had a very narrow escape last fall, being saved only by the efficiency of the Native engineer who managed to get the motor started, and kept it running in a very high sea until they reached a safe anchorage. Such cases fortunately are not the rule and motor-boating constitutes one of the joys of the country.

The inconvenience of poor communications was illustrated during a trip to Padler [Padle Fiord—Ed.], Davis Straits, I took with Dr. Stuart, to bring in a young Native who had been injured in a fall from a cliff. He was hurt on December 26, 1930, suffering a broken elbow, one fractured collarbone and the other dislocated. The news reached Pang on January 12, 1931, by two Natives from Padler. Because there was not sufficient dog feed in Pang to carry us over to Padler, our Natives were dispatched immediately to hunt seals, but as these are pretty scarce and hard to procure in the dead of winter, it was not until January 18, that they returned with enough food for the trip. We started the next day, and reached Padler on January 26, one month after the accident occurred. Fortunately he was young and the fractured and dislocated collarbone knitted themselves again and are quite alright. The broken elbow however, while knitting, formed new bone in the joint and ruined its working. The most Doc could do, when we got him back to Pang, was to reduce the stiffness slightly so that he still has considerable use of his arm.

It was on this trip that I also received my first lesson in dentistry. Doc was suffering from a toothache when we left, and on the second day out, he couldn't stand it any longer. I was delegated to have out the tooth. We were stopped at a Native camp and had only a candle for light. Doc held the candle, while I clamped the forceps on the tooth and pulled. He sure had plenty of sand to stand it and I'm darned sure that I was shaking harder than he was when I finally got it out. Later on at Pang, I had to pull another tooth for Doc and this ordeal was no more pleasant than the first one. I also participated in three operations with Doc giving anaesthetic, so I have had several good experiences during the year.

One of the most interesting events of the year is the HBC's white whale drive, which takes place as soon as ice conditions permit boats to run. The whale fat produces a very fine oil and the hides make up into quillcases and leather bags etc., while the meat is used for dog feed. The drive is held in a fiord about 80 miles from Pang, and occupies a full week, thus furnishing a very pleasant outing. The whales are absolutely harmless and are easily frightened, so it is an easy matter, for several motor-boats, by running back and forth across the fiord and gradually working into it, to drive the whales to the end where they are left high and dry at low tide. They are killed and skinned on the spot, the hides and meat are salted, and the oil put in barrels to await shipment. We got about 450 whales which netted about 200 barrels of oil. The police, of course, take part in the drive merely to procure dog feed, of which we realized about six boat loads.

The unfortunate Cramer and Paquet landed here on August 3, on their way to Copenhagen, Denmark, and left the next day. They naturally caused a great deal of excitement amongst the Natives — it was the first plane they had ever seen. We now hear, with much regret, that the plane was lost and that Cramer's body has been picked up off the coast of Norway. Luck certainly was against poor Cramer on his third attempt to reach Europe over this route. He had lost a plane at Port Burwell, Heron Straits, a few years ago, and another on the Greenland ice cap. And now, when he had put practically all the hazardous part of the journey behind him and was almost within sight of his goal, his luck turned against him once more and he lost everything. Paquet was the radio operator and was just newly-married, which adds more tragedy to the affair. They were both splendid fellows and deserved the success that they so nearly achieved but it all goes to prove that Fate is a queer personage.

I am more or less undecided about plans for the future, now that things are so bad outside. I hope to have about fifteen hundred dollars in cash when I get out, and if money is worth what it seems to be, I should be able to do things with it. Keep your eyes on anything that looks like a good proposition until I get out next year and we will see what we can do.

Right now we are in the midst of "Customs and Fur Export Tax" duties for the HBC ship, so I will have to close this now. I hope you will all be well when I get out next year, and I am certainly looking forward to it. I will not undertake that trip all the way to North Sydney, as I will have to take the train for Ottawa a few hours after getting off the boat, so it would hardly be worth it. The best thing would be to visit Uncle Fred when I can get leave from Ottawa.

Goodbye & love until next year,

P.S. Broadcasts to the North will start on Saturday October 3, and continue every Saturday, as well as on December 24. Station KDKA continued to send messages until quite late last Spring, after the schedule was finished, so that although the schedule is supposed to be finished on February 27 1932, you will be quite safe in continuing to send messages until the end of May.

Editor's Note

Obviously, Constable T.A. Bolstad describes his own unique view of the North.

East Through the North-West Passage

RCMP *Quarterly* Staff

Skippered by the veteran Arctic navigator, Sergeant Larsen, the eight-ton RCMP patrol ressel *St Roch* proudly sailed into Sydney, N.S., on Oct. 8, 1942, after a history-making voyage of ten thousand miles from Vancouver across the roof of the world.

The recent voyage of the *St Roch* through the North-West Passage is destined to rank high in the annals of the Force. Twenty-eight months after leaving Vancouver — months of relentless winter, isolation, the monotony of vast space devoid of vegetation, gigantic icebergs threatening to crush and destroy — the *St Roch* dropped anchor in Halifax Harbour. Sgt. Henry A. Larsen, captain and navigator, manoeuvered through ice, snow, fog and treacherous currents, much of the time in uncharted waters, and brought his crew safely to port. The venture was another of those routine jobs that make history.

Completely equipped for northern work, even to two-way radio, the RCMP auxiliary schooner *St Roch* is powered with a 150 h.p. Union Diesel engine, supplemented by an eighteen h.p. auxiliary Diesel to operate pumps, lighting plant, generators and so on. She is 105 feet long with a twenty-five-foot beam and was built in Vancouver during the winter of 1927–28. Her timbers are two thirds heavier than normal and her outside hull construction is unique in that the hull is sheathed with a layer of Australian 'iron bark' — the only wood known that will resist the grinding effects of ice pressure. The schooner has been used to distribute supplies to RCMP detachments in the Western Arctic, occasionally returning to her home port at Vancouver for repairs.

Reg. No. 10407, Sergeant Larsen, was born forty-three years ago in Fredrikstad, a community adjoining Sarpsborg, Norway, where Raold Amundsen — the only other man to conquer the North-West Passage — hailed from. Since boyhood Sergeant Larsen has looked upon Amundsen as a man whose accomplishments he wished to equal; in backtracking his hero's course, Larsen, unexcelled Arctic skipper, has realized a life-long ambition. He joined the Royal Canadian Mounted Police at Vancouver in 1928 after becoming a naturalized Canadian. He has served continuously on the *St Roch* from that time. Previously he had spent six months in the Norwegian Navy, and after leaving his home country he made two voyages to the Arctic as mate on Captain Klingenberg's ship, *Old Maid*; on both occasions he was the sole navigator. He is a graduate of the Norwegian Polytechnic of Navigation and has served as first officer on a trans-Atlantic liner. In February, 1941, Larsen was commended by the Commissioner for his skill and excellent judgment in navigating the *St Roch* safely into winter quarters. He is married, has two children, and when he's at home it's 1090 Victoria Ave., Victoria, B.C.

On June 21, 1940, the *St Roch* with her crew of eight, her safety bulwarks and lifelines rigged up to ensure the safety of the men while on the Pacific, sailed from Vancouver, carrying a total cargo of 151 tons — coal, fuel oil and general supplies for Western Arctic RCMP detachments.

Upon reaching Atkinson Point, the ship developed engine trouble, and Reg. No. 8406, A/Cpl. M.F. Foster, chief engineer, deemed it advisable to put about for repairs to the deck machinery.

Corporal Foster, who is forty-one, joined the RNWMP in 1919 and took his discharge when his term expired in 1924. Two years later he re-engaged in the RCMP at Vancouver, and was present at the installation of the *St Roch*'s engines in 1928. He has served at Regina, Vancouver, Victoria, Edmonton, Ottawa, Bache Peninsula, NWT, Rockcliffe, Aklavik, NWT and Prince Rupert. He was engineer on the *St Roch* on her maiden voyage and has since proved himself, many times over, a competent mechanic and Diesel engineer. He is married, his home is at Vancouver.

On June 23 the *St Roch* was on her way again and proceeded up the Inside Passage, anchoring next day at Boat Harbour to overhaul the fuel pressure pump. A hazardous trip lay ahead; everything had to be at the peak of perfection, and the veteran skipper was taking no chances.

At times he conferred with his forty-one-year-old first mate, Reg. No. 10607, Cst. F.S. Farrar, who joined the Force in 1929 and has served at Regina, Edmonton, Vancouver, Esquimalt, Kamsack and Weyburn. Born in Liverpool, Eng., Constable Farrar holds a British Board of Trade certificate as a navigating officer in which capacity he worked on mail boats and auxiliary transports during the last war. He is single.

The voyagers reached Alert Bay at noon of the same day. Here the engine was given a final going-over before the schooner put out to sea on a westward course for Unimak Pass.

On June 25, sail was used to advantage and fine weather prevailed during the crossing to Unimak Pass. On July 4 they entered the Bering Sea and ran into strong winds, rains and poor visibility which lasted all day and all night, forcing them to seek shelter for a few hours in a small cove on Akun Island. When the gales subsided the *St Roch* proceeded, and in a short time tied up at the American Pacific whaling station wharf at Akutan Harbour in the afternoon of July 5. Here the engineers checked over the fuel valves; Reg. No. 12740, Cst. P.G. Hunt and Reg. No. 10155, Cst. A.J. Chartrand, deckhands, filled the fresh-water tanks.

Constable Hunt, 28, is an excellent sailor. He is interested in law and aviation, has served in the Force for over seven years on detachments at Regina, Moose Jaw and Kipling, and in 1940 was to be stationed at Coppermine, NWT, but was retained on the *St Roch* because of his ability.

Cst. A.J. Chartrand was on his last voyage, for he was destined to die before the trip was over.

Next day Dutch Harbour came into view, and later in the afternoon Unalaska was reached. Here the *St Roch* rested over Sunday, July 7, while her crew were entertained by officers and men of the U.S. coastguard cutter, *Shoeshone*.

Monday was a busy day: a consignment of fresh supplies was loaded on, and the vessel set out for Dutch Harbour again where 2153 gallons of fuel oil was taken aboard. Weather conditions forced the travellers to stay there until July 9, when they left for Teller. After a mean trip in the face of wind, rain and fog they arrived on July 14, but a strong south-south-west gale prevented them entering the harbour until the next evening. Here they took on dry fish, checked over the engine and proceeded to Cape York where they encountered rain and fog, passing through Bering Strait into the Arctic ocean without a single glimpse of landmarks.

Meanwhile Reg. No. 7756, Cst. W.J. Parry, the fifty-eight-year-old cook, was busy contributing much to the welfare and happiness of his ship-mates. He is Welsh by birth, married and has one child. All-round handy man, willing to turn his hand to any job, he has seen service at "Depot" Division, Regina, Edmonton, Fort Norman, NWT, Macpherson, NWT, Aklavik, NWT, Ottawa, Vancouver and Esquimalt.

Land wasn't sighted until the *St Roch* approached Cape Lisburne when Sergeant Larsen decided to head for Point Hope. This was reached on July 18 after travelling through heavy fog banks, with only occasional glimpses of land. On July 22 they anchored off Cape Smyth, Point Barrow settlement, after a run during which scattered pieces of ice were seen.

From then on more ice was encountered, getting thicker as the *St Roch* proceeded eastward. Progress was slow, and on the 24th the engines were stopped and the schooner was allowed to drift with the ice-pack. Cape

Halket was reached at noon of the 25th; the ice was solid to the shore, and the vessel had to follow the floe off-shore until late afternoon when she was moored to the ice. Beset by heavy, old ice, the vessel kept on the move to avoid being crushed, making slight headway eastward as small openings occurred. Young ice formed at night, binding the floes together.

Contact with civilization was maintained by wireless. At the controls was Reg. No. 13013, Cst. E.C. Hadley, 23, who joined the Force in 1938. He is unmarried, comes from Weyburn, Sask., and his chief interest is radio.

By July 31 the vessel had worked her way to anchorage close inshore off Beechey Point, but as ice began to set she was moved out and moored to a grounded floe to avoid being pushed ashore. On August 2 she began working eastward again, tying up every now and then when the ice got too heavy. Five days later when within sight of Cross Islands she got caught in a pocket and was unable to budge. A strong north-west wind pressed the ice in from the north; towards shore the ice was aground and the little schooner was caught in the middle — a virtual prisoner until August 10 when the icc, weakened by wind, blasting powder and vicious rammings from the vessel herself, gave way and afforded a passage into open water close to shore.

Here, although the ship almost scraped bottom at times, the going was much better; the wind calmed down and the ice was scattered.

Barter Island was passed on August 11. The crew saw very little ice between there and Herschel Island which they reached at midnight of the 12th, and moored alongside the beach for oil refueling. Next day the RCMP *Aklavik*, with Inspr. S. Bullard, Officer Commanding, RCMP Aklavik Sub-division, aboard, appeared and remained while both ships took on coal and miscellaneous stores from the island detachment.

Strong easterly winds and fog kept the vessels in harbour until August 17, on which day they attempted to reach Tuktoyaktuk near the mouth of the Mackenzie River. But owing to a heavy swell they could make no headway, and were forced to turn back. The following day both vessels reached Toker Point where they remained until the fog lifted and landmarks of Tuktoyaktuk were discernible. At Tuktoyaktuk coal was discharged and dry fish taken aboard as the *St Roch* awaited the arrival from Aklavik of Reg. No. 12704, Cst. G.W. Peters, 32, who joined the ship on August 23 as second engineer. He is from Winnipeg where he joined the Force in July, 1935. Before being assigned to his present station two years ago, he served at Winnipeg, Vancouver and Aklavik. He is a good engineer and general seaman.

On the 24th, Inspector Bullard and Reg. No. 12958, Cst. J. Friederick, who had acted as second engineer up to this time, went ashore. A native woman and child from Aklavik hospital were taken aboard on their way to Cambridge Bay and the *St Roch*, with the RCMP *Cambridge Bay* in tow, set sail. Dirty weather and dense fog met them shortly after their departure from Tuktoyaktuk but they continued, reaching Pearce Point in two days where the fuel taps were cleaned and the main engine checked.

Bad weather imprisoned the ships here until August 28. Next day they reached Bernard Harbour where a strong gale delayed them again and put off their arrival at Coppermine until the last day of August.

At Coppermine coal and supplies were unloaded and three dogs, to be used for patrol work, were taken aboard. Constable Hunt, who had been assigned to duties at this detachment, was retained on board in place of Reg. No. 12582, Cst. J.M. Monette who had suffered constantly from seasickness. On September 3, Sergeant Larsen and his crew bade good-bye to this far northern point and headed for Tree River, where a thousand gallons of fresh water was taken on, then proceeded to Wilmot Island. Strong north-west winds forced them to seek shelter in the inside harbour. On September 7 when the weather improved they set sail again and anchored outside Simpson Rock.

Next day Cambridge Bay was reached. Supplies for the detachment here were unloaded and the RCMP *Cambridge Bay* was delivered in good order. Four more dogs were taken aboard and the *St Roch* got ready to put to sea; on the 10th she was away. But bad weather and strong winds forced her to run for shelter behind Finlayson Islands where she remained for two days then proceeded westward and anchored off Kent Coast. Fog and bad weather held her there until September 15 when she started back to Coppermine to attend to various duties.

All this was routine to the *St Roch* and her crew. It was the ship's custom to travel into the Western Arctic each autumn and freeze in at some officially determined point to serve as a floating detachment up there in the land of long nights, ice and snow. This time, however, she had hoped to penetrate the Northwest Passage. But the weather had been against her, and now the season was too far advanced for her to proceed on that venture. In addition, Corporal Foster had discovered that he would need some parts for the main engine, and these could only be obtained through the winter mail. Accordingly, Sergeant Larsen thought it advisable to go either to Banks Island or Walker Bay and winter in.

On September 20, the *St Roch* anchored off Holman Island in a fine deep harbour. Fog held the vessel at anchor for two days, then she headed for De Salis Bay, Banks Island — an enormous harbour well protected from east winds by a long sandspit. The spot seemed ideal for winter quarters. But Skipper Larsen's experienced eye caught sight of something that made him decide against the location: high mounds of rock and pushed-up gravel, indicated heavy ice pressure in the spring; in such a large harbour, the *St Roch* would be exposed to heavy ice-floes and in addition the nearest fresh water was five or six miles away. A quick decision had to be made for it was the time of year when the weather in the Arctic is very uncertain — there was no time to prospect around. So the schooner crossed over to Walker Bay, on the west coast of Victoria Island, arriving on September 25. A site was chosen in the south-eastern part of the bay, about three hundred yards from shore in ten fathoms of water.

Unloading began at once. All fuel oil, coal and boats were stowed on the beach; fish nets were set, but the season was too far advanced — the fish run was over. October was windy and this kept the bay from freezing over. It wasn't until October 30 that the *St Roch* was in position for her winter clothes — a wooden framework from fore to aft covered with canvas. Ice conditions between Point Barrow and Herschel Island had been extremely bad, and the weather was, in general, the worst ever experienced by the *St Roch*. Severe bumps and squeezes caused a small opening through which some waver trickled into the forepeak. When the vessel broke clear of the ice pressure this aperture closed up again, and the leakage ceased.

The cold came, and the blizzards and gales. The *St Roch* rested, "cemented" in the ice. But not so her crew. Dog patrols were carried out to near-by Banks and Holman Islands. Scattered Eskimo tribes were visited, their health checked and investigations were conducted to see that the NWT Game Act was being observed. Doing the ship's chores and going on hunting trips relieved the monotony; in between times the crew read, or listened to the radio, especially when the "Northern Messenger" brought them news of the outside world and the folks back home. The Arctic cold and darkness was hard, but these men were accustomed to it, had tasted it before.

For ten months the *St Roch* remained fast in her wintry berth. Then, on July 31, 1941, after she had been scraped and painted, her machinery overhauled and examined, the winds slackened enough to allow her to leave winter quarters. Progress was slow. After a few hours she was blocked by large ice-floes between Mount Phayre and Pemmican Point; however, she reached Holman Island that night.

At this point an investigation was made of the accidental shooting of a native boy, Jack Goose, who had to be taken aboard for transportation to Aklavik for medical attention. Upon leaving Holman Island the *St Roch* encountered vast quantities of scattered ice and thick wet fog. Progress was slow and finally she had to be moored to an ice-floe so she wouldn't become entangled in blind leads. In this manner the vessel inched her way along, stopping often to avoid danger; on August 2 she anchored off Cape Bathurst in an impenetrable fog. Next day the voyage was continued and at midnight the ship hove to in very shallow water near Toker Point.

Several times the little schooner almost lost the struggle against a fierce gale as she fought to get back in deep water. But finally she won through and on August 4 the wind and sea abated, allowing her to round Toker Point and put in at Tuktoyaktuk.

The following day, as the *St Roch* rested alongside the Hudson's Bay Co. wharf, Inspector Bullard came aboard; the loading of freight for Coppermine and Cambridge Bay detachments began at once.

Departure for Coppermine was delayed by fog and dirty weather until August 8. Two native boys, Jimmy Panaktuk and David Adam, from the Anglican mission at Aklavik were taken aboard. Fair speed was made through scattered ice and rain, and on August 9 Baillie Island was passed. From this point the ice became very heavy with large unbroken floes. But good time was made by proceeding inside these and on the 10th the vessel passed close inshore at Booth Island, working various leads eastward. A few hours after passing Pearce Point a stop was made because of dense fog. The vessel worked its way to open water and reached Krusenstern on August 12. After putting David Adam, the native boy, ashore, she proceeded on and reached Coppermine the same day.

Here supplies were unloaded and empty drums taken aboard. August 14 saw the gallant little ship departing for Cambridge Bay, and the following day she dropped anchor off Finlayson Island where she remained until 2 a.m., August 16, timing it so she would approach Cambridge Bay in full daylight. At Cambridge Bay Jimmie Panaktuk was put ashore, supplies were unloaded and spare fuel oil was emptied from drums into the tanks. All the drums were then filled with water and stored in the hold for ballast. The *St Roch* left Cambridge Bay on August 19 and continued on by way of the famed North-West Passage — the coveted route that had baffled so many early explorers intent on finding a short cut to the wealth of the orient.

Extremely adverse conditions were encountered while proceeding to Peterson Bay, King William Island. Bad weather forced a delay at Simpson Rock until the 20th, when an advance was made by skirting the coast. The ship's compass was now useless owing to the nearness of the Magnetic Pole. Lind Island was reached that night. The *St Roch* remained there four days before proceeding eastward in Queen Maud Gulf. Soundings were taken at frequent intervals and good sailing was found south of Geographical and Nordenskjold Islands. The vessel anchored at Etah — a small group of islands — which she left on the 25th, working cautiously towards King William Island. Soundings were taken continually as no vessel of the *St Roch*'s draft had ever before entered these

waters. The coast was sighted about mid-morning, Terror Bay was nego-
tiated and a stop made at the islands in the entrance of Simpson Strait
in mid-afternoon.

From the *St Roch*'s motor launch some of the crew took soundings
among the small rocky islands which crowd this narrow strait. The bottom
was found to be uneven, but general conditions were better than Sergeant
Larsen had expected.

On August 27 the vessel continued eastward in a strong current. At
7 a.m. Tullock Point was passed; the strait widened and the water grew
deeper. Booth Point was passed and anchor was dropped at Gjoa Haven,
Peterson Bay.

When the schooner continued on August 30 shallow water was again
encountered, and soundings had to be taken continually. The weather
grew worse; hail and snow forced the vessel to seek shelter in the lee of
Mount Matheson, and a very poor shelter it proved to be when a strong
north-west gale arose and caused the *St Roch* to roll and pitch like a cork.

On September 1, the weather cleared and as the vessel proceeded one
of the crew remained at the lead while another stayed by the masthead —
both of them on the look-out for shoals. At a spot between Spence Bay
and Matty Island which was reached after much dodging and turning to
avoid shoals, progress was stopped by a solid pack of ice that extended
from shore to shore. The vessel was anchored off a grounded floe in a very
strong current.

Ice began to close in on the vessel threateningly, so a new position was
taken beside a rocky islet. A heavy snow storm raged all night, great floes
struck against the ship but the two anchors held fast until morning when
the wind changed and eased the ice northward.

About noon the *St Roch* moved along with the ice and anchored close to
shore while the motor launch was used to take soundings in the entrance
to a small cove that looked like a good place to shelter. But the water
was too shallow; the vessel had to remain out in the open and weather a
violent snow squall with changeable winds that night.

Even in daylight it was difficult to distinguish the shore line as the
beach and ice were covered with snow. On September 3 the vessel continued cautiously and at 5 p.m. an inlet was sighted in Pasley Bay, Boothia
Peninsula. The *St Roch* entered it to avoid being pushed up on the beach
by incoming ice.

Early next morning a trip was made ashore and, from a near-by hill,
ice conditions were observed. As far as the eye could see, ice had been
pushed up against the coast and the inlet entrance was blocked. The
St Roch, completely surrounded by ice, was forced further down the bay —
her engines were useless against the terrific pressure. On the 5th, when

the movement of the ice slackened, anchors were heaved in and the vessel made for a patch of open water and anchored. Late that night strong winds again forced ice close to the vessel which was carried along—a helpless hulk locked between heavy floes.

On September 6 she struck a shoal, pivoted around twice, listed to port then to starboard but fortunately the continued pressure pushed her over a shoal with seven feet of water, dragging her anchors and ninety fathoms of chain. Shortly afterwards she was again afloat and moving with the ice. Back and forth she shifted, avoiding destruction many times by hair-breadth escapes until finally she jammed close by the beach. On September 11 the whole inlet froze over solid. The ice was cut away four days later and the *St Roch*, aided by her engines, pushed out about fifty yards where she was moored to a floe of old ice outside the tide crack. Before the month ended, some gear and fifteen tons of coal were taken off and piled on the ice. The canvas housing was erected over the decks fore and aft.

And then began a real arduous winter. Hellish gales struck at the marooned craft, the montony of the vast open snow-laden spaces gnawed at the men whose only pastimes were reading and listening to the radio.

But there was also work to be done—work that helped to pass the time; the crew made long dog patrols, taking the Eskimo census and attending to various police duties. The longest trek was made by Sergeant Larsen and Constable Hunt in taking the Eskimo census. They were out sixty-one days and travelled eleven hundred miles in weather never milder than forty-eight below. There were some interesting sidelights; for instance, Skipper Larsen came across the wintering place of the good ship *Victory* which was abandoned by Sir John Ross at Victoria Harbour over a hundred years ago. Rope found close by was as good as new and just as tough. The iron of the old ship's engines was being used by Eskimos for making tools.

And then tragedy struck.

On Feb. 13, 1942, Constable Chartrand was stricken with a heart attack. He died within a few minutes. Sergeant Larsen and Constable Hunt got in touch with a Roman Catholic priest, Father Gustav Henry, while out on their long patrol. At their request, Father Henry mushed to Pasley Bay to perform the burial ceremonies, after which members of the crew erected, on the shore overlooking the bay, a large stone cairn and cross to mark the grave of their departed comrade. (For obituary see RCMP *Quarterly* 9, 470.) On a name plate surmounted by an RCMP crest was inscribed the following legend:

THE NORTH-WEST PASSAGE

8th October, 1904–13th February, 1942
Regimental No. 10155
Constable Albert Joseph Chartrand
Royal Canadian Mounted Police
Schooner *St Roch*
Pasley Bay, N.W.T.

The long winter wore on as the men carried out their duties. In the spring, all machinery was given an overhaul, and on August 3, after eleven months at Pasley Bay, the *St Roch* broke free and worked her way about fifteen miles northward. Here, in a narrow lead extending a few miles westward, the ice was unbroken, so the vessel rested and awaited developments. Shortly afterwards this lead closed and the *St Roch* was again a prisoner.

While she waited, the crew had a busy and exciting time of it. Severe pressure at times lifted the vessel over four feet, heeled her over from side to side. This was relieved somewhat when the crew set off charges of black powder close to the vessel, cracking the ice which up-ended and formed a kind of cushion. The crew constantly plied ice chisels, cutting away ice from rudder and propeller so they would not get damaged. Whenever an opening occurred the main engine was used; thus, little by little, the *St Roch* made headway. Back and forth, an egg-shell in a giants' playground, she drifted with instant death and destruction always hovering in the background. On several occasions the skipper himself feared that the doughty little vessel was doomed. On August 12, No. 1 cylinder head broke and caused the main engine to flood. The piston from No. 1 cylinder had to be drawn, and from then on the *St Roch* operated with only five cylinders.

On August 24, a strong northerly gale split the ice, opening a lead southward from the most westerly point of the Tasmania Islands. The *St Roch* gained the lead and by noon of the 26th had reached comparatively safe anchorage in deep water that lay between the islands. This, according to Sergeant Larsen, was the worst part of the voyage. She remained alongside a steep beach three days. Meanwhile from a vantage point on high land Sergeant Larsen observed ice conditions in Franklin Strait. On August 29 the vessel pulled out and reached Dixon Islands off Cape Prince of Wales Island. From here on ice conditions were favourable and when abreast of Bellot Strait the vessel cut across and entered it. The western end of this stretch of water was clear of ice but in the centre there was an impassable, tightly-jammed ice barrier two or three miles wide.

Aided by the tide, the *St Roch* rammed into this frozen wall and attempted to drift through. The current was very strong and ice whirled,

191

up-ended, and closed in from all sides. But finally the vessel drifted through and anchored off the Hudson's Bay Co. post, Fort Ross, on the east side of the strait. Here Sergeant Larsen reported to headquarters at Ottawa that there had been a partial break-down of the main engine and that the *St Roch* would have to proceed at reduced speed.

Until September 2 the *St Roch* remained at Fort Ross, changing anchorage continually because of moving ice and a strong north-westerly gale. Then passing through the narrow strait between Possession Point and Brown Island she continued along the coast of North Somerset Island. Headway was greatly hampered by large floe-ice which clung stubbornly until the half-way mark between Prince Leopold Island and Cape York was reached. Ahead, there were only scattered pieces of ice, but, whenever the wind subsided young slush ice formed rapidly and slowed the vessel down.

Navy Board Inlet was entered on September 4; no ice was visible except for a line of icebergs in Eclipse Sound. Early in the morning of September 6, anchor was dropped at Pond Inlet where stores and coal were discharged, some fuel oil taken on, and the dogs remaining (some had been mercifully destroyed) were taken ashore.

Reg. No. 11768, Cst. J.W. Doyle, who was due for relief from northern service, came aboard as a member of the crew to replace the late Constable Chartrand. Constable Doyle is from Campbellton, N.B., and has been in the Force for over ten years, serving at Winnipeg, Regina, Charlottetown, Rocksliffe and Pond Inlet, NWT. While at the latter detachment he investigated the case of Joshie—R.v. Joshie (RCMP *Quarterly* 9, 364). He is thirty-three and unmarried.

On September 10 the *St Roch* weighed anchor and in Davis Strait—home of the icebergs—ran into a strong south-east gale, violent squalls. Several small icebergs appeared and, as all headway was stopped by the mounting swell, the schooner was hard put to dodge them.

All the way down Baffin Island and the coast of Labrador the weather was bad, with rain and poor visibility persisting.

The first vessel sighted by the *St Roch*'s crew was a small Newfoundland fishing schooner off Bateau Harbour, Southern Labrador. This was on September 22. The *St Roch* was detained at the harbour by bad weather until the 26th. From there she proceeded southward, anchoring one night at St. Charles and two nights at Forteen Bay because of violent gales. On September 30, Corner Brook, Newfoundland, was reached; fresh water was secured, and temporary repairs were made on the broken cylinder head by engineers of the Bowater Pulp and Paper Mills.

The *St Roch* bade good-bye to this port on October 5. A small convoy accompanied her, but outside the bay she couldn't keep up owing to a strong south-west gale. She headed off shore and on October 8 arrived at Sydney Harbour, Cape Breton Island, which she left next morning. She arrived at Halifax, via Bras d'Or Lake, at 3.30 p.m., October 11. There she will undergo a general outfitting and have more powerful engines installed, for duty on the east coast.

In his official report covering the voyage, Sergeant Larsen stated that the 1941 and 1942 seasons were very bad from the view-point of sailing weather and, had they missed the opportunity — the only one that offered — of getting out of Pasley Bay when they did, the *St Roch* would still be up there; due to north-westerly and westerly winds which prevailed all summer, the ice never left the bay nor the west side of Boothia Peninsula.

Spick and span in a fresh coat of grey paint, the schooner looked none the worse in Halifax Harbour for her long and arduous struggle. She had received many hard knocks and bumps; but having been built for such treatment, she took it in her stride.

The historic voyage is over. Averaging six knots, the *St Roch* travelled in all 9,745 miles: on the first leg of the voyage, to Walker Bay, 5,240 miles; from there to Pasley Bay, 1,666 miles; and on the home stretch to Halifax, 2,839 miles.

Chancing their strength and stamina against the toughest elements in the world, the *St Roch* and her crew challenged a route strewn with the skeletons of ships and men of former years — and won!

Editor's Note

This laconic account of the *St Roch*'s battle with ice in the North-West Passage gives only a minimum of insight into the dangers faced by the crew during the nearly two years they navigated unchartered and ice-bound waters. The complete voyage from Vancouver to Halifax lasted two years and three months. On July 11th, 1944, the *St Roch* began the return east-west journey to Vancouver. It arrived on October 16th the same year, taking only three months.

In April 1950 it sailed from Esquimalt, B.C., via the Panama Canal to Halifax, N.S., arriving on May 29th. Thus it became the only ship to ever sail around the North American continent, the first to sail through the North-West Passage from west to east, and the second to sail through the passage from east to west. The first to do so was the *Gjoa*, skippered by the famous Norwegian explorer, Roald Amundsen, 1903–06. During his voyage Amundsen requested assistance from the North West Mounted Police in the North and they sent him ten of their dogs.

Humour

22

The 'osses et 'em!

Ex-Cpl. T.E.E. Greenfield

In July 1926, while I was still a constable in British Columbia, Sgt. T.C. Brice, Cst. M.T. Berger and I made a patrol from Telkwa Detachment to Fort Babine. We rode the saddle horses over 60 miles of dirt road to Topley, where we arrived by the end of the second day.

As it was necessary to carry food and bedding, two packhorses were hired from B. McCrea of Topley. We started early on the third day over the rough trail to Topley Landing on the west shore of Babine Lake. The lake, 120 miles long, is the source of the Babine River, one of the largest tributaries of the Skeena River.

On the third day, we reached Big Meadows, a natural meadow with good grass for the horses and a creek on the south side. The meadow is entirely surrounded by a dense spruce, jack pine and birch forest.

While Berger and I unloaded our supplies from the packhorses and unsaddled the three saddle horses, Sgt. Brice went back up the trail a short way and put up four poles across it. Horses will feed until satisfied, then wander around looking for the trail back. When they come to the bars they will just stand there, never going around the ends through the bush.

The tent was erected in the open and the evening meal was cooked and the blankets were spread at dark. After our meal, I took a fish hook and line and fished about a dozen 8-inch Dolly Varden from the stream, cleaned them and put them in a large fry-pan of water and set the pan on top of the saddles and grub boxes. During the night, I was wakened by Sgt. Brice stumbling over me and going out of the tent. I heard him chasing the horses away from the grub boxes. He paid particular attention to my saddle horse, named Byng.

I was first up next morning and started our campfire for breakfast. When I went over for the fish, I found the fry-pan empty on the ground. I told Sgt. Brice and Cst. Berger that the fish were gone. Berger said that a mink had gotten them. Sgt. Brice said, "No! The 'osses et 'em."

This remark brought a laugh from Berger and me. So. we had to make do with bacon, eggs, pancakes and coffee, with honey and butter for the hot cakes.

In 1927, in August, Cst. Berger was promoted to corporal and he led the patrol to Fort Babine. We made the 28 miles from Topley to Topley Landing in one day and were ready to leave by boat and 5 horsepower Elto outboard motor the next morning. I rowed the boat out into the bay at the mouth of the Fulton River and trolled a 6- or 8-pound lake trout. I came ashore then and cleaned the fish, leaving the head, fins and insides on the sand for the mink. The horses had crowded up near the camp to get in the smoke to keep the flies away and, as soon as Byng saw the fish, he came down to the shore and ate the fish head, fins and innards. I called to Berger and said, "The 'osses et 'em." Berger was as amazed as I was. Two or three weeks later, I had a prisoners' escort by train to Prince Rupert and by C.N.S.S. *Prince Rupert* to Vancouver and to Oakalla Prison Farm. I had to wait for the biweekly boat back to Prince Rupert. so I obtained leave and visited Sgt. Brice who was lingering in Vancouver Hospital with terminal cancer. I said that I owed him an apology for laughing at him when he said the "'osses et 'em." He replied "there are a lot of things you fellows will learn as you go along."

Sgt. Brice had been a member of the RCMP expeditionary force which had served in Eastern Siberia from 1918 to 1919. He said that they had bought hay for the horses from the Russian peasants but their ponies had stampeded into the camp and whatever hay had not been eaten was trampled into the snow and mud. So learning from the peasants, the police fed their horses smoked fish (salmon), when short of hay. In 1919, one hundred remounts were returned to Canada (Vancouver) and Byng was one of the hundred.

23

My Soul for a Salad

Brenda Fingler

On March 7, 1978, I signed the largest grocery cheque I had ever written — $3,500.

Now, six months later, as I glance out the living room window of our hilltop house in the tiny Inuit settlement of Lake Harbour (Baffin Island, NWT) and watch the community come alive, I am filled with anxious anticipation. People from six to sixty scurry about, soon lining the edges of the shoreline. My husband, Walt, pokes his head in from the detachment office at the end of the hallway. "Sea lift's in!" he calls.

Sea lift! The very words send shivers of anticipation down my spine.

The ship laiden with provisions, sailed months ago from Montreal. It travelled through the St. Lawrence Seaway, around the Newfoundland/Labrador coast, across Davis Strait until finally it now noses into the mouth of the deep narrow channel that leads to our community.

Somewhere in the hold of the ship lies a pallet with our name on it holding a year's supply — $3,500 worth — of groceries. Even just thinking about the shipment I can taste meat, milk, eggs and real potatoes — not instant, canned or dried but fresh, with skins — potatoes that can be peeled or boiled or lazily baked in their jackets.

Quivering with excitement, I slip on my jacket and step into my Territorial "tap shoes" (commonly known as rubber boots). Clutching my small daughter's hand I eagerly join the press of people along the shore. At five feet nine inches I am taller than the majority of my Inuit companions so do not need to jockey for position. Walt hoists our daughter up on his shoulders where she has an enviable view of events meaningless to her.

Everywhere I look people are peering through binoculars and cameras as the ship, growing larger by the minute, makes its stately way up the harbour. I glance at the usually impassive faces on either side of me and absorb the smiles and animated chatter in a tongue still strange to my ears.

Walt hands me the binoculars and I focus on the approaching ship. When it comes sharply into view I laugh out loud. Lining the railing on one side of the ship is nearly every member of the crew eagerly peering at us with cameras and binoculars. The irony of the situation appeals to me. I raise my arm and wave. The crew, to the delight of the landlubbers, waves back in unison.

The shoreline erupts into a colourful, noisy array of people waving and cheering. There will now be new stock on the shelves of the tiny local Hudson Bay store and an end to soda pop grown stale and flat from a year's rest in the Bay's warehouse. There will also be sleek new snow machines to facilitate the coming winter's hunting season. And finally, the RCMP detachment's new four-wheel-drive, royal blue, 3/4 ton Ford truck with the official emblem on its doors.

The truck is eagerly awaited by the three hundred people in this community. It means Walt and I no longer have to haul our supplies laboriously by wheel barrow from the shed on the beach, a half mile up-hill to the house. It means also that the nurse will no longer have to use the Muskeg, a painfully slow tank-like vehicle with a box on the back, as an ambulance. The new truck means, too, that the very young and the very old, the sick and the infirm, will no longer have to climb the steep road to the tiny airstrip to greet family and friends arriving and departing.

The bright red ship drops anchor a quarter mile out from the shore at high tide. Its freshly varnished booms and rigging glint in the afternoon sun. The crowd along the shore begins to disperse, returning to their homes as they are sure it will be morning before the ship begins to unload its precious cargo.

I cannot leave my spot. I've waited months for this moment: months as I've watched my storage room's supplies dwindle, months when in desperation for fresh food I would have sold my soul for a salad. Our small family stands alone on an outcropping of rock perched over the steep cliffs that protect the harbour. We are silent. We wait.

Our patience is soon rewarded. A small outboard boat is swung over the edge of the supply ship. A lone man gets into it, starts the engine, and heads for shore. Quickly, wordlessly, we scramble from our perch and hurry to meet him. As he beaches his boat and walks toward us I'm surprised at his appearance. He is older than I would have thought, having seen his agile movements on the large ship. He wears a matted black cap which he removes as he approaches. His heavy wool sweater is a grimy grey as are his pants tucked into green rubber boots.

"Bonjour, comment ça va?" the sailor says as he offers his hand to Walt. Walt does not speak French and is at a loss after they clasp hands. I offer mine, "Bonjour, ça va bien. Et vous?"

The sailor smiles warmly at me as he grips my hand. He crouches down in front of my daughter and murmurs something I'm unable to decipher. She smiles shyly as he shakes her hand.

My French is rusty and I struggle to tune my ear to his speech. With much laughter and apologies on both sides we make the arrangements he requests. He surprises us by saying they will begin off-loading now as the ice is already forming and their time in our harbour must be short.

A small group gathers on the beach to watch. The first item off is the truck. It is slowly lowered over the side of the ship where it neatly lands on the flat deck barge. The barge is then pushed to shore through the choppy waves. Once it hits bottom, two men place long heavy planks from the barge to the shore. Walt's job is to drive the truck off. He's nervous. He pulls at the brim of his cap but casually strides up the heavy plank.

There is an anxious moment when one of the planks supporting a truck wheel slips away from the rocking barge. The truck teeters precariously. I clutch my throat and watch in fascination while the crew force the plank back under the wheel. Walt sits immobile behind the steering wheel, tension etching his face. They signal to him to proceed — quickly. The truck thumps into the soft damp sand. A gleeful cheer arises. The barge returns for another load.

Suddenly, Inuit children appear as if out of the rocks. They gaze silently at the shiny new vehicle, their dark eyes snapping. They maintain a respectful distance while my husband inspects the new vehicle. He runs his hand carefully along the gleaming exterior, raises the hood and nods over the engine. He opens the doors and the crowd of eager children move closer. Our daughter scrambles up into the back of the truck where she dances around. Soon a group of youngsters join her there and the truck becomes a mass of squealing, dark-haired, bouncing children.

The barge docks for the second time. A front-end loader cautiously navigates the planks and begins to stack the plastic-wrapped pallets well past the high water line. Our pallet is the third one off. We hold our breath as the loader deposits it in the back of the truck.

Back at the building that we call home, we frantically tear off the heavy plastic wrap and begin unloading our groceries. There are cases of soup, juice, crackers, salmon, soap. Everything is carefully stacked on the shelves until we reach the case of popcorn. We haven't eaten popcorn with butter in four months. I hurry to the kitchen and pop a bowl full while my friends continue unloading. A big city, movie-theatre smell fills our small living quarters. Just as I set out the bowl the power clicks off — a regular occurence in our community with its temperamental diesel generator. We light candles, or what we affectionately call our "Arctic fireplace", and sit on the floor and munch popcorn and praise the sea lift.

24

Alpha Pie à la Black Market

Const. W.P.M. Kirkman

In those days not long gone when "black market" was on every tongue, most investigations of that nature were grim and seamy; but one, at least, had its lighter side.

Black market! The very words conjure up images of swarthy-faced gangsters and desperadoes slinking down shadowy lanes and whispering behind closed doors. However, as all investigators who have worked in the devious channels of "black marketeering" know, our pedlar of hard-to-get articles doesn't operate that way. True, he is sly, unscrupulous and crooked, but with all that he usually goes about his business with a happy-go-lucky air that completely disarms the uninitiated and unwary. His victim, as a rule, seldom realizes until too late that he has been party to a shady deal, one in which he has come off second best. More often than not the willing prey salves his conscience by telling himself that he hasn't actually been dealing in the black market; he's just a little smarter than the next guy at getting goods that are in short supply, that's all.

The black market deals that thrive on this sort of attitude, which was not rare, offer little in the way of excitement or adventure for the investigator. With the advent of gas rationing, however, members of RCMP black market squads across the country found themselves leading the lives of story-book detectives. They then got enough thrills to do them for a lifetime. As an ever-increasing number of stolen and counterfeit coupons flooded the market, investigators got tangled up more and more in situations distasteful to them. Many an ambitious energetic young constable wondered why, in the name of all that is holy, he ever undertook to do work so subtly apt to reduce the normal span of three score years and ten.

Practically all investigations in the black market field are grim and involved. There is little cause in any of them for joy and laughter. After a while the investigator begins to view life with a jaundiced eye and to look on every acquaintance with distrust and suspicion. Even an innocent phrase can take on a sinister meaning if one yields to such a complex.

A case in point concerns two members of the Force who had come to the conclusion that everyone in creation was buying, selling or making counterfeit gas coupons. Day in and day out they had done nothing but chase down leads and keep a suspicious looking character under observation, always in the high hope that eventually the cause of all their grief would fall into their hands with his stock of phoney coupons. But the character in question proved to be extremely cagey and elusive, invariably just one jump ahead of them.

Then one hot summer's day, after pursuing a trail that finally ended up a tree, the policemen decided to take time out and give the matter a good "think", over a refreshing drink. Fitting their actions to the thought, they soon were propped up on stools in a greasy little restaurant in a disreputable part of town. The proprietor, they thought as they sucked up the cool concoction through the straws, would bear watching. A shifty-eycd bird, if ever they'd seen one, who looked for all the world like he'd cut anyone's throat for a dollar.

Their suspicions deepened a few minutes later when an equally seedy-looking individual entered the cafe and within their ear-shot started talking to the proprietor in an undertone. The low mutterings were barely audible.

"How many can you take, Joe?"

"Oh, about 25 will do."

"Same as last time?"

"Yeah. Ten A's, ten B's and five C's. Take 'em to the back, I'll pay you there."

Now thoroughly aroused, the sleuths scarcely contained themselves. Here, right before their very eyes, was a deal in gas ration books — in all probability counterfeit. Like leashed foxhounds waiting to join the chase, they followed with bated breath the conspirators' every move. After a whispered consultation one of our heroes took up a position that commanded a view of the rear of the premises.

Followed an eternity of waiting. Then Joe took a wad of bills out of the cash register and hurried to the back. This was the cue the officers had been waiting for. Hot on Joe's heels, they streaked past the counter and, amid an assortment of pots, pans and other kitchen paraphernalia, the heavy hand of justice fell on the partners in crime who were in the process of paying and being paid.

"Where are the gas ration books?" demanded the law.

The startled suspects protested that they hadn't any. But the very vehemence of their protestations served only to confirm the belief in the "hunters" minds that at last the quarry was in their grasp. Hadn't they virtually witnessed 25 books being bought — at least heard the deal going through?

"All right Joe. We heard you make the deal with Charlie here. You bought 25 books. Where are they?", said one.

"I didn't buy any 25 books", insisted Joe, unhappily.

Cold eyes narrowed, sceptical lips curved, "Do you mean to stand there and tell me that you didn't order ten A books, ten B's and five C's from Charlie?" accused the other. "We heard you while we were sitting out front, so you may as well tell us where they are."

An expression of profound relief and understanding softened the faces of both Joe and Charlie. Striking an impressive stance, they pointed to a neat stack of 25 pies on the table.

"There's your gas books", Joe indicated triumphantly. "Ten Apple, ten Blueberry and five Cherry."

And, sure enough, examination of the pie crusts disclosed on each the letter A, B or C, according to the filling therein.

Editor's Note

These investigators were not entirely disappointed. They checked the gasoline ration books of both the restaurateur and the delivery man, and found that each book contained a number of counterfeit four-coupon pages, for which the offenders paid heavy fines.

25

Scandalous Behaviour of Blackie the Bear

Cpl. D.G. Crater

A friendly bear romps about in an amusing drama and indulges in anti-social antics that present a difficult problem to the law and to the residents of a Western community.

Ten years ago while I was stationed at Leader (Sask.) Detachment a member of the *Ursus Americanus Pallas Carnivora* family was the central figure in an exciting case that pursued a merry course and concluded only with her demise. She was a wild mischievous young thing sporting a black fur coat when she came as a gift to Frank Bean at Prelate, Sask., from friends in the northern part of the province.

It was inevitable from the beginning that Bean's clumsy and lovable protégé should appeal to him for he was of a pleasant and jovial nature. But he was shrewd, too, and realizing her potentialities as a drawing card for his garage-and-filling station business, he installed her as a partner.

All went well for several months. The playful little cub wandered about the place and made friends with everybody; she was a general favourite among passing motorists who upon seeing her suddenly remembered they needed gas. The partnership thrived; Bean's business seemed to grow as the cub expanded and developed into hale robust "Blackie".

But every rose has its thorn. The village fathers grew apprehensive of 200 lbs. of unpredictable bear meat free to roam at will. They lodged a complaint and Bean was penalized under the Fur Act for keeping Blackie in captivity without authority. The Department of Natural Resources asserted strongly that they had no desire to own the animal but signified their willingness to issue Bean a licence. The local council however refused to grant the ancillary bylaw permit required to keep a wild animal within the village limits, even if a cage were provided.

Bean was loath to part with Blackie much less destroy her. By this time a genuine bond of attachment had joined the two. But he was a peaceful man anxious to stay on the good side of his neighbours, and despite the benefits she brought to him he decided their partnership must dissolve. With heavy heart and an uneasy conscience he offered her to the wild animal park at Moose Jaw, Sask., but like the Dept. of Natural Resources, they didn't want her either — no bear being needed.

Desperate and now really up against it, the garage owner sought out Frank Mikal, who owned the livery, and persuaded him to give Blackie sanctuary. The livery stable was within the village limits and, though the council did not wholly approve, they seemed to prefer having the bear there than at Bean's garage and decided that so long as she behaved herself they would wink at this less flagrant violation of one of their by-laws. As for Blackie, she was quite content to be left in the seclusion of a pasture behind the livery stable.

Like all bears Blackie was fond of sweets and after school the village youngsters usually gathered there to give her bon-bons and marvel as she begged for more. She was tethered to a big stake. For diversion, the kids sometimes teased her. Often on these occasions she became cross and tugged to get free from her yoke.

One day, when nobody was around she managed to break loose. With dangling chain she ambled out onto the street and climbed a telephone pole. In joyful mood at her new-found freedom she proceeded to show off from the top of this perch and venturing out on the wires gave an exhibition that surpassed by far the gymnastics of the Man on the Flying Trapeze. Somersaults and near falls thrilled most of the townsfolk who had assembled to watch, and evidently aware that she was the cynosure of all eyes she excelled herself with each fresh stunt.

But calamity was near at hand; the performance was swiftly drawing to a close. All this time the loose chain had been wrapping itself around the telegraph wires. Shorter and shorter it got until the gymnast found herself hanging by the neck some distance from the pole. Excitement by now was at fever pitch. As the noose tightened about her neck she pawed the air as if to grab some for her lungs, but each jerk only sewed her up tighter. Her struggles became weaker until finally they stopped altogether. It looked like Blackie had joined her forebears.

She was still suspended precariously about 30 feet above the crowd, a helpless prisoner, when Mikal with most of the fire brigade and equipment rushed to the scene. A long ladder was quickly hoisted and the on-lookers held their breath as men mounted to its swaying summit. Advice came gratuitously from all sides as the rescuers unwound the entangled chain.

For weeks some of them had striven to get rid of Blackie, and now they were risking their necks to save hers. Man indeed is a complex creature.

Our star came to life for a moment in this final act, but was given no opportunity to take her curtain call. She dropped to the ground like a sack of oats and was knocked out cold. Once again her trials and tribulations appeared to be over for all time. But alas, they weren't. In about 15 minutes she stirred, came to, regained her feet unsteadily, and except for an apparent dizziness seemed none the worse for her experience.

At her old post in the livery yard, she resumed her less-dramatic role of entertaining juveniles. As time wore on and the torments of her audience increased she began to show signs of viciousness to such an extent that Mikal decided he couldn't keep her any longer. One evening he entered into a conspiracy with two friends from across the South Saskatchewan [River] who consented to spirit Blackie away in a car while he, himself, for the benefit of the owner, spread the sad tidings that she had escaped.

Up to a point everything went according to plan. Bean played his part like a trouper, a willing prey to the conspirators who plied him with drinks until, like an innocent babe, his head bowed on his chest and he slept. Unfortunately Blackie didn't know her lines so well. In the still of the night her chain was broken as pre-arranged. Quietly she submitted to being herded into the back seat of the waiting vehicle behind a makeshift barrier of lumber. But when the car started moving, like the sociable creature she was, she "ad libbed" by leaping over the obstruction into the front seat. With words that weren't in the script the kidnappers made a hasty exit, their unmanned transport plunged on and crashed into the fence of a nearby lumber yard, and Blackie, unscarred and undismayed, was returned once again to her post.

After that Mikal flatly refused to retain his holding equity in Blackie and took her back to her owner at the garage. Here she entered into domesticity readily and became quite friendly with the mechanic. Either to satisfy her curiosity or her desire for company she always joined him beneath any automobile he was fixing and grunted her approval of his dexterity. When she got in the way, as frequently happened, a persuasive dig in the ribs invariably caused her to move over. Then one balmy day a farmer named Joe appeared and took a shine to her. In response to inquiries, Bean talked like a radio announcer selling soap and the upshot was that Blackie was exchanged for a dilapidated car that could be junked for spare parts.

Joe led his new love away and installed her in his barn for the night. Next morning when Joe's kids went out to do their chores they found that the horses had broken loose and that they refused with indignant snorts to return to the stable. Unaware that the farm live-stock had been added to, they were wide-eyed to find a big black bear where the team belonged. The place was a wreck—stalls had been damaged, hay pulled out of the snow, and amid a tanglefoot of broken halter shanks and other harness the shaggy new-comer was foraging about in complete possession. Dad was summoned.

Doubtful, when he viewed the destruction, that he had acted wisely, Joe dispossessed Blackie and moved her to new quarters. But when the Mounted Police visited him and pointed out that a permit to keep the bear would be necessary he was certain that he had been rash. He told his callers he would think the matter over.

Meanwhile Bean had been fined for trading in fur without a licence. He told me later that for awhile every time he saw a policeman he expected to receive another summons.

Joe, who disliked red tape and government formalities, didn't relish his position. Fearing that Blackie might involve him, too, in a snag with the courts, he pondered the problem deeply. One evening he drove to the Bean garage and explained that he had brought along a hog but was unable to locate the butcher. Would Bean mind keeping the pig which was in a sack until such time as Joe could transact a business deal? Bean was glad to oblige and being courteous helped Joe carry the heavy bundle into the garage.

"Grunts kinda funny, don't it?" he remarked as they deposited it in a corner. "More like a growl."

"Throat trouble", Joe said blandly.

He climbed back into his seat, offered his thanks and as he started off shouted, "You was right about them growls. It's that dang bear. She's all yours and don't bother about returnin' the Chev."

After that, Bean and his friends discussed the parlous question many times. One proposal was that Blackie be crated and presented on the first dark night to the RCMP detachment. Fortunately, this idea was not acted upon. Instead, she was taken south to the sand hills and turned loose. Some concern arose over the safety of stock in the vicinity, but no complaints were received.

I often wondered what became of her. In later years I learned that actually she had been taken to a farmer who was willing to try his hand at keeping her. Due to an ever-increasing tendency to answer the call of the wild, however, she was doomed. The farmer shot her. All that now remain of poor Blackie are ten retractable claws which he removed from her carcass before consigning it to the good earth.

26

My Most Memorable Meal

D/Commr. W.H. Kelly (Rtd.)

Over the past half century I have eaten meals in the best restaurants of North America and Europe. I have been the guest at lavish state dinners in at least a dozen countries, thanks to the RCMP for allowing me to be its representative at such functions. I remember with particular fondness a meal in Paris, at a restaurant in the Bois de Boulogne; another in the city hall of Stockholm, a state dinner; and yet another in Norway, in the city of Bergen, where the pièce de résistance was reindeer chauteaubriand. Still another memorable feast was at the Dorchester Hotel of London, England—in spite of the English reputation for mediocre cuisine—when Lord Thomson of Fleet gave a dinner in honour of the ailing Lord Beaverbrook.

However, my most memorable meal was Christmas dinner at the RCMP Depot Division, Regina, in 1933, the year I joined the Force. By then I had been living in barracks nearly six months. The daily meals were plain, but the food plentiful. Only the fussy eaters—of whom I was not one—complained among themselves about the lack of variety, or that a meal was not hot enough, or that Sunday supper was always a cold salad plate. But such persons never made their complaints official, even when the orderly officer visited the mess each day at noon and loudly enquired, "Any complaints?"

The best meal of the week was always on Saturday at noon. The commanding officer and his aides, after inspecting other areas of the barracks, would end his inspection in the men's mess. I never heard that he found anything to criticize. I would have been surprised if he had, for every Saturday morning recruit mess orderlies (of whom I was one quite often) scrubbed everything from utensils and tables, to floors and walls, while the cook and his two assistants prepared the noon meal.

By the time the inspection party arrived the noon meal had begun. The room would be called to attention, then put at "ease" as the inspection continued. Someone in the party would call out, "Any complaints?" The answer, usually from a staff member living in barracks, was invariably,

"None, Sir!" It would have been a brave recruit who beat him to the answer with a "Yes, Sir." But this never happened in the nine months I lived in barracks.

In the kitchen the cook and his assistants were ready for the inspection, dressed up in their white jackets and pants, newly laundered, and wearing the high, white, traditional cooks hats. The C.O. would look at what was being served, and usually took a sip of the soup. One of his aides, the Division Orderly, stood by with his writing pad ready to make note of anything that needed correction. The C.O. would then march out of the mess, followed by a line of his several aides.

I never saw the Division Orderly make a note of anything in the mess, although I had seen him make the necessary notes when the barrack room was being inspected, or when the men who lived there were being inspected — from head to toe — every Saturday morning.

There was one occasion, however, when the daily orderly officer's query of "Any complaints?" might have been answered in the affirmative, but it wasn't. For two or three days in a row we were not provided with butter at the noon meal and no explanation was given to us for its absence. When butter returned once again to the table, the matter appeared to have been forgotten. When a mess meeting was scheduled sometime later, 3/Cst. Ted Atherton, miffed about the missing butter, called a preliminary meeting in our barrack room to plan strategy for the mess meeting. (Such mess meetings were called mainly to accept the mess financial statement and vote the monthly bills be paid.) We all agreed that no one would make a motion to pay the bills, nor would we vote on a motion made by one of the staff.

The meeting was always "chaired" by Sergeant Major E.O. Taylor, one of the most gentlemanly sergeants major that ever held such a position. When he called for a motion, nothing happened. After some delay a staff member made it. Then, Atherton, who had been chosen as spokesman, got up and explained very respectfully that our attitude was not solely due to the fact that we hadn't been given any butter at several noon meals, exactly, but that by not giving us an explanation we had been treated as juveniles instead of the grown men we were! (I am sure that some of the staff considered all this disobedience and insubordination.) Atherton's remarks were accepted with good grace by S/M Taylor, and we were then asked to vote again. All recruits abstained. But the staff voted, and the sergeant major said that that was enough to have the bills paid. The meeting was adjourned and we were dismissed.

Strangely, we heard no more about our behaviour at the mess meeting. Even more strange was that our drill instructors, Robbie and Griff, who enjoyed giving us a little extra drill for any perceived misdemeanor, said not a word. However, we did not have another mess meeting as long as I was in Depot — about another four months.

The system of feeding recruits at that time in Depot Division was based on a thirty-cents-a-day meal allowance for each recruit, or ten cents a meal. A regular member was the mess secretary whose job it was to purchase foodstuffs — no doubt with the assistance of the cook — and to keep within the thirty-cent limit. At the time of the butter incident no small part of the criticism was aimed at him, which of course questioned his competence for the job. We had no experience on which to base an opinion about whether or not it was difficult to feed healthy young men with large appetites on thirty cents a day. (In 1986, although the system is now different, a recruit who eats three meals a day at Depot Division is charged $9.50 per day: $2.90 for breakfast, $3.30 for lunch, and the same for dinner.)

In 1933 the Force was celebrating its 60th anniversary, its Diamond Jubilee, so an extra effort was made to see that Christmas dinner suited the occasion. The time for the meal was set for about 3.00 p.m. The decorations in the mess created a festive atmosphere to which was added the colourful uniforms of officers and NCOs. We recruits wore our brown jackets, of which we were just as proud as the others were of their scarlet tunics. At each place on the table was a four-page, orange-coloured menu. Pages two and three listed the menu. (See box.)

There was such a variety of food that making a choice seemed overwhelming, but as young recruits we overcame the problem with little difficulty! Having been raised in a temperance home it took very little wine and beer to satisfy my uneducated taste. As we sat eating and drinking we couldn't help but express our amazement to each other that such a meal could even be served in the mess hall at Depot. Sometime during the meal the C.O. spoke a few words, wishing us all a Merry Christmas, and good fortune on our future transfers to actual police work. My friend Bob Lough quietly wondered aloud if the C.O.'s benevolent Christmas spirit would relieve him of his night guard duties that night. This brought the expected horse laugh from those within earshot.

Usually we left the mess as quickly as possible, but on this occasion we lingered at the tables long after the meal had ended, reluctant to bring such an occasion to an end. It was an evening of which could be truly said, "a good time was had by all". Our spirits were so high we were oblivious to the cold, bitter, prairie wind blowing across the parade square when we finally did return to our barrack rooms in old B Block.

As we lay on our beds, satiated with food and drink, we could not stop talking about the meal we had just finished. We wondered how the mess secretary could provide such a meal on thirty cents a day. Some wag said he must have scrimped, not only on the butter, but in numerous ways all the year round that we had not detected. In spite of the Christmas spirit that abounded we were not prepared to give him full credit for such a meal without some criticism. We found it difficult to believe — as someone suggested, and which was probably true — that because it was such a special occasion, Headquarters in Ottawa had given the mess a special grant for the Christmas dinner.

However the meal was paid for, we were happy to have partaken of the most sumptuous meal most of us had ever had up to that time in our lives. Whatever elaborate meals came our way in the years that followed, I doubt if there was any meal more memorable than that Christmas dinner at Depot Division in 1933. I know that for me, it was indeed my most memorable meal.

1873–1933
MENU
MERRY CHRISTMAS

RELISH
Sweet Pickles   Ripe Olives   Celery Hearts

COCKTAIL
Tomato Juice   Cocktail

SOUP
Tomato Bouillon   Oyster Soup

SALAD
Lobster Salad Mayonnaise

ROASTS
Roast Young Saskatchewan Turkey   Chestnut Dressing
Cranberry Jelly
Baked Ham   Champagne Sauce

VEGETABLES
Mashed Potatoes in Cream   Potatoes Duchess
Buttered Brussel Sprouts   Cauliflower (Maître d'hôtel)

DESSERTS
English Plum Pudding   Hot Mince Pie
Sixtieth Anniversary Christmas Cake
Comport [sic] of Fresh Fruits
Oranges   Grapes   Bananas   Apples   Raisins
Mixed Nuts

BEVERAGES
Tea   Aerated Waters   Coffee   Wine   Beer

27

Mounted Police and Motion Pictures

H. Bruce C. Carruthers

Mr. Carruthers is well qualified to give advice to the film-makers on matters concerning the Force for he spent nearly four years in the Yukon as a Constable, later Corporal. At 18 he engaged in the RNWMP at Battleford, Sask., on July 14, 1919, with Regimental Number 8332. A Prince Edward Islander by birth ex-Corporal Carruthers travelled extensively in Central and South America before settling in Hollywood. He is married, has three children and resides at 5155 So. Wilton Place, Los Angeles, California.

Doubtless, many Members of the Force have walked out of theatres very much disappointed with the way they have seen themselves portrayed on the screen. For five years I have been applying all of my efforts to the education of those connected with the motion-picture industry and it is a task with many hidden difficulties. In Hollywood I am known as the Technical Advisor on all matters pertaining to the Royal Canadian Mounted Police from its origin to the present time.

This work requires vast quantities of research and material regarding every detail of uniform, equipment and action; a good imagination, patience and fortitude. It also calls for many contacts with Governmental departments and civilians for immediate and minute non-Police information from all parts of the Dominion and, most of all, the kindly and ever-efficient cooperation of the RCM Police headquarters, without which my difficult task could not be carried on. I am very grateful for this assistance.

I have acted as technical advisor on productions ranging in cost from $50,000.00 to $2,500,000.00 and I find that the technical questions on one are as numerous as on the other. There is the same amount of work to be done on both but on the lesser productions there is practically no time for preparation so all possible corrections are made while the cameras are turning.

Some of these questions seem inconsequential, nevertheless, they have to be correctly answered as small errors rob a story of its feel of authenticity.

In one instance they had a Mounted Policeman about to enter a trading post, a drunken Indian staggered out, bumped into him and he, the Policeman, laughed at him and went on in; in another case a Sergeant was thrown into jail with Indian prisoners for insubordination, his "pals" tied up the guard, gave the Indians whiskey so they wouldn't tell and rescued the Sergeant; another had a Court scene with the Judge pounding a gavel and shouting for order; in another script a man was apprehended for having stolen goods in his possession, the Police third-degreed him, forced a murder confession, tried, sentenced and hanged him in twenty-four hours; in still another case an Inspector dismissed a man from the Force then reinstated him at the end of the story without the Commissioner's approval in either instance.

You see how things develop?

One erroneous assumption in this country is that we are soldiers doing Police work. My constant effort is to raise the standard of intelligence of the "motion-picture constable" to a par with our men and to inject a friendly feeling between the officers, NCOs and men without having the Commissioner passing out the cigars every time he walks down the corridor.

Another problem is the miscasting of Mounted Policemen. I strive for a clean-cut, intelligent-looking individual, well-proportioned, of good carriage and able to ride correctly.

Recently I had fifty Hollywood cowboys sent to me to use in a sequence around an early Divisional Headquarters. When they rode, their arms were even with their shoulders; when on foot, they had no pride in uniform and if one button was fastened they considered themselves dressed. The riding-boots in Hollywood are of an inferior style and quality and these fellows would not keep them clean or properly laced.

One day I needed a man for a "close-up" and out of these fifty not one had a chest, they were all stomach. Luckily, I had six men whom I had chosen for build and carriage who were working with another unit of the Company miles away so I requisitioned: "one man with a chest!"

A condition prevalent in Hollywood is the insatiable desire of some studios to make a laughing-stock of Peace officers. They call it "comedy relief". I call it "moronic reaction". This I will not stand for. It is insulting, reflects the attitude of those making the picture and is conducive of disrespect for Law and those enforcing it and my continuous objection to such cheapness causes my unpopularity at times.

In a production recently released the Mounted Police lead is cast as a bloated, moronic type who is always getting into trouble and trembling in his shoes. Throughout the picture he portrays a half-wit and, literally, is constantly falling all over himself and doesn't even know how to salute. A picture of this type should not even be granted a release.

There is so much story value actually in the Force it is assinine to develop the unnatural ideas we see on the screen.

Some years ago when serving in B Division under Supt. R.E. Tucker, I learned one lesson never to be forgotten. Irrespective of the question asked, he would not tolerate the answer: "I don't know, Sir!" The only way you could get by was to reply: "I'll look it up, Sir." but within a reasonable time you had better have the answer because "R.E." could reduce the stature of a man to that of a midget at a glance while, on the other hand, there was nothing too good for his men.

This apparently simple principle has been the basis of my accumulation of knowledge since that time and it is a splendid rule for any men called upon to answer innumerable questions — be he a Policeman in Canada or a Technical Advisor in Hollywood!

My business is that of guiding producers, writers and directors in the preparation and filming of motion-picture productions. They know nothing about the Mounted Police and little about Canada.

The studio purchases the screen rights to a Mounted Police story whose author may or may not have ever seen a Mounted Policeman. Invariably they decide that the story would not make a good picture but the title, being catchy, is retained and writers are assigned to formulate new story ideas which may contain a skeleton of the original plot. These various ideas are passed on to two new writers who are assigned to do the screen adaptation.

When the semblance of a story is compiled, the technical advisor is called in and handed the script. His business is to suggest necessary changes and to guide the new writers in the final script; the more intelligent and pliable the writers, the easier the task. If the studio executives desire nothing but blood and thunder then the technical advisor has a truly difficult job and he has to convince forcefully those with whom he is dealing — or quit. Not only does he have to show them they are wrong but he has to substitute acceptable changes in story and *they must be good*!

As the story progresses the Art Department works out details for construction of the buildings which play a prominent part in the picture and the technical advisor provides the ideas as to their appearance without and within, including the furnishings. In some cases the suggestions cannot be met and substitutes have to be made.

When the story and construction have been completed and the "shooting" begins, it is the technical advisor's duty to be ever-present to supervise the action in accordance with the story and to see that it has the right "feel". The director's interpretation is what you see on the screen, hence, if the story seems faulty in action, changes have to be made.

While making *Heart of the North* for Warner Bros. in 1938, we changed about 90% of the story. My Inspector was still very faulty and the only way he could be changed was by voice inflection but James Stephenson gave me his whole-hearted co-operation and did a beautiful piece of work, resulting in his being the most effective Inspector I have yet seen portrayed on the screen.

The most disheartening part of my business is to work on a good screen story, erect suitable buildings, see the whole story photographed according to script and then, when the picture is released, find that all authentic incidents have been cut from the film, everything you have striven so hard for has been sacrificed for hundreds of feet of "close-ups" of the star!

These and many others are the problems of a technical advisor in Hollywood. As I sit in my chair on a "set" watching a Police picture being "shot" I have the thought of 2,500 Members of the Force around me as my one great desire is to turn out a truly, worthwhile production in order that you men may come out of the theatre with a smile and saying to each other:

"That was really a good Mounted Police picture!"

RCMP in Wartime

28

Battle-Dress Patrol

Asst. Commr. L.H. Nicholson, M.B.E.

Our Force has many traditions, most of them built around accomplishments in maintaining and enforcing the law or in storied patrols of the West and North. A few of these traditions that are especially inspirational are founded upon gallant but fatal attempts to finish a job at all costs.

There is also a bright, if for the most part unwritten, chapter of tradition which concerns the Force's association with Canada's Armed Services in times of war. This chapter of our story, though never stressed, comes more and more into focus as effort is added to effort and sacrifice to sacrifice. Every time Canada has gone to war, the Force has shown an eagerness to serve which of necessity was tempered by genuine and reluctant realization that all could not go. Only a lucky and envied few were privileged to carry the name of the Force into action in the two World Wars.

Back in 1885, in the North-West Rebellion, practically the entire Force was committed in one way or another. Squadrons, troops and details fought under their own officers as components of the North West Field Force, while smaller parties acted as scouts for other units.

In the South African War a total of 245 NWMP officers and men were granted leave of absence to serve with the 2nd Canadian Mounted Rifles and Lord Strathcona's Horse. It is of interests to recall some of the well-known names on the roll-call of that famous group. A few that spring to mind are the late Col. L.W. Herchmer, then Commissioner; the late Major Gen. Sir Samuel B. Steele, K.C.M.G., C.B., M.V.O., ex-superintendent; the late Lt. Gen. Sir Archibald C. Macdonell, K.C.B., C.M.G., D.S.O., ex-superintendent; the late Major Gen. Sir James H. MacBrien, K.C.B., C.M.G., D.S.O., ex-Commissioner RCMP; Lt. Col. G.E. Sanders, C.M.G., D.S.O., who received his decoration for gallantry upon being recommended for the Victoria Cross, ex-superintendent; the late Sgt. A.H. Richardson, V.C., ex-sergeant major of the Force with Regimental Number 3058.

In the First Great War the Royal North West Mounted Police, as the Force was then designated, supplied two squadrons of mounted men — A Squadron going to the Western Front where it became part of the corps troops cavalry regiment, and B Squadron to Siberia in the autumn of 1918 where along with other Allied units it played its part in the policing of Vladivostock and surrounding area during the chaotic aftermath of the Russian Revolution. In these two squadrons were many men who are in the Force today, including our present Commissioner.

A large number of Imperial Reservists, moreover, took their discharge in 1914 from the RNWMP when called back to their original units, and many of those who survived re-engaged with the Force after the Armistice. A famous warrior among these reservists was Reg. No. 5685, ex-Cst. Michael O'Leary, V.C., one of the earliest winners of the empire's highest military award in the 1914–18 conflict. Incidentally, a member of our company met him in 1943; again in uniform, O'Leary proudly mentioned that his seven children, both sons and daughters, were in the Armed Services.

Another notable who left us in 1915 to gain rank and fame was Reg. No. 5529, ex-Cst. G.R. Pearkes. Now Major General Pearkes, V.C., D.S.O., M.C., M.P., he won his Victoria Cross at Passchendaele while a major in the 5th C.M.R.

In 1939, when war again threatened, it was in accordance with tradition for the Royal Canadian Mounted Police to seek once more the privilege of participation with our country's armed forces, and the Commissioner offered the services of the RCMP in any capacity, either at home or abroad.

It was realized then, however, that we would have a heavy load to carry at home and on Sept. 18, 1939, the Rt. Hon. Ernest Lapointe, P.C., M.P., Minister in Control of the Force, made clear in a letter to the Commissioner just how important the government considered these duties in Canada would be. Mr. Lapointe outlined some of the essential functions the Force would be called upon to perform and then went on to say, "Furthermore, it must be obvious to all members of the Force that these important duties can only be efficiently performed by trained personnel, and for these reasons, I shall not be able to consent to granting any leave of absence to officers, non-commissioned officers or constables for the purpose of serving in any expeditionary force that might leave Canada on active service, with the possible exception of a representative unit to be recruited from the RCMP. Neither will it be possible to grant discharges from the Force to enable non-commissioned officers or men to enlist for overseas service. No discharges by purchase will be authorized until further orders". Following this directive, it was decided that the Force could best contribute by providing a provost company. This, it was thought, would utilize to most advantage our special qualifications without exceeding the limitations of our man-power possibilities.

Here, it is well to pause and say that while this article refers only to the men of the Force who served with the Provost Corps of the Canadian Army, we of that group wish to pay tribute to our brothers in arms who joined the Royal Canadian Navy and the Royal Canadian Air Force—the members of our Marine and Aviation Sections. Theirs is another story, but one whose bits and pieces we followed eagerly as they reached us from time to time while we were away and on more than one occasion we were cheered by their accomplishments.

No. 1 Provost Co. (R.C.M.P.) was a unit of the 1st Canadian Infantry Division, and its history must always be regarded as belonging to the larger story of that formation. To be included in the "order of Battle" of a fighting division is an honour, and to the men of the 1st Division—the wearers of the "red patch"—it was a special one jealously guarded and later upheld when the test came. So the company was not only senior in its own corps; it was also a small but important part of the senior Canadian field formation and could justifiably claim pride of place.

The decision to send a provost company was not, it must be admitted, popular at first. But looking at it today it was a good decision, one that had far-reaching consequences as the extent and importance of provost work for a modern army became apparent. The first impression of our volunteers was that they would have to work under the proverbial stigma which attached to military police, coupled with a disappointment in not being able to go as fighting troops. But this impression gradually faded in England and completely disappeared when our men moved into battle. At the end there was pride in having served with the Canadian Provost Corps and special satisfaction in having been one of that Corps' first units—No. 1 Provost Company (R.C.M.P.).

Though we always had to enforce discipline, the troops soon got to know that we aimed at doing it fairly and impartially, and that part of our job was to help any soldier who was lost or in trouble. First adopted by our company this policy soon earned respect. Subsequently, the same policy was adopted by new companies formed as units of other formations, until in 1940 it was taken into use as service doctrine when the Canadian Provost Corps came into being. We do not claim to have set the pattern, but at least we anticipated what it would be and proved, by example, that it was workable.

Linked with the company's determination to make the job of enforcing discipline a respected one was a growing realization that the provost men of a field formation had a heavy responsibility of traffic control in the forward areas. This was demonstrated in study and exercises, and later proved as our formations moved into action. When the fighting troops saw that provost men stayed with them under fire, manned traffic points that were, to put it mildly unhealthy, and shared the hardships of combat zones, they accepted us. The man who shared a slit trench and helped to evacuate your wounded one night could scarcely be damned the next if his duty required him to warn you off the street at curfew in a rest area.

Apart from the work No. 1 Company discharged as a unit, more and more of its members were posted to other duties as time went on and in a broader field served the Canadian Army in a manner that the authorities are quick to praise.

It is not boasting to say that No. 1 Provost Company (R.C.M.P.) was unique in the Canadian Army, perhaps any army. By virtue of its origin, the individual member was, according to military standards, of high mental and physical calibre, educated above the average, had received first-class semi-military training, possessed police experience and had through his service in the RCMP been tried and found efficient.

It was inevitable that this concentration of highly-trained personnel would not long be left undisturbed when the men could fill a wider and more useful purpose in other provost capacities in the young but rapidly growing army. And so soon after it arrived in the United Kingdom, No. 1 Company began to break up as members were transferred to positions of greater scope and responsibility.

Altogether 58 members of the company were commissioned and throughout the war they constituted the bulk of provost officer personnel posted to staffs of formations, and a considerable number served with other provost units. There were numerous staff positions to be filled. At Canadian Military H.Q., London, there were a deputy provost marshal (colonel), an assistant provost marshal (major), a deputy assistant provost marshal (captain), an administrative officer and one or more lieutenants, while at Army H.Q. there were a D.P.M., two A.P.M.s and two or more D.A.P.M.s. Each of the two corps had an A.P.M. and a D.A.P.M., and each of the five divisions an A.P.M. Behind the field formations there were A.P.M.s, D.A.P.M.s and provost companies in lines of communication and base area formations and in the United Kingdom.

Not all but a great percentage of these posts were filled by No. 1 Company men. Our men were also prominent in phases of provost work to which little thought is generally given. They were employed at detention barracks, field punishment camps, a training depot in England and special investigation sections and subsections — wherever Canadian troops were to be found. Even at a Corps of Military Police (British) Depot on the slopes of Mount Vesuvius where reinforcements for 1st Canadian Corps provost units were trained, No. 1 Company supplied instructors. Again, some of our men were selected for duty with the Allied Military Government branch and after special training found themselves in occupied countries, reorganizing and directing civilian police systems, fire departments and civil defence — reestablishing order from the chaos and ruin that follow defeat. For these various duties we supplied a goodly number of officers, warrant officers and senior NCOs.

Before the war the conception of provost duties in the field did not go beyond traffic control and the taking charge of stragglers, prisoners of war and refugees, while out of action the work consisted principally of maintaining good order and discipline by uniform patrols. Crime was investigated in a direct manner and if civilians were involved the cases, in the main, were handed to the civil police.

However, to meet present-day requirements the need for trained investigators within the army organization became more and more apparent and early in 1941 a Special Investigation Section was created at London. From a staff of two or three, the section grew rapidly until by 1942 investigations were being conducted throughout the British Isles by plain-clothes men from London. Subsequently further sections were formed and included in the WEs [War Establishment] of formation H.Q. No. 1 Company men were, of course, particularly suited to the work. From first to last the S.I.S. was predominantly RCMP, and in this particular connection the dispatch of our unit proved to be of outstanding value to the Canadian Army.

The work of S.I.S. included the investigation of crimes committed by Canadian soldiers, the tracing of deserters, illegal sale of army property and all matters with which uniformed provost personnel could not cope. In the United Kingdom many extensive investigations of considerable interest and importance were conducted by the S.I.S., while later in Italy and on the continent the scope of their work was greatly enlarged.

The nature of its duties brought the S.I.S. in close contact with the civil police of the British Isles, particularly Scotland Yard, and our men not only added to their knowledge of police work but formed lasting friendships with many stalwarts of the police system devised by Robert Peel.

In field formations the position of a provost staff officer was a busy one, for his responsibilities as detailed officially were: (a) advising his commander and the staff on all provost matters; (b) the general efficiency of the provost unit or units within the formation; (c) detailing the duties of provost units and issuing the resulting orders; and (d) certain administrative functions handled from his own office.

Continuous close contact existed between provost staff and unit officers, and in action A.P.M.s and D.A.P.A.s spent much time reconnoitring roads and areas so as to be in a position to anticipate requirements and allot duties as new ground was taken over.

Bearing in mind these widely-scattered and varied duties, the reader should not think only of No. 1 Provost Company (R.C.M.P.), but of the many men who went from it to strengthen and support the whole fabric of the Canadian Provost Corps abroad. The company was always the focal point, but of the 215 men who went through its ranks only some 30 were in it at the war's end. Most of the others were placed through out the entire Canadian Army, doing every conceivable variety of provost and police job, and their efforts reflected credit not only on the RCMP but on the small unit that had launched them on their army careers.

No definite analysis is possible but the writer ventures to suggest that No. 1 Provost Company (R.C.M.P.) fed more officers, warrant officers and senior NCOs to other units than any body of comparable size in the whole Canadian Army.

Early steps in the formation of the company in Canada and in its training are well known. Volunteers were called for from all divisions of the Force and those finally selected were assembled at N Division, Rockcliffe, Ont., in November, 1939. Documentation and the metamorphosis from policemen to soldiers were completed and training commenced at once. The men first "met" their motorcycles at this place and toward the end of November police uniforms were put aside in favour of battle-dress.

Commissioner Wood inspected the unit on December 6 and saw with pride the men who were again to carry the name of the Force into action.

The company left Rockcliffe by troop train for Halifax on December 8. To meet security requirements, it had for several days been confined to barracks. At the time much was being made of "hush hush" and the importance of secrecy, so there was no official send-off or formal good-byes. Consequently it was a refreshing surprise to the men when a brass band turned up at the Ottawa railway siding to speed them on their way.

At Halifax, or, as it then was known, "an Eastern Canadian port", units of the first flight of the 1st Canadian Infantry Division united and boarded troop-ships. Our company found itself on E4, the famous liner *Aquitania.*

The convoy sailed under a strong naval escort on December 10. Among other well-known ships in the convoy were *Duchess of Bedford, Empress of Britain, Empress of Australia* and *Monarch of Bermuda.* The escort included the battle-ship *Resolution,* the battle-cruiser *Repulse* and the aircraft-carrier *Furious* — all of the Royal Navy — and four destroyers of the Royal Canadian Navy — *Ottawa, St. Laurent, Fraser* and *Restigouche.* The whole presented an imposing sight that will not soon be forgotten.

The *Acquitania* anchored off Greenock, Scotland, on December 17, and our company moved from there to the garrison town of Aldershot in

Southern England, where it was greeted by two NCOs who, attached to the divisional advance party, had preceded them by some three weeks.

The company settled down with the division for the winter, one of the coldest and most disagreeable from a weather standpoint that England had experienced in years. Its first billet was Barrossa barracks but after a few days they moved into Ramilies barracks for the remainder of the winter. These venerable brick-and-stone structures consist of separate barrack rooms, each little building is an exact copy of its neighbour — alike in primitive plumbing and heating arrangements, lack of insulation, dreary discomfort and inconvenience.

Barrossa and Ramilies barracks are full of history. For many decades soldiers have gone from them to fight Britain's wars and to police the Empire. But to men accustomed to the steam-heated barrack-room life at Regina, Sask., and Rockcliffe, the warmth and colour of history failed to compensate for the deficiencies. Native ingenuity, however, helped to make the best of things, though it caused dismay to the barrack wardens who frequently discovered extemporized heating equipment and stove-pipes jammed into ancient chimneys through holes not in the original design. On these occasions there was talk of payment for damages, courts martial and threats of awful retribution, but somehow nothing ever materialized from it.

Leave to one half of the company at Christmas and the other half at New Year's gave most of the men a chance to see London, and, as rationing didn't start until January, 1940, life in that metropolis was still more or less normal — the dreary years of scarcity and the Woolton sausage came later.

The full impact of war and all its consequences had not as yet been felt. So far the Canadians were finding life interesting in another land. To the average citizen of the United Kingdom, Humanity was drifting toward a sombre shadow. But it was still the unknown, with few foreseeing the long wearisome years of darkness, scarcity and semistarvation ahead; the telegrams of personal tragedy; the nights of terror and destruction and the constant threat of peril to the nation.

Though the streets were blacked out, people passed freely along them, snatches of song and laughter were to be heard, cinemas and theatres flourished, and from Piccadilly and Leicester Square or the little streets of Soho one could push through the blackout curtains to the warmth, light and gaiety of restaurants, good food and wine.

However, this strange unreal interlude was short. The beginning of the interminable dismal years came quickly and the Canadian soldier, despite his sufficiency of good food, warm clothing, cigarettes and many things designed to keep him content, shared to some extent the unpleasantness of life that was the daily lot of the British civilian.

At Aldershot the days were spent in acquiring and testing the vehicles and multiplicity of other equipment that a modern provost company takes to war, and in obtaining a specialized training such as no one had previously imagined.

In traffic control and convoy work, the men soon received a foretaste of what was to come. To anyone who has not done it, the hazards of shepherding a convoy over narrow, unmarked, unknown roads in almost total darkness are difficult to visualize. Those who did it will recall that it was as arduous as any work undertaken later in a battle area, if not more so. Large "exercises" were to come — exercises in which divisions, corps, even armies ranged over many counties. But that first cold, dark winter gave our men a vigorous introduction to the full meaning of motorcycle patrol and point duty.

In addition to the strenuous program of training, in which all troops engaged, our men had their normal duties to discharge in policing a large area around Aldershot and Farnborough and in assisting the British Corps of Military Police in London. One section at a time was stationed in the metropolis, being relieved periodically so that the whole of the company could gain experience in that particular line of duty.

Spring of 1940 brought Dunkirk — the first taste of action to ten of our men who accompanied the Division Commander, Major Gen. (later General) A.G.L. McNaughton on a reconnaissance in the Dunkirk coastal area. This manoeuvre was a preliminary to advancing the 1st Canadian Division into action on the Continent. But the plan had to be abandoned when the overwhelming superiority of the enemy and the imminent breakdown of Allied defences caused the situation to deteriorate beyond hope. So fierce was the offensive action of the Germans that the destroyer which carried the "recce" party was under persistent and heavy attack from the air and was fortunate indeed to escape with no casualties from the hail of bombs and machine-gun bullets to the protection of the R.A.F. fighter cover above the English coast.

Meanwhile, the 1st Infantry Brigade, augmented by a considerable number of attached troops and units from other arms of the service, had moved to Dover under the traffic control of No. 1 Company and was prepared to embark for immediate action.

Quite a few of our men will remember the tenseness and urgency preceding that movement which now is referred to as the "Dover Dash". They will recall the wild careering of the convoys through Southern England; the suspense at Dover, heightened by the scurrying of little craft to and from France and the ominous rumble of heavy guns from across the Channel; then, finally, the disappointment and chagrin when the last signal came, the drawbridge of Fortress Britain was raised and the troops returned to Aldershot.

With the approach of summer the company vacated Ramilies barracks for Blenheim barracks near Farnborough, a group of spacious, modern wooden buildings, steam-heated and very comfortable, but stayed there only a few days after Dover before moving with the division to Northamptonshire. The invasion of Britain being expected hourly, it seemed odd that the Canadians should have been moved to the centre of England, far from the coast. But actually the new location was a strategic one from which the division could be hurled against the invader at any of many threatened points.

Eight days later, accompanying the 1st Brigade, the company again moved quickly, toward the south coast — bound for Plymouth, France and the abortive landing at Brest. At Plymouth our men loaded their vehicles on the transport *Cyclops* and sailed on the *Ville d'Algiers* — a French luxury cruise ship that had yet to assume battle-dress. The brigade group landed at Brest during June 13 and 14, 1940, and on antiquated French trains rolled up country into the region of Le Mans. Then, with the tanks of the leading Panzer regiments only 20 miles away and French resistance practically at an end, the Canadian force was withdrawn and returned to England.

The movement orders of the remainder of the division which had prepared to follow the 1st Brigade group to France, were cancelled and eventually the whole division was reunited at Aldershot, thoroughly disgruntled at the turn events had taken a second time to keep them out of action. Probably the best recollection of this episode retained by our company is the tiresome, uphill march under a sweltering sun and over the uneven cobblestone road from the dockside at Brest to its first French billet.

After the return of the 1st Brigade from France, the all-important task was the defence of England. Soon, the Canadians were ordered to the Oxford area, which entailed several days and nights of arduous convoy duty for No. 1 Company. Then a week later the procedure was repeated when the division moved to Surrey. The company found itself billeted at Merstham near Redhill where during a waiting period of over a year it performed provost duties within the division and policed the divisional area and neighbouring towns of Croydon, Redhill, Reigate, Epsom, Dorking, Oxted, Bromley and Sutton.

In retrospect those busy, active years in England resolve into a kaleidoscope of towns and villages; green hedgerows and country lanes, ancient castles and slumbering country houses set in rolling parks; historic buildings and city streets; barracks, billets and camps; moves and exercises; aerial dogfights over the Downs viewed from slit trenches, and weekends in London punctuated by the unearthly moan of the sirens, with the crash of the barrages attending the probing fingers of the searchlights.

The full story of those waiting years in besieged Britain cannot be told here, but it is forever etched on the minds of those who were there, along with an infinity of personal memories and individual stories.

It must not be thought that the term "waiting period" denotes any degree of idleness, or that the busy life our men were accustomed to in the RCMP was exchanged for a state of inactivity until action came. The fact is that No. 1 Company was never idle, for in or out of action there always is work to be done by the military policeman. Furthermore, from their landing in England until their departure for Sicily, the Canadian troops were immersed in a steady round of training that invariably approximated conditions of actual warfare. Our years in the United Kingdom bore not the slightest resemblance to the desultory existence of garrison troops in peacetime.

Two main problems were studied by the High Command: the defence of the United Kingdom, and the invasion of Europe. Every possible form either might take was examined, and detailed plans were formulated for it. These plans were put to test in mock battles, or "exercises" as they were called, and, large or small, the exercises followed one another closely and kept the cogs of the huge military machine well oiled and in motion.

Exercises are not far behind actual operations for testing the efficiency of the military machine, and they are the only means of detecting weaknesses and determining remedies. Planned and executed with all the exacting forethought and security precautions of operations against a real enemy, these manoeuvres were designated by code names, and, though the names were meaningless in themselves, "Beaver", "Bumper", "Tiger", and "Spartan" will provoke vivid memories in the minds of No. 1 Provost Company men.

The company, through the training movements in which it figured, acquired a wide and many-sided experience in moving mechanized troops over England's devious highways.

Besides this testing of the plans made by the General Staff to meet any eventuality, the operations continually in progress served to confuse enemy observers and cloak the troop movements to battle areas overseas. There was no way of knowing what a code name stood for, and when thousands of troops and large numbers of vehicles and guns swept from one end or side of the British Isles to the other, the civilian had no idea at all of what was going on and only at the last moment might the troops be told their final destination. Dieppe, Sicily and the beaches of Normandy began ostensibly as simple exercises.

Most of the exercises were designed to give maximum practice in bringing troops quickly into action and, while they were critical trials of their planners' skill, the practical implementation of the movement aspect rested on the shoulders of provost personnel.

In modern warfare, mobility is of vital importance and the recent world conflict proved beyond any doubt that an army's striking power depends largely on that army's ability to advance and grapple with the enemy. Efficient traffic control is essential in military operations, and the tide of battle may well turn on how it is carried out by the provost personnel responsible for it. Certain it is that a traffic jam at a crucial moment, with masses of vehicles piled up and blocking the way, can be as disastrous as any set-back engineered by the enemy. England offered ideal training conditions. Few of her roads are straight or broad, and during exercises there were amazing tie-ups that pointed up many lessons and prepared us for the real thing. Each exercise added to our experience and ensured that in battle our company would function more smoothly, be better able to cope with any complexity likely to arise.

Editor's Note

This article is made up of excerpts from a much longer article. The author later became Commissioner of the RCMP.

29

The Marine Section of the Force

Sub-Inspr. R.A.S. MacNeil, O.B.E.

When in September, 1939, Canada elected participation in the greatest drama the world has ever known, she like every other democracy, was woefully unprepared. Her Navy, comparatively tiny but highly efficient, was, like its sister services, pitifully inadequate. The extent to which that Navy grew and the responsibility it shouldered in six years of war undoubtedly comprise one of the brightest chapters in the history of Canadian arms. And into this chapter a few modest sentences were written by the ships and the men of the Royal Canadian Mounted Police Marine Section.

For several years before the war, an agreement existed between the Naval Service and the Force whereby, in the event of war, the ships of our Marine Section would be transferred to the Royal Canadian Navy and the personnel allowed to volunteer. Though more or less informal, the arrangement assured the Navy of the immediate use, when they would be most needed, of some 30 vessels of various sizes and a number of trained and experienced seamen. Consequently between Sept. 3, and Sept. 10, 1939, most of our ships were on duty at sea wearing their new white ensigns. Of the personnel, 155 officers and men had volunteered for and been accepted by the Navy; the remainder were in the R.C.A.F., forming the nucleus of its new Marine Section for Air Sea Rescue.

The War at Sea

Some of these volunteers took part in the early anti-submarine patrols and examination duties at the Approaches to Halifax. Those duties, however, were but a forerunner of many grimmer ones which in the next six years exacted a sickening cost in ships and lives and took our men to minesweepers, corvettes, frigates, destroyers, aircraft-carriers and battleships on the convoy routes to the Western Approaches to the United

Kingdom, to Iceland, Murmansk, the Mediterranean the Pacific and ultimately to the invasion of Normandy.

To most of our men — and most of the Canadian Navy for that matter —
it was an anti-submarine war. So much has been and will be written on
the Battle of the Atlantic that it is not this writer's purpose to enlarge
on it except as it affected RCMP Marine Section ships and personnel.
Yet in that respect the battle cannot be lightly dismissed here, for some
of our members saw their most arduous and bloodiest service in that
campaign. We were denied the preliminary inactivity that preceded the
fighting on land and in the air. At sea the war opened with the torpedoing
of the *Athenia* and mounted with murderous intensity until V-E Day, when
hundreds of U-boats still were deployed against us.

The reason for the battle at sea is readily understood. Munitions,
food, fuel and other vital supplies in prodigious quantities, also troops,
had to be transported to Britain. It was done in ships, and the U-boats
concentrated their efforts against those ships. The strategy was sound —
that of severing the supply lines and denying us use of the oceans.

Our problem in turn was to protect the merchant convoys — by driving
off or destroying the enemy. The phrase "The safe and timely arrival of the
convoy" appeared throughout the years with constant reiteration in the
sailing orders for the convoy escorts; and with good reason, for it held in
check the temptation — often very great — to ignore the convoy and fight
it out with the Hun.

In the early stages, we could afford to view the battle with some confidence. The enemy confined his attacks for the most part to the Western
Approaches — of grim memory — and assisted by the powerful French
Navy we were able to provide reasonably adequate protection. Furthermore the U-boat at that time favoured the submerged attack in daylight,
and this, considering the A/S (anti-submarine) resources at our disposal
and the effectiveness of the still secret Asdic equipment, resulted in a
heavy destruction of these vessels with relatively low Allied merchant
shipping losses.

But with the fall of France the situation changed abruptly. Our
troubles multiplied to the point where many times they seemed insurmountable. U-boats appeared in ever-increasing numbers and, instead
of concentrating on the Western Approaches, attacked convoys all over
the Atlantic. Our forces, now tragically reduced by the loss of the French
ships, had to be stretched almost to the breaking point to provide close
escort for the entire Atlantic passage.

Then, on top of all this, the enemy changed his tactics. The secret of the
Asdic was out, and he quickly grasped the futility of submerged attacks.
His wolf-pack surface attacks at night against thinly defended convoys

brought him great success; but the development of radar and the acquisition by the Allies of many more escort ships checked his aggressiveness to some extent.

The battle seesawed up and down with heavy losses on both sides until eventually, due to many factors, the enemy was beaten. At the peak of the fight our losses were enormous but they were always replaced; the enemy sank many more ships than we did submarines. But still he was beaten. Because, as in the Napoleonic wars, though our losses in ships ran into thousands as against his in hundreds, replacements always filled the gaps.

It was into this battle that most of the RCMP Marine Section ships and men were absorbed.

Our larger ships — *French, MacDonald, Laurier, Fleur-de-lis, Adversus* and *Alachasse* — at first were employed on anti-submarine patrols and the Examination Service. After a few months, when the convoys from North America to the United Kingdom were inaugurated, they formed part of the outward local escort for the convoys leaving the Nova Scotia ports of Halifax and Sydney. These duties necessitated heavier armament and the installation of depth-charge gear and Asdic equipment, with the result that our normally peaceable-looking ships fairly bristled with guns and presented a very war-like appearance. The ships continued on the duty of local escort — that is to the Western Rendezvous, as it was known at that time — until the new construction program produced more suitable ships to take over the escorting of the convoys. Our ships then were relegated to the familiar and exacting if less exciting duties — patrol and examination.

It was well that Canadian ship-yards accomplished the magnificent job they did, for very soon the convoys required close escort for the entire cross-ocean trip. The old police vessels lacked the endurance necessary for such work. Nevertheless many bitter comments were heard on board anent N.S.H.Q.'s lack of perception in denying our ships the opportunity to take part in it. The impatient ones, however, were to see plenty of action in European waters.

A number of experiences befell our ships and men about this time, and unfortunately some of them already have been forgotten. *Adversus* was lost at sea; there were no casualties and the captain even saved the ship's confidential books. *Laurier*, with a Marine Section officer in command, had the honour of being senior ship of the inward escort for the Netherlands cruiser that brought Princess Juliana and the two infant princesses to Canada in 1940. She later formed part of the outward escort for the convoy so courageously defended by Capt. Fogarty Fegan, V.C., in H.M.S. *Harris Bay*, when attacked by an enemy surface raider.

One evening at dusk shortly after this, *MacDonald*'s former captain experienced the doubtful glory of being bombed by friendly aircraft off Nova Scotia. The ship was almost capsized by near-misses, the exchange of signals being highly diverting but unpublishable.

As the ships retired from escort duty, most of them passed into other hands, and Marine Section personnel were required to man the new corvettes and minesweepers coming forward from the ship-yards. In these ships and later in frigates and destroyers some of our officers served throughout the remainder of the war in command at sea. To relate their experiences would take volumes; little more than passing reference and a very sketchy recapitulation may be given here.

Our men, in several cases as Senior officers, served all over the ocean in close escort groups, and in striking forces comprised of corvettes, frigates and destroyers. Service in striking forces, or support groups as they later were known was highly prized, and within certain limitations these groups were free to roam the ocean and seek out U-boats for destruction. There was no convoy to worry about, except of course when such a group was used to reinforce the close escort of a heavily attacked or threatened convoy.

On one occasion while leading a group of three lend-lease destroyers one of our officers gained contact with a U-boat at the end of a four-day hunt by aircraft and surface vessels. The U-boat surfaced in the dark, fired two torpedoes at a flank destroyer, then dived. The torpedoes exploded harmlessly on the surface. The destroyers searched for the submarine but poor weather prevented further Asdic contact. The next afternoon, while still hunting, the ships heard Haw Haw gloating over the sinking of two British destroyers in that locality.

One gratifying aspect of the battle was the association it offered with the stout-hearted men who carried on the fight at sea after their countries had been overrun. None who had the privilege of serving with French, Polish, Norwegian and Dutch units will ever forget their high sense of duty and boundless determination to ensure Germany's defeat at whatever cost. And the cost for some of them was great.

Sometimes they worked in separate groups, but more often as ships became available they were welded into mixed fighting units — especially when the fight was toughest. And they worked superbly together. One group consisted of a British destroyer, H.M.S. *Harvester*, commanded by the Senior officer, one Free Norwegian, two Free French, one Free Pole and one "Free Canadian", H.M.C.S. *Dauphin*. The Polish destroyer was the Q.R.P. *Garland* famous for her exploits; H.M.S. *Harvester* gave a similarly magnificent account of herself before she was sunk with very heavy casualties.

One Marine Section officer, in command of a frigate, was credited with a confirmed submarine kill, and several others participated in actions assessed as "probables", "possibles" and "certain destruction". Survivors from torpedoed merchantmen and their escorts were brought to shore by the hundreds. There is no way of knowing how many actions our men fought in in defence of convoys, but the total over six years is very high. Some indication may lie in the ten decorations, including two foreign and six mentions in dispatches, awarded Marine Section personnel in the Navy. Yet honours and awards do not tell the whole story; usually, in sea warfare, they go to the few for the devotion and courage of the whole.

While the more fortunate of our men were serving operationally and at close grips with the Hun, many others were filling a variety of important and difficult administrative posts on shore — all part of a gigantic and complex organization designed to cope with the multitudinous tasks involved in keeping a fighting fleet at the peak of efficiency. What these men accomplished, working at all hours of the day and night, year in and year out, was one of the factors which contributed to victory in the Battle of the Atlantic.

Ships at the end of a long hard ocean crossing had to be made ready for sea again in a matter of days — sometimes hours. The combined operations of the enemy and the assaults of North Atlantic winter gales imposed a back-breaking task on the repair staffs at the dockyards. And always there were the routine jobs of providing each ship with fuel, victuals, ammunition and man-power, which usually were done in a race with the operations staff who ultimately ended the contest with the signal that began with the familiar sentence: "Being in all respects ready for sea and prepared to engage the enemy. H.M.C.S. will proceed at . . . ."

Our people fitted into this vast organization like pieces into a jig-saw puzzle and a list of their duties reads like a dockyard nominal roll. "Port Minesweeping officer", "Boom Defence officer", "Assistant King's Harbour Master", "Berthing Master", "Compass Adjuster", "Engineer officer i/c Repairs", "Chief Examination officer", "Staff officer Local Craft", "Staff officer to Captain (D)" and "Port Signal officer" are some of the jobs "taken in hand and made good" — to use the ancient and yet ever new sailor's phrase — by Marine Section members whose peacetime experience so admirably fitted them for their war duties.

With their comrades at sea, these men, striving toward the same great goal produced a united effort that contributed largely to the attainment of that goal. Theirs was a privilege which by the very nature of things was denied the great majority of members of the Force — that of direct participation in the war against Hitler. That privilege was accepted with a high sense of duty and responsibility. In the words of the Chief of the Naval

Staff, "These vessels with their trained crews were an important factor in the build-up of an efficient escort Navy, and gave us a real measure of help at a time when it was most needed".

About 25 of the officers and men of our Marine Section best qualified by their knowledge of small craft volunteered for the R.C.A.F. Marine Section for Air Sea Rescue. With them went *Arresteur* and *Detector*, two high speed launches that already had proved their worth during a short span of anti-smuggling service; in the years that followed, they rendered worthy service in succouring the distressed.

Round these ships and few men was built an organization which in a few years numbered its small craft in hundreds, its personnel in tens of hundreds. The value of the service rendered by the R.C.A.F. Marine Section in saving lives is incalculable. Ditched aircraft were salvaged, their crews saved, supplies were transported to outlying or otherwise inaccessible posts and a host of other duties were discharged in a manner of which many an airman has cause to be proud.

It is a curious anomaly that, while all were working toward the same goal, the energies of many of our men were concentrated upon killing and destruction and those of many others were absorbed into the loftier task of saving human lives and succouring the unfortunate. But whether their work called for destruction of life or the saving of it, we feel they did that work well.

30

Gold Smuggling to the U.S.A.

A/Cpl. W.E.L. McElhone

High grading in Canada's mining industry is a serious evil. Not only are the mining companies and their share-holders robbed of their property—The government loses revenue which is needed in our fight for freedom.

Since mining began in northern Ontario many years ago, thefts of gold and silver by employees of the mines have been frequent. The practice, known as "high grading", that is, the theft of high-grade gold or high-grade silver, has been a headache to the police and a continual drain on the mining companies' profits.

When the mining industry opened at Cobalt, Ont., where fabulously rich deposits of silver ore were discovered, high-grading activities likewise swept into being; later, when other mining camps opened up, especially in the rich gold-mining areas of Porcupine, the high graders moved in there also.

The enforcement of the mining laws and sections of the Criminal Code relating to theft of gold was in the hands of local municipal police and special enforcement bodies in each camp. But these officers were handicapped as they lacked adequate facilities and did not have sufficient personnel.

In the next few years the high-grading racket became so serious that the problem of eradicating it was placed in the hands of the governments of Ontario and Quebec. The provincial police of these provinces working under the direction of departments of the Attorneys-General and in conjunction with the Provincial Mining Associations, took over the responsibility of enforcing laws against high grading. As a consequence, many persons were prosecuted and sent to jail. But high grading continued to such an extent that it was felt even these measures were inadequate.

In 1938, the Attorney General of Ontario appointed special agents to conduct a thorough investigation. These men cooperated with the enforcement officers already in the field, but were specially empowered to examine bank accounts, money transfers and so on. Subsequently, a series of prosecutions arose which revealed to the amazement of all concerned that the loss of gold through high grading was in excess of a million dollars a year.

Fourteen high graders were convicted on conspiracy charges at Toronto — four of them going to the penitentiary and ten to the reformatory. The evidence showed that gold was stolen from the mines in the form of high-grade quartz. It was then sold by the thief to men in the high-grading business — usually men who lived in the mining towns, so-called good fellows who made it a point to become acquainted with the miners. The high-grade buyer upon gaining possession of the quartz melted it down crudely into buttons containing seventy to ninety-five per cent pure gold, which were disposed of through Toronto "dealers" (some in the jewellery business), who in turn sold them to local gold-refining companies where they were refined properly and entered in the legal gold channels.

These cases were proved in part by the records of gold receipts at the refining companies, and those of payments by the companies. Judge James Parker of York County Court, who presided at the trials, severely criticized the refining companies concerned, although none of them was included in the indictment, stating that surely they were aware the transactions were illegal; that they must have known the gold they were buying was stolen, because it was mined gold, not gold that had been recovered from scrap jewellery or scrap gold coins.

The upshot of his censure was that the refining companies in Canada have since refused to accept any gold suspected of coming from mines through illegal channels — in other words, high-grade gold.

Meanwhile, although some men had gone to prison, their wives, families and friends were ready and willing to carry on. Conditions, however, had changed: the gold could still be stolen, could still be melted down and taken to Toronto, but no longer could it be sold to Canadian refineries.

New outlets had to be found. There were, of course, refineries and manufacturing jewellers in the United States who, if they desired, could use high-grade gold in their businesses just as readily as gold obtained through legal channels.

So matters stood in the spring of 1940.

The Dominion Government, however, had passed an order in council — the Foreign Exchange Control order — which prohibited the export of any property from Canada without a permit from the Foreign Exchange Control Board. Obviously permits would not be granted to anyone for the purpose of exporting stolen gold, so Toronto high graders, who in the meantime had found a market for their gold in New York City, resorted to smuggling gold out of Canada, and Canadian money back.

In July, 1941, these activities came to the attention of Foreign Exchange Control Board officials and members of the RCMP employed in the enforcement of the Foreign Exchange Control Regulations. Working full time, four men, two from the Board and two from the Force, investigated the matter. When necessary they were assisted by RCMP personnel from the detachment and division headquarters at Toronto, by the Ontario Provincial Police, by the Toronto, Kirkland Lake and Timmins city police departments, by mine investigators and others.

Observations, which usually began at an assay office in Toronto where a large number of gold samples were brought, led to information concerning certain high graders and their *modus operandi*. It was noticed, for example, that when a load of gold reached Toronto through a particular channel it invariably went to a man named Sydney Faibish.

Many persons were bringing the gold from the north, but in general they belonged to either of two groups — the Labrecque or the Quaranto group. The first consisted of Alphonse, Ernest, Albert, Lionel and Paul Labrecque; the other of Joseph (Tony) Quaranto, Frank DeLuca, Willie Franciotti and Albert Mazucca. All these men were residents of the Timmins district.

When a runner arrived in Toronto with a load of gold he would pass it to a woman named Annie Newman. If Annie knew and trusted the runner she would accept his assay figures and sell the gold to Sydney Faibish. But if there were any doubts in her mind she would send sample drillings of each gold button over to the Heys office for a check assay. The payoff took place when all parties were satisfied that the gold was genuine and not just some base metal plated over. Crooked dealings were common in the high-grade racket; there are even cases on record in which fake gold was paid for in counterfeit money.

After three months' intensive investigation, a fairly complete history of the gold's movements in Canada was outlined in notes and reports submitted by the investigators. But the first real evidence that the gold was being exported came on Sept. 13, 1941, when an automobile bearing New York licence plates was followed from the Faibish residence in Toronto to Fort Erie. The automobile with its two occupants crossed the Peace Bridge and went on to Buffalo where a check-up disclosed that the car belonged to a local man named Charles Abrahams and that he had driven it to Toronto.

All relevant information was accordingly passed on to the United States treasury officials in Buffalo whose inquiries subsequently uncovered the American end of the chain along which the high grade was passing to New York City.

At the same time the Canadian investigators continued to add to their evidence. It was learned that for over a year Abraham's automobile had been making almost weekly trips to Canada. On each occasion it was in this country only a few hours — just long enough to drive to Toronto and back.

Arrangements were made to conduct simultaneous searches in various northern Ontario and Quebec towns and in Toronto. The orders for search, written and signed by an inspector of the Foreign Exchange Control Board, were issued under s. 34(i) Foreign Exchange Control order. A number of persons were to be detained for questioning.

Abraham's automobile made another trip to Toronto on September 26. By this time it was fairly well established that this automobile was the means by which the gold was being exported, and it was decided that at the next opportunity an attempt would be made to seize the gold in transit.

Thus on the evening of October 4 the automobile was searched by United States customs officials as it entered Buffalo from Canada. Approximately $10,000 in gold bullion was found in a vest worn by Harry Julius, a passenger in the car. The vest, worn under Julius' shirt, was of canvas, specially made with large pockets and shoulder straps. It was later learned that Julius was a New York City taxi driver who lived in the Bronx.

As soon as word of the seizure reached the Canadian investigators the pre-arranged plan swept into action and during the next day — Sunday, October 5 — eight searches were carried out in Toronto simultaneously with others made of premises in Timmins and Kirkland Lake, Ontario, Val d'Or and Perron, Quebec. In all, more than sixty policemen took part.

The results were most gratifying. Numerous articles were found which were later used as exhibits in court. In the Faibish household investigators located over $8,000 in Canadian currency, a gold button worth approximately $1,500, scales, weights, acids and drills used in handling gold; also some slips of paper and note books in which were figures pertaining to weights, assays and values of gold, as well as telephone numbers linking Faibish up with other persons involved. Similar seizures were found in other places, but not in such abundance. Valuable exhibits were also found at Annie Newman's residence, at the many residences of the Labrecque family, and at those of Frank DeLuca and Willie Franciotti.

During this activity it was learned that Tony Quaranto was in the hospital suffering from an incurable cancer. His doctor stated he had only a very short time to live. It was therefore decided that Quaranto should be named in the indictment as a co-conspirator, but that he should not be charged.

All the evidence was presented to a grand jury of the Supreme Court of Ontario, who returned a true bill on an indictment which contained twenty-two counts. The eleven accused involved were arraigned before Mr. Justice Keiller MacKay and granted bail ranging from $3,500 up to $20,000.

The charges included five of Conspiracy, s. 573, Cr. Code, with which each accused was charged and other substantive charges under the Foreign Exchange Control order and the Criminal Code, against one or more persons with either the illegal export, or the illegal possession of, or dealing in, gold bullion.

Four of the charges dealt with the illegal export of gold under the Foreign Exchange Control order, and the fifth with Illegal Dealing in Gold, s. 424, Cr. Code. The Crown's evidence was prepared by two Toronto barristers, R.M. Fowler and J.J. Robinette, who had been specially appointed by the Department of Justice to cooperate with Foreign Exchange Control Board and Royal Canadian Mounted Police investigators.

The accused appeared before Mr. Justice MacKay and jury in a trial that began on May 4, 1942, and lasted five weeks. Of the original panel of one hundred persons only eleven jurors were chosen, making it necessary to bring in new jurymen to obtain the twelfth juror. The five charges of conspiracy were heard as soon as the trial opened, and eighty witnesses for the Crown produced some 150 exhibits.

On June 5, the jury brought in their verdict after deliberating sixty-nine hours — the longest time a jury has been out on any trial in Canada. Their verdict held that Sydney Faibish was guilty on five charges of conspiracy, Annie Newman was guilty on one charge — they disagreed on a second charge and acquitted her on three others.

Frank DeLuca, Ernest and Lionel Labrecque were each found guilty on one charge, and acquitted on four.

Alphonse Labrecque was found not guilty on four charges, and the jury disagreed on one.

Benjamin Faibish, Albert Mazucca, Willie Franciotti, Paul and Albert Labrecque were found not guilty on five charges.

There are substantive charges pending against Sydney and Benjamin Faibish, Annie Newman, Albert Mazucca, Paul and Lionel Labrecque, but the hearing of these was set over.

The charges against Albert Labrecque and Willie Franciotti were dismissed.

These sentences were imposed:

Sydney Faibish — four years' imprisonment and $7,000 fine; in default of payment eighteen months' imprisonment.

Annie Newman — three years' imprisonment and $5,000 fine; in default of payment one year's imprisonment.

Ernest Labrecque — two years' imprisonment and $3,000 fine; in default of payment eighteen months' imprisonment.

Lionel Labrecque — two years' imprisonment and $1,000 fine; in default of payment one year's imprisonment.

Frank DeLuca — imprisonment for fifteen months definite and three months indeterminate.

Forfeiture action regarding the money and gold seized will come before the Exchequer Court at a later date.

In the meantime, as a result of the investigation in the United States, five persons were charged in Federal Court before Judge John Knight and jury at Buffalo, N.Y. The five were Charles Abrahams, Harry Julius, David Roth, Jack Rubin and Bernard Kushner. Roth and Rubin were Julius' brothers-in-law, and the taxi driver had acted as runner for them, getting $50 a trip plus expenses. Abrahams' pay was $25 for driving Julius from Buffalo to Toronto and back. Roth and Rubin had been selling the gold to the Kushner and Pines Refinery in New York City of which Bernard Kushner was the owner and operator.

Tried on a conspiracy charge relating to United States customs laws, Rubin, Roth, Julius and Abrahams pleaded guilty and thereafter gave evidence for the government. Kushner was found guilty, sentenced to four years' imprisonment and ordered to pay a fine of $3,000. It is understood he is entering an appeal.

Rubin was sentenced to eighteen months' imprisonment.

Roth was released on two years' suspended sentence and placed on probation.

Julius was sentenced to one year and a day in jail.

Abrahams was sentenced to six months' imprisonment.

The results of the Toronto case were not as satisfactory as might have been expected. It was apparent that the jury took the attitude that any of the accused who had been ignorant of the fact that the gold was for export to the United States could not be convicted of conspiracy to export. Although properly instructed in this regard by the trial judge, they brought in a verdict against only Sydney Faibish of conspiracy to export; the others accused were merely convicted of conspiracy with Faibish of dealing in high-grade ore.

The sentences imposed both in Canada and the United States were severe, but they closed the channel through which the gold had been smuggled.

A word may be said regarding the seriousness of stealing and smuggling gold from Canada. The Foreign Exchange Control Board is attempting to conserve foreign exchange to purchase war materials from the United States. It is the policy of the United States Government to pay $35 in American funds per ounce for gold. It will therefore be seen that gold produced in Canada which is sold by the Dominion Government to the American Government is as valuable to our Foreign Exchange position as are United States dollars.

The operating cost of the mines remains the same whether any gold is stolen or not. Loss by theft is, accordingly, a direct loss of profit. Since the outbreak of war, owing to high taxes on mine profits, such loss to the government is a serious one. High grading is a weighty problem — one angle alone, is that it places huge profits in the hands of unscrupulous persons, a situation similar to that which existed in the bootlegging days of the prohibition era.

Editor's Note

This was one of the most important cases investigated in Canada under the war regulations. During the trial the police suspected that someone had tampered with the jury. At one point the Crown prosecutor asked one of the two men who were later found not guilty, if he was known around Timmins, Ontario, as the king of the highgraders (those who trafficked illegally in gold ore stolen from the mines). Laughingly, he replied that he was not the king but perhaps the crown prince. Not only this but also most of his other evidence was equally self-incriminating. However, he was acquitted.

31

Tashme

Const. W.R. Cooper

For security reasons it became necessary early in 1942 to evacuate the Japanese people from the protected area of the Pacific coast. A matter of military strategy, the undertaking was the biggest emergency transfer of population in Canadian history. In its initial stages, some 8,000 Japanese were given temporary accommodation at Hastings Park, Vancouver, B.C., and from there, as settlements were established, moved to their new homes.

Six of these relocation centres are still operating, all of them in British Columbia, the province in which most of the Japanese in Canada are located. They are known officially as interior housing projects and it is incorrect to refer to them as internment camps.

Tashme, most isolated and most complete of these projects, is situated in a valley 2,300 feet above sea level on the site of old 14 Mile Ranch so named because it was 14 miles from Hope, B.C. Giant mountain barriers hem the place in and invest it with an aloof beauty and mystical aura of a Shangri-La.

The name Tashme though it sounds typically Japanese is of thoroughly Canadian origin. It came about this way. When the evacuation took place the British Columbia Security Commission, now Department of Labour, Japanese Division, whose primary function, in the words of Order-in-Council P.C. 1665, was "to plan, supervise and direct the evacuation" and "to provide for the housing, feeding; care and protection" of the evacuees, consisted of Mr. Austin C. Taylor, a prominent Vancouver industrialist, Asst. Commr. (now Deputy Commissioner) J. Shirras of the British Columbia Provincial Police and Asst. Commr. (now Deputy Commissioner) F.J. Mead of the Royal Canadian Mounted Police. The first two letters of the surname of each of these officials were linked together to form TA-SH-ME, a word destined to outlive the settlement for already it has been used to name several Japanese babies.

All the lumber used for renovating and construction work at Tashme was obtained on the spot. The supply was unlimited as the settlement lies not only in the heart of the mountains but in the heart of some of the richest forests of the province. Timber limits were leased and from the outset many experienced Japanese loggers were employed at felling trees.

A saw-mill was erected on the grounds to cut the logs into lumber, and soon a number of dwellings began to take shape. As each little hut was finished it became the home of an evacuee family and gradually the congestion at Hastings Park was relieved.

Wood and lumber continued to be the main product of the settlement even after building operations were completed. It is marketed elsewhere by the Department of Labour and some of it in 1943 helped to alleviate the acute fuel shortage in Vancouver.

On the property, when the security commission acquired it, were a small ranch house, two large barns and several outbuildings. One of the barns was quickly converted into a two-storey apartment house by Japanese carpenters and workmen; the other served first as a hospital but now is a recreation hall, and one of the outbuildings became a well-equipped butcher shop.

A large U-shaped structure was erected and divided into three parts: one side provides office accommodation, the middle is a store and the other side is a warehouse. Subsequently a school, quarters for the occidental staff, and the hospital were finished.

There are ten avenues in the settlement, each with approximately 30 houses resembling army huts, that have no basements and are covered on the outside with tar paper. Each hut accommodates a large family or two small ones, and in the latter case both families share the middle room which in every house serves as a kitchen, dining-room and living-room, and from which the bedrooms are separated by curtains.

Outwardly the huts seem alike with their adjoining flower gardens, tiny and colourful, their wood piles neat and all of a size. Inside, however, some are interestingly different; it is remarkable what a little originality and effort have accomplished.

Several are well finished and have built-in tables and cupboards. Some have been partitioned, and in a few instances other rooms have been sectioned off; this practice, however, is discouraged as it involves the use of extra stoves and heaters. The beds are built purposely high off the floor so as to provide storage space underneath for trunks and boxes. When company comes, quaint little wooden benches appear from nowhere and a cushion for each is gracefully placed in position as the visitor sits down.

Four apartment houses near the centre of the settlement provide living quarters for some of the older people and numerous families. Each apartment consists of a large room, and large community kitchens, one to a floor, furnish facilities for cooking and eating.

244

Down on what is known as Pig Avenue, a bunk house some distance from the others and locally called the "bull pen" has been assigned to a dozen or more undesirables who are feared and ostracized. After dark this abode is shunned by all but the brave.

The bachelors live in bunk houses where at all hours of the day a queer type of card game is in progress. These tenants are always complaining, for Japanese object strenuously to sleeping in upper bunks and judging from the many requests made they never seem to have enough space for their personal belongings.

The huts have no running water or electric lights. Taps placed at intervals along the streets supply the water, oil lamps the illumination. Electricity is confined to street lighting and to the store, hospital and other public buildings.

Administration at Tashme is handled by a small staff of occidentals headed at present by Mr. Walter Hartley, whose assistant supervises such outside work as cutting logs, saw-mill activities and general maintenance. The office staff consists of a chief clerk, an accountant, a welfare manager and a junior clerk. Occidentals are also in charge of the hospital, the store, the warehouse, the butcher shop and the post-office.

The welfare department, under the management of a trained social worker, is responsible for housing, clothing, financial, personal and other matters. Its chief function is to supervise full and supplementary main-tenance — a system of support similar to public relief.

Residents must subsist on their private assets, if they have any, down to a certain amount — namely, $260 (1,000 yen) for each adult and $50 for each child. The reason for setting this limit was to preserve for the Japanese a measure of independence, a nest-egg from which they could draw in post-war contingencies.

Maintenance is based on the size of the family, large families with earnings below the usual allotments getting supplementary maintenance. Where circumstances warrant it, clothing may be supplied, but the requi-sition, which is filled at the central office in Vancouver, must be supported by the welfare manager's recommendation.

A high moral standard obtains at Tashme and only a negligible amount of actual child welfare work is handled. Nor is there much call for the welfare department to sit in on personal problems; very few cases come of-ficially to its notice, for the Japanese have an inherent aversion to sharing family matters with outsiders.

At Tashme, as at other Japanese relocation centres, a committee of the more prominent residents represents the people in an advisory capac-ity and performs certain minor administrative duties, but of course it is always subservient to the authority of the occidental supervisor. There is no lack of would-be politicians eager for prominence in civic affairs, and a place on this committee constitutes the realization of their highest aspirations.

Local problems and grievances are brought before this tribunal and each is discussed at a general meeting before being referred to the proper authority for attention. The committee very often acts as arbiter in family disputes and its rulings are usually accepted and followed. Judgment is sometimes difficult though, for no Japanese will admit he is in the wrong if there is the slightest possibility that by doing so he will lose face among his people. The Japanese are a race given to censure and bitter criticism of one another, and to lose face is a calamity of the worst kind.

There are three main religions at Tashme—Buddhism, Church of England and United Church. The population is preponderantly Japanese nationals and Buddhism therefore predominates. The other two denominations are represented by missionaries who concentrate on secular education.

Education upon which the Japanese place great importance, has not been neglected. All instruction is in English and students are encouraged to use this language, their weakest subject, in everyday speech. Indeed, they are also urged to develop all their thoughts along Canadian lines.

Ninety per cent of the students attend the public school, grades I to VIII inclusive, where the regular British Columbia provincial curriculum is followed. Teachers are chosen from the best educated young Japanese Canadians and given a brief but thorough training sponsored by the Department of Labour. The bulk of education work at Tashme devolves upon this school whose classes begin at 8.30 in the morning and end at 3 in the afternoon. Attendance is good and the results have been extremely satisfactory—in fact they compare favourably with the accepted grade standards of elementary Canadian schools anywhere.

There are also subsidiary schools at Tashme. The kindergarten is run by Church of England missionaries with two classes a day, one in the morning and one in the afternoon.

The high school, grades IX to XII, with an attendance of about 100 pupils, is conducted by United Church missionaries. By special arrangement with the Department of Labour, the public school classrooms are made available for the high school students at 3 in the afternoon and 6 in the evening. Japanese graduates assist the occidental teachers, and courses in commerce and home economics are given. The evening classes enable day workers to take up studies, and though the "double duty" entailed is rather onerous to some students, all do surprisingly well.

The social side is a very important part of life at Tashme. The Boy Scouts, numbering about 150 members, Girl Guides and Wolf Cubs come under the Tashme Young People's organization and have been doing splendid work. The Parent Teachers' Association also is very active, and it is considered an honour to belong to it. There are several other prominent groups: The Shin-Wa-Kai, an adult society; The Tashme Young Buddhists' Association; The Anglican Young People's Association, and so on.

These groups meet in the recreation hall. Formerly a cow stable, the lower floor of the same building is used as an assembly-room by the economics and music groups, and the stalls, though attractively painted in green and white, seem an odd setting for piano and music book. The musicians — some of them are accomplished artists — occasionally give concerts, and dances and other entertainments are staged there in the Christmas season.

Conforming to native habit, residents of Tashme, save for some of the girls accustomed to the privacy of a modern bath tub or shower, obviously enjoy public bathing. Bath houses have been built for the purpose, but unlike the ones in Japan, those for the men and boys are separate from those used by the women and girls. These ablution centres are popular resorts, for there the local gossip is bandied about while the bathers sit on little benches and soap themselves, before soaking in the large community reservoir.

Food is always a topic of interest. The impression that rice and plenty of it will alone satisfy the Japanese inner man is quite erroneous. Raw tuna fish flavoured with soya sauce and mustard, or rice cakes garnished with seaweed, are favourite dishes at Tashme, though one doubts if either would appeal to many Canadians. Most Japanese in the settlement relish occidental as well as oriental food, and only one oriental meal a day is customary — usually rice and chopped fried meat, or fish and vegetables. In the hospital both kinds of food are served.

Medical service for all residents is free and Tashme is fortunate in its modern, well-equipped hospital. An occidental doctor is in charge and has as assistants a Japanese doctor, a Japanese dentist, three trained nurses one of them Japanese, and many Japanese nurses' aides. Every precaution is taken to maintain the good health of Tashme's 2,300 residents, and consequently there is very little illness — 20 patients in the hospital at one time is unusual although there is accommodation for 50.

Soya sauce is as essential to the Japanese diet as olive oil is to the Italian. A small soya factory operated by the Department of Labour and manned by Japanese workers manufactures enough of this commodity and miso paste, a byproduct, at Tashme to supply the needs across Canada.

Tashme is too high above sea level for good all-round farming, but the residents are encouraged to till land in unused parts of the valley and free seed is provided for the purpose. The Japanese are excellent gardeners and many have private plots that not only help materially to reduce the maintenance cost of the settlement but provide good farm training for the workers. Barley, oats, celery and cabbages are grown in gardens that are planted and tended with characteristic care. With live-stock however the Japanese are not successful; pigs were raised at first, but the experiment proved uneconomical.

The people have other occupations also, and many are employed as stenographers, truck drivers, mechanics, butcher shop helpers, store clerks and so on throughout the settlement.

The general store stocks groceries and dry goods of all kinds, and like the butcher shop receives payment in coupons, not money. Books valued at $2.50, $5 and $10 containing coupons worth from one cent to 50 cents are purchased from the cashier. Shopping therefore has its headaches, involving as it does both scrip and ration coupons.

As in most isolated places a great deal of merchandise is bought through catalogues, and every day finds the post-office jammed with parcels from well-known mail order firms.

Tashme is invariably a surprise to visitors. It is hard for the stranger to believe that this snug, self-supporting little principality is tucked away in such an isolated spot. But the settlement is real enough, and it is dependant upon few other than its own resources.

A bakery furnishes the entire settlement with bread; laundry and pressing concerns are open for business; dressmakers and tailors are plentiful. There is also a shoe-maker with an efficient staff, and a barber shop where shampoos and face massages soothe tired nerves with city efficiency and technique. On 9th Avenue the jeweller's long nimble fingers deftly repair the community's timepieces, while on 10th Avenue Joe the photographer, who shaves only when called upon to take pictures of weddings, gives good 24-hour service on films.

There is a marked difference in the outlook of the Canadian-born Japanese (Nisei) and that of the nationals (Issei). Yet the former differ just as much from occidentals in this respect. Caught in a conflict between two cultures these Canadian Japanese are in a class by themselves and at Tashme as elsewhere theirs is the problem faced by all first-generation children of foreign parents who have settled in America. But the difficulties of the orthodox oriental are even greater for he does not take readily to the customs and laws of our country.

Strict parental authority, traditional among Japanese, is the source of much family trouble. In a great many cases the fathers frown on the freedom enjoyed by young Canadians and do everything in their power to counteract its influence on their own offspring. Ordinarily, Japanese children submit implicitly to their parents' will and even an adult seldom makes a decision without first consulting his father. Thus, with little or no contact with the outside, the young Japanese at Tashme and the other relocation centresy are now much more oriental in their views than they were three years ago.

Many and varied are the duties of the RCMP detachment at Tashme. In the beginning, the Force established road blocks on the communication routes where every passer-by is checked by a guard. It was deemed inadvisable to allow the Japanese to wander at will, so all their movements are kept under surveillance by means of a rigid permit system. No resident is permitted to leave the settlement without adequate reason being shown. Death of a relative seems to be the best and therefore the most popular excuse, and it is astonishing how great in number are the relatives each deceased Japanese has.

Invariably the residents bow politely as the police make their regular patrols through the settlement. The constable finds himself instinctively returning the gesture, and after a few months he begins to wonder whether he will be able to break himself of the habit by the time duty calls him to some other detachment.

Preparing the monthly report is always a task, for many parole certificates suffer a tragic fate — according to the harassed owners some go through the family wash, others become part of baby's breakfast and still others simply disappear into thin air.

Japanese reluctance to discuss private matters with persons not of their race seems to dissolve where the Force is concerned. Each day a steady stream of worried faces flows into the detachment office. There is seldom a dull moment. Just as the constable through an interpreter is trying to untangle the snarled skeins of a family difference he is interrupted by a rush call from the bunk houses where a fight, usually of the verbal kind, is in progress. That settled, and the participants friends once more, a new problem is awaiting him back at the office.

Tashme and its sister settlements were the solution to a very serious problem. The mass migration, affecting more than 21,000 persons, an undertaking unique in the annals of this country, was effected without mishap. In sharp contrast to the sufferings of refugees in other parts of the world, scrupulous attention to the needs of the evacuees was observed. And it is gratifying to record that the residents of these relocation centres, many of whom plan to return to their homeland, have frequently remarked the impartial and courteous treatment they have always received at the hands of the RCMP.

32

The Black Market

D/Commr. W.H. Kelly (Rtd.)

In the Spring of 1942, government regulations to control prices and wages came into effect and the rationing of some goods had already started. Price and wage controls were designed to battle the certainty of inflation, and rationing was to ensure a fair supply of goods for everyone according to what was available. Shortages of such goods were the ingredients of black-market activity and it had already begun. I was told to set up a black-market squad concentrating on infractions of the war regulations. I was given an assistant, Constable Barry Graham. The squad soon grew to eight men and at times even more.

The government had appointed dozens of wartime administrators and controllers, mostly dollar-a-year men, from business and industry, all of whom issued regulations under the War Measures Act. The responsibility of administrators was to ensure the proper distribution of goods not directly associated with the war effort, and to ensure proper price levels. The controllers were responsible for ensuring that goods and materials directly related to the war effort, such as steel, gasoline, vehicles and machine tools, were generally allotted to users through a priority and rationing system.

From the outbreak of war in September 1939, there had been partial price controls in Canada on such things as rent, sugar, timber, milk, steel and clothing. But by the Fall of 1941, the federal government decided that if proper control was to be maintained, a price ceiling had to be imposed on everything, a much fairer system than was then in effect.

This decision was brought about by the heavy demand from manufacturers and industrialists for basic commodities so that they could build up inventories in anticipation of continued price increases. This created a shortage of materials. When a price ceiling on all items came into effect demand began to decrease and fears of further price increases abated. The next step was taken when the government decided that prices between September 15 and October 1, 1941 were to form the basic prices of commodities. There could be no change in price without authority from the Wartime Prices and Trades Board.

A Crown Company known as Commodity Prices Stabilization Corporation was established to provide subsidies to certain industries to offset the rise in the cost of raw materials, often purchased out of Canada and beyond the control of Canadian regulations. The price ceiling to the consumer was therefore maintained. But even this system was ideally suited to those people in industry who, through lack of ethics or integrity, were prepared to defraud the government by falsifying their claims for subsidies.

There were two sets of regulations with which I was mainly concerned: the Wartime Prices and Trade Board Regulations which generally dealt with matters of interest to administrators, and the Wartime Industries Control Board Regulations covering those matters of interest to controllers. Both sets of regulations were enforced, where possible, by hundreds of civilian inspectors across Canada, mostly men whose regular jobs had become redundant by the war.

A typical "price check" case occurred soon after the regulations came into effect. An inspector found Simpson's main store in Toronto selling a briefcase above the ceiling price. It had a markup of 137% over cost price, whereas Eaton's across the street was selling the same briefcase at only 67% above cost, but within the ceiling price. Simpson's was warned by an inspector that they were breaking the law and advised to lower the price. When this had not been done within a week, prosecution was contemplated, but only after giving them another warning. As prosecution might take place, a member of the RCMP Black Market Squad went with the inspector when the second warning was given. Simpson's still did not reduce their price so they were prosecuted and heavily fined.

Civilian inspectors could do all the work that required checking under the regulations, but when it came to prosecution it required police experience. Neither could they investigate black-market offences which required police techniques, hence the RCMP Black Market Squad.

The federal government program at this time covered five points: curtailment of public spending by taxation and borrowing by way of war bonds, industrial priorities in relation to war material and food, ceilings on wages and salaries, subsidies to supplement agricultural income and the income of specified industries in order to hold down retail prices, and a price ceiling program. Each one of these involved thousands of regulations.

When I realized what the Black Market Squad had to enforce and saw the obvious areas that could be abused, I knew that we would not be short of enforcement work until the war's end. But at least we would be working now directly in helping Canada's war effort.

That the government program was a success can be seen from the fact that although the cost of living between September 1939 and October 1941 had risen by 18%, it rose only 3% between October 1941 and September 1944. In a similar period during World War I, the inflation rate was 65%.

It soon became obvious that black-market transactions were not the kind of offences that encouraged citizens to give information to the police. The Black Market Squad itself would have to ferret out offences. To prosecute consumers would be a never-ending task so it was decided to concentrate on traffickers in black-market goods, all of whom were out to make "a fast buck" at the expense of the war effort. Some consumers would inevitably be prosecuted.

The war regulations provided for the licensing of all forms of business as a means of controlling the behaviour of those businessmen who might transgress the law. This meant that when a businessman was prosecuted he was in double jeopardy. He could be fined and/or sent to gaol, and his license could be revoked by government. This, no doubt, had an effect on most, but not all.

The Wartime Prices and Trade Board (WPTB) Regulations had broad powers of enforcement. An officer of the Board could authorize the police to search without a search warrant. There was even authority in the regulations to prosecute by way of Summary Conviction, charges of "conspiracy to commit summary conviction offences". This was unheard of in criminal law, where conspiracies involved only indictable offences. This particular power was incorporated into the regulations so that offences dealing with matters important to the war effort could be disposed of quickly. The system could not afford to have cases remain in the court process for long periods of time.

In addition, there was a change in the normal appeals procedure. Normally appeals from a summary conviction would be heard by a District or County Court judge and there the matter ended. But under war regulations the decision of such a judge could be appealed to the Supreme Court of a province. Experience showed how wise it was to have this provision in the regulations.

The Wartime Prices and Trade Board had regional offices throughout Canada under the direction of enforcement counsel. In Toronto, Mr. Dalton C. Wells, later Chief Justice, was in charge. He came under the direction of the chief enforcement counsel for Canada, Mr. Wishart Spence, later a Justice of the Supreme Court of Canada. The nature of black-market work necessitated close cooperation with Mr. Wells.

THE BLACK MARKET

As we were preparing to look for our first black-market activity, a case was given to us by the Toronto City Police, beginning a practice that was to continue throughout the war years. Police work in the city had lessened because many of those with whom the police were ordinarily involved were now in the armed forces. Whenever there was a suggestion of black-market activity arising from their enquiries into other matters we were always informed. The first two cases (in Canada) involved young men found in possession of loose legal gasoline coupons. They were suspected of selling coupons at 25¢ each. It was a simple case of possession and they were each given a month in gaol. Black-market work had begun.

The smallest gasoline ration book issued was an AA category. Each car driver received one for pleasure driving. The categories then progressed from A to E, according to one's occupation and its importance to the war effort. The abuse of gasoline rationing regulations resulted in more offences than the total of all other offences in Canada during the war years. The police were able to deal with only a portion of them.

It didn't matter where gasoline ration coupons were handled, offences were committed. Where they were manufactured, the employees stole them in loose sheet and book form and sold them to traffickers. In the Oil Controller's offices a number of offences were committed. First, there was the false application, applying for a category higher than the law allowed. Then there was the crime of bribery when those employees who were authorized to set categories were paid to authorize a category higher than one was entitled to. If a ration book was issued after the ration year had started, a number of its coupons had to be removed. These coupons should have been destroyed and most were, but a number of employees stole them and sold them on the black market.

Consumers abused the regulations in a number of ways. They would purchase gasoline without coupons where they could; they would use ration books not issued to them or tender loose coupons that they had received from friends or purchased on the black market. Offices that issued ration books became the target for thieves as did the offices of large trucking firms which had a ration book for each of their trucks. Truck drivers for these companies often used the books to purchase gasoline for themselves. The theft of legal ration books at one period in Hamilton, Ontario, allowed several million gallons of gasoline to be sold on the black market, and the thefts in Toronto were much greater than in Hamilton.

After the coupons were tendered at service stations they were supposed to be collected and destroyed at an authorized place. But even at this type of place, employees had a system which prevented the coupons from falling into the incinerator and those they retrieved became available on the black market.

The real control of gasoline rationing was intended to take place at the service station but more offences took place at service stations than anywhere else. In Windsor, after arresting a service station operator, members of the RCMP stayed to operate the pumps. Nearly every motorist who went there broke the law in some way because he knew the operator disregarded the law. Service stations accepted loose coupons and sold gasoline without coupons. When they did this they went to the black market to get coupons to turn them in to their gasoline suppliers for the gasoline they received.

Then there were counterfeiters. As soon as rationing went into effect there were counterfeit gasoline ration coupons on the market. Their first efforts did not produce good coupons; the paper used, or the printing and even the inks used gave them away. However, counterfeit coupons continued to improve each year and when the government took off rationing in 1945, the counterfeits were as good as the legal ones, even though they were nearly as difficult to counterfeit as paper money.

Counterfeiting of gasoline ration coupons gave rise to a tremendously increased black-market activity. This added supply of ration coupons spawned large numbers of traffickers, who in turn sold coupons to smaller traffickers who operated in war plants and other places where there was always a ready market among employees.

In order to stop, or at least lower the amount of abuse, in 1943 it was decided that coupons should have a space on them to include the car license number which was to be written in by the book holder. Along with this, service station operators had to open bank accounts for ration coupons in the same way they would open accounts for money and their used coupons had to be deposited just like their money. The system was unwieldy, however, because too many coupons were involved and bank clerks took the word of depositors because there were too many coupons to count. Some "cooked" the accounts in favour of the depositor, and others stole coupons and used them or sold them to friends.

But the inclusion of the license number on the coupon enabled the Black Market Squad to check the consumer to see if indeed he had purchased gasoline at a particular service station. This was to result in large numbers of service station operators being prosecuted. But before reaching this stage, many other cases were investigated. Persons from all levels of society were involved in the gasoline rationing black market: ministers of the gospel, businessmen of all kinds, a lawyer or two, and even a policeman. The head of a national film distribution company was arrested and fined, along with a nationally-known orchestra leader at the King Edward Hotel in Toronto and a well-known radio organist at the Royal York Hotel. A check at Simpson's service station on Adelaide Street, across from their main store, resulted in some counterfeit coupons being found. Early the next Sunday morning one of the most senior officers of the company was knocking on my door at home admitting he was the guilty party.

On one occasion during this period I had to go to Montreal on duty, and while getting gas I handed a service station operator my ration book. He told me to put it away because "every time I take a coupon from one of those things I get into trouble. I would rather get into trouble for not having them." This indicated to me the widespread use of counterfeit ration coupons. I was there for several days and invariably I could have obtained gasoline for my car without coupons.

One of the most spectacular arrests I have ever seen made was in connection with the theft of legal ration books from the Ontario Motor League offices on Bay Street in Toronto. An informant of mine had agreed to buy some of the books from a well-known thief. They were to be delivered to him on Centre Street, behind the General Hospital in Downtown Toronto, a short street with a few small residences and some vacant lots. The informant was to wait in his car and the thief would drive up and deliver the books. We wanted to arrest the thief before he reached the informant so that the latter could say he knew nothing of what was taking place. This would be difficult for anyone to believe but it would leave a doubt in the mind of the thief. He might think the police had received their information elsewhere.

Several members of the RCMP were on the street disguised in some way. One or two were lying in the grass as though they were deadbeats sunning themselves. Another worked under the hood of an old truck and so on. Eventually the man we were waiting for came along and parked his car about fifty feet behind the informant. He shut off his engine and, as he opened the car door, we rushed toward him. But he saw us coming and, propelling himself off the runningboard, ran across a vacant lot making for a hole in the fence and freedom.

The nearest member to him was Constable McIver, barely tall enough to be a member of the RCMP and of slight build. The escaping criminal was tall and fast. McIver kept up to him as they crossed the lot but soon McIver realized he was losing ground to his faster opponent. He made a diving leap through the air to try to grab the fleeing man, though when he was in mid-air, completely parallel to the ground, he realized he could not reach his running quarry. As quick as a flash he flipped over and when he next stretched out, feet first, the propulsion of the somersault was just enough for his feet to connect with the fleeing man between the shoulder blades. With a loud grunt the suspect crashed to the ground, with the stolen ration books flying from his pocket. In seconds McIver had plenty of assistance.

Constable McIver was a quiet, introverted type. He seldom had a chance to show the stuff he was made of, but that day he did and made the most of it. He retired many years later as a staff sergeant, having spent most of his life in an office and I am sure that many who served with him over the years did not know the kind of man he could be in an emergency. I made sure it was a matter of record.

One of the earliest cases involving an employee of the Oil Controller occurred when we arrested a fur dealer on Bloor Street for having a gasoline rationing book of a higher category than he was entitled to. He admitted that he had a friend in the Oil Controller's office who had given him the category after he had paid him some money. At this stage it was just the fur dealer's word against the employee and we needed more evidence to prosecute. The fur dealer agreed I could use his name to introduce myself to the employee.

Posing as a chocolate salesman, an occupation I knew could not get more than an A ration book, I met the employee in my car close to his office as arranged by telephone. I told him I wanted an E category and if he could get it for me I would pay him for it. He said there would be no difficulty in getting me a D category but an E was quite difficult, no doubt making this pitch so that he could charge me more. I knew it was just as easy for him to write E on my application as D. After a while he said he would try, but that it would cost me $75. I filled out an application for a ration book which he had brought with him. He told me to leave my occupation blank and we arranged to meet at a nearby cafe when his office closed at five o'clock.

I knew exactly what he had to do. As a categorizer after filling in my ostensible occupation in keeping with an E category, he would put the Oil Controller's stamp on it and sign it. There was no check on him at all in the office and, with the application duly approved, I could get my ration book at one of several places.

At 5.00 p.m. I met him as arranged. He handed me the authorized application and I saw that he had approved a category E ration book, and that he had filled in my occupation as that of a "cattle buyer." I paid him the $75 and we left the cafe. On the sidewalk, two members of the RCMP were waiting for him and when I nodded my head they arrested him, searched him and found the $75. I had paid the employee in marked money.

He elected to be tried by judge and jury and when he was found guilty the judge wanted to send him to the penitentiary for a term much longer than two years. But the prosecutor, J.C. McRuer, later Chief Justice of Ontario, insisted that a common gaol sentence was sufficient for him, so he was sentenced to two years in the common gaol. It seemed that most of the employee's customers were in the fur trade so we checked out a number of fur dealers and found that their applications had been falsified. They were all charged and served short terms in gaol.

The regular eight men in the Black Market Squad were not enough to keep up with the work required of them. So from time to time we were assigned help from various other squads at RCMP headquarters, as well as some who had been transferred from western Canada (on temporary duty) to Toronto. With this manpower there was enough administrative work to keep me busy. But it wasn't my nature to sit in an office when there was an opportunity to be outside, so along with other members I handled casework.

About this time a fairly extensive black market was operating at various army camps in Ontario, particularly at Camp Borden. A number of soldiers were given short terms in gaol. Similarly, in plants and factories in southern Ontario it was not unusual to seize gasoline ration coupons, legal and counterfeit, in large amounts. The coupons seized from each individual would have permitted the illegal sale of 40–50,000 gallons of gasoline. All were prosecuted and duly punished.

The Black Market Squad was not employed solely on gasoline cases. One case I investigated involved an employee of the Machine Tools Controller, Byron Dewey Snell, who had accepted the gift of a yacht valued at $3,000 from a machine tool dealer at the base of University Avenue in Toronto. We presumed the gift had been made so Snell would show some favour to the dealer in authorizing a supply of machine tools. The dealer was also charged but we wanted the Snell case to be disposed of first. When the jury could not agree on a verdict, even though the judge had strongly charged for a conviction, we suspected interference. A new date was set for the trial and Snell was allowed out on $6,000 cash bail.

When the date for the trial arrived Snell was not there so bail was forfeited. We later learned that Snell was working for Henry J. Kaiser, the American industrialist, in San Francisco, helping to make war freighters. At least his forfeited bail was a substantial penalty. The case against the dealer was withdrawn.

Another non-gasoline ration case was that investigated under the Metal Controller's Regulations. Information had been received that Bill Lewis, who ran a men's clothing store on Dundas St. W. in Toronto, was buying cadmium from employees of a plating plant nearby. Cadmium was so scarce that it was only being used to plate special parts of radios for fighter planes. The employees were stealing the cadmium in the form of round balls weighing about one-and-a-half pounds each, then selling them to Lewis. Strangely enough the regulations did not make possession of cadmium an offence, but disposing of it in any way without a permit from the controller was.

I went to Lewis posing as a man from Montreal who ran a plating plant. I needed, I said, the cadmium in my business and asked him to sell me what he had. At first he denied that he had any, but when I told him my source of information was a plant employee who had sold some to him, he agreed to sell it to me. We agreed on a price and he agreed to pack the cadmium in two strong boxes and deliver them to the freight shed on Front Street, all ready to be shipped to Montreal. He delivered all right and I paid him. But he, too, was arrested by two RCMP constables standing close by. He was heavily fined.

About this same time, Constable Barry Graham and other members of the squad were busy rounding up a number of people involved in a black-market ring arising from the theft of gasoline ration coupon sheets just after they came off the presses at Rolph, Clark, Stone, the lithographers who had the contract to print them for the federal government. They suspected a man named "Duke" Marshall, a former employee of the company who still maintained contact with many of them. At first they began to interview people found in possession of sheets of coupons with more than four coupons attached. This meant that the source could not be anyone who tore up legal books because there were only four coupons to the small sheet. They must originate from the manufacturer in some way. Inquiries led back to Marshall and other traffickers, and then to four pressmen in the plant. All were taken to court and Marshall got the heaviest punishment—two years in gaol.

This case raised a point that came to our notice frequently. Although under normal circumstances employees found stealing company property would be fired, during the war skilled labour was so scarce that after an employee had been through the courts, his company would take him back to continue his service with them. This did not apply to government workers who were only being employed during the period of rationing.

One evening an informant of mine whom I did not completely trust came to my home and showed me several uncut sheets of sugar ration coupons. He said he had received them from an employee of Consolidated Press on Adelaide Street who was a pressman there. I knew this company had a contract for printing ration coupons and there was some information that coupons were finding their way out of the plant illegally. Despite the aid of the informer I had reached an impass, so I decided, with proper authority, to search the employee's home. The search revealed a number of large uncut sheets of coupons and I told the employee he would be charged in due course. I didn't arrest him as I wanted to make further inquiries at the plant.

As I left I lectured him a little. I said it was a shame that our sailors had to risk their lives escorting freighters loaded with sugar so that people like him could arrange for people to buy more than they were entitled to. This was Friday. On Monday the city police asked me to go to the morgue as they thought I could identify a body for them. It was the man from whom I had seized the sugar ration coupons. He had a son in the Navy employed on escort duty in the Atlantic Ocean.

If there was one thing to be learned from black-market cases, it was that normally law-abiding citizens didn't give much thought to the law if they saw an opportunity to obtain something they wanted or to make a fast dollar. There are always those in society who are willing to cater to such people, at a price. But without "customers" these people could not exist. The black market operated very much the same as present day organized crime. If the general public did not purchase the services provided by organized crime, organized crime could not exist.

The fact that there was a war going on and that the goods and materials handled on the black market were putting a strain on the country's war effort did not matter to such people. The war was somebody else's business, not theirs. Seldom did a judge when convicting such people fail to mention that while they were hindering the war effort, young men were giving their lives in Europe in order to protect folks back here. The more I dealt in black-market cases, the more I wondered how so many people could lack a sense of loyalty, if only enough to obey the laws which were made to support the war effort.

33

The Force's Siberian Patrol

S.W. Horrall, RCMP Historian

On a spring afternoon in May 1919, a freight train slowly pulled out of the First River railway station just outside Vladivostok in eastern Siberia. Earlier that day, its long line of freight cars had been loaded with war supplies for the White Russian armies fighting in the Ural Mountains.

Ahead was a long and dangerous journey across central Asia — 4,000 miles on the Trans-Siberian Railroad. For protection, it carried an escort of heavily-armed Russian soldiers under the command of a British Army officer, Capt. Montagu Smith of the Royal Artillery. Its final destination was the wartorn city of Yekaterinburg, the headquarters of the White Russian forces, where just ten months before the Czar and his family had allegedly been executed.

Russia in 1919 was the scene of a bitter civil war between the forces of the Soviet government which had come to power following the revolution and the anti-Bolsheviks or White Russians who sought to regain control of the country.

In 1918 the Allied powers decided to send an international force to Siberia to aid the Whites. By the summer of the following year the port city of Vladivostok was crowded with Allied troops — American, British, Canadian, French, Japanese, Serbian, Italian and Czech. They saw little action but their presence prevented the local Bolsheviks from seizing power and kept open the Trans-Siberian Railroad, the vital life line along which Allied war supplies were channelled to the White Russians fighting in the interior.

The supplies under Captain Smith's charge however, were unlike any others destined to participate in the Russian civil war. On board the train stabled eight to a boxcar and originally from the ranches of Alberta and Saskatchewan, were 154 horses of the Royal North West Mounted Police. With them, to ensure their safe journey, went six members of the Force's Siberian squadron. Before they reached their destination more than a month later, these men would experience one of the most unusual episodes in the Force's history.

A squadron of Royal North West Mounted Policemen arrived in Siberia as a result of the Canadian government's decision to join with the other Allies in intervening in the Russian civil war. Czarist Russia had entered the war against Germany in 1914 on the side of Britain and France. As long as Russia remained in the conflict, Germany was forced to divide its military strength and fight its opponents on two fronts one in eastern Europe, the other in the west.

Following the October Revolution of 1917 however, the Soviet government decided to bring the war between Germany and Russia to an end. In March 1918 in the Polish border town of Brest-Litovsk, a Soviet delegation under Leon Trotsky signed a peace treaty with Germany. The withdrawal of Russia from the war enabled the Germans to concentrate their forces on the western front. In the spring of 1918 the German armies made important gains in France and Belgium.

The successful outcome of the Allied cause was further threatened by the outbreak of civil war between the rival factions in Russia. As order in the country broke down the oil and grain resources of the Ukraine lay open to German domination. In addition, more than 60,000 Czech troops who had formed part of the imperial army were in danger of being imprisoned by the Soviet government.

In an attempt to reopen the eastern front, prevent strategic resources from falling into German hands, and to ensure the safe withdrawal of the Czech troops, the Allied powers agreed in July 1918 to send a military force to Siberia to aid the anti-Bolshevik elements in their struggle to regain power. A few weeks later — on August 12 — the Canadian government sanctioned the formation of an expeditionary force of 5,000 men for Siberia, including a cavalry unit.

Within a few days of the government's decision, Commissioner Perry was given authority to recruit a cavalry squadron of six officers, 184 other ranks and 181 horses for service in Siberia. The government's announcement was welcomed by the members of the Force, many of whom had been anxious to see active service ever since the war began.

The squadron, later known as B Squadron, RNWMP, was quickly organized and trained at Regina. More than half the volunteers were seasoned men brought in from detachment duty. The remainder were mainly youngsters in their late teens from the farms and ranches of Alberta and Saskatchewan, who jumped at the chance to serve overseas with a mounted unit they knew and respected.

On Oct. 1, 1918 members of the Squadron were granted leave of absence and transferred to the Canadian Expeditionary Force, Siberia. A few days later, an advance party of one officer and 20 other ranks left for Vladivostok to arrange accommodation for the rest of the Squadron. The remainder sailed from Vancouver aboard the S.S. *Monteagle* on November 17, under the command of Maj. (later Asst. Commr.) G.S. Worsley. With them went the Squadron's horses, many of which had already served the Force for many years on the prairies.

The Squadron's stay in Siberia was only to last a few months. Even before it sailed, the war in Europe had come to an end. With the signing of the Armistice on Nov. 11, 1918, the main cause for the Allied intervention disappeared. For B Squadron the next few months were spent carrying out routine duties in and around Vladivostok, without seeing any action.

Public opinion in Canada meanwhile, had become increasingly hostile toward the presence of Canadian troops in Siberia. The Canadian government had been uncertain of the soundness of intervening in the civil war from the outset. Early in the new year Prime Minister Borden decided that starting in April 1919 the Canadian forces would gradually be withdrawn.

Before they left however, the Canadians were to hand over some of their equipment and supplies to the White Russians. Among the items to be left behind were the horses of B Squadron. They were to be shipped by rail to Yekaterinburg in the Ural Mountains, more than 4,000 miles west of Vladivostok, to reinforce the White Russian cavalry.

On May 17, 1919 the horses were reluctantly moved from the Squadron's barracks to the railyards at First River. The decision to leave the horses behind was not a popular one with the members of B Squadron. They had grown attached to their mounts. Some of them had ridden the same horse on detachment duty back on the prairies.

At First River Station they were handed over to Captain Smith, the officer in charge of remounts from the British Military Mission, who would be in command of the supply train. With only a squad of Russian soldiers as guards, Smith needed experienced horsemen who could take care of the animals on the long journey ahead.

To assist he obtained six volunteers from B Squadron: Farrier Sgt. J.E. "Teddy" Margetts, Reg. No. 7373; Cpl. P.S. Bossard, Reg. No. 7398; Troopers L.B. Clare, Reg. No. 7484; H.O. Nunnemaker, Reg. No. 7434; G.A. Pilkington, Reg. No. 7368; and M. Wright, Reg. No. 7442. Teddy Margetts' willingness to accompany the horses was not unexpected. Born in Oxfordshire, England, he had earlier served with the British Army in the South African War, where his keen nose for adventure and his ability to handle horses had already established a colorful reputation. George Pilkington was another Englishman. The remainder of the party, like many of the members of B Squadron, were young Americans who had emigrated to western Canada after the turn of the century. Philip Bossard came from New York state, Mitchel Wright from Colorado. Luther Clare was one of three brothers in the Squadron who hailed from Virginia.

The horses had a long journey ahead. Work on the Trans-Siberian Railroad had begun in 1891. Czar Alexander III had hoped a rail link between the heartland of Russia and the Pacific Coast would open up Siberia for settlement and development as railroads had done in North America.

With the agreement of the Chinese government, the original line took a short cut through Manchuria, reentering Russian territory a few miles outside Vladivostok. Through service on this line, from Moscow to Vladivostok, a distance of 5,542 miles, was opened in 1903. The longer all-Russian route which passed north of Manchuria was not completed until 1914. By the time the train reached Yekaterinburg it would be closer to London than Vladivostok.

Travel over the Trans-Siberian Railroad during the summer of 1919 was not without hazards. Long sections of the line were guarded and patrolled by Allied troops. It was impossible however, to maintain security over every mile of track. The White Russians had little control in the Siberian countryside through which the railroad passed. In the interior, Red partisans had been organized among the peasants. It was not difficult for them to attack the railroad, creating delays on the already congested line. In the summer of 1919 the partisans were particularly active in an area west of Lake Baikal.

Leaving Vladivostok on May 18, 1919, the trainload of horses headed west for Yekaterinburg over the shorter route through northern China. Sergeant Margetts had been seconded by Smith to take charge of the animals to their destination. The other five members of the Squadron had permission to assist Smith as far as the Manchurian city of Harbin.

Once there they would return to Vladivostok to rejoin the rest of the Squadron which was preparing to leave for Canada. Smith found, however, that he could not rely upon the Russian guards to help Margetts with the horses. Frequent stops had to be made to obtain fresh water and give the animals a chance to exercise. By the time the train reached Harbin, several of them had become ill. Unless the other men continued to help, many of the horses would never reach Yekaterinburg. Smith decided therefore, to disobey orders and take them all the way, a decision they readily complied with.

On June 4, 2 1/2 weeks after leaving Vladivostok, the horses and the men of the RNWMP suddenly found themselves caught in the midst of the Russian civil war. West of Lake Baikal, near the remote Siberian town of Tayshet, the train was "attacked and wrecked by Bolsheviks". The derailment took place on a steep enbankment. Nineteen of the boxcars were "smashed to atoms". Two of the Russian guards and 15 horses died in the crash. Another 24 Russian soldiers were injured.

The members of the Force set about handling the situation in a manner which was to win them high praise and recognition. With the assistance of the remaining Russians, Teddy Margetts took charge of the rescue operation. Many of the horses were still trapped inside the overturned boxcars, others lay tangled in the wreckage. A number were so badly injured they were later destroyed. However, Margetts' prompt action and leadership enabled many of the trapped animals to be rescued. "By his example and energy," the official citation later stated, "many valuable horses were saved."

Meanwhile some 20 to 30 horses had broken loose from the overturned cars. Badly frightened, they quickly decided to put as many miles as possible between themselves and the noise and confusion of the railroad. Like Margetts, Corporal Bossard acted quickly to save the horses.

He was determined they should not be left to an uncertain fate in the Siberian wilderness. Although under sniper fire from the retreating partisans, he rallied three other members of the Force behind him, and securing injured mounts, took off into the countryside after the escaping horses. Risking capture by the Reds, the four men rode several miles before the last of the runaways were turned and headed back to the train.

It was several days before the remaining horses and their escorts were able to continue the journey to Yekaterinburg. They finally reached there June 25, 1919 — 38 days after their departure from Vladivostok. Behind them was probably one of the longest journeys ever made by a trainload of military horses. Once they were handed over to the White Russians, the men had to face the long trip back to the coast. B Squadron meanwhile, was already crossing the Pacific on its way home.

Captain Smith had nothing but praise for the conduct of the members of the Force. To Commissioner Perry he wrote: "All of your men behaved splendidly ... I could not wish for a finer lot." He especially singled out the action taken by Farrier Sergeant Margetts and Corporal Bossard at the time of the derailment.

For the way in which they distinguished themselves, both men were eventually decorated. Teddy Margetts was awarded the Meritorious Service Medal. To Philip Bossard went the Military Medal for "Gallantry and Distinguished Service".

With the exception of George Pilkington and Teddy Margetts, all the members of the train squad took their discharge shortly after returning to Canada. George Pilkington remained in the Force until 1922 as a member of the riding staff at Depot Division. Philip Bossard eventually opened a locksmith business in Calgary, which he ran until his death in May

1968. Today his son, who carries on the business, is the proud owner of his father's Military Medal. Teddy Margetts retired to pension in 1937, after spending many years at N Division. He passed away at Winchester, Ontario, Nov. 3, 1969.

As for the horses, their fate remains unknown. Shortly after they were turned over to the White Russians, the Red Army launched a new and decisive offensive. Yekaterinburg was captured by the Bolsheviks a few days after the horses were delivered. The Whites were soon in full retreat.

By October 1919, all opposition to the Soviet government in central Siberia had been crushed. In all probability, the horses eventually fell into the hands of the enemy. Perhaps they ended up as remounts for Trotsky's Red Army.

Whatever their fate, the inscription on the Force's Guidon "Siberia 1918–19" is a lasting reminder of their participation in the Russian civil war.

Horses

34

How the RCMP Came to Have Black Horses

D/Commr. W.H. Kelly (Rtd.)

During the early days of the Force when horses were the only means of transportation, the NWMP found it difficult to obtain a sufficient number of the right type of horses for the patrol work required of them—long arduous patrols, often with little feed. The "march west" resulted in the death of many horses as well as leaving a large number of them in poor health with a condition known as "Alkalied".

As a result, Assistant Commisioner Macleod, who was in charge of their first post—later to be named Fort Macleod—was forced to send some members into the United States to buy horses, and such trips continued for a number of years. The only horses the Mounties were able to purchase were unbroken bronchos, which in time became just the kind of horses the Force required.

In addition to the horses purchased in the U.S., the NWMP managed to acquire some horses raised by local ranchers to augment the periodic shipments of eastern horses. The latter were never really suited to Force requirements in the west, but because of the general difficulty in obtaining horses it was a number of years before the Force could replace the eastern mounts with horses raised in western Canada or the United States.

Suitability being the determining factor in selection, the NWMP made no attempt to obtain horses of any particular colour. For example, when the Force began its march west to the prairie region from Fort Dufferin in 1874, the mounts obtained from Ontario were so varied in colour that each of the NWMP's six divisions had a predominently different hue of horse: A Division had dark bays; B Division, dark brown; C Division, bright chestnuts; D Division, grays and buckskins; E Division, blacks; and F Division, light bays. The horses on the march included the forty or so that had been purchased by Acting Commissioner W. Osborne-Smith around Winnipeg in 1873, in preparation for the arrival of the NWMP in the late fall of that year.

When the prairies began to be settled, western businesses and ranchers competed for the type of horse required in the west, so the difficulty in obtaining the right kind of horses for the Force remained. This problem still existed at the time the RNWMP began to mechanize its transportation. Westerners who had used horses began to use mechanical means of getting around. This caused the many horse breeders to go out of business, giving the Force even less choice as to the colour and quality of horses it purchased. Up until the time when black horses were introduced into the Musical Ride, the colour of RCMP horses was generally bay of one shade or another.

It was over sixty years after the inception of the NWMP that the idea of standardizing the colour of its horses came to a man who was in a position to do something about it. In 1935, Assistant Commissioner S.T. Wood had been in London, England, taking a *modus operandi* course at Scotland Yard, and he was there again as the officer in charge of the RCMP King George VI coronation contingent. On both occasions he saw the scarlet-coated Life Guards on their black horses and was very impressed with their appearance. Some years later, Commissioner Wood told me that seeing the Life Guards with their black horses had given him the idea that the RCMP should turn to black horses, first for the Musical Ride and then for recruit equitation training.

During this time and for many years thereafter, and as had been done since 1873, the Force purchased its remounts when they were three years old. They were often small in stature, but with proper care and feeding usually grew to the standards required by the Force — 15.2 hands in height and weighing between 1,100 and 1,200 pounds. They were initially roughly broken in and only after an additional four to six months training, when a recruit could safely ride them, were they used for recruit training.

When S.T. Wood became the eighth commissioner of the Force in 1938, word went out to purchase as many black horses as possible. It was soon apparent that a suitable number of horses of this colour could not be obtained, and equally apparent that if the Force was ever to get black horses in sufficient numbers it would have to raise its own. And so it was that, in 1939, a limited breeding program began at the Depot Division stables in Regina.

World War II began that fall and this undoubtedly slowed the implementation of any plans for an extensive breeding program. A few mares were purchased and some of the older equitation mares were transferred to the breeding program. The stallion "King" was purchased at this time.

270

He was black in colour and was the son of an American saddle horse sire and a Thoroughbred/Percheron-cross mare. He clearly showed the Percheron strain.

"King" was not particularly successful as a sire and was replaced by a black Thoroughbred stallion named "Fred Tracey", rented from his owner in Ottawa at the rate of $35 a foal. However, it soon became clear that the facilities at Regina were not suited to a breeding program commensurate with the needs of the Force, so consideration was given to moving them elsewhere.

S.T. Wood was familiar with the horse-breeding area of southwestern Saskatchewan. This area included the Cypress Hills and the site of old Fort Walsh, a former headquarters of the NWMP, which later became one of Canada's official historic sites.

The RCMP purchased 706 acres of land, which included the location of the old fort. Suitable buildings were erected on the exact site of the fort, and a manager (soon to be known as the "wrangler") was engaged. The Force also leased 2,305 acres of adjacent range land from the provincial government.

There was some delay in acquiring and developing the properties because war duties required all possible manpower and money, and later it was necessary to temporarily abandon equitation training of recruits as well as the colourful Musical Ride. Nevertheless, by the spring of 1943 the property, now referred to in the Force as "the ranch", was ready to receive the nucleus of the proposed expanded breeding program from Regina: twenty-three mares, eleven foals and the rented stallion "Fred Tracey".

The problem of obtaining the right kind of stallion was ever present during the early years of the breeding program. Among the stallions used for breeding purposes, one or two were actually chestnut in colour, a colour the Force expected would dominate in the foals thrown by the black mares. During the early period, stallions other than Thoroughbreds were also kept. Later on, (with one exception, when "Hymeryk", a stallion of the Trahkener breed was used), only Thoroughbred stallions were accepted. Although most of these stallions appeared to be black in colour, some of them were actually registered as dark brown.

By the 1950's, black foals began to appear with some regularity, while others were various shades of brown. Occasionally a bright chestnut foal was born, sometimes to a black mare by a black or dark-brown stallion.

The breeding program at Fort Walsh was based on the hard style of raising horses. The animals were kept outdoors summer and winter, fending for themselves on the natural grassy range, with practically no supplementary feeding. The Force horses were rounded up in the fall, identified among others belonging to neighbouring ranchers by the fused MP brand—the Force brand since 1887. The young stock was branded and then put back on the range after the three-year-old remounts had been selected.

Those responsible for the program believed that raising horses in this manner would produce a horse with strong muscles and good bone, and generally tough enough to carry heavy policemen in the saddle. No doubt there was some merit to this view, but some authorities now believe that these good characteristics were offset by the fact that the remounts began saddle work only a few months after leaving the ranch. In the 1950's, a program of regular supplementary feeding was put into effect, and this not only improved the appearance of the stock but produced better breeding results as well.

Commissioner Wood retired from the RCMP in the spring of 1951, and was immediately appointed a special constable of the Force (without pay) so that he could officially remain involved in the breeding program which he had begun. He spent every summer and fall at the ranch until 1965, when he was stricken with a serious illness which eventually resulted in his death.

By the mid-1950's the Force was still not producing either the quantity or the quality of remounts that it required, so the purchase of remounts continued mostly in colours other than black. On the advice of several experts, the breeding program was expanded, so as to ensure not only an increase in quantity of foals but in quality as well. The first obvious step was to purchase suitable mares and the price for them was set at about $250 each.

About this same time there was a fear that with the continuous use of Thoroughbred stallions the horses were developing too fine a bone for the work required of them. As an experiment, two purebred Clydesdale mares were obtained from the Dominion Experimental Farm at Indian Head, Saskatchewan, and bred to a black Thoroughbred stallion. No one expected that the result of this mating would produce black saddle horses for Force use, but that the filly foals through subsequent breedings might produce a heavier-boned black horse. The experiment was limited to the extent that only a few filly foals were used in this way, leaving a residue of Clydesdale blood even in some of the beautiful three-quarter or more black Thoroughbred horses the Force uses today.

In spite of the prolonged efforts of the Force to raise its own horses, it wasn't until the mid-1960's, 25 years after the breeding program began, that all the horses in the Musical Ride were raised by the Force. Even then, there were a few whose colour was dark brown, not black. Not until the mid-1970's were all the RCMP horses — breeding stock (except stallions), Musical Ride and equitation — of the Force's own breeding.

Before this period, however, a great change had taken place in regard to RCMP horses. In the summer of 1966 the federal government, as an economy measure, decided that RCMP recruit equitation training should end, but the RCMP Musical Ride should be retained as a permanent public relations attraction. The government also decided that the Musical Ride operations base should be transferred from Regina, Saskatchewan, to Rockcliffe, Ontario, and, that the breeding operation should be moved from Fort Walsh to some place near Ottawa.

The Force realized that if recruits did not take equitation training it would be necessary to retain a number of equitation horses — in addition to those used in the Musical Ride — to train those members in equitation who would volunteer for Musical Ride duty. Thus a number of such horses were also retained, and the remainder were sold in Regina at public auction. At the same time plans were being made to ship the breeding stock to Ontario.

Soon the Force purchased 345 acres of farmland at Pakenham in the pastoral Ottawa Valley, about 30 miles northwest of Ottawa. New buildings and fences were erected and by late 1967 and early 1968, the breeding stock from the ranch found themselves in completely different surroundings. Instead of grazing on the hilly range land at Fort Walsh, they now grazed on the flat prairie-like pastures at Pakenham. Whereas the range at Fort Walsh had never seen a plough, the pastures at Pakenham had been farmland for more than 150 years. Instead of living outdoors all year round, the horses could now be taken indoors during severe weather. In addition, the farm soon began to produce enough hay to feed not only the Pakenham breeding stock, but the Musical Ride and equitation horses at Rockcliffe as well. Despite these differences, there is one great similarity between the ranch at Fort Walsh and the farm at Pakenham: both have fine fresh-water creeks running through their properties.

In the 15 years since the Pakenham remount station was officially opened on December 1, 1968, it has developed into a model horse-breeding station. It was at first under the management of Ralph Baumann, who came to Pakenham from Fort Walsh, and later under the watchful eye of Bruce Parr, Baumann's assistant at Fort Walsh and later at Pakenham.

The breeding program has not only resulted in the black colour of RCMP horses being stabilized, but to a remarkable degree it has been responsible for their standardization in size, conformation and temperament. These horses must be considered as a definite type of Thoroughbred, even though not of full Thoroughbred blood. However, they cannot be

273

considered as a separate breed, as one international writer on horses has concluded.

The present horses of the RCMP are three-quarters to seven-eighths Thoroughbred, with a few pure Thoroughbreds among them, but there is no great concern about these and future horses being too fine-boned for the work they are required to do. Continued attention to the type of stallions and mares used in the breeding program, as well as the continuing practice of not using remounts until they are 5 to 6 years old (by which time they have had about two years' training), has resulted in a satisfactory type of horse.

It is now 46 years since the late Commissioner S.T. Wood conceived the idea of the RCMP using black horses, and during that time many of our members have helped to develop the breeding program which today is at peak efficiency. Our beautiful black horses are now seen by more people, at home and abroad, than ever before. As long as the RCMP have such horses they will remain a tribute to Commissioner S.T. Wood. But even he could not have foreseen the high degree of success the breeding program has reached today.

35

Lady Dewdney's Own
The Beginnings of the RCMP Musical Ride

Stan Horral, RCMP Historian

It is not widely realized that the RCMP Musical Ride is almost 100 years old. Although it sometimes said that the first ride was organized in 1876, no evidence has ever been found to support this claim. There seems little doubt that the first musical rides performed publicly by the North-West Mounted Police took place at Regina in the winter of 1887. Constable John Stewart, who participated in those original performances, described them many years later in an article entitled "How the Musical Ride Started". Known today throughout the world for its skill and appeal, the RCMP Musical Ride traces its humble beginnings back to the Canadian prairies nearly a centry ago.

Mounted displays by units of cavalry are probably as old as warfare itself. Over the centuries there are numerous records of soldiers engaging in mounted tournaments, cavalcades and sports as an occasion to show off their ability to ride and their prowess with weapons. During the last quarter of the nineteenth century it became popular for cavalry regiments througout the British Emprie to give public demonstrations of their military proficiency. These usually involved a mounted troop being put through its drill movements, and was often followed by a mock battle on horseback, or contests in swordsmanship and the use of the lance. In February 1885, the Royal Cavalry School (ancestor of the Royal Canadian Dragoons) in Quebec City gave a public exhibition of cavalry exercises without music. In July of the same year, the NWMP held a field day at the Barracks in Regina which included several mounted events organized by Sergeant George Kempster, who was to be a key figure in the presentation of the first musical rides two years later.

What distinguished a musical ride from these exhibitions of cavalry movements and tactics was the substitution of a brass band for a drill instructor. Instead of responding to words of command, the change from one formation to another was signalled to the mounted troops by a change of tempo or tune in the accompanying music. The result was a non-stop harmonious blend of music, movement and horsemanship. The first known public performance of what was from the start termed a "musical ride" was given by the 1st Regiment of Life Guards at the Royal Military Tournament in London, England, in June 1882.

The Royal Tournament, as it is called today, had its start in 1880 as "A Military Tournament and Assault-at-Arms". The inaugural performance was held in north London at the Agricultural Hall, Islington. At first it consisted largely of competitions between contingents from several British regiments. There were shooting contests, sham battles, jousts with various weapons and riding events like tilting the ring and slicing the lemon. Much later the Royal Navy, Royal Marines and the Royal Air Force added their own contributions to the annual event to turn it into a vast military pageant. The first tournaments lasted for about a week. It was intended to use the profits to assist the widows of soldiers. Unfortunately, for the first two years, 1880–81, the public stayed away in droves and it was a financial flop.

This all changed in 1882. That year the 1st Life Guards introduced a musical ride into the program. It was an instant success and the hall which seated 4,000 persons and had standing room for 10,000 more was packed for every performance. Thereafter the musical ride became a permanent and popular part of the spectacle. For many years the 1st and 2nd Regiments of Life Guards took turns annually to put it on. Another popular innovation at the Royal Tournament occurred in 1884 when a display of cavalry movements was presented by the 3rd Hussars. The origins of these first musical rides and mounted displays remain very obscure. Tradition links them with tournaments held earlier by British Volunteer regiments. It is also likely that they had some tie with the experience of the British Army in India, where military pageants that included mounted events had been taking place for some years. There are, however, good reasons to link these developments in London with what was to occur in Regina in 1887.

It was the fortunate conjunction of several factors which brought about the appearance of the first Mounted Police musical rides. Strangely enough, Louis Riel and the rebellious Metis of 1885 had a big part in it. It was the unrest of that year and the possibility of further trouble that prompted the government to expand and reorganize the North West Mounted Police on a more permanent footing. The strength of the Force was increased from 500 to 1,000 men. Annual expenditure upon it also doubled to over one million dollars. An extensive building program was planned for many of the major posts. Among the organizational changes was the establishment of a "Depot" Division at Regina as a permanent training centre.

Also planned for Regina was the erection of a large wooden indoor riding school. Hitherto, all mounted training had taken place out of doors. Needless to say, in severe winter weather it was disrupted. A riding school was essential to the organization of a musical ride because it was only during the winter, when the men had been brought in from summer detachments, that there were sufficient riders available to train one. Construction on the riding school began in the summer of 1885. It was not completed until May of the following year. The building which cost $30,000 dwarfed everything at Headquarters. It was 60 metres long and 36 metres wide with a gallery at one end for spectators and a band. The *Regina Leader* described it as "one of the finest in the country."

The riding school provided the necessary accommodation. Three key individuals now entered upon the scene. The first of these was Reg. No. 1120, George Kempster, who took his discharge from the Life Guards in London in 1884, and came to Canada and joined the Mounted Police in December of that year. The thirty-year-old Kempster had also served for several years in the 11th Hussars. Whether he was involved in the first musical rides in London from 1882–84 is unknown, but as a member of the Life Guards stationed there it is unlikely that he would not have known about them. In fact, Kempster turned out to be an outstanding horseman and by 1886 he was the senior riding instructor in Regina with the rank of sergeant major.

Next to appear was Reg. No. 1365, Jacob (Jakey) Farmer, a short, stout man with an unmistakable Cockney accent, who joined the Force in May 1885. Farmer was another veteran of the British Army. He had spent 10 years in H.M. King's Own Regiment and had considerable experience with military bands. Commissioner Herchmer was a strong supporter of bands in the Force, and in 1886 he appointed Farmer bandmaster with the task of reorganizing the mounted and dismounted bands in Regina. The Commissioner later commended him for their high state of efficiency.

Finally, and probably most important, there was Inspector William George Matthews, a forty-year-old former lieutenant and riding master of the 3rd Hussars, a regiment which had had a prominent part in presenting mounted displays at the Royal Tournament. Matthews had also spent several years of his service with the regiment stationed in India. He was commissioned an inspector in the NWMP on October 20, 1886. Shortly after his arrival at Headquarters Herchmer appointed him riding master. He took up his new duties just as the men of B Division returned to Regina from their summer detachments to spend the winter at mounted and dismounted drill. Just what Matthews and Kempster knew about musical rides at this point, no one will ever know for sure. They were certainly experienced and accomplished horsemen, and together with the new riding school, the men of B Division and Jakey Farmer and his band, it was their expertise that put together the first musical rides of the NWMP.

There were five public performances of the ride during the winter of 1887. The records of the NWMP reveal very little as to the nature of them. Although they sometimes comprised 16 men instead of 32, from the descriptions of them in the local newspapers they appear to have had most of the elements which are to be found in the RCMP Musical Ride today. The first performance took place in the riding school on Saturday afternoon January 15, 1887. In the spectators' gallery were Commissioner and Mrs. Herchmer, several other officers and their spouses, as well as a number of guests from town who braved a blizzard and sub-zero temperatures to attend. The reporter from the *Regina Leader* described the scene:

> The band, under Mr. Farmer, was playing a spirited march, and sixteen Mounted Policemen, with lances at rest ... were putting their equines through a series of geometrical and other figures with remarkable accuracy and skill, with a most pleasing effect.
>
> After going through a number of interesting gyrations, radiating circles and other odd figures, now walking, the next minute trotting, and then breaking into a gallop, the horsemen formed into a line at the opposite end of the pit from the gallery, and as the band struck up 'Bonnie Dundee,' cantered forward to the other end, keeping exact time with the music, halted abruptly, broke in the centre, wheeled sharply to right and left, formed fours and cantered back along the sides.

Apart from the number of riders it sounds very similar to the present RCMP Musical Ride. Interestingly enough, the Ride still performs to the sound of "Bonnie Dundee".

The second performance took place on Wednesday, January 26th, but the newspapers did not cover it. The third occurred a month later on February 26th. This time it was a state occasion with His Honour Lt. Governor Dewdney and Mrs. Dewdney in the gallery, and there were 32 riders instead of 16. The newspaper's brief account describes it as being "heartily applauded by the spectators," and reflecting "great credit on the drill officers".

The next musical ride was presented a few days later on Saturday, March 5th. Once again the Lt. Governor of the NWT attended, along with deputy ministers from Ottawa, the territorial justices and other local dignitaries. The *Leader* found this ride similar to the others, but "more interesting and exciting". Once again there were 32 riders. The charge at the end was so warmly received that at the request of the ladies in the audience Inspector Matthews had it repeated. The final ride of 1887 took place on April 5th. As on former occasions the music was under the direction of Bandmaster Farmer. This time the ride commenced with the horses dancing slowly to the accompaniment. Then according to the *Regina Journal*, "The company of sixteen horsemen proceeded to go through the drill, evolutionizing and manoeuvering so rapidly as to make it difficult at times to keep track of their movements." A few days later B Division headed out for Wood Mountain and its summer detachments.

The only illustration depicting these first musical rides is a drawing by the well-known American frontier artist Frederic Remington, which appeared in the December 24, 1887, issue of *Harper's Weekly*, a New York magazine. It shows 16 riders charging. The scene, however, is set on the barrack square rather than in the riding school. Whether Remington actually witnessed one of the first performances is not known, although he certainly was in western Canada about that time. The editor of the *Regina Leader*, who did see the rides, described the drawing as "pretty accurate". Indeed, the detail of the uniform and saddlery is so good it is hard to believe that Remington was not working from real life.

Several years would pass before there would be another performance of the musical ride. There were a number of reasons for this. The first and most immediate was that on November 26, 1887, a fire was started in the riding school by a faulty stove in an adjacent harness room. In bitterly cold weather the fire extinguishers were found to be frozen and within minutes the showplace of Headquarters was reduced to a pile of ashes and rubble. In addition, the principals behind the first rides soon moved on to other things. In October 1887, Sergeant Major Kempster purchased his discharge to try his hand at farming. He eventually died in Calgary in 1920. During the winter of 1888, the band was temporarily suspended due to a lack of musicians. It was revived again, but Sergeant Jakey Farmer took his discharge in 1890 to go into business. He turned out to be a much better bandmaster than a businessman and was soon trying to re-engage, but there were no vacancies. Inspector Matthews, meanwhile, had been transferred to Lethbridge where there was a shortage of officers for field duty. Mrs. Matthews had detested Regina. Lethbridge did not improve her view that life on the Canadian prairies was dull and unsophisticated, a colonial backwater. In 1893 Matthews resigned his commission and returned to England.

More important in the long run, however, was newspaper criticism. A satirical Toronto weekly called *The Grip* saw the rides as an example of extravagance by the Conservative government of Sir John A. Macdonald, which was sensitive to allegations of misuse of public funds. It published a cartoon which labelled the musical rides as "Lady Dewdney's Own", and suggested that murder and robbery were taking place while policemen were being used to entertain the Lt. Governor's wife and her friends. The message hit home. It would be a while before the Mounted Police again engaged in any such "frills". Nevertheless, the 1887 rides were well received by the citizens of Regina, who, in an age when the horse was still an important means of transportation, were qualified to recognize the skill they represented. They would not be forgotten. Eventually, there would be requests for a repeat performance. As to the Mounted Police, they saw the potential of the musical ride for promoting goodwill in the community. A tradition was in the making. The riding school was rebuilt in 1889, but with the departure of Matthews and Kempster it would be a few years before circumstances would again favour the organization of another musical ride.

36

The Evolution of the Horse

D/Commr. W.H. Kelly (Rtd.)

Whenever we see or think of the RCMP Musical Ride, we appreciate the beauty of the horses and enjoy watching them perform. But rarely do we think that these beautiful animals, and others of different breeds and sizes, evolved from the small rabbit-like creatures found on the North American continent, millions of years ago. There is evidence to show that the evolution of the horse predates that of man by some sixty million years.

During the Eocene period, some sixty to forty million years B.C., the earliest ancestor of the horse, *Eohippus* (*eos* meaning dawn and *hippos* meaning horse) was only fifteen inches (four hands) high, and lived on leaves and plants. In the next 20 million years, its successor, *Mesohippus*, had reached a height of 20 inches. Over the next 25 million years, or so, to about 10,000 years B.C., through the Oligocene, Miocene, Piliocene and the Pleistocene periods, the horse lost its toes, gained a hoof and had grown to about 53 inches (13 hands) in height. Since then the horse has evolved into the beautiful animal of the present day.

Bones have been found in North and South America which show that horses existed on these continents in the Pleistocene period, about 1,000,000 to 10,000 years B.C. But they disappeared from these areas and are believed to have crossed into Asia by way of the Siberian Isthmus, to appear again only when the Spanish conquistadores brought them back in the 16th century.

Meanwhile horses had been evolving in Asia and Europe. They were first hunted for meat and, later, kept in herds much as cattle are kept today, long before men learned to domesticate them for other purposes. The Chinese are thought by some to have been the first horsemen, but this is disputed by others who believe the Brahmans were the first.

It is also known that there were skilled riders in Asia, Europe and North Africa as early as the third millenium B.C. Some time before that man had already begun to value the horse as a draft animal, and harness in a crude form is known to have existed as early as 4,000 years B.C.

THE MOUNTIES AS THEY SAW THEMSELVES

In 1600 B.C. in the general area of today's Middle East, the Hittites, who had used horses in battle over a long period, wrote the first cunieform text on the raising and care of horses. About this same time the Egyptians are known to have used horses to draw chariots, but this was thousands of years after the Assyrians had done the same thing.

It was inevitable that man would use the horse to help him in battle against his enemies. This had been done thousands of years before Alexander the Great, in the 4th century B.C., crossed the Hellespont, not only with tens of thousands of soldiers on foot, but 5,000 mounted on horses. It soon became common for all armies in Europe to have a complement of mounted troops.

Large horses were developed to carry heavy armour into battle, in the days when the broad axe was considered a useful weapon, and later to draw heavy cannons and mortars. Much later, the idea began to prevail that speed and surprise were useful qualities in winning battles, and so lighter horses and cavalry tactics came into use.

After centuries of being used on the battlefield the horse eventually gave way to mechanization. Nevertheless, horses played an important part in World War I, and even at the beginning of World War II in some European countries. Today, in countries such as Switzerland, they still are used in mountainous regions to haul equipment over rugged territory, where soldiers have to patrol.

As the horse was being developed for war, it was also being put to other uses. From the time it was domesticated, man used horses for his own welfare. But until the eighteenth century, usually only people of means could afford to keep them. But as society evolved, more people began to own horses when they were able to use them in commercial ventures. As the only means of land transportation it became necessary to put the horse to work in the interest of the community and not just in the interests of the wealthy.

From very early days the horse has been used for recreation and entertainment. At first the horse was used by some men to hunt for food; later, the hunt became part sport as well as necessity. Soon the horse became part of the pomp and pageantry at Royal Courts. History is replete with details of chariot races, and even polo was played in the 4th century B.C. Romans are known to have raced horses and imported stallions and mares to breed the types of horses they desired.

In medieval times, jousting took place at tournaments, and very early the horse became part of the bullfight. No one knows exactly when steeple-chasing and flat racing first took place, but they were given a tremendous boost when the English, in the late 17th and early 18th centuries, imported Turk, Barb and Arab horses, which became the foundation stock for all thoroughbred horses in the world today. In America where all the European sporting uses of the horse were accepted, some additional ones were added, such as rodeos and stampedes. A new type of horse, some may call it a breed, was especially developed to run a quarter of a mile — the quarter horse.

While all these things were going on, ponies were not forgotten. Some were used for work purposes, such as the pit ponies, where height is a consideration, but ponies were mostly kept for recreational purposes, such as light carriage work and the show ring.

Although the horse as a work animal has greatly diminished, it is still used for farm work in many countries, and it has not altogether vanished from the North American farm scene. Some religious sects, such as the Mennonites, refuse to mechanize their farm operations, or even to use cars to go to market. But the recreational horse is more popular than ever today. In this category can be placed the draft horses that are specially bred, not for work purposes but for the purpose of improving the breed, or as is done by some breweries, as an advertising gimmick.

Our affluent society has enabled more young people than ever to own their own horses, or to take riding lessons on rented horses. Horse racing is as popular as ever, and harness racing probably more popular than ever before, although this can be attributed as much to love of gambling as love of horses.

During its history, the RCMP has used horses as draft, military and recreational animals. As in the case of work horses, generally, mechanization gradually spelled the doom of the RCMP patrol horse. The recreational use of RCMP horses, as seen in today's Musical Ride, brings pleasure to hundreds of thousands of people, worldwide.

The Musical Ride's popularity can be partly attributed to its pageantry and colour, but it is not difficult to believe that mostly it is the enjoyment of seeing beautiful, well trained horses perform. When watching them perform, even when one knows that it took them over sixty million years to evolve into the noble creatures they are, it is difficult to appreciate the fact that their ancestors were once small dog-like creatures only two or three hands high.

Policework

37

The Coquitlam Bank Robbery

Const. R.W. Morley

At 10.30 a.m. on Apr. 3, 1956, the bank alarm that will ring down through the history of the RCMP suddenly shattered the early morning routine of the Burnaby Detachment office, in British Columbia. Immediately the terse message that has lately been heard all too frequently in the Vancouver area, crackled over the police radio:

"Burnaby to all cars and stations.... A bank alarm.... The Royal Bank of Canada, Lougheed Highway and North Road. ... All other stations please maintain radio silence.... "

Over and over the message was repeated. While speeding police cars converged on the bank, an attempt was made to contact the premises by phone, a routine practice, to ascertain if the switch had been accidentally tripped. When no answer was received, all cars were notified that this was no false alarm.

The first car on the scene was one from nearby Maillardville Detachment, with Csts. H.M.C. Johnstone and A.L. Beach. When the car slowed near the bank, Johnstone leaped out and ran toward the side of the building. While Beach drove around to the parking lot in front of the bank, Johnstone headed for the front door. Everything inside appeared normal as he entered. The manager, J.D.W. Howat, was standing behind the counter. Johnstone asked if everything was all right.

Menaced by a sawed-off shot-gun in the hands of a masked bandit standing out of Johnstone's line of vision, Mr. Howat shook his head. At the same instant, Herbert Howerton, his face also masked, sprang from behind the counter and fired a .38 slug point-blank at the policeman, now only about 15 feet away. Falling to the floor and completely unprotected in the main lobby of the bank, Johnstone was suddenly the target for a barrage of shots from Howerton and Howard Folster who now ran, screaming hysterically, from the vault toward the main door, his only avenue of escape.

Drawing his revolver, Johnstone snapped one shot at William Banks as he attempted to leave the manager's office. The bullet struck Banks in the left shoulder, spinning him backward and knocking the shot-gun out of his hands. Johnstone next turned on Folster who was charging toward him, emptying all five shells from his .32 revolver as he ran. Most of these found their mark in the Policeman's body. His empty gun still clicking, Folster raced through the door, attempted to climb on the speeding get-away truck driven by the fourth bandit, William Gordon Garry Owen, but fell off and collapsed in blind terror under the wheels of another parked truck. Then Howerton, clutching $10,000 under his arm, leaped the bank counter and sprinted past the prostrate form of Johnstone, firing madly as he ran. One of Johnstone's bullets ripped through Howerton's left arm, and as he opened the door the bandit became a target for the bullets of both Constables Beach and Johnstone, who now staggered up from the floor and chased the fleeing man. About 15 feet from the door of the bank, Howerton suddenly stumbled and was probably dead the instant he hit the sidewalk, shot cleanly through the heart.

Banks surrendered meekly to Johnstone who was now sitting on the side-walk in front of the bank, covering Folster and Howerton with his empty gun.

Cst. U.J. Schroeder who had arrived, threw Banks to the ground, searched him, then directed the bank manager to cover him. Schroeder next took Folster into custody while Beach tried to intercept the youthful Owen who was attempting to escape in the truck, a fully loaded Thompson sub-machine gun still clutched in his right hand. Beach fired his remaining shots at Owen, and then hurled his empty revolver at him, shattering the side window of the vehicle. He then turned and assisted Johnstone into the Police car, radioing the description of the getaway truck and its driver as he raced to the Royal Columbian Hospital in New Westminster.

Meanwhile Owen sped along North Road, then turned west along Cameron Ave., attempting to reach a second car which the quartet had parked approximately two miles away. He was hotly pursued by two civilians and when he missed a turn, his truck skidded into a deep ditch. He scrambled out, still clutching the "Tommy Gun", and sprinted into the nearby woods. On his way through the brush Owen concealed the weapon under a log and continued across the Lougheed Highway where he was spotted by Csts. J.A. Fielders and L.W. Hanson, speeding toward the bank in an unmarked car. After a short chase, Owen surrendered.

The services of Police Dog "Rip" and his master, Cpl. I.E. Hall, were then requested, and the dog soon recovered the concealed machine gun.

Subsequent investigation at Langley B.C., where the homes of Howerton, Folster and Owen are located, revealed a second sub-machine gun, owned by the dead bandit, together with over 200 additional rounds of ammunition. This gun was a souvenir brought from Korea by Howerton, who served there with the Canadian Forces. It is apparently of Chinese manufacture, and a weapon deadly in its very simplicity.

Thus came to an end the wildest gun battle in the history of the RCMP. Fortunately the ending was a happy one. The conduct of all members who came under fire was worthy of the highest praise. Constable Johnstone, although wounded in the left little finger, left palm, left shoulder, right chest, right side, right forearm and left hip, was not injured in any vital organ. The bullet which entered his chest had been deflected from his heart by a button on his tunic. He was released from hospital approximately a week later, after having been promoted to the rank of Corporal by Commissioner Nicholson on the day following the robbery. His courage and devotion to duty are best summed up in the words of a *Time* magazine correspondent, for in those few seconds when he lay on the bank floor, lead ripping into his body from all directions, yet nevertheless fighting back with deadly accuracy, Johnstone was truly "outgunned but not outfought".

Two newspaper editorials, perhaps typical of the press comment generally on an efficient piece of police work, are reprinted here:

> For rootin' tootin' six-gun shootin' heroes, Canada does not need to look to its history or across the line for Davy Crocketts and assorted U.S. marshals. Constable Bud Johnstone of the Royal Canadian Mounted Police, 1956 version, makes them all look pretty soft.
>
> For the West is still wild and Constable Johnstone has shown that there are still men who are men away out West. In a pistol battle with bank robbers in Burnaby, B.C., the constable wound up with 12 [sic] bullet holes in his body and was still able to hold a press conference before doctors picked out seven bullets, with one still to come. . . .
>
> True to the tradition of the RCMP, Constable Johnstone did not draw his gun first and come in fighting ... the robbers started shooting. The bank robbers' union has every right to expect that a policeman with a bullet in him will lie down and take no further interest in their felonious proceedings.
>
> But eight slugs in him and The Law still shooting — son, that's enough to turn a crook to honest labor
>
> From: *The Calgary Herald*

> The Royal Canadian Mounted Police staged an exhibition of speed, efficiency and raw courage this week that has stirred the public's admiration.
>
> In less than 20 minutes after a Coquitlam bank was held up ... one bandit was dead, one suspect wounded and two other suspects were behind bars. . . .
>
> The hero of the piece is RCMP Constable (now Corporal) H.M.C. "Bud" Johnstone, 29, of Maillardville, who was hit eight times by slugs from

.32 and .38 calibre guns but who, despite his wounds, killed one of the bandits and felled another.

This is the sort of thing that makes a great police force.

All the electric warning systems, two-way radios and fast police cars are no substitute for the nerve that sends a young police officer dashing into a hail of lead determined to do his job, regardless of consequences.

Johnstone did his law-enforcement job and did it magnificently. He upheld the highest traditions of one of the world's finest police forces, and we are all thankful that he survived the heavy odds that were against him.

His performance, and that of the three other RCMP officers who were with him, is more than a great example of bravery.

It is a warning to all gunmen in this vicinity that they are taking their lives in their hands when they try to stage a hold-up. There is no better insurance against bandits than courageous straightshooting police.

From: *The Vancouver Province*

38

They Tamed the East Also

Insp. J.P. Blakeney (Rtd.)

In 1920, the Dominion and the Royal North-West Mounted Police, two federal police forces, amalgamated and became the RCMP. We in Nova Scotia were charged with the enforcement of all federal laws including the guarding of the naval dockyard and magazines.

At that time there wasn't an organized provincial police force, just the odd county and provincial constables. Should the Attorney General's Department require assistance, they would ask Ottawa and we would give them the help required.

I received instructions in May 1922 from my O.C., Insp. C.D. LaNauze, to go to Sydney and report to Mr. Patterson, the Crown prosecutor, as he wished several arrests made in Cape Breton. We did not know any facts. Inspector LaNauze told me to take Constable Cooke, the only man he could spare from regular duties at Halifax.

Constable Cooke and I went to Sydney on the night train and reported to Mr. Patterson, who later became Attorney General for the province. He asked how many men I had and I told him one. Mr. Patterson said I couldn't make the arrests with only one man, because the facts of the case warranted a much larger force.

The facts were that on the coastal steamer *Aspy*, which carried freight and passengers from Sydney to Bay St. Lawrence on a weekly schedule, four men from Bay St. Lawrence, travelling in the late fall of 1920 caused a great deal of trouble and damage. Under the influence of liquor, they smashed all cooking utensils, broke the engine-room skylight and performed such other acts that the captain had to return to North Sydney where the four somehow escaped back to their homes.

Warrants were issued for each and several county and provincial constables were sent to make the arrests. However, the four were all robust men in their 20s and the constables were not able to make the arrests. Then as winter was coming on and travelling in the district was next to impossible, nothing was done until the spring.

Mr. Patterson told me the only person at Bay St. Lawrence who would give assistance or information was Father MacDonald, the parish priest. All others were afraid on account of their size and conduct, especially while under the influence of liquor. Mr. Patterson said Father MacDonald was pleased the RCMP had been called in and hoped they would be successful.

After discussing the matter with the Crown prosecutor, I went on board the *Aspy* which was lying at a wharf in Sydney. I told the captain who we were and that we would be passengers on his boat the next day en route to Bay St. Lawrence. The captain said he didn't want to discourage me, but with only one constable I wouldn't be able to arrest the four men and return to Sydney. He said they had caused a terrible disturbance on his ship.

I told the captain I couldn't ask for assistance until I had made an effort to bring them in and hand them over to the authorities at Sydney. The captain said the only thing he could do was to wish me luck.

We went on board the *Aspy* early next morning and it blew up a gale almost from the north, causing the ship to plunge and roll continuously. Constable Cooke became seasick and couldn't eat all day. The heavy wind and rough seas delayed the ship so that we couldn't get up around Cape North and into Bay St. Lawrence, so the captain decided to go into Neil's Harbour until next morning when he thought the wind would decrease.

Neil's Harbour was almost 30 miles by road from Bay St. Lawrence. The captain said he knew a man who had a good horse and a double seated wagon who he thought would make the journey for us. He said his regular procedure was to leave Bay St. Lawrence about noon on his return trip to Sydney and he would not be back again until the following week, but if I could get to Bay St. Lawrence by road, he would wait there the next day until 2 p.m., but no later.

The man the captain referred us to agreed to take us, but the arrangements took time and we didn't leave Neil's Harbour until 9 p.m. The roads were muddy and Constable Cooke and I had to do a great deal of walking to help the horse on the long hills and by 1 a.m. it got tired. The driver said he knew a man who lived on the same road and he would try to borrow a horse to finish the trip.

We stopped at this man's house. He was asleep, but woke up and told our driver he could borrow the horse. We left with the fresh horse and arrived at Father MacDonald's about 4 a.m.

Father MacDonald was glad to see us, but said the men we were after were fishing lobsters from a factory at Meat Cove, six miles away and there wasn't a road, only a footpath. He said while we were resting he would see if he could get someone with a boat to take us to Meat Cove. He came back in about an hour and told us he wasn't able to get anyone—

their excuse being they wanted to tend their lobster traps, but he felt sure it was because they were afraid and did not wish to assist in the arrests.

Father MacDonald said he would call his housekeeper and we would all have breakfast, after which he would go with us as he thought we wouldn't be able to follow the path without a guide. He stayed with us until we were in sight of the factory.

On arrival I asked for the boss and he told me the four I was looking for were out in boats. He said he would not be able to give any assistance in connection with the arrests. He informed us we could go into the can shop, a small building apart from the factory.

There was a temporary stage built near the factory where the boats could unload lobsters at high tide, but this could not be done at low tide, which was the case on our arrival. Boats arriving at that time had to land at the beach — about 100 yards from the factory — and the men would carry their lobsters in hand barrows.

There was a young lad who came to the can shop for empty cases and he found out who we were and became interested in our work, so I told him who we were after and to tell us when any of them arrived at the beach, which he did.

When the first boat arrived he told us it contained John and Neil MacLellan. When these two started up the beach, we walked down and met them. I asked if they were John and Neil and the latter said they were and asked why we wanted to know. I told them who we were and why we were there.

Neil said, "Oh yes, you and who else ?"

I told him Constable Cooke and myself were the only ones. He looked at Cooke, who had been seasick all day, travelled all night and then gone another six miles on foot, and said he did not look as if he could put up a good fight.

It was raining and I noticed an empty shack near the bank and asked them to go to it so I could explain who else, if necessary, would help to effect their arrest.

When we got in the shack John, the elder of the two said to Neil, "These men are from the Mounted Police and we should go along with them without any trouble." Neil agreed to this, but at first it looked as if he was going to give some trouble. They said their brother Murdock would soon be in and they would call him up to the shack.

Murdock arrived shortly after and they told him who we were and that they were going back to Sydney with us without causing trouble. Murdock asked if they had turned "chicken" and they said no, but under the circumstances they thought they should go along without causing trouble. He agreed.

I told the three we would stay in the shack while they delivered their lobsters. I said I knew they had relations working in the factory and it would be embarrassing for them to be followed around by two Mounted Policemen. They seemed to appreciate this, but I told them not to stop for dinner as we had to be back to Bay St. Lawrence by 2 p.m. They said they knew a man with a boat who would take us there, saving that six-mile trip over the path.

Fraser, the fourth wanted man, did not come ashore in time for us to arrest him, so I had one of his relations come down to the shack where we were waiting and told him we had a warrant for Fraser's arrest. I told the relative to advise Fraser to come to Sydney on the *Aspy*'s next trip and surrender to authorities there.

The man with the boat arrived and we embarked for the *Aspy*, arriving shortly before two. The captain seemed surprised that we had three prisoners. I told him none of us had eaten dinner, and he said he didn't think the cook would give them any as they had made a shambles of the galley the last time they were aboard. I told the captain I would talk to the cook, which I did and he told me he would not give them food.

He called them some bad names and said he wouldn't even allow them in his department, but after talking to him and explaining that I would be responsible, he agreed to give us all some dinner. He also gave us supper as we did not arrive at Sydney until about two the following morning.

On our arrival at Sydney, the captain said he would call at the police station and have them come down with their patrol wagon to take the prisoners to the jail. I told him this was not necessary, we would walk there as it wasn't far from the wharf and I knew the way.

At the station the night sergeant was also surprised that we had brought in the three MacLellans. He said that when these men worked in Sydney, it would always take several of their force to effect an arrest of any one of the brothers.

Fraser came to Sydney the next week on the *Aspy* and surrendered. All four were properly dealt with later. Our duty was only to see that they appeared at Sydney.

Editor's Note

This tale is an example repeated many times in various forms. Just the mention of the term "RCMP" as a means of identification or the appearance of a member in uniform made the work of members easier, often under very dangerous circumstances.

39

Fourteen Hours With "Satan"

Const. R.W. MacKay

June 18, 1957, will be a day long remembered by Police Service Dog "Satan's" handler. At 4.30 p.m. the day before, the O.C. Truro Sub-Division was advised by the O.C. Moncton, that Wilfred Joseph Gauthier, an inmate of Dorchester Penitentiary, had escaped from a work party on the Prison Farm. As the dogmaster at Moncton was on leave, the assistance of "Satan", stationed at Truro, was requested to aid in the search.

Road blocks had been set up on all roads around the prison and on No. 2 Highway at the Nova Scotia-New Brunswick border, and were manned by both prison officers and RCMP personnel. After arrival at the scene, the dog was used, without success, until the late evening in the area where Gauthier was last seen. As there didn't seem to be much more the dog could do that night, and it looked as if he might be quite busy the next day, he was rested until morning. Road blocks were maintained throughout the night, and Gauthier's description was circularized by radio, TV and newspapers, so the public were well aware of the search.

Around 4.15 a.m. on the 18th, a car went through a road block on No. 2 highway near Dorchester without stopping and nearly ran down a prison officer. It stopped about 300 yards down the road, and when the prison and RCMP officers got to it, there was no one in it. It was still quite dark and it was impossible to see on which side of the road the driver had disappeared.

A call was put in for the dogmaster, who was a few miles away and when he arrived with "Satan", the dog was given scent from the front seat of the car. He followed a track leading across a field into a brush-covered gully, across another field and then into the woods. The track continued through the woods and the searchers saw footprints in muddy places. Some five miles later, and after crossing two dirt roads, "Satan" stopped tracking and started pawing at the ground, where a still-burning cigarette butt was found. The track was again continued and about a half-mile farther on, "Satan" lifted his head and dragged the dogmaster around a tree where he found himself face-to-face with two youths.

They were quite surprised at the sight of the dog and extremely indignant at being tied together with "Satan's" leash. It had taken the dog an hour and a quarter to work the track at a fast trot. The suspects gave their names as Ronald Brown and Samuel Ball, and said they had been hitch-hiking from Ontario. Ball, who did most of the talking, claimed no knowledge of the car and said they had gone into the bush to sleep, a distance of some four or five miles from the highway.

They had some $70 in bills and change, and after they were escorted to the highway, they were turned over to Moncton C.I.B. Later in the day, after some questioning, Brown admitted to breaking into a store at The Range with Ball, stealing some money and later stealing the car. The road blocks were continued that day, and "Satan" was used to check different reports that came in. At 6.30 p.m., a call was received at Sackville Detachment from a woman who said she had seen a man answering Gauthier's description, cross a field and enter the woods about two miles out of Sackville. "Satan" was taken to the scene and indicated a track leading across the field and into the bush. The dog continued tracking through dense bush and swamps, occasionally stopping to pick up pieces of newspaper. After about 2 1/2 miles of tracking, the dog came out on a field where a group of sheep were grazing. They tried to get into the act and were a bit of a hindrance to the dog, but nothing like the two large pigs which were on the other side of the next fence that was crossed. These were, undoubtedly, two of New Brunswick's largest and most inquisitive pigs, and it took the combined efforts of both "Satan" and dogmaster, aided by a few well-placed missiles, to discourage them from taking over the track. Another fence was crossed and after a short distance through the bush, "Satan" tracked right up to the escapee, who was hiding under a tree.

He was still in prison garb but had a piece of a rubber cape over his shoulders. He had slit pockets in the lining of his jacket and in these were concealed, a file, knife, small piece of wire mesh, and a short piece of cord. He also had a skinned partridge wrapped in newspaper, and it was pieces of this paper that "Satan" had picked up. Gauthier had killed two partridges with stones and had eaten one of them raw, and a can of sardines which he had taken from the prison. His main complaint, other than being caught, was the flies which had kept him awake all night.

Upon reaching the highway, the dogmaster tried to flag down some passing cars to get word to the nearest road block. This was a bit too much to ask any motorist, owing to the publicity the escapee had had. The cars would slow down, but as soon as the occupants got a good look, they sped off. Possibly, this was due to the fact that Gauthier was lying on the ground nearby out of sight of any motorist and the dogmaster was dressed in mud-spattered khaki pants, a khaki hunting jacket, and answered the description of Gauthier fairly well, even to the color of hair. Within a matter of minutes, a few Police cars arrived on the scene, having been told by passing motorists that Gauthier was trying to flag down a car on the highway.

It was a busy and profitable day for "Satan". In a matter of some 14 hours, he had worked two tracks totalling about nine miles, and had captured one definite and two possible candidates for Dorchester Pen.

Editor's Note

"Satan" was one of the many dogs the RCMP has acquired, or bred, over the years since they purchased their first dog, "Black Lux", in the mid-1930s. This dog was a son of Dale of Cawsalta, which had been used as a private tracking dog by RCMP Sergeant J.N. Cawsey in the course of his duties, several years before "Black Lux" was purchased. Dale was purchased from Cawsey and became the second tracking dog owned by the RCMP.

40

R.v. Schwalb et al.

RCMP *Quarterly* Staff

Murder — Geneva Convention — Nazi Brutality in Internment Camp
— Prisoners of War Subject to Laws of Detaining Power — Long Com-
plicated Investigation Involving Numerous Interviews — Retrial Because
Juror Under Age — Convictions — Appeals — Execution

Because he was anti-Nazi in his convictions and believed that Germany
was losing the war, August Plaszek, a 42-year-old German prisoner of
war, was beaten, stoned and hanged by an angry mob of fanatical fellow-
prisoners. After a long difficult investigation by the RCMP, the guilty
were brought to Canadian justice.

In May, 1943, an internment camp was established at Medicine Hat,
Alta., and about 500 quite tractable P.o.W.s were incarcerated there, the
majority of whom had belonged to Rommel's Afrika Korps and been taken
prisoner in North Africa by British forces. In June about 1,000 more
P.o.W.s were moved in from internment camp 133, Lethbridge, Alta.,
among them many unruly individuals some of whom were agents of the
Gestapo. Later still more were transferred from other parts of Canada until by July of that year the population of the camp had swollen to between
4,000 and 5,000.

Among the more docile P.o.W.s were some who upon Hitler's rise to
power prior to the war had, for political reasons, left Germany and gone
to France where they enlisted in the French Foreign Legion and later were
posted to Morocco for duty with the French Army. When the Axis overran
North Africa these exiles were captured but instead of being treated as
prisoners they were conscripted into the German Army as German nationals to fight against the British Eighth Army which subsequently took
them prisoner.

Due to the common bond of their former associations these P.o.W.s more
or less banded together in the Medicine Hat camp, a fact that tended
to isolate them from the other inmates and thus bring them under the

suspicions of the newly-arrived Nazi element which attempted at once to impose its will upon the camp and claimed that this minority conspired to overthrow the camp authorities.

The upshot was that late in the afternoon of July 22, 1943, the German camp-leader ordered an inquiry into the activities of certain ex-legionnaires who were accused of allegedly holding anti-Nazi sympathies and of spreading defeatism within the camp. A German law student in civil life presided over the tribunal which was conducted along typical Nazi lines. Escorted to what was called the orderly room the suspects were cross-examined by this German officer in the presence of another examiner and a typist. Three other inquisitors, whose function presumably was to furnish corroboration of incriminating evidence, listened in an adjoining room where they could hear without being seen.

One ex-legionnaire, Christian Schultz by name, after being questioned, was told that he would be detained for two or three days pending further inquiry into his case. Having knowledge of similar occurrences Schultz knew that detention in these circumstances generally meant a severe beating and sometimes even death. Reflections along this line must have occupied his mind as he was led away, for at the door of the hut where he was to be confined he suddenly broke free, raced round the building and straight west across an open space to the warning wire that surrounded the compound, the while waving a white handkerchief and shouting in German for help from the Canadian authorities. On the other side of the enclosure at this point was a sentry post, and realizing that something was amiss the veteran's guard on duty there phoned to the office for help.

Some 20 Nazis who soon were joined by about 200 others chased and stoned Schultz as he ran. He ducked under the warning wire and two of them crawled after him but hastily withdrew when the guard levelled his rifle in their direction, leaving the fugitive safe for the moment between the wire and the main fence. Before reinforcements arrived, it looked as though the crowd might attempt to rush the lone guard but when he fired a warning shot they apparently decided against doing so. Then reinforcements arrived and Schultz was saved.

The rescue seemed to touch off an interval of mob mania among the irate Nazis whose number at the scene had now increased to almost 1,000, and precipitated the action that followed. Shouting and cursing, they returned to where the inquiry still was in progress and demanded that the remaining suspects be given up to them. It was then a few minutes before 6 p.m.

Plaszek, an ex-legionnaire about to be interrogated, was thrown out of the orderly room to the rabble, and was stoned, kicked, and beaten. He fell to his knees yelling that he was innocent, but several men in the crowd dragged him by the feet to the recreation hall where, with blood gushing from his head and still pleading weakly for mercy, he was hanged.

The hall, situated in the north-west corner of the camp, measured 115 feet by 130. Its main entrance was in the middle of the south side and consisted of sliding double doors. Inside, the west wall was divided by heavy stanchions into eight 14-foot-wide bays, and on the third of these stanchions from the southwest corner was a 2 by 4 beam used as a support for an improvised punching bag which was suspended four feet above the floor. It was on this beam that Plaszek was hanged.

When Canadian camp officials forced their way through the crowd and finally reached the scene, the body had been cut down by order of the camp P.o.W. doctor, and was lying on its back on the floor. A strand of quarter-inch sash cord was wound tightly twice round its neck and knotted below the right ear. Tied to the punching bag support between the bag and the wall was a piece of similar cord whose hanging free end was cut close to the beam and soaked with blood. The adjacent wall bore splashes of blood, and though the cement floor had been washed this had obviously been done in haste and traces of blood were still on it.

Next day an autopsy, performed at Medicine Hat by Capt. W.F. Hall, M.D., of the R.C.A.M.C., with Lt. Col. H.B. Kenner, M.D., of the same unit in attendance, disclosed bruises and abrasions, a fractured rib and two severe scalp lacerations on the back of the head, apparently inflicted by a blunt instrument. Death was due to strangulation by hanging.

A military board assisted by an RCMP investigator questioned a number of P.o.W.s, but little evidence was obtained and from August 8 on the Force worked independently. Though the procedure subsequently followed was mainly routine in nature so far as criminal investigations go, the case is notable because of the lengthy chain of inquiries that had to be forged to bring the offenders to justice and it demonstrates once again that dogged persistence alone can lead to the successful detection of certain crlmes.

Difficulties were encountered from the outset. Few if any of the legionnaires had been eye-witnesses to the slaying as they had kept out of the way lest the same fate overtake them. In other words all those who might have been expected to shed light on the case had been compelled for reasons of personal safety not to show too much curiosity about what was going on. The language barrier, too, complicated things, and an interpreter had to be employed in nearly all the interviews. Moreover, there was the fact that all the P.o.W.s were approximately the same age and dressed alike; because of warm weather no tunics were worn.

Apart from these obstacles there was the sullen, antagonistic and sometimes arrogant attitude of the Germans interviewed. When P.o.W.s were wanted for questioning outside the camp they first were interrogated by the ruling class inside, who told them what to say. Upon their return they were again interrogated as to exactly what had been said. Thus before being interviewed many of those questioned were thoroughly conversant with the police interrogation procedure and schooled in what attitude to adopt toward any questioner.

Scores of these young Nazis, all typical products of the Hitler youth movement, were quite arrogant, defiant and surly as they recited their rehearsed stories, and they openly declared that even if they knew who the murderers were, or of anything that might help to clear up the mystery, they would not tell. "I am a good German, but actually I do not know who did it", or, "I could not tell you who killed him, as that is entirely a matter for our German military authorities to decide on", they would say.

Great caution had to be exercised in all the interviews lest the responsible faction, which if anything became more despotic as the investigation proceeded, send out — and it seems probable that they did so — purely "built-up" witnesses who were carefully coached to play a double game, one calculated to mislead the police as well as to find out just how much the police knew.

No one could be traced who had witnessed the hanging. The nearest sentry, the guard who had saved Schultz, had noticed the commotion but was too far distant to see details; he had seen a man whom he was unable to identify being dragged through the main entrance into the building where Plaszek's dead body was found, had seen the big doors swing shut, but was unable to identify any of the individuals involved. Afterwards almost 1,000 P.o.W.s were paraded through the recreation hall to view the hanging body, presumably as an object lesson to any whose loyalty to the Fatherland might be wavering. But the investigator could locate no person who would admit to being there when the murder occurred or who knew of others that had.

To appreciate the difficulties involved one must first know something of how these internment camps operated and of the methods employed by those who condemned the former legionnaire to his death.

In accordance with Article 18 of Convention Relative to the Treatment of Prisoners of War concluded July 27, 1929, each camp was in charge of a Canadian army officer known as the Commandant. Upon the recommendation of the P.o.W.s themselves the Commandant appointed certain inmates to act as camp leaders, block leaders and hut leaders, whom he held accountable for the maintenance of camp discipline. To carry out their functions in this regard these P.o.W. officials were perforce vested with a certain amount of authority; and military tribunals were set up to hold formal inquiries into any breach of the camp rules and regulations, to pass sentence and to punish any offender they found guilty. These tribunals were not empowered to question the political ideologies of any P.o.W. nor certainly not to pass the death sentence on anyone, though as the present case reveals they arrogantly assumed both these rights.

The oral statements of P.o.W.s and certain seized documents early suggested that the P.o.W.s in the Gestapo or "pressure group" paid first allegiance to a lieutenant-general who was the highest ranking Nazi officer interned in this country. In supreme German command of all P.o.W.s throughout Canada this individual was enabled to keep in touch with and issue instructions to leaders in the main camps by a system of communication made possible through transfers of P.o.W.s from one camp to another which for security reasons were necessarily frequent.

After the murder it was obvious that the Medicine Hat camp was feared by many P.o.W.s whose loyalty to the Third Reich was doubted by the Nazis. Several ex-legionnaires from the Riding Mountain National Park camp in Manitoba, for instance, asked for protective custody when they learned that contrary to their wishes they were to be sent there. It developed that the camp leader at Riding Mountain, who had been instructed to segregate the prisoners selected for transfer, had for reasons best known to himself included their names in the list.

P.o.W.s not known to be imbued with the Nazi philosophy were practically outlawed as enemies, and an atmosphere of tension and mistrust pervaded the whole camp. Everyone suspected the other of being a spy; and contributing to the terror was a rumour bandied about that all the ex-French legionnaires were to be herded into a hut which would be sprayed with gasoline and set afire.

The investigator felt that when the true course of the war dawned on the P.o.W.s some of them would become more amenable to being interviewed. But the impending repatriation of the P.o.W.s made it necessary to bring the investigation as soon as possible to a point where it could be decided what P.o.W.s would be needed for the successful prosecution of the case in order that they could be held in Canada to appear at the trial.

Another factor hampering the investigation was the privilege that permitted camp leaders to send news to Germany for, fearing reprisals on relatives at home because of it, anti-Nazi P.o.W.s were reluctant to talk. More rigid censorship relieved this situation, but even at that the investigator was hard put to it to convince prospective witnesses that the Canadian authorities could shield them against retaliatory action of their own countrymen.

Conditions bearing on the investigation generally improved, however, when several ex-legionnaires whose lives had been threatened sought protective custody. In the late autumn of 1943 these men were placed on farms away from the influence of the camp. Branded as traitors and struck off the rolls by the camp leaders they were encouraged in their new-found security to overcome their restraint and tell what they knew of the affair. And thus the opening wedge in the long-drawn inquiry was made.

As a consequence of these moves and of the many transfers of P.o.W.s from one camp to another, the investigation branched out to other points in Alberta and to Manitoba and Ontario. When it brought encouraging signs of progress, one German camp leader objected to P.o.W.s being taken out of the camp for questioning. He forbade any of them to discuss the murder, and to ensure that his orders were carried out posted NCOs strategically about the camp to listen in on any attempts to talk confidentially. After that, private conversations would be rudely interrupted by the nearest satellite whose business it was to learn what the talk was about.

Through the months the investigation continued. As it became clear that Germany was doomed to defeat so the morale of the Nazis in the camp deteriorated and bit by bit more direct evidence was gathered and correlated. After Germany's unconditional surrender the P.o.W.s became noticeably more communicative, and by July, 1945, five suspects were implicated.

Further inquiry cut this number down to three, and the next month it seemed that enough evidence had been procured to establish a *prima facie* case against them. On Oct. 11, 1945, an information and complaint was laid before Magistrate W. H. Ellis at Medicine Hat charging *Feldwebel* (sergeant major) Werner Schwalb, *Soldat* (private) Adolf Kratz, and *Gefreiter* (lance corporal) Johannes Wittinger with Murder, s. 263 Cr. Code. The accused were arrested on October 15, four days later, at the Lethbridge internment camp to which they had been transferred.

Article 45 of the Geneva Convention reads:

> Prisoners of war shall be subject to the laws, regulations, and orders in force in the armed forces of the detaining Power.
>
> Any act of insubordination shall render them liable to the measures prescribed by such laws, regulations, and orders, except as otherwise provided in this Chapter.

In all respects the provisions of the convention were strictly observed. Article 60 lays down:

> At the commencement of a judicial hearing against a prisoner of war, the detaining Power shall notify the representative of the protecting Power as soon as possible, and in any case before the date fixed for the opening of the hearing.
>
> The said notification shall contain the following particulars: —

(a) Civil status and rank of the prisoner.

(b) Place of residence or detention.

(c) Statement of the charge or charges, and of the legal provisions applicable.

If it is not possible in this notification to indicate particulars of the court which will try the case, the date of the opening of the hearing and the place where it will take place, these particulars shall be furnished to the representative of the protecting Power at a later date, but as soon as possible and in any case at least three weeks before the opening of the hearing.

During the war the Government of Switzerland through its consul exercised the role of protecting power, but with the defeat of Germany the Government of Canada assumed that office; accordingly notice of prosecution was served upon the Commandant of the Lethbridge camp who on this occasion was selected to represent the protecting power.

Article 61 of the convention provides:

No prisoner of war shall be sentenced without being given the opportunity to defend himself.

No prisoner shall be compelled to admit that he is guilty of the offence of which he is accused.

Article 62 provides:

The prisoner of war shall have the right to be assisted by a qualified advocate of his own choice, and, if necessary, to have recourse to the offices of a competent interpreter. He shall be informed of his right by the detaining Power in good time before the hearing.

Failing a choice on the part of the prisoner, the protecting Power may procure an advocate for him. The detaining Power shall, on the request of the protecting Power, furnish to the latter a list of persons qualified to conduct the defence.

The representatives of the protecting Power shall have the right to attend the hearing of the case.

The only exception to this rule is where the hearing has to be kept secret in the interests of the safety of the State. The detaining Power would then notify the protecting Power accordingly.

The Commandant explained to the accused that these articles gave them the option of three methods of defence: they could (a) engage their own private counsel; (b) apply to National Defence headquarters for military counsel, or (c) to the Department of Justice for counsel.

Meanwhile to ensure a just trial most of the P.o.W.s required as witnesses either for the prosecution or defence continued as helpers on farms or in hostels, isolated from each other and away from dominating influences. Dr. Hall who had performed the autopsy on Plaszek's remains was in England on duty, and arrangements were made for his return to Canada for the preliminary hearing.

The preliminary hearing was held at Medicine Hat from November 13 to 16 before Magistrate Ellis. Walter D. Gow, K.C., Agent for the Attorney-General, Medicine Hat, represented the Crown and L.S. Turcotte, barrister of Lethbridge appointed by the Minister of Justice, appeared for the defence. The three prisoners were committed to stand trial at the next court of competent jurisdiction to be holden in Medicine Hat.

At this time general repatriation of German P.o.W.s to Europe was in full swing and it was necessary to halt the transfer of any of the principal witnesses or of other persons connected with the case.

At the regular sittings of the Supreme Court of Alberta which opened at Medicine Hat on Feb. 25, 1946, the three accused appeared before Chief Justice W.R. Howson. The prosecution was conducted by H.J. Wilson, K.C., Deputy Attorney-General for Alberta, with Mr. Gow as associate counsel, while Mr. Turcotte continued to act for the defence.

Before the arraignment defence counsel applied for separate trials, arguing that unless these were granted the interests of each accused would be jeopardized. Mr. Wilson opposed the motion on grounds that the evidence was applicable to all three accused, since they had participated in the same crime at the same place and at the same time. His objection was overruled, however, by His Lordship who remarked that the case called for the fairest trial possible and exercising his discretion ordered that each accused be tried separately. (See notes to s. 858, *Tremeear's Criminal Code*, 5th edition.)

Schwalb pleaded not guilty. Prosecution witnesses testified that he had helped drag Plaszek to the recreation hall, that he had stood in the middle of the hall with blood on his hands and clothing immediately after the hanging, that he had left with the blood still on his hands and when asked what he had done had replied, "Go into the hall where one is hanging there." One witness swore that Schwalb had entered a hut and while washing the blood-stains away had said, "It was I who asked for the rope." Another witness stated that days later Schwalb had complained to him of not being able to sleep because he had taken part in the crime at Medicine Hat. Schwalb had admitted to still another witness that he had been present at the murder but intimated that if brought to trial his alibi would be that he was on the sports field at the time.

No evidence was offered for the defence. In his address to the jury defence counsel pointed out that Plaszek was killed by mob violence during the heat of passion and argued that the accused should therefore be found guilty of the lesser offense of manslaughter.

In summing up, His Lordship observed that there was no evidence that Plaszek had provided any provocation such as would cause a person to act in the heat of passion.

On March 5, the jury after an hour of deliberation found the accused guilty as charged and he was sentenced to be hanged in the provincial gaol at Lethbridge on June 26, 1946.

Next to be tried was Adolf Kratz. Arraigned on March 7, he elected for trial by jury and pleaded not guilty. Evidence of the Crown, entered up to March 15 with the exception of March 11 and 12 when court was adjourned, was largely a repetition of that heard in the preceding trial.

One witness identified Kratz as being among those on the office steps when Plaszek was thrown out and as having struck the victim on the head with a heavy stone which he held in his both hands. After being hit by the stone Plaszek slithered down the steps to the ground. Another witness testified that, after Schultz had escaped into protective custody, Kratz had declared, "There are some more in the head hut and if I see one I know I am going to help hang him," also that later Kratz had said, "Well I have helped hang one of those swine." Another witness heard him say that he had taken part in the hanging because it was his duty, as all the swine—referring to the ex-members of the Foreign Legion—should be hanged. Other witnesses stated that Kratz took an egg and remarked, "This egg will taste as good again since I helped hang a pig."

No evidence was offered for the defence, and on March 16 His Lordship charged the jury. Several hours after retiring, the jury returned, stating that they had been unable to reach a verdict, and asked if they could add a recommendation. After further deliberation they again returned, this time with a verdict of guilty coupled with a strong recommendation for mercy. Before passing sentence, the Court assured the accused that it would forward the jury's recommendation for mercy to the proper authorities with all haste. The death sentence was then imposed to be carried out on June 26, 1946, at the provincial gaol.

The trial by jury of Johannes Wittinger proceeded on March 18. This accused had frequently boasted that he had taken part in the Nazi putsch at Gratz, Austria, in 1934 after Dollfuss was assassinated in Vienna, that he had undergone a long term of imprisonment, and that upon his release when the Hitlerites took over that part of the country he was given a high position in the Nazi party.

Evidence for the Crown was almost completed when defence counsel objected to the proceedings on grounds that one of the jurors was under 25 years of age, and moved for a dismissal of the jury. S. 921 Cr. Code, lays down that "Every person qualified and summoned as a grand or petit juror, according to the laws in force for the time being in any province of Canada shall be duly qualified to serve as such juror in criminal cases in that province", while s. 3 of the Alberta Jury Act, Chap. 130, R.S.A., 1942, provides that "any inhabitant of the Province of Alberta over 25 and under 60 years of age . . . shall be liable to serve as a juror. . . . " Defence counsel submitted that as this juror whose age was just a few days over 24 years and three months was not liable for service under the Alberta Jury Act he could not qualify under the Criminal Code. His Lordship took this matter under advisement and later, remarking that he had been unable to find any cases of a similar nature in Canadian legal reports, dismissed the jury and sent the case forward for retrial at the October assizes of the Supreme Court of Alberta at Medicine Hat.

Wittinger's second trial started at the adjourned sitting of the Supreme Court which opened on June 17. Twenty-nine witnesses were called by the Crown whose case closed at noon of June 21, 1946. Testifying in his own behalf, the accused denied all evidence of the Crown, stating under cross-examination that he was unable to explain why several witnesses should perjure themselves against him. On June 22, His Lordship charged the jury who retired and returned in two hours with a verdict of not guilty. The case against Wittinger was dismissed.

Appeals were entered on behalf of Schwalb and Kratz to the Appellate Division of the Supreme Court of Alberta on grounds of non-direction and misdirection by the trial judge, but neither appeal was allowed.

Since the end of hostilities the Canadian Government had assumed the role of protecting power and as subsequent action lay within the discretion of the Governor-in-Council notice of the conviction and sentence was immediately served upon the latter, in accordance with the provisions of Article 66 of the Geneva Convention.

Kratz' sentence was commuted to life imprisonment in Saskatchewan Penitentiary at Prince Albert, Sask., but on the appointed date Schwalb paid for his crime on the gallows.

In a letter to the Force, after the conclusion of these trials, Mr. Justice Howson commented:

> It was more than a difficult matter to even get a sort (in the investigation and preparation of these cases), because of the Nazi organization in these P.o.W. camps. After listening to the evidence in two prosecutions and a part of the third, I think that I understand, to a degree at least, the methods employed by the top-ranking Nazis in these camps and I am quite amazed at the success achieved by your men. They deserve great credit. Their method of presentation of their evidence also deserves a word of praise. It was all that could be desired.

I was very pleased also to see that the R.C.M.P. officers all appeared in Court in their scarlet tunics. To my mind that is important, particularly where there is a large percentage of our people of foreign birth or foreign extraction.

41

Security Service
Nabs Soviet Spies

G.J.I. Saunders, RCMP *Gazette* Staff

Introduction

However much we may lament international tension, however much
we may decry the abuse of a trust which one country extends to another, however highly we may value the ideal of global harmony—
well, we still love a good spy story. We all do. The tricks and tosses of
intrigue appeal to a romantic suspicion that the affairs of men, and
indeed of the cosmos, are not governed entirely by the geometric logic
of bilateral trade agreements or public treaty, but also by clandestine meetings, faceless beings, disguises, secret codes, underground
networks, dark fates.

Canadians will agree with the Federal Government that such espionage cannot be tolerated. It may be fascinating to read about, but
the spies must be expelled, their Government rebuked and notice of
Canada's indignation publicly displayed. Logic and a civilized view of
the matter prevail—as they must.

Perhaps the most noteworthy aspect of the year-long affair is that the
RCMP succeeded in getting their men without, apparently, breaking
a single Canadian or international law.

They opened no private mail, burned down no barns, broke into no
offices without warrants; instead, they relied upon sound detective
work, legitimate investigative craft.

The Government may present the affair as evidence of the RCMP's
skill and dedication (and so it is). But the affair also provides clear
evidence that effective police work and respect for the law are readily
compatible, as well as essential.

Editorial, *The Globe and Mail*, Feb. 11, 1978

Canadian Government officials summoned Soviet Ambassador Alexandr Yakovlev to state Ottawa's displeasure over spy activities, exactly

309

one day after he had received a note demanding compensation for Canadian recovery costs incurred in the North West Territories, involving radioactive COSMOS 954 satellite parts.

On February 9, 1978, Ottawa lunched on headlines that read: Mounties Smash Soviet Spy Ring. Of 64 officially resident Soviet embassy members in Ottawa, eleven had been expelled, and two others on leave were refused re-entry.

The Minister of External Affairs' announcement created a furor unequalled in Canada's capital since the Gouzenko case hit the streets.

> At noon today, on my instructions, the Under-Secretary of State for External Affairs requested the Ambassador of the Soviet Union to withdraw eleven Soviet nationals from Canada for engaging in inadmissible activities in violation of the Official Secrets Act and of course of their status in Canada.
>
> Two other Soviet nationals who were involved have already departed Canada but will not be permitted to return. A strong protest has been conveyed to the Soviet authorities about these activities.
>
> The Soviet ambassador was informed that the Canadian government had irrefutable evidence that all 13 persons had been involved in an attempt to recruit a member of the RCMP in order to penetrate the RCMP Security Service.
>
> Nine of the Soviet nationals still in Canada are employees of the Soviet embassy, one is an official of the Soviet trade office in Ottawa and one is a member of the International Civil Aviation organization secretariat in Montreal.
>
> The Soviet nationals involved are: Igor P. Vartanyan, First Secretary responsible for sports and cultural affairs, Soviet Embassy, Ottawa; Nikolai M. Talanov, counsellor, Soviet Embassy, Ottawa; Anatoly A. Mikhalin, official of the Soviet foreign trade office, Ottawa; Vadim A. Borispolets, Attache (consular affairs) Soviet Embassy, Ottawa; Vladimir L. Souvorov, Second Secretary, Soviet Embassy, Ottawa; Vladimir I. Oshkaderov, translator, International Civil Aviation Organization (IACO, Montreal); Yevgeniy K. Koblov, clerk, Soviet Embassy, Ottawa; Gennadi V. Ivashavitch, Third Secretary, Soviet Reztsov, employed in the library of the Soviet Embassy, Ottawa; Pyotr R Linnenurm, Second Secretary (consular affairs), Soviet Embassy, Ottawa; Voldemar P. Veber, formerly Second Secretary in the consular division, Soviet Embassy, Ottawa, returned to the USSR July 1977; Andrea V. Drysin, economist, Soviet foreign trade office, returned to the USSR December 1977.
>
> Early in 1977 two Soviet intelligence officers approached a member of the Royal Canadian Mounted Police and offered him an unlimited sum of money to spy for them. This member of the force had, on an earlier posting and in the normal course of his responsibilities, come into infrequent contact with one of the Soviet officials in this case.

To establish the ultimate purpose of the Soviet approach, the member of the force was authorized, by the RCMP, under carefully controlled circumstances, to meet with the principal agent, Mr. Vartanyan, in accordance with elaborate instructions he had received from the two Soviet officials. Between April 1977 and the present, he met secretly with the principal agent on seven occasions.

The twelve other Soviet nationals identified with this operation, were involved in different support functions including transportation, counter-surveillance and regular weekly observation activities.

This case proved to be a classic example of an intelligence operation, involving complex signalling systems, coded passwords, secret concealment devices, all for the purpose of arranging clandestine meetings between the RCMP member and the Soviet agent.

As an example, on different occasions, filmed instructions were passed to the RCMP member in a hollowed-out stick and a specially prepared package of cigarettes. The RCMP member was instructed by the agent to obtain information on such subjects as the methods the RCMP security service employed against Soviet intelligence services in Canada, character assessments of RCMP personnel and details regarding RCMP counter-espionage cases.

The RCMP member in return provided the Soviets with carefully screened non-sensitive information or completely fabricated material. The fact that he was paid $30,500 for information of no consequence provides an indication of the importance the Soviet intelligence service attached to this operation. The important point for the House to note, however, is that this case has involved no compromise of Canada's security.

This Soviet recruitment attempt is nevertheless a source of serious concern to the government. Its importance should be seen in the context of the unusual lengths to which the Soviet intelligence service was prepared to go to suborn a member of the RCMP. The case did not have any other implications for Canada's security. The evidence derived from this operation indicates that it was directed solely against the RCMP.

The firm action taken by the government in this case will remind the Soviet Union of our determination to deter foreign espionage.

The government regrets that activities of this kind should be conducted at a time when there are efforts under way, to which both Canada and the Soviet Union have subscribed, to reduce the level of international tensions by overcoming mistrust and increasing confidence. Activities such as those I have disclosed to the House are contrary to that objective and represent a serious setback in our bilateral relations.

This incident and the action we have had to take today, will inevitably place strains on our relations with the Soviet Union. Nevertheless, the Canadian government continues to attach importance to Canadian-Soviet relations and hopes the Soviet government does likewise.

How Did It All Start?

In the shadowy world of espionage, intrigue is a major factor, and trends can be very significant. When one day flows into the next with hardly any fluctuation in activity, both sides can assume the other isn't on to anything big. But the crunch came when, in less than three months, seven persons had been expelled from Canada for engaging in spy activity. This was especially significant when only twenty or so had been expelled in the previous thirty years.

The first jolt the Soviets felt came when Assistant Air Attache, Vladimir Vassiliev, was expelled in December, 1976, for " ... activities incompatible with his diplomatic status". He had been trying to obtain classified material from a contact he had made, unaware that the contact was keeping the RCMP informed of his every move.

The second jolt came on January 6–7, 1977, when five Cubans were expelled from Montreal and Ottawa. They had actively recruited, trained and tasked an American mercenary who had entered Canada in September, 1976. It didn't take the Security Service long to "twig" what was happening, and in four months all those involved in the operation were on their way out of the country. No double agent this time, just good counterintelligence work.

The trend was continued when a Soviet exchange scientist, Lev Grigoryevich Khvostantsev, working at the National Research Council, tried to persuade another exchange scientist who had access to classified material to turn some material over to him. The other exchange scientist of course, told the Security Service and in February, 1977, yet another Soviet spy was expelled from Canada.

There is little doubt that by this time KGB Headquarters in Moscow were upset by what was happening, and their diplomatic pouches probably burned with instructions to " ... get on the ball and find out!!" The Soviets here decided their best bet was to penetrate the Security Service and looked around for a possible contact. They chose an RCMP officer who for simplicity, will be referred to as M-13.

Igor Vartanyan, described as the operation's kingpin, was alleged to be the Soviet Embassy's first secretary responsible for sports and cultural affairs, although he had no apparent background in sports administration. He had KBG training, however, plus he had received permission to leave Ottawa's confines at least 41 times. (By law all Soviet Embassy residents wishing to stay out of the National Capital Commission area longer than 48 hours must file for permission at the Department of External Affairs. Canadian Diplomats are similarly restricted by reciprocal diplomatic arrangements. In practice, however. Canadians find it more difficult to tour

Soviet areas that they would like to see — except for Leningrad — than their Russian counterparts — free to travel to most regions in Canada. Many Soviet diplomats have taken advantage of this situation to tour the country from Halifax to Vancouver. In fact, some Canadian organizations sometimes send Soviet officials on junkets in the interests of cultural exchange, a measure hardly reciprocated in Moscow.)

Previously, M-13 had met one of the spies during the normal course of his duties and had infrequent subsequent contact with the Soviet official in question. This official and Igor Vartanyan approached M-13, offering him "an unlimited amount of cash" for his cooperation. M-13 reported these facts to his superiors, and he effectively became a triple agent. The Soviets were confident that they were dealing with a "high level government agent".

The Soviets sought information on RCMP anti-Soviet operations, specifically:

1. How the Mounties were learning about Soviet undercover operations in Canada.

2. Names of personnel involved in these operations, their character assessments, traits and weaknesses, financial standing.

3. Intricate details of RCMP counterespionage operations.

4. Security Service methods employed to expose Soviet espionage attempts.

5. What common information exchange exists between RCMP, CIA and FBI.

In return, M-13 supplied the Russians with carefully screened non-sensitive information or completely fabricated material and stories of no real consequence. The fact that the Soviets paid M-13 $30,500 Canadian dollars certainly indicated the length to which they were prepared to go to infiltrate the RCMP Security Service, and the importance they attached to this operation.

The Canadian Government had reportedly been told of these Soviet activities during the course of the investigation. In 1977, three other Soviet officials had already been expelled for spying. On each occasion the "attention of the Soviet authorities had been drawn to the damaging consequences of those inadmissible activities on relations between Canada and the Soviet Union." (Wording of diplomatic communique.)

Chronology of Meetings

The first encounter occurred on April 21, at the home of M-13. Our triple agent received his first instruction film of negatives in the form of signal codes plus verbal guidelines on how to signal for the next meeting at a Towers store in Ottawa. Towers, on Cyrville Road, is a shopping centre situated in a primarily residential area. It is readily accessible from the Queensway, or by bus. The number of shoppers varies, ranging from a constant trickle at the beginning of the week to near capacity by Friday night and Saturday. The "signal" was a piece of coloured tape stuck on the outside of a roof support pillar. Tape width, height on the post from the ground, vertical or horizontal placement were key factors to the message conveyed. Thus the Soviet contact need only drive into the lot past the post to get the message.

Once M-13 called for a meeting, the Soviet reply tape was to appear on the east crosswalk post at Kent and Gilmour Streets. Kent Street is a one way northbound street running between the Queensway and Parliament Hill. Rush-hour traffic and the height of the tape from ground level demanded that M-13 drive in the right-hand lane in order to see the tape at all.

There were four different meeting categories, roughly classified as: Constant, Regular, Instant or Brush, and Reserve.

In "Brush" meetings, few or no words are exchanged. Information is passed on by quick hand movements — like a relay race where the baton changes hands, or a pickpocket in a crowd where your wallet instantly disappears before you have a chance to miss it — the piece of paper or microfilm landing in the contact's pocket. This technique is frequently used in crowds, where such movements succeed unnoticed.

The tape colours, placements and meeting locations changed slightly for each set of instructions passed, and each could only be used once.

First "Constant" Locale

A certain colour, width, locale and tape placement in the city would specify a "Constant" meeting place in Gatineau Park, in the front parking lot of the M & R Food Centre, a variety-cum-restaurant food store. With the latest issue of *Maclean's Magazine* showing in plain view in his rear car window, M-13 was to park in front of the store at 6 p.m. He would raise the hood of his car, then wait until the Russian agent's car arrived. Once confirmation was made, using stilted passwords, he was to follow the car to a more secluded spot for a lengthier discussion.

Password Conversation would go like this:

> Question: Can you show me the way to Pink Lake?

> Answer: Sorry, I know Pink Lake, but in Ontario Province.

(Actually Pink Lake should be properly spelled as Pinks Lake and it is situated a mere two miles up the road from the M & R store.)

Thus, other meetings were scheduled.

Dead Letter Boxes

DLB's or drops as they are known in spy parlance, are convenient ways of passing messages along to one another without arousing too much suspicion. They should, in fact, never be known to anyone except the parties involved in drop and pickup. They have been used by spies world-wide. To the Soviets, setting up an elaborate system of Dead Letter Boxes was a natural instinct, probably covered in the KGB spy manual.

One such drop was located 10 miles northwest of Hull. The drop location was beside a bridge abutment under the Gatineau Parkway on Notch End Road. The container used was to be a Coca-Cola tin.

When the system was to be used, the Soviets would signal that a container held a message by placing a green tape on the right window of a telephone booth at the Parkway General Store. To later confirm the pickup, a similar tape was to be placed on the left post of the sign "Booth Terasse de pique". The pickup must be made before 6 p.m. on Wednesday.

A Meeting

On a clear day, the Gatineau hills can be seen from the north side of the RCMP Headquarters complex. Situated in the province of Quebec, across the Ottawa River, they are less than 10–15 miles distant. The Gatineaus are renowned. In winter, they are famous for numerous downhill and cross-country ski trails and toboggan runs — many of which are free to the public. In other seasons, they afford some of the most scenic viewing readily available to city dwellers. They are frequented by hikers, nature enthusiasts, amateur ecologists and others just wanting a pleasant drive in the countryside. Anyone visiting the ski slopes or lookouts must drive through the hamlet of old Chelsea. In fact, it is so small that only a few houses, a Fire-cum-Police Station plus a couple of shops exist to cater to visitors on either their way up or down.

Old Chelsea is within the Ottawa-Hull designation. No special permit is required to travel there. The area is very popular, yet far enough out of the way to provide concealment for clandestine activities.

On the last Thursday of June, M-13 went to the M & R store at 6 p.m. His identifier—*Maclean's*—in place, he parked in front of the store with his engine hood up. Then he began his 5 minute wait for his contact. Vartanyan was hiding in the bushes for our man. Disguised as a hiker twiddling a stick, he met M-13. Vartanyan joined M-13 in his car and they drove together to the St. Louis Hotel in Hull. Here, over talk, the stick was slipped to our man under the table. No money changed hands at this point. They verbally agreed to another meeting.

Vartanyan's stick demonstrates another spy technique. It is hollow and contains another set of filmed instructions. If caught, Vartanyan could easily discard the stick without arousing suspicion.

This set of instructions held new directives, including new sites located in Montreal, as well as Ottawa.

Just off St. Laurent Boulevard near the Queensway entrance is a shopping centre where an IGA food store and K-Mart dominate the vast parking lot. The building which houses both stores has a flat overhanging roof with support pillars at regular intervals the entire length of the building. These exposed columns were sequentially numbered, no. 1 being front left-hand side. Pillar no. 1 was known as Station "K", and was used by the Soviets to call for an operation. Here is an example:

1. Soviets to M-13: Signal "K" (K-Mart Store). M-13 would read a signal Monday afternoon. The same afternoon he would confirm the operation by placing a signal at "T" (Towers Shopping Plaza) before 6 p.m., meaning the message had been received.

2. M-13 to Soviets: Signal placed at "T", Monday afternoon before 6 p.m. Soviets placed confirmation signal on Tuesday afternoon at signal place "K", that the message had been received. The same colour of tape was to be used for sending and confirming the message. And, oh yes, "Please remove your signals after 6 p.m." (Actual Text.)

M-13 and Vartanyan met once more on October 20. The Soviets paid him $5,000 for some of the fabricated information which had been passed on earlier.

The scene then shifted to Montreal. The Soviets obviously needed a larger city and bigger crowds to protect their operatives. M-13 passed on more worthless data to the Soviets on December 17, and at another meet one week later, Christmas Eve, received $13,000. They offered M-13 $250 to buy the latest Minox EL 35 spy camera, ideal for photographing secret documents, and another $250 to buy Christmas presents for his family.

January, 1978, in Montreal

Into the New Year, M-13 and the Soviets discussed the possibility of going abroad. The RCMP agent had made a good impression, and the Soviets wanted to "perfect" his seemingly rudimentary knowledge by sending him to spy school.

Back in Ottawa, M-13 collected his last $12,500 for "services rendered". Another meeting was agreed to, where the Soviets were prepared to advance M-13 a further $4,000 to pay for his tickets overseas. The meeting was never held. The Department of External Affairs, in cooperation with the RCMP, chose the very date of their next meeting, February 9, to denounce the Soviets' actions in the House of Commons.

During the last eight weeks of the case the Ministry of Justice, the office of the Solicitor-General and the Ministry of External Affairs were kept informed of every movement of the operation. One of the leading Justice Department prosecutors was involved in the case from its earliest stages, and offered valuable advice on the legal aspects of the case.

Canadian and Soviet Reactions
(excerpts from the media)

At his weekly news conference, Prime Minister Trudeau reacted cynically to suggestions that the decision to banish 13 Soviet officials was timed to buff up the image of his government and the RCMP.

> I'm sorry if this is going to give a good image to the RCMP and its efficiency.... It's too bad it's happened at this time when we're in an election year.... Maybe the Soviets are trying to help the government.

The timing was not in the hands of the RCMP. The ripe moment was determined by the circumstances of the case. Only so much false information could be fed before suspicions were aroused. The RCMP does not have unlimited resources. After the net was full, the police had nothing to gain, and much to risk, by continuing the deception.

"Uncovering the spy ring ... was disturbing to the government," Trudeau said. "But we will continue to try to have good relations with the U.S.S.R."

Although the two latest breakthroughs have clearly opened a significant crack in Soviet espionage operations in Canada little hope is held out that the operation will be pulled back or discontinued.

"They will probably continue spying and we will continue trying to prevent them," Prime Minister Trudeau observed.

Soviet press officer, Igor Lobanov, said the charges of spying against the 13 were "laughable accusations". Asked why Canada would risk harming relations between the two countries if the charges were not true, he replied: "It will make easier the life of the RCMP now. They will get good press coverage from now on."

Soviet Ambassador Alexandr Yakovlev scrubbed a press conference which was to be held February 10 at the National Press Building to hear noted Soviet cosmonaut Georgi Beregovi talk about the U.S.S.R.'s space program. "The news conference was cancelled because of the new situation that has developed," said an embassy spokesman.

There's no grass growing under the feet of the administrators at 10 The Driveway. The name of expelled Soviet spy Igor Vartanyan was removed from the apartment building's tenants' list even before the Soviet's wife had been informed she was to leave the country with her husband. The building manager who removed the name from the registry was asked why the rush. "Why not," he said. "They haven't left yet, but the apartment is as good as vacant."

The Russian-speaking wife of the expelled diplomat sat seven floors above, in her plush one-bedroom apartment with a woman friend, waiting for the return of her husband, unaware that she had been ordered to leave the country along with him.

At the airport, she was quoted as saying, "I'm happy to be leaving, I want to be home with my sons in Moscow."

After a brief stop at the Charlotte Street embassy for final farewells, the cavalcade — a convoy of five diplomatic vehicles carrying three Soviet diplomats, their families and belongings — headed east toward the Quebec border.

Before reaching the Queensway, the cars stopped and gassed up for the trip ahead. In what was perhaps a final acknowledgement of North American customs, a credit card was produced to pay for the gas.

Comment

Working toward the security of a nation is constant ongoing procedure. There were countless individuals behind the scenes that made this operation a success. They cannot, however, in the interests of security be mentioned here. They must, as is necessary, work in the shadow of anonymity, never receiving public acclaim for their valourous and unselfish deeds. The story that unfolded here could certainly not have met with the success it did without their nameless help, without their devotion and dedication to their country. Our thanks must go out to those who shall perforce remain faceless and nameless in the constant battle for freedom against tyranny. Perhaps by publishing this story we will, in some small way, show the appreciation of a grateful nation.

Editor's Note

In this article there is a good description of the *modus operandi* of Soviet spies communicating with their agents. The use of signs on posts, and "dead letter" boxes appears to be so simple that it might be easily detected. However, this is not the case. This method in which the agent receives instructions to carry out his assignments, and often to receive his pay, without meeting the spy, has usually escaped detection.

42

A Daring Switch

Insp. J.P. Blakeney (Rtd.)

Prior to 1930 according to Customs laws in force up to that time, any vessel with a cargo of contraband liquor on board could legally enter any port of entry for various legitimate reasons, such as landing a sick mariner, weather, taking on food or water, or for making emergency repairs. But as soon as it entered the master must go immediately to the Customs House where he would declare the nature and quantity of the cargo.

Then the Collector of Customs would go on board and place his seal on all doors and hatchways leading to the contraband liquor. He would station a Customs watchman on the vessel. The watchman's wages and maintenance were paid by the captain or owners of the cargo.

The duty of the watchman was to remain on board during the entire stay in port and to see that the seals were not broken or tampered with. He, of course, would come ashore when the vessel sailed for the high seas, but it was unlawful and made vessel and cargo liable to seizure if the seals were broken while the vessel was still inside the three-mile limit.

After she got beyond she was in international waters and the seals could be broken. This three-mile limit was later extended to 12.

I had reason to believe the privilege of allowing these liquor-laden vessels to enter port was being abused, although I could get no definite proof.

This had no reflection on the Collectors of Customs at the various ports. They were all as far as I was aware, conscientious and good reliable government employees, but unfortunately some of the watchmen they hired were not trustworthy and could be bribed to allow the seals to be broken and some of the contraband disposed of in Nova Scotia ports.

I received a phone call one day about noon from a man in one of the Lunenburg County towns, telling me he had some information which might be of interest, but he would have to see me that afternoon or evening, otherwise it would be too late. He thought it advisable to bring a couple of men with me.

As this man had given me valuable information on previous occasions, I arranged to meet him late that afternoon at an isolated spot on a side road near an old vacant farm. I took a corporal and a constable.

My informer told me there was a large sailing vessel with a full cargo of liquor anchored in a small harbor in one of the large islands lying off the coast. On arrival the captain had come to the Customs House on the mainland — the port of entry for that district — and stated that his reason for coming into port where he expected to remain for several days, was to make some necessary repairs to his engine.

The liquor was intended for the American coast and he was going to proceed there as soon as repairs had been made. This rumrunning vessel, in addition to a complete set of sails, was also equipped with a diesel engine.

My informer said Customs had placed a watchman on board, but according to his information, arrangements had been made to allow the seals to be broken and a portion of the liquor smuggled into the province.

I was also advised that repairs were just an excuse to enter port. Since arriving the captain was known to have been ashore and made contact with a person strongly suspected of large-scale smuggling operations in the province.

On one trip ashore he had met this person by appointment at a local hotel where the captain was introduced to a prospective buyer and arrangements were made to purchase $3,000 worth of the captain's cargo. My informer knew that this purchase consisted of rum and whisky, but did not know the exact quantity of each.

In this case as in most large-scale liquor transactions, there are usually two or more men, but one is usually the man with the money or the "higher up". He never actually handles the liquor personally or puts himself in a position where he could be charged with possession.

The buyer, after the preliminary arrangements had been made, explained to the captain that he had a partner and it would be the latter who would actually receive the liquor. It was arranged the captain would come in his dory equipped with an outboard motor and be at a certain wharf on the mainland at 11 that night.

The partner would meet him with a large motorboat. They would go to the vessel lying out four or five miles where the actual transaction would take place. The partner of course, was to have sufficient money to pay for the liquor.

The buyer did not have his partner with him at the hotel. He was accompanied by a man sometimes employed by them, but this man was not actually in the room where the arrangements took place. Neither was he introduced to the captain and as far as we knew, had not been pointed out to him.

As the partner and the captain had not met, it was arranged they would use the password "dory". The captain, who would be in his dory concealed under the wharf when the partner arrived, would listen for the word, come out from hiding and they would proceed out for the liquor.

I was assured by my informer that if I decided to take the place of the partner, when the real partner and his crew attempted to start their motorboat to go the eight miles, their engine would not start. By the time they discovered the trouble and got the new part it would be too late to keep the appointment. My informer, while not definitely sure, said as far as he knew the buyer had not given the captain a description of his partner or of the motorboat he would be using. Their identification depended solely on the password.

After deciding to go ahead with the scheme, I discussed with my informer the matter of hiring a boat. He told me of a man who owned a cabin cruiser used for a legitimate business such as carrying passengers on the La Have River and taking picnic and other pleasure-seeking parties out to the islands. As far as he knew the boat owner was not in any way connected with illegal liquor traffic.

Accompanied by the corporal and constable, I proceeded to the home of the boat owner, arriving just about dusk. He did not at first seem very friendly, and after a few remarks I asked him if I could hire him and his boat to do a job for me that night. He asked if we were in the rum business and I told him, "in a way, yes we are."

He said, "I thought so. Well you can't hire me or my boat for that purpose. You fellows think you are smart but you sometimes get caught, and if caught with your rum in my boat she will be seized and I don't think you fellows would pay for her loss."

The reason I approached this man cautiously was because I wanted to first try and determine what his attitude was toward the rumrunners and whether or not he could be trusted. I felt I could come out in the open and told him who we were and showed my Writ of Assistance and other police credentials.

As soon as I did this, his attitude changed. He said he was interested in the work I was doing along that part of the coast in an effort to put down the illegal smuggling of liquor into the province. He agreed for a very reasonable price to go with us, but hoped there would be no shooting. I assured him there would be none so far as the police were concerned.

I told the boat owner I wanted to arrive at a certain wharf about eight or nine miles from his place at 11 sharp and for him to gauge our time of starting and the speed accordingly.

We concealed the police car behind the boat owner's barn and shortly after dark started away in his boat. It was a dark night with overcast skies but not much wind. We went in slowly to the head of the wharf and I gave the password and heard it repeated. A dory came out with three men on board — the captain and two of his crew.

The captain came on board and the two crew members remained in the dory. The first thing the captain asked was if I was Mr. so-and-so's partner. I told him I must be, otherwise I would not be there and in possession of the password. He said he was satisfied. We started out across the bay to the harbor where the vessel was lying, taking the dory in tow containing the two crew members.

During the discussion with my informer that afternoon, there were two things we did not know: what quantity of the order was rum and how much was whisky and the price per gallon of rum or per case of whisky. The only thing we knew was the total cash involved.

We had a fairly good idea of the current prices charged by rumrunners, so we used these and added up a certain amount of rum and another of whisky until the total came to $2,970. I put these quantities on a sheet of paper without, of course, quoting my price and I had this when I met the captain.

When proceeding out to the vessel, the captain and I had the cabin to ourselves. The two policemen remained with the owner of the boat. In order to try and avoid embarrassment when we got on board the vessel, I told the captain that since my partner had been talking to him, we had found it necessary to make some changes in quantity, but the total value would be about the same as agreed upon.

I said I had a list of the quantities but we would have to make up the total price when we got on board. He said it did not matter to him which kind we wanted as he had lots of both.

I also discussed the matter of the Customs watchman and he said I need not worry as he was a good fellow and arrangements had been made for him to be in his bunk asleep. We arrived alongside the vessel shortly after midnight and I noticed there were five men on board. That made a crew of eight including the captain and there were only three of us, but I did not anticipate any serious trouble although some of the crew members looked as though they were capable of anything.

I went on board and the two policemen remained in the motorboat. The captain took his mate and myself into his cabin where he took the list the informer and I had prepared and added up the amount which came to $3,010. This was $40 more than our estimate which I considered a fairly good guess.

The captain prepared a list of the quantities copying from the slip I handed him. He gave his list to his mate and told him to check as it went over the rail. He handed my list back. He told me to pay him and they would load the liquor into my boat.

I told the captain I was not going to pay until the liquor was piled on deck and some of it at least loaded on board my boat.

As I was handling the money for others beside myself, I had to take every precaution for its protection. I displayed a roll which looked like a lot of money when really it was less than $100.

I told the captain that the Customs watchman appearing just at the right time may already have been arranged between them. This was a mistake and almost fatal to the whole scheme as the captain became very angry and told me to go and get my liquor somewhere else. I realized I had blundered and would now have to make the best of it. I told the captain that from past experience in liquor transactions, I had learned that anything could happen where large sums of money were concerned. I told him I could easily get the liquor from other sources and with this remark I walked to the cabin steps and started up, feeling that I had made the wrong approach and our plan had ended in failure.

I knew that the Department at Ottawa took a serious view of cases where Customs seals were illegally broken and if I saw these broken even though no liquor was actually removed, I would place the vessel and cargo under seizure. However, when about halfway up the steps, the captain called me back and told me his mate was waiting for orders at the top of the steps to go ahead and put the men to work and get my liquor.

The captain and I went on deck, but by the time I got there both hatches were open so I could not tell if the seals had been intact or not. I did notice however, that there was quite a vacant space directly under the hatches. This would indicate that some of the cargo had already been landed somewhere in the province, although I had no actual proof.

The men worked both hatches, the rum coming out of one and the whisky from the other. They seemed to be anxious to get the job over with so they could go to bed. Very little of the liquor was remaining on deck. It was passed immediately over the rail to the men on the motorboat and they were assisted by the boat owner, who I think was as interested as we.

After this had been going on for some time and a good portion of the liquor was already on our boat, the captain said that I should come to the cabin and pay him.

I knew the time had come for a showdown and I had sufficient evidence to support the seizure of the vessel and cargo. I told the captain we were members of the Royal Canadian Mounted Police and I was also a

Customs and Excise officer and that his vessel and cargo were being place under seizure.

I realized there was a possibility of trouble as the captain might think we were hijackers and not officers at all. In order to prevent this I produced my writ and other identification as quickly as possible. By the light of the lanterns, he glanced over my documents and in a very surprised voice said, "Why, you are Blakeney."

As soon as I told the captain who we were, the two policemen came on board. One took up a position on the side of the vessel where the boats were tied to prevent anyone from leaving and the other toward the bow where he had a view of the whole deck.

The owner of the motorboat who, before starting out had given the impression that he was a little nervous, did not act like a man who was afraid. Instead of going in the cabin of his boat where a frightened man would naturally have gone, I noticed he was out on the forward deck with what I think was a gaff in his hand — it looked as if he was ready to assist if required.

After they realized their vessel was seized, the crew appeared in an ugly mood and I asked the captain to call them together. In his presence I advised them not to attempt to cause any trouble, for they would find that interferring with an officer in the execution of his duty was a much more serious offense than being found on a rumrunner.

The captain agreed and told them the vessel was seized and there was nothing they could do about it. He advised them to go to their bunks, which they eventually did and we had no trouble. Only one member of the crew was a Nova Scotian. The others were from points outside the province, mostly from Newfoundland.

Sometime after the crew had gone to their bunks, the Customs watchman came on deck. He recognized me and asked what I was doing on board. I told him I was going to ask him the same thing. He said he must have fallen asleep. I told him he could finish his nap at home as the vessel was under seizure and his services were no longer required.

After things had quietened down we placed the liquor all back on board. As I knew the corporal with me would be urgently required at headquarters to resume his normal duties I sent him back on the hired motorboat early that morning, instructing him to ask Inspector LaNauze to get in touch with the Customs preventive patrol boat which I knew was somewhere along the south shore and have the captain come and take charge of the seized vessel and tow her to Halifax.

I also asked the corporal to get in touch with a constable, on leave and visiting his parents who lived on the mainland not far from where the seizure was made, and ask him to come and stay on board the vessel, also for the use of his father's motorboat for a ferry to and from the mainland.

We remained on board, getting our meals and sleeping, but with one man always on guard in the event of trouble. The second day after the seizure the Customs patrol boat arrived and towed the vessel to Halifax with the entire crew still on board except the captain, whom I brought ashore and took to Mahone Bay where the magistrate resided.

While proceeding to Mahone Bay, the captain suggested his best procedure would be to plead guilty to smuggling, but as no liquor had actually been landed from his vessel, he thought the Department at Ottawa might see fit to impose a $400 penalty on the vessel as he knew it had done in previous cases.

If so he could then — after paying this penalty and the one imposed by the magistrate — continue on his voyage to the American coast which he was most anxious to do. He said he knew a firm of lawyers in Halifax he would consult and they would assist in the matter.

I told the captain it was his privilege to take whatever steps he saw fit as my responsibility ceased after I had him arraigned. The captain appeared before Stipendiary Magistrate Holloway at Mahone Bay, pleaded guilty and was fined $200.

In the meantime the seized vessel was towed to Halifax and tied up at the naval dockyard. The captain and owners, through the efforts of their lawyers were able to bring the seizure before the Exchequer Court at Halifax, where some evidence was taken.

The case continued at Ottawa and was attended by a capable lawyer from Halifax, who represented the Crown and by myself. The final decision by the judge of the Exchequer Court was that the vessel and cargo remain forfeited to the Crown.

43

Couriers Wanted:
No Experience Necessary

Sgt. Carl MacLeod

The Phillip Tse case has already received widespread publicity. Newspapers around the world carried the story when the initial arrests were made. It was the subject of a feature article in the March 1981 issue of *Reader's Digest*. And now a feature film by Tom Gould, a former Far East correspondent for the CBC, is being planned.

Sgt. C.B. MacLeod, the author of the following article, worked on the case as a handler of undercover agents. He has been in drug enforcement with the RCMP for more than 15 years and in his words, "It was the most exciting case I ever worked on." In early 1979, two female members of the RCMP, posing as couriers, and two cover teams, each consisting of four male members of the Force, infiltrated a major drug-importing ring based in South East Asia. The investigation lasted approximately one month and took place in some of the world's most beautiful and exotic cities. By the time the case was closed, 20 million dollars worth of heroin had been seized and six ringleaders arrested. Sgt. MacLeod tells his story. Ed.

It was one of those rare cases that you only read or fantasize about but never actually happens. In December 1978, in Toronto, Ontario, however, the fantasy became a reality. A police informer reported to the Metropolitan Toronto Police Department that a Chinese man, later identified as Tse, Wo Kong, was in town to recruit two Caucasian female heroin couriers for a Chinese organization centred in Hong Kong and the Netherlands. In recent years Caucasian couriers, as opposed to the once traditional oriental courier, were preferred. Posing as North American tourists, leisurely wending their way through the Far East and Europe, they could more easily avoid the suspicion of alert law-enforcement personnel. Toronto Police called in the RCMP which, with a network of liaison officers in Europe and Asia, was in a better position to deal with the case.

Initially, we considered that Tse, Wo Kong, might be attempting to recruit two unwitting females into white slavery under the guise of a world tour sweetened by the promise of substantial financial rewards. We quickly became believers that Tse was a bonafide drug dealer, however, when our liaison office in Hong Kong informed us that he had been arrested in Amsterdam in 1976 in possession of half a pound of heroin and had served 16 months in gaol. We also discovered that he was more than the charming oriental he appeared. Approximately one month after having been released from gaol, he participated in the brutal beating, torture and attempted murder of a Chinese male suspected of being responsible for a missing heroin shipment in March 1978. We also learned that he had an eye for pretty women.

The informant who had tipped off Toronto Police agreed to introduce an undercover operator to Tse. On January 2, 1979, S/Cst. Helen Destefano, portraying an attractive secretary, desirous of seeing the world — and if a bit of risk was involved and as long as she would be paid handsomely, so be it! — was introduced to Tse in the bar of the Harbour Castle Hilton Hotel in Toronto. Tse was immediately impressed by her confidence and savoir faire and it was not long before he was making his offer. Tse, or Phillip as he was also called, told her he wanted to hire a second female courier and without seeming too obvious, Helen gave her assurance that she had a friend who fit the bill.

Three days later Cpl. Dianne Wright, C Division, Montreal Security Service, was hired. The price agreed upon was $5,000 U.S. for each courier and an expense-paid trip to Hong Kong. Tse could not believe his good luck — nor could we believe ours.

At the early stages of planning this investigation it was realized that we would possibly require the most senior cover team ever assembled by the RCMP. At the risk of being a bit melodramatic, I would like the reader to consider some of the problems we faced: tentative travel schedule changed on a moment's notice; temperature variation from 115°F in Malaysia to 40°F in France; and most important, two undercover operators who had to be protected at all times. A formidable challenge. Tse had informed our operators that they would be separated once they received the suitcases containing heroin. For this reason a cover team of four members was assigned to each operator. Team No. 1 was responsible for Cpl. Dianne Wright and consisted of Insp. W. Stefureak, O.I.C. coordinator; Sgt. John Pielechaty, in charge of technical aids; myself, the undercover handler; and Cpl. Al Roach, in charge of travel arrangements. On Team No. 2, responsible for S/Cst. Helen Destefano, were S/Sgt. Tom Brown, coordinator; Sgt. Larry Tronstad, i/c technical aids; Sgt. Al MacDonald, undercover handler; and Sgt. Reg Chad, travel arrangements. In addition to the assigned duties, each man conducted surveillance when required. Duties were also interchangeable. An especially invaluable member of the group was S/Sgt. Brown who had been our liaison officer in Bangkok, Thailand, from 1976 to 1978. He knew the climate and the culture of the orient, and more important he had an insight into the oriental criminal mind.

From comments Tse had made to Wright and Destefano, we were reasonably sure that the heroin would be picked up somewhere in South East Asia and delivered to either Europe or possibly North America. It was here that our liaison officers were invaluable because every possible country through which we might travel had to be briefed on our operation and several important issues had to be resolved before we could think of continuing the operation. The feedback from the liaison officers was that we could expect total cooperation on condition that no part of the heroin shipment remain in any one of the countries, a totally reasonable and acceptable condition.

In addition to our operational plan, we devised a series of verbal and visual communications in the event that we were unable to meet privately with our operators. Perhaps the most memorable one was the word "Maple Leaf". It meant that the operation was being terminated and that seizure and arrests were being made.

Meanwhile, Tse, who had now obviously made the decision that he had found his two couriers, started to reveal details of the routing, conveyance and time frame. The girls would be travelling 10 to 15 days and the first stop would be Hong Kong. There, they would receive further instructions. Somewhere in Asia they would pick up false-sided suitcases containing heroin. Once loaded they would travel separately and enter Europe through Spain or Switzerland.

Knowing this, on January 15, 1979, an advance party of Insp. Stefureak, S/Sgt. Brown, Sgts. Pielechaty, MacDonald, Tronstad and Cpl. Roach departed for Hong Kong via Los Angeles. They were met in Hong Kong by our liaison officer, S/Sgt. Neville Gillespie and Insps. Donaldson and Mutch of the Royal Hong Kong Police Department (RHKPD) Narcotics Bureau who had been assigned to our case. There, preparations were made for surveillance coverage, hotel accommodations and up-to-date briefings for the Hong Kong police department.

Two days later, on January 17, we got the green light we'd been waiting for. Tse met our operators in Toronto and supplied them with airline tickets for a Trans International Airlines charter flight departing Niagara Falls, New York, for Hong Kong at 10.30 p.m. that evening. He gave instructions to the operators, or "Phillip's Angels" as he was now calling them, that he would meet them on January 20 at the Hong Kong Hilton

Hotel. He also supplied each operator with $160 to cover the cost of the suitcases he had requested they buy at an earlier meeting.

We discovered in the nick of time which airline Tse had booked the girls on and just managed to get seats for Sgt. Chad and myself. We had been assigned to accompany the operators and it was our intention to identify the Chinese controller who Tse said would be on the same flight. What we didn't know in advance was that this was a charter designed for Chinese people going home for the Chinese New Year and it had an extra row of seats added for that reason.

We arrived at the airport before the operators and were watching as they checked in. The situation was ridiculous. Ninety-five percent of the people checking in were Chinese and there was no way we could identify if one Chinese male was paying unusual attention to these two good-looking Caucasian females.

At 10.30 p.m. January 17, 1979, Trans International Airlines charter flight #TV95021 departed Niagara Falls, New York, for Hong Kong via Chicago, Anchorage (Alaska) and the island of Okinawa. Estimated time of arrival — 4.00 p.m. January 19. Total flying time — 21 hours. Jet lag took on a new meaning!

Shortly after our arrival in Hong Kong, a reporter from the South China Post was alerted by a member of the hotel staff where we were staying that there were a number of RCMP members staying in the Hong Kong Hilton. The reporter, suspecting he was on to a scoop, contacted the RHKPD. It was only through quick thinking and the promise of an exclusive story that the case was not over before it had even begun.

On January 20, Tse held his first meeting in Hong Kong with Destefano and Wright and gave them additional travel information and instructions. Once they received their loaded suitcases in Malaysia, they would discard their personal suitcases — the ones he had reimbursed them for in Toronto. They would then travel to a small town outside of Amsterdam. Most of the travel in Europe would be by train during the night.

On January 22, Tse met the operators and told them he suspected he was under police surveillance. He instructed them to check out of the Hilton Hotel, take a taxi to the airport, wait half an hour, and then go to the Sheraton Hotel in Kowloon. The operators followed his instructions. Tse called them at the Sheraton to tell them everything was airight. The next night he was to have dinner with the women in the Eagles Nest, an exclusive eatery in the Hilton. He cancelled out. Hong Kong Police watched him call from the lobby of the hotel making excuses why he couldn't attend the dinner. We suspected either that he was showing the operators to an associate or that he had spotted the surveillance.

Several meetings were held during the next few days. At one meeting the operators were told that the new suitcases were not ready, at another, that the volume of Chinese New Year traffic was making it difficult to get flight reservations. The reason for the constant changes in plans, we were sure, was to test the operators' ability to take instruction and to shake surveillance.

Waiting for Tse to make his move, the girls toured Hong Kong — followed at a discreet distance by the cover team. The first thing that struck us about the city was the extreme wealth and extreme poverty. No clearer example of class distinction existed than when we looked down on the boat people from our luxurious rooms in the Excelsior Hotel. Most of these people, we were told, were born and would die on those sampans.

When we weren't needed as covers, we passed the time playing poker in our hotel room. None of us was sad when Sgt. Pielechaty left with the advance party for Penang. He gave us several costly poker lessons which seemed magnified because the currency was almost five Hong Kong dollars to one American dollar.

As the days wore on, the strain of waiting began to tell and poker playing and sightseeing in Hong Kong quickly lost their earlier glamour. We were particularly concerned because each passing day increased the chances of our cover being spotted. The operators also felt the strain. It was now time, we decided, for them to become aggressive and demand that Tse give them some definite travel plans and get them on a flight to Penang. We felt confident that he had tested them sufficiently and was committed to using them. Cpl. Wright and S/Cst. Destefano, therefore, told him that they had to get back to Canada and that they wanted to get on with the job.

The approach worked. On January 26 Tse came to the operators' room with more expense money and plane reservations on a flight leaving that afternoon for Penang, Malaysia, 1,500 miles southwest of Hong Kong.

Insp. Mutch of RHKPD somehow found a seat on the same plane for Sgt. Pielechaty who, as the technical person on the team, was deemed the most important member at this point. One Chinese passenger, I might add, was most agitated with the airline on finding out they had overbooked the plane.

The only seats Brown, Chad, Tronstad, Roach and I could get were first class leaving two days later. You have not experienced service until you have flown first class on Japanese Airlines. The customer's comfort is paramount and the stewardess's first duty is to offer slippers to all first-class passengers. Sgt. Chad was celebrating his 20th anniversary in the Force and it was quite obvious that he thought he had died and gone to heaven.

The luxury and comfort were short-lived, however, because when the aircraft touched down in Kuala Lumpur, we got our first taste of the equatorial climate. Malaysia is close to the equator and our first thought was, how can people live in this heat. S/Sgt. Brown was the only member who had experienced the climate. Somehow the description of it he had given us back in Toronto took on a new meaning. The first few days were spent buying sun hats, lighter clothes and looking for shade.

Penang Island is a vacation paradise commonly frequented by German and Australian tourists. Our job was, therefore, much easier because we were able to blend into the scenery. On one occasion, however, we felt that Sgt. Pielechaty was taking the "blending in" a bit too far. He tried to convince two of us to join him on the beach for a card game. This might seem like a reasonable request. It was not. Pielechaty had seen a group of Malaysian fishermen playing cards and he wanted to get into their game. Our role?—to protect him in case he won and they took exception to a Caucasian taking their hard-earned money. We had visions of fileting knives and angry fishermen and quickly talked him out of such bravado. After the poker lesson he had given us in Hong Kong, there was no doubt in our minds that he had the ability to quickly master whatever game they were playing and relieve them of many Malaysian dollars.

Tse finally arrived in Penang on January 30, having had, like us, problems getting reservations during the holiday season. During the next few days he held a series of meetings. At each meeting he changed the route slightly. One thing that seemed certain, however, was that after flying into Zurich, Switzerland, the operators would take an overnight train to France and Holland. Tse also stressed that the girls would be followed by a European controller and that there was a total of seven people in his organization: two Japanese; one Chinese; one Malaysian; one European; and two Canadians.

On February 3, Tse and a Chinese male, who was later identified as Ko, Chi Keung, arrived unexpectedly on the beach in front of the Rasa Sayang Hotel. I know it sounds like a scene from a James Bond movie but Tse approached S/Cst. Destefano underwater. You can well imagine how startled she must have been. A briefing followed on the beach where Cpl. Wright was sunbathing. It was the most significant meeting thus far. Tse, with Ko watching on, illustrated the travel plans by making drawings in the sand.

After this meeting we were reasonably sure that our operators would be flying from Penang on February 7, stopping briefly at Kuala Lumpur and Singapore, then onto Zurich where they would stay overnight. From Zurich they would travel by train to Paris where S/Cst. Destefano would check her suitcase at the Gare de l'Est and Cpl. Wright would check hers at the Gare du Nord. Wright and Destefano would then go to the Sufferin Le Tour Hotel where they had reservations.

On February 4, Insp. Stefureak, Sgts. Chad and Pielechaty and I left Penang for Vienna. In Vienna we split up, Chad and Pielechaty going to Zurich, to brief the Swiss authorities, Stefureak and I to The Hague to brief the Dutch authorities.

On February 6, Insp. Stefureak, S/Sgt. Van de Graaf, liaison officer at The Hague, and I left The Hague for Brussels to brief the Belgian authorities and then continued on to Paris for a briefing of French authorities.

In Penang, meanwhile, events were unfolding which would ultimately put our operators in possession of 14 pounds of Chinese #3 heroin worth in the vicinity of 20 million dollars on the European market. It is necessary to describe in detail how this was staged because the first exchange by Ko was made to appear like a mistake. In actual fact it was only a dry run and clearly displayed the cunning of Tse and company.

On February 4, Cpl. Wright and S/Cst. Destefano had been switched to the Palm Beach Hotel. At 5.35 in the evening of that day, Ko, the man who had helped Tse draw the travel route in the sand, came to the girls' room and introduced himself as "Paul". He said that Tse would bring the loaded suitcases to the room at 7.00 p.m. Instead, Ko returned to the room five minutes later carrying two suitcases saying that they both contained heroin. He then left and was observed entering a neighboring hotel room. At 6.30 p.m. Tse arrived and told the girls that "Paul" had brought the wrong suitcases. He attempted to cover the "mistake" by saying that there were numerous similar suitcases in his hotel. He also said that the suitcases were loaded but that because of poor craftsmanship would have to be replaced. As he was leaving, Tse did an about face and said that the suitcases were not loaded and that he would come back to get them on February 5.

The next day Tse attempted to move the operators into the Mandarin Hotel in Georgetown. This hotel is well known by the Malaysian enforcement community as a favorite hotel used by couriers exiting Malaysia. Destefano and Wright questioned the unnecessary packing and unpacking. Tse agreed that they could stay another night where they were but would have to check into the Mandarin on the following day because the loaded suitcases would be delivered there at 12 noon. During Tse's final meeting he attempted to remove the suitcases which Ko had delivered "in error". Due to congestion in the corridors, however, he left them for later.

At 8.00 a.m. the next morning, Tse was back at the operators' hotel room followed a short time later by Ko carrying two suitcases identical to the "wrong" ones which had been delivered on February 4. Tse instructed Cpl. Wright to take control of these suitcases. A short time later Ko had her check the hallway for surveillance. She reported an oriental male watching the corridor. Ko quickly revealed that he was one of their people. Cpl. Wright then removed her personal belongings from her old suitcase and packed them into the two new ones which Ko had just delivered. Cpl. Wright's suitcases were loaded, Tse said, in the sides; Destefano's would be loaded in the top and bottom. Because their suitcases were different, Tse said, his boss had decided that it would not be necessary to check into the Mandarin and also that the operators could now stay together in Zurich.

It was obvious that Tse and company were starting to feel a bit easier because S/Cst. Destefano received her loaded suitcase in a much more expeditious manner. Tse arrived as promised and helped S/Cst. Destefano carry her personal suitcases into a waiting car. They then set off for the nearby Rasa Sayang Hotel where, Tse said, Destefano would receive the loaded suitcase. At the Rasa Sayang, however, Tse did not stop, temporarily throwing Destefano's cover team into a very tense situation because it was not immediately prepared to observe another area. In actual fact, however, Tse had the loaded suitcase in the trunk of his car and was only trying to locate a taxi to return S/Cst. Destefano to the Palm Beach Hotel. When she realized what he was doing she convinced him that the diversionary tactics were not necessary and that he could drive her back to the Palm Beach. Tse followed Destefano's advice and returned her to the hotel himself.

When the dust had settled and the cover teams discovered what Tse had done, the pulse rates began to return to normal. Destefano and Wright were now finally in possession of the heroin, six kilos of it packed in small plastic bags pressed to a thickness of a little over one inch and skillfully hidden between the lining and the outside cover of the three suitcases. We all knew that the delivery would take place as quickly as possible now that the "mules" were taking all the risks.

On February 7, MacDonald and Roach left for Zurich followed shortly afterwards by our operators. Covering them were S/Sgt. Brown and Sgt. Tronstad. Also watching their every action was Tsang, Ching Wah, one of Tse's associates.

At Zurich a police vehicle camouflaged as a taxi was conveniently waiting for Wright and Destefano. If any counter-surveillance existed it was quickly lost. The Swiss police were most kind and gave the girls a tour of Zurich and the surrounding area including a ride into the Alps. This was the first time in almost three weeks that they could relax knowing that they were safe from Tse's surveillance. It was just what the doctor had ordered. It helped break the tension and recharge the batteries for the final run into France and Holland.

During the stopover at Zurich S/Sgt. Brown and Sgt. MacDonald conducted field tests on the heroin. A common practice by some trafficking organizations is to load couriers with substitutes such as flour in an attempt to establish if authorities are on to their particular group. Large organizations spare no expense to avoid detection. It is merely a business overhead. Fortunately for us, the results of the field test were positive.

On February 9, Destefano and Wright boarded a night train for Paris. Tsang, who had been assigned to watch the girls on the Penang to Zurich flight, actually assisted them with their luggage without revealing that he was one of Tse's associates until afterwards at the Paris train station when he told them to check their loaded suitcases and go to the Sufferin Le Tour Hotel. After checking into the hotel, Destefano and Wright went to the Paris Hilton Hotel coffee shop, the spot agreed upon in Penang for meeting Tse. He arrived at 10.30 a.m. with more instructions. They were to obtain bus schedules for Amsterdam, Rotterdam and The Hague because they could be travelling by bus to any one of the three destinations. Their stay in Paris would be four or five days. They should get their loaded suitcases from the train station and secure them in their hotel rooms. He then supplied expense money and said he would call to check on them every morning between 10 and 11.

Over the next couple of days telephone contact was maintained between Tse and the two women. On February 11, sharp at 10.00 a.m., Tse telephoned and requested that the bus schedules be checked and arranged a meeting at the Hilton Hotel coffee shop for February 13. He also informed the operators that they would be travelling separately to Holland, one leaving in the morning and the other one at night.

At the meeting on the 13th Tse asked Cpl. Wright to accompany him outside because, as he said, he wanted someone to have a look at her. After returning Wright to the coffee shop, he took both women for a walk, parading them, as we later discovered, past their next controller Lee, Tang Ming. Tse then showed them a large bundle of money, hinting that this was their final payment. Next, he directed Cpl. Wright to leave on the 6.45 p.m. train for Rotterdam where she would be met at the train station by either Ko or Tsang.

By the time Tse left and this information was relayed to the cover team, very little time remained to pack and we were most fortunate that Insp. Stefureak and Cpl. Roach got on the same train as Cpl. Wright. Assistant Commissioner Oosterbroek and other members of The Hague National Narcotic Unit who had been in Paris awaiting the departure for Holland now had to race back to make preparations for Cpl. Wright's arrival. They caught up with the train in Belgium and succeeded in getting a member on board. Lee, Tang Ming, for obvious reasons, had no trouble making the train. I wasn't so lucky. I missed it.

One week earlier I had taken a taxi from Le Grand Hotel to the Canadian Embassy and tipped the driver the amount prominently displayed on the chart. I can only guess that because I had business at the embassy, the driver must have assumed that I was a well-heeled VIP and should have given him a bigger tip. Whatever the reason, he left in a cloud of diesel smoke while using a string of expletive deleteds that certainly assisted him in remembering me and vice versa. When the Hague liaison officer, S/Sgt. Gerry Van de Graaf, and I needed a fast ride to the train station, who did we flag down ... ? You guessed it! My friend, the expletive-deleted taxi driver. Gerry and I agreed that it was the slowest cab ride on record.

Tse now concentrated his efforts on his final courier, S/Cst. Destefano. He seemed to be uncertain as to exactly what he wanted her to do because he instructed her to change hotels, then changed his mind, and told her to check the loaded suitcase in a locker at the train station and then, without warning, arrived at her hotel room. These indecisions were Tse's way of checking for police surveillance.

No course on police stress could have slowed the heartbeat or reduced the adrenaline rush caused by what happened next. Tse helped Destefano check out of her hotel room. The two of them got into a taxi in front of the hotel and took off for the train station. The French surveillance team inadvertently followed the wrong taxi. I realized what had happened but could not communicate with the French surveillance member. Fortunately, Insp. Pruneau, the RCMP liaison officer in Paris, who had been in the hotel providing translation and coordination on Tse's last move, returned shortly after Tse and Destefano's departure and we picked up the trail. By the time the rest of the French surveillance team had caught up, we had been following S/Cst. Destefano with one car for approximately 14 blocks through Paris traffic. What then seemed like an eternity was in retrospect only a few minutes.

We were the only ones worried though. S/Cst. Destefano later told us that she never thought for a moment that we were not with her — and even if we hadn't been, she felt that Tse could have been manipulated until we did catch up. This is a clear example of the confidence and grit displayed by both women throughout the entire exercise.

While we were careening through Paris traffic trying to keep up with Tse and Destefano, he was giving her the next set of instructions. She would be leaving for Brussels on the 11.23 p.m. train.

In preparation for the trip she checked her loaded suitcase at the Gare de l'Est and received a ticket stub. Her personal luggage she checked at the Gare du Nord and then accompanied Tse to a cafe where he told her the name of her hotel in Brussels and the date and time he would be contacting her. Tse and Destefano then returned to Gare de l'Est where Tse disappeared into the subway.

On her own now, Destefano went to the holding area to get her loaded suitcase. I was nearby and could see a look of consternation on her face. It was obvious that she had to meet the cover team. She went into the women's lavatory. Having little choice I followed her in — choosing that moment to enter that I thought was most "cool", though I don't suppose it could ever be too "cool" meeting in a women's lavatory. Inside the lavatory, she told me that her ticket stub was missing; without it she could not retrieve the loaded suitcase. This information was quickly relayed to Insp. Robert Peru, in charge of the French police operation, Paris, who easily made arrangements for the release of the loaded suitcase. Suitcase in hand at last, Destefano took a taxi to the North Station, purchased a ticket for Brussels and waited on the platform for the 11.23 p.m. departure.

From the beginning of this undercover operation our objective had been to follow the heroin to the highest possible level while at the same time providing unfailing security for our operators. Because Dutch authorities were close to arresting the conspirators on Cpl. Wright's delivery, and since we had insufficient lead time to properly brief Belgium authorities, a decision was made to terminate the Paris phase of the operation.

For those of us who were covering S/Cst. Destefano, the ending in Paris was not as dramatic as we had anticipated. In fact, it was quite anticlimactic, not the stuff from which great movies are made. After living in a state of continuous watchfulness and considerable pressure for almost a month, we felt only relief — and the ultimate in job satisfaction.

At 10.50 p.m. S/Cst. Destefano stood on the platform at Gare du Nord, loaded suitcase in hand, waiting the departure of the 11.23 train for Brussels. Two new overseers, Fong, Fook Wing, and Chan, Wing Woo, who had been implicated by French police surveillance, stood on the platform with her, pretending not to know her or each other. Occasionally they glanced up at the huge digital railway clock, occasionally at S/Cst. Destefano. Less than one half hour before departure, scattered throughout the crowd, a 12-man team composed of members of the Paris Narcotics Bureau and the RCMP stood watching. Seconds later they closed in. Fong and Chan were arrested. S/Cst. Destefano turned over the suitcase to Insp. Pruneau, who gave it to the French police. It contained over five-and-a-half pounds of Chinese #3 heroin. A short time later French Police arrested Tse at a downtown hotel.

At the same time as the arrests in Paris were being made, the situation in Rotterdam was very quickly approaching termination. Waiting at the train station at Rotterdam when Cpl. Wright arrived was Tsang. She followed him outside the station where he explained that Ko had got the instructions all mixed up and instead of arriving yesterday he had only arrived today and because of that there was no car ready to place the loaded suitcases in. Cpl. Wright suggested that she check into the Hilton Hotel until the problem was straightened out. Tsang agreed.

A truly frustrating and fairly common occurrence with undercover work is not being able to talk to the operator at critical times. This happened to the Dutch Police. They had been watching the operation and, seeing Tsang meeting with Ko and Lee, thought that a loaded suitcase had been delivered to them. As a result, when they saw Ko and Lee leave the train station they arrested them. Fortunately, the arrest took place out of Tsang's sight, because the suitcase, though similar to the loaded ones, was empty.

At midnight and in a state of nervous exasperation, Tsang called Cpl. Wright. He couldn't locate Ko and Lee. Wright, by now acting on instructions from Stefureak and Roach, took the offensive and expressed both annoyance and fear. Tse had promised her, she said, that she would be relieved of the loaded suitcases the moment that she arrived in Rotterdam. She was going to move to another hotel, she told Tsang, and if he wanted the suitcases he had better get over to her hotel right away and get the key for the room. She wasn't staying there a minute longer. She'd meet him in the lobby.

Tsang asked her to be patient. He would try and contact Ko again and call her within the hour. At 12.55 the phone rang. It was Tsang. He tried to convince her to spend another night at the Hilton. He hadn't been able to contact Ko. Cpl. Wright refused. Feigning annoyance and paranoia she told Tsang that this was totally out of the question and if he didn't come right away she was going and would leave the suitcases in the hotel room. Now, boxed in and having no choice, he instructed Wright to meet him in the hotel lobby with the key.

When Tsang arrived ten minutes later he found Cpl. Wright sitting in the lobby with the two suitcases. From their posts in the lobby Insp. Stefureak and Cpl. Roach could see he was upset. Wiping perspiration from his face he ordered Cpl. Wright to return the suitcases to her hotel room. A heated argument ensued, Tsang finally agreeing to take the suitcases. He beckoned Wright to follow him outside to a waiting taxi. Cpl. Wright, a smug look on her face, took a 360° trip in the hotel's revolving doors, returning to the safety of her cover. Tsang, seeing he was being deserted stepped into a waiting taxi where he was arrested in possession of 7.7 pounds of heroin.

Back in Paris, the celebration had already begun. The four bottles of champagne which Insp. Stefureak had entrusted to Sgt. Chad to be shared by all the team when the case was finished were quickly consumed — so quickly that when Sgt. MacDonald and I returned from the Paris Police Station at 1.30 a.m. looking forward to sampling the famous French grape, none remained. The team in Holland also missed out. I suspect, however, that if the positions had been reversed, the champagne would have had the same fate.

Our case caused much discussion among high level officers of the Netherlands National Narcotic Unit as well as state and municipal police. Under Dutch law it is an offence to assist in committing a crime. Cpl. Wright was viewed as a party aiding an offence or as an agent provocateur, and her evidence, consequently was nullified.

As a result, the case against Tsang, Ko and Lee could not successfully be prosecuted in Holland. Nor could Tsang, Ko or Lee be extradited to France because no extradition treaty existed between the two countries.

They were, however, British citizens and on this basis were ordered deported to the nearest British soil, England. This deportation was effected on February 16. An extradition treaty exists between France and England, therefore once the men were in England, French authorities immediately commenced extradition proceedings.

The extradition hearing was held in London, England, on July 18–19, 1979. Insp. Stefureak, Cpls. Roach and Wright, and S/Cst. Destefano were in attendance as witnesses for the Crown. The magistrate ordered the extradition of Ko and Tsang but discharged Lee. A French legal expert testified on the conspiratorial nature of the evidence on Lee and its acceptance in France but his extradition was denied. Lee was, however, arrested under the Immigration Act as an undesirable alien and deported to Hong Kong.

France has a judicial system referred to as Napoleonic Law or "code civil", which is totally different from the system we know in Canada. Briefly, police officers are required to give depositions to a senior police officer and this document is then used at the trial. Police officers are seldom required to give evidence and in fact only our operators were required to give depositions. Nor did they have to attend the trial. The onus rests heavily on the accused to prove his innocence and to stand mute all but seals one's fate.

At the French trial held later Tse, Ko and Chan were sentenced to 10 years and Fong and Tsang each received a six-year sentence. Lee was sentenced to six years in absentia. In France the full term is served and only under exceptional circumstances are prisoners released before the expiration of their sentence.

This case illustrates the professionalism and superb cooperation received from eight countries and countless jurisdictions around the world. We would not have succeeded without their help.

All of us who worked on the case will not easily forget the experience. We were together for over a month under some very stressful situations yet would all jump at the chance to work on this type of case again.

Editor's Note

S/Cst. Helen Destefano and Cpl. Dianne Wright were presented with Commissioner's Commendations for outstanding service on November 23, 1983.

This article illustrates the importance of police cooperation if attempts at controlling international drug trafficking are to be successful.

The Golden Dog Press

This volume was produced using
the TeX typesetting system, with
Adobe New Century Schoolbook
PostScript fonts.